Cost-Benefit Analysis
for Public Sector
Decision Makers

Cost-Benefit Analysis for Public Sector Decision Makers

Diana Fuguitt
and Shanton J. Wilcox

Q

QUORUM BOOKS
Westport, Connecticut • London

Library of Congress Cataloging-in-Publication Data

Fuguitt, Diana.
    Cost-benefit analysis for public sector decision makers / Diana
Fuguitt, Shanton J. Wilcox.
      p.   cm.
    Includes bibliographical references and index.
    ISBN 1–56720–222–5 (alk. paper)
    1. Public administration—Decision making.   2. Public
administration—Cost effectiveness.   I. Wilcox, Shanton J., 1973–   .
II. Title.
JF1525.D4F84   1999
352.3'3—dc21   99–18646

British Library Cataloguing in Publication Data is available.

Library of Congress Catalog Card Number: 99–18646
ISBN: 1–56720–222–5

First published in 1999

Quorum Books, 88 Post Road West, Westport, CT 06881
An imprint of Greenwood Publishing Group, Inc.
www.quorumbooks.com

Printed in the United States of America

The paper used in this book complies with the
Permanent Paper Standard issued by the National
Information Standards Organization (Z39.48–1984).

10 9 8 7 6 5 4

Copyright Acknowledgment

Julia A. Welch has generously given permission to use a case scenario and value
estimates from a research paper, ''Cost-Effectiveness Analysis of Three Proposals
to Save the Fort DeSoto Seagrass,'' she completed as a student at Eckerd College
in 1992.

Contents

Illustrations

TABLES

Preface

This book presents step-by-step how to perform, interpret and assess cost-benefit analysis. Numerous books have been written on the subject of cost-benefit analysis, so it might be asked, why one more? The primary reason is that this book focuses on the practical analysis. Traditional cost-benefit analysis texts delve with great detail into the economic theoretical foundations for the analysis, discussing at length the theoretical disputes that have yet to be fully resolved. In contrast, this book concentrates on the practical steps and techniques involved in an actual cost-benefit analysis. Our concern is the challenges that arise in applying theoretical concepts to real-world situations. Furthermore, we provide a more comprehensive encounter with the analysis, addressing many procedural steps that other books assume the reader already understands.

Cost-benefit analysis has proven to be a useful decision-making tool with widespread application. The analysis provides information to aid public (as well as private) managers who are considering any of a number of policies with social goals or consequences (e.g., environmental policies, health and safety regulations, transportation and water resource projects, recycling programs, youth programs, etc.). In-depth knowledge of the practical steps in an objective cost-benefit analysis can enable these decision makers to understand, interpret and critique a particular analysis and thereby make more informed decisions.

Moreover, both the procedure and its conclusions have been the subject of substantial scrutiny by interested and concerned parties. The nature of the conflict and some of the issues involved are perhaps best illustrated by a hypothetical example. Suppose after conducting a cost-benefit analysis, a regulatory agency recommends that the federal government require farmers in the Tampa Bay area to construct retention ponds, thereby reducing agricultural runoff into the bay. The farmers, outraged at yet another costly regulation, challenge the recommendation. They argue that the agency grossly underestimated the cost of retention ponds and that the analysis is faulty because "net present value," not the "benefit-cost ratio" calculated by the agency, is the appropriate decision criterion. In contrast, commercial fishers support the recommendation, citing evidence that the regulatory agency's estimates of fishing benefits are actually conservative and the ratio is too low because the agency used a high discount rate. To complicate matters further, environmental advocacy groups contend enhanced bay habitat will support more endangered manatees and that this (unmeasured) benefit by itself warrants the regulation.

As this hypothetical but realistic scenario suggests, cost-benefit analysis can be shrouded in controversy. Although a useful tool in deciding whether to pursue specific policies, cost-benefit analysis is scrutinized in the real world by competing political interests and special-interest groups with conflicting ethical values. They rightly question the objectivity of those carrying out the analysis and the accuracy of the results. Ironically, these groups often use the same tool to challenge local, state and federal mandates and policies. At the same time, their arguments often reveal misconceptions concerning the appropriate rules and purpose for doing a cost-benefit analysis. Cost-benefit analysis is such a standard economic tool in policy making that its use will only increase in the future. It is imperative, therefore, that those who perform a cost-benefit analysis, those who make recommendations based on its results, and those whose lives are affected by the recommended policies all understand this tool for its real-world impact.

Accordingly, we have written the book with this wide range of readers in mind. Most cost-benefit analysis books, by focusing on theoretical foundations, require at least upper-level undergraduate, and often graduate, economic knowledge. Moreover, our experience in the classroom, as teacher and student, indicates that even if theoretical concepts are understood, students generally encounter difficulty applying these concepts to analyze real-world situations. Our handbook seeks to overcome these limitations. Written assuming the reader has little or no prior knowledge of economics, it is accessible to a broad audience. Welfare economic concepts are explained, though in simple terms, so the reader can intelligently recognize the assumptions and values embodied in the analysis. In addition, the book offers step-by-step principles for how to do a cost-benefit analysis, grounding theoretical economic concepts in realistic scenarios complete with illustrative hypothetical examples. The recommended principles are enumerated in each chapter in Parts II and III and then summarized for comprehensive and easy reference in each part's concluding chapter (Chapters 15 and 23, respectively).

Furthermore, our scope is broader than economics; we recognize that cost-benefit analysis is used within an interdisciplinary decision-making context. Critics scrutinize the cost-benefit framework's inherent "soft spots"— hard-to-quantify parameters that include subjective human preferences, controversial ethical values, theoretical economic disputes and uncertain policy effects.

We directly address these "soft spots" so the reader can see their effects on this relatively objective economic analysis and understand their implications for rational decision making.

In all, the book provides a straightforward, detailed, step-by-step presentation and assessment of cost-benefit analysis, delineating the practical techniques along with their interpretation and contribution to complex decision-making processes. The book is thus intended for a wide spectrum of readers. These include public (as well as private) decision makers, future analysts, undergraduate and graduate students in applied economics and interdisciplinary programs (environmental studies, public policy, public health and the like), concerned citizens, special-interest groups, corporate and legal communities—anyone interested in learning how cost-benefit analysis impacts real people and how the techniques can be best applied in the real world.

At the outset, we want to call the reader's attention to our choice of pronouns that refer to an individual's gender. In writing this book, we found the "he/she" and "him or her" pronoun combinations to be difficult to employ throughout the entire text. This is especially the case when making reference to one of the two main "characters" in the book, the decision maker and the analyst. We have decided to use feminine pronouns when referring to the decision maker and masculine pronouns when referring to the analyst. This practice is particularly advantageous when discussing the characters' interaction with each other, for the selected pronoun should identify clearly which one of the two (decision maker or analyst) is the focus of a particular statement. When referring to other hypothetical individuals, where the individual's gender could arguably be either male or female, we will use "he or she." Also, when a specific real-life individual is mentioned, we will use pronouns befitting that person's actual gender.

We wish to thank several people for their help and support during this project. In particular, we want to express our gratitude to Joan Wilcox for providing editorial comments as well as general guidance in the initial stages of formulating the book. We are also grateful to Russell Bailey and Cynthia Nuhn, former and current instructional services librarians, respectively, at Eckerd College, for their assistance in finding bibliographic sources over the years. Special thanks to Linda O'Bryant, collegial secretary for the Behavioral Sciences, Eckerd College, for her enlightening sense of humor, her constant moral support and her exemplary dedication and deft skill in helping to prepare the final manuscript. Immense thanks are due to Dr. Lloyd Chapin, Dean of Faculty at Eckerd College, for granting Diana a year-long hexennial leave in order to complete the book. Finally, a very special note of gratitude goes to the many Eckerd students who have valiantly performed cost-benefit analyses as part of their course work and whose practical questions inspired this book. Needless to say, any errors in the text are ours.

We also want to express personal notes of gratitude. Diana thanks her parents, for their love and support in sharing the value of education and the joy of learning, and her many Eckerd colleagues, for creating a warm, supportive community where devoting the time and energy to write a book is encouraged. Shanton thanks his family for their support in taking the nontraditional job, his friends for their interest and help and, finally, his wife for her love and encouragement.

Part I

Cost-Benefit Analysis in Practice

Chapter 1

A History of Application

INTRODUCTION

The formal practice of cost-benefit analysis began in the public sector as an aid to government decision making. First adopted by the U.S. federal government during the 1930s to assess select public project expenditure decisions, the technique developed and took shape thereafter, eventually spreading to Britain in the 1960s as well as to other Western countries. The traditional technique therefore evolved within the context of the more advanced industrialized countries. A variant, referred to as "modern" cost-benefit analysis, was created in the 1970s, adapting the analysis to address the special circumstances of less developed countries and inform multilateral funding decisions. Meanwhile, the use of the traditional analysis continued to grow. In the United States in the 1980s and 1990s, interest in requiring federal regulatory agencies to undertake cost-benefit analysis for proposed major regulations spread to several levels of public decision making, including both the executive and legislative branches of the federal government as well as state and local governments.

In addition to the growing application of the analysis in the United States and around the world, the technique's versatility is suggested by its extension to a wide variety of decisions in numerous fields. Cost-benefit analysis has been applied to appraise such public expenditure alternatives as water resource projects, transportation projects, urban programs, education programs, health and nutrition policies, pollution control projects and endangered species preservation, as well as to assess government regulations in the areas of health, safety and the environment. All together, an extensive record of more than 60 years of experience has accumulated in the practice of cost-benefit analysis. Today, cost-benefit analysis embodies a diverse set of valuation techniques that are available for the prospective analyst to assess any of a large number of policy options in a variety of fields. Also, another variant of the technique, cost-effectiveness analysis, has been (and is) widely used in the areas of military spending and health policy decisions.

This chapter sketches the evolution of the application of cost-benefit analysis. Attention is devoted to public decision-maker objectives in adopting or requiring the technique. The response of constituencies to applications of the analysis within specific fields is also highlighted. Most notably, environmentalists have expressed serious concerns regarding the use of cost-benefit analysis to assess policies with environmental consequences, while businesses have endorsed the analysis as a rational means to control growing regulatory costs. In light of both groups' viewpoints, the discussion concludes by exploring President Reagan's executive order that required every proposed "major" federal regulation to pass a cost-benefit analysis before promulgation, followed by controversial Congressional legislation in 1995 that, if passed, would have expanded the role of the analysis in regulatory decision making.

1930s: U.S. FEDERAL WATER RESOURCE PROJECTS

Cost-benefit analysis was originally devised to inform U.S. public decisions for funding water resource projects. As early as the 1800s, U.S. legislation authorized engineering surveys of water resource needs and technical feasibility assessments of proposed federal water resource projects; economic evaluation, however, was introduced only gradually in a series of legislation passed decades later. Notably, the River and Harbor Acts of 1927 and 1928 authorized the Army Corps of Engineers to survey the nation's river basins comprehensively; the engineers also included in these "308" reports the estimated construction costs for proposed projects, thereby taking the first step toward economic evaluation (McKean 1958: 18). However, the question remained as to how legislators could justifiably prioritize the possible projects. What would be gained in exchange for the expense incurred by the taxpayers? If projects did not generate sufficient revenues to reimburse the U.S. Treasury—a likely possibility given the very nature of noncommercial public projects—on what grounds might their construction be warranted?

Congress answered these questions with the Flood Control Act of 1936. This act recognized controlling flood waters to be "in the interests of the general welfare" and stipulated that specific projects were economically justified "if the benefits to whomsoever they accrue are in excess of the estimated costs." Thus, Congress acknowledged that public flood control projects generate value in the form of products or services benefitting members of society. Prevention of flood damage, for example, can raise property values, increase agriculture crop production and the like. The legislation authorized the Department of Agriculture to estimate such public benefits along with costs.

The 1936 act marked the beginning of the application of economic principles to assess public expenditure decisions. The act is thus credited with initiating the practice of cost-benefit analysis, whereby both social gains (benefits) and costs are measured and expressed in monetary value, thereby facilitating easy comparison and rational project assessment.

The requirement that the benefits and costs of water resource projects be assessed became even more widespread with the 1939 U.S. Reclamation Project Act. This legislation authorized the Bureau of Reclamation in the western United States to commission irrigation and related water projects if the costs could be repaid by the farmers who used the irrigated water and/or, taking a comprehensive public viewpoint, could generate sufficient benefits to other members of society (McKean 1958: 19). Thus, the value of improved navigation, enhanced recreational and commercial fishing, increased water recreation activities and electric power generation began to be measured and included in project analysis. Once again, benefits were to be weighed with costs in the economic calculation. Moreover, the major federal agencies entrusted with applying cost-benefit analysis to assess select water-resource projects elected to employ the technique to appraise other projects as well.

Cost-benefit assessment thus evolved as a tool to inform the decision-making process, and as McKean observed, ''cost-benefit analyses clearly play an important role in the determination of budgets and in the selection of particular projects'' (1958: 20). Nevertheless, it must be emphasized that from the beginning the analysis was intended to be only one component of the information considered by public decision makers. As McKean reports,

The purpose of cost-benefit analysis, as it developed, was and is to *help* determine both the size of the Agencies' budgets, or the number of projects, and the particular projects that are to be undertaken. . . .

Naturally, this . . . is not regarded as the only piece of information which is relevant to these decisions. This is clearly recognized by the Agencies which prepare and use the analyses and by Congressmen, who also use them in reaching their decisions. (1958: 19, 20; emphasis in original)

Thus, cost-benefit analysis emerged as a *decision-making tool*, a useful source of information to aid the decision-making process but not the sole determinant of a given decision.

1950s: COST-EFFECTIVENESS ANALYSIS FOR MILITARY AND HEALTH EXPENDITURES

In the postwar era, as U.S. public expenditures grew, a rational analytical framework for determining budget priorities became all the more important. Accordingly, the principles underlying cost-benefit analysis began to spread to other decision areas. Noteworthy during the 1950s was the adaptation of the principles to create a related tool, cost-effectiveness analysis. This technique enables application of rational economic logic to assess policies for which it is extremely difficult if not impossible to value benefits in monetary terms.

Cost-effectiveness analysis developed specifically as part of efforts to extend economic criteria to assess military spending alternatives. To enhance military decision making, the RAND Corporation devised rules for allocating resources to achieve military objectives. In theory, benefits might be conceived as gains in military strength or national security or, perhaps more promising for valuation purposes, as the potential reduction in damage due to defense expenditure. However, even for this last, monetary measurement proved difficult. A more useful approach was to identify quantifiable objectives (such as the expected number of enemy targets destroyed or early detection of an enemy assault) and to determine which alternative expenditures were relatively cost effective in achieving each quantified objective (Hitch and McKean 1961: 110–20; 1967: 72–84). This reformulation of the analytical technique initiated the practice of cost-effectiveness analysis.

Also during the 1950s, health economics emerged as a field in its own right. Several alternatives including cost-of-illness analyses (COIAs), cost-benefit analyses and cost-effectiveness analyses were applied. By the late 1970s, cost-effectiveness analysis became the preferred technique for assessing health care when the saving (or premature loss) of a human life was involved. COIA values human life in terms of the individual's expected contribution to national income through labor productivity (a monetary value), while cost-benefit analysis values individual preferences for saving a human life in monetary terms. Many found these two techniques' monetary valuation of human life to be questionable. Cost-effectiveness analysis escaped this scrutiny by expressing health outcomes in such units as number of lives or life years saved (and more recently, quality-adjusted life years [QALYs] saved). To determine which policy options are relatively cost effective, the decision maker must still employ some implicit value of human life. However, the use of implicit values in the decision-making process can be less controversial than explicitly including such values in an analysis.

1960s: THE SPREAD OF COST-BENEFIT APPLICATIONS

By the 1960s, cost-benefit analysis had played a role in the political allocation of budgets for over twenty years; during that time, it had carved out a niche as a useful tool informing U.S. federal government decision makers. Not surprisingly, practitioners encountered problems with limited data and information constraints, yet some economic analysis was needed to aid rational assessment of public expenditures. The private sector's economic alternative, financial analysis, could not account for the gains achieved by non–revenue-generating expenditures; and cost-effectiveness analysis, although preferred in some fields, provided less information to the decision maker than did cost-benefit analysis. Cost-benefit analysis offered the most comprehensive and informative systematic technique to assess decision choices involving output or services not priced in markets.

Accordingly, the application of cost-benefit analysis continued to spread to other fields as well as to other countries.[1] Britain in particular began to explore use of the analysis to assess proposed transport investments. By the 1960s, economic principles had extended the methodology to the area of transportation, for instance, establishing how to value such transport benefits as the time savings to travelers. Cost-benefit analysis was first applied when the British government considered constructing the London-Birmingham motorway in 1960. Thereafter, although not a government requirement, application of the analysis continued to assess major British transportation projects. Then, in 1967 a Government White Paper gave the analysis "a limited role" in appraising decision alternatives for nationalized industries. The White Paper declared that managers of nationalized industries should make their decisions consulting financial business criteria; but when reason suggests the social benefits or costs might make a marked difference, the government would perform a cost-benefit analysis to assess the decision options (Pearce 1971: 15).

During the same decade, the cost-benefit methodology expanded to address policy decisions in additional fields. In the United States, for example, the principles were applied to assess alternative methods of pollution control. This launched an extensive research effort in the ensuing decades to develop valuation techniques for estimating the economic value of environmental quality and natural resources.

Indeed, in the 1960s an entirely new field, environmental economics, was born, with the cost-benefit framework forming the theoretical foundation for analyzing public policy options for managing environmental quality. Initially, the approach had little impact on environmental policy; such legislation as the U.S. Clean Air Act of 1970 and its 1977 amendments established air quality objectives with no apparent consideration of the associated benefits or costs. By the late 1980s and early 1990s, however, economic considerations had become a part of Congressional thinking and were explicitly incorporated in U.S. environmental legislation (for example, the 1990 U.S. Clean Air Act Amendments).[2]

1970s: CHALLENGES TO ENVIRONMENTAL VALUATION

During the 1970s, the practice of cost-benefit analysis continued to flourish in the United States as well as in many other countries. At the same time, the environmental movement began to challenge the method's application in Britain. The initial protest focused on the Roskill Commission's proposed Third London Airport location at the beginning of the decade. Supported by a cost-benefit analysis, the commission recommended the airport be constructed at a controversial inland location rather than at a more politically acceptable coastal site. The proposed inland location's closer proximity to residences offered reduced traveler time costs but greater noise pollution costs. The recommendation sparked a cry of outrage from the British environmental community, which found the seemingly low values of the noise pollution inconsistent with political preferences. In later years, with the advantage of hindsight, Pearce indicates that while there were methodological difficulties in the study's approach to valuing time saved, other studies' estimates do "not . . . suggest any significantly higher valuations for noise nuisance" (1983: 19). However, at the time, the outcry drew attention to the practice of environmental valuation.

Thereafter, critics began to question more broadly the application of cost-benefit analysis to value environmental quality. Most notably, Self (1975) and Schumacher (1975) challenged the very idea of assigning a monetary value to an environmental attribute. Despite such criticisms, the application of cost-benefit analysis in the environmental field continued to grow, especially in the United States.

1970s: LESS DEVELOPED COUNTRIES

Beyond the United States and Britain, the analysis spread to other regions, including less developed countries. In the 1950s and 1960s, project aid from the Western nations to less developed countries increased, leading in turn to numerous questions concerning the gains these projects achieved. Citizens of donor countries required justification from their governments for investing their tax monies in less developed countries. Agencies responsible for allocating these funds likewise sought an appraisal method for comparing investment alternatives. All led to a surge of interest in cost-benefit analysis. However, the economic circumstances characterizing the less developed world differed greatly from those in the West. Most notably, market prices were highly skewed (because of extensive government intervention in markets, limited competition and substantial unemployment and underinvestment) and thus were not useful measures in determining social value. In addition, high risk and uncertainty prevailed as a result of political unrest and specialized monocrop economies; also, the distribution of income and consumption was extremely unequal. Scholars therefore devised new analytical techniques, including a complex calculation of shadow prices (involving conversion factors, exchange rates and international price adjustments) as well as the determination of distributional weights (reflecting existing economic disparities and both present and future government redistribution objectives).

Manuals with guidelines detailing these techniques were written for the Organization for Economic Co-operation and Development (Little and Mirrlees 1969, 1974), the United Nations Industrial Development Organization (UNIDO 1972) and the World Bank (Squire and van der Tak 1975). These texts constitute the classic sources for the application of "modern" cost-benefit analysis in less developed countries. The intricate complexities of the approach are beyond the scope of this book, which limits its focus to the traditional analysis. Thus, we refer the interested reader to these and more recent sources, such as Ray (1984) and Dinwiddy and Teal (1996).

1980s AND 1990s: U.S. FEDERAL HEALTH, SAFETY AND ENVIRONMENTAL REGULATIONS

Within the United States, the federal government's role in the economy continued to expand throughout most of the postwar era. Federal spending grew as a percentage of gross domestic product. In addition, new regulatory agencies were established with authority over a broad range of industries, giving rise to a marked increase in federal regulation of the private sector.

Private businesses felt the federal government's influence most directly through these regulations and other bureaucratic decisions. By the late 1970s, the private sector expressed growing dissatisfaction, arguing that the private costs incurred to comply with federal regulations were excessive. In calling for deregulation, businesses eventually perceived cost-benefit analysis as a potential ally. Requiring regulations to satisfy a cost-benefit analysis offered the prospect of limiting the regulations and bringing rationality to regulatory decision making.

It is noteworthy that public outcries have been substantially greater in support of applying cost-benefit analysis to ensure the efficiency of regulations than ever was the case for public projects. This is not surprising, considering the likely distribution of benefits and costs from each. Public projects concentrate benefits on individuals in specific geographic areas, while the costs are dispersed across the nation's taxpayers. Thus, it is likely the prospective beneficiaries find it in their interest to seek the public expenditure, while the individual taxpayer gains little from challenging a project. In contrast, the benefits of regulations are often diffuse, spread across the nation—although sometimes they are intended to meet the needs of an identifiable select group (such as individuals suffering from a particular health condition). The costs, however, are generally concentrated, incurred by a small number of identifiable firms, often belonging to a particular industry and perhaps located in a specific geographical area. These businesses, each bearing a sizable share of the imposed costs, seek financial relief and thus challenge the regulations' rationality and fairness.

Meanwhile, the federal government's executive branch began to require cost-benefit analysis in the regulatory process. In 1974, with double-digit inflation in the U.S. economy, the possible inflationary effect of new regulations became a significant consideration. Accordingly, President Ford directed agencies to discuss the economic implications of select proposed regulations. This marked the first time that benefits and costs were officially part of the assessment of federal regulations.

Thereafter, U.S. presidents explicitly endorsed the objective of easing the regulatory burden on industries. As part of a broader deregulation strategy, President Carter promulgated Executive Order (E.O.) 12044 on March 23, 1978.

Among its stipulations, E.O. 12044 instructed agencies to perform an economic analysis weighing the potential regulatory costs with the potential benefits for all proposed "major" regulations, that is, any regulation that "would result" in (1) $100 million or more in annual costs to the economy or (2) "a major increase in costs or prices for individual industries, levels of government or geographic regions."[3] Thus, cost-benefit analysis became an important part of regulatory assessment. At the same time, as Alviani notes, "broad discretion remained for continued regulation in areas where costs and benefits were neither quantifiable nor measurable" (1980: 289).

The Reagan administration took markedly greater strides to incorporate cost-benefit analysis in the decision-making process and reduce regulatory burdens. President Reagan's E.O. 12291 on February 17, 1981, broadened the number of proposed rules requiring an economic analysis weighing benefits and costs— called a Regulatory Impact Analysis (RIA). For instance, the definition of a "major" rule was expanded to include any regulation "likely" to result in (1) $100 million in costs to the economy, (2) major cost or price increases or an added, third possibility, (3) "significant adverse effects on competition, employment, investment, productivity, innovation," or competition with foreign-based firms.[4] E.O. 12291 also allowed the Office of Management and Budget (OMB) to designate any rule or set of rules it so deemed as "major." Moreover, Reagan's E.O. 12291 responded to lobbyists by requiring for each proposed major rule, a rigorous demonstration that the potential benefits outweigh the potential social costs, *before* the rule can be promulgated. Thus, prior to being considered for a ruling, a new major regulation must pass a cost-benefit analysis, and federal agencies assumed the burden of proof for such economic justification (Alviani 1980).

After the announcement of E.O. 12291, concerns were expressed about the increased time required to propose, approve and promulgate new regulations, resulting in a slower and more cumbersome process. In addition, the ability of cost-benefit analysis to "pass final judgment" for all proposed major regulations was questioned from the standpoint of both data availability and measurement expenses, especially for health, safety and environmental benefits (Baldwin and Veljanovski 1984: 59). Despite such concerns, Reagan's E.O. 12291 remained in effect until the 1990s, when President Clinton issued E.O. 12866, which, for all intents and purposes, retained most of the Reagan order's provisions.

In the 1990s, national attention focused on the role of cost-benefit analysis in the regulatory process—this time in a new arena, Congress. A coalition of business representatives and state and local government officials, whose budgets were saddled with high compliance costs, sought further control over the federal regulatory process. The issue surged to the forefront in Congress when many well-known environmental regulations, including the Endangered Species Act and Superfund, were scheduled for reauthorization. In September 1994, Republicans in the House of Representatives unveiled the Contract with America promising, among other things, to bring "regulatory reform" bills to a vote in the first 100 days of a Republican-controlled Congress. In what was generally perceived as a public mandate, Republicans successfully gained majority control of the House in the November elections. During 1995, a number of bills were proposed specifying differing requirements for cost-benefit analysis in the regulatory process. The most prominent of these bills was the Risk Assessment and Cost-Benefit Analysis Act of 1995 (H.R. 1022).

Among H.R. 1022's specifications, the following were the most controversial.

- A risk assessment and cost-benefit analysis would be required for all proposed major regulations, with "major" defined as any rule with annual compliance costs to governments and the private sector of $25 million or more.

- For proposed regulations entailing more than $100 million in costs (and for any others designated by the head of the OMB), agencies must develop a program for *peer review* by a panel of outside experts, which "shall not exclude peer reviewers with substantial and relevant expertise merely because they represent entities that may have a potential interest in the outcome."

- After completion of the risk assessment, cost-benefit analysis and peer review, the agency head must "certify" the regulation's benefits are "likely to justify" the costs— a requirement that would "supersede" any conflicting criteria. Therefore, similar to Reagan E.O. 12291, establishing sufficient evidence that a proposed rule is expected to achieve positive net benefits and thereby passes a cost-benefit analysis is a necessary requirement before a final ruling.

- After agency certification and before the final regulatory decision, the proposed regulation is subject to *judicial review*. An individual or entity who perceives the data and analyses do not justify agency certification, and thus a final regulation, can pursue this argument in court. Final ruling is prohibited until (and if) any such court case is resolved and the agency's decision is upheld.[5]

Among the proponents' strongest arguments in favor of the bill was the desire for a rational regulatory process. As Mr. Walker, chair of the Committee on Science, urged, "Congress must help ensure an effective and workable system of accountability, disclosure, peer review, and careful analysis of alternatives. In the end, we must ensure that the federal government can stand behind and justify regulations based on the facts." Also, "careful consideration and objective information will help ensure that hundreds of billions of dollars in annual economic costs are focused on real and substantial risk reduction" (U.S. House 1995).

At the same time, numerous criticisms challenged the proposed legislation. Several members of the Science Committee submitted a dissenting statement, declaring that HR 1022 "sets up a cumbersome and costly procedural maze which is much more likely to lead to gridlock and costly new bureaucracy rather than to faster and more rational rulemaking"; also, the bill "turns what is a laudable goal—encouraging better cost-benefit analysis—into an inflexible and unobtainable prerequisite for any regulation" (U.S. House 1995). Environmental

Protection Agency (EPA) Administrator Browner, in a public interview, concurred with this last statement. She endorsed the importance of cost-benefit analysis and noted the EPA's increased use of the tool in recent years. At the same time, she explained that "to require in every single instance that the dollar amounts be applied to human lives, to IQ points lost in our children . . . and to deny us the right to act when the benefits [of providing protection] are not such that they clearly outweigh the cost is unfair to the American people" (Browner 1995). Moreover, unlike analyses of public projects where the main costs are government expenditures, regulatory analyses confront the task of collecting estimated costs from the to-be-regulated businesses (who are sometimes wary of supplying confidential information that may become known to competitors, or who may overstate their costs so the regulation appears less favorable).

Many opponents questioned the extension of the risk assessment and cost-benefit analysis requirement to regulations involving annual costs as low as $25 million, noting the additional expense to the federal government of performing such analyses (for instance, see Greer 1995). For example, a single cost-benefit analysis prepared by the EPA reportedly cost on average $675,000, ranging from some $200,000 to more than $2.3 million (U.S. House 1995); in addition, the bureaucracy would grow in size with the hiring of additional staff to perform these analyses. In another area of disagreement, conflicting views were expressed about the validity of allowing experts with possible vested interests to be peer reviewers (for example, see Stevens 1995). Finally, the judicial review provisions were criticized. Without HR 1022, businesses were pursuing numerous lawsuits challenging regulations after passage; the bill would enable judicial challenge before passage. In such a case, implementation of the regulation, along with its benefits, would be postponed, and the challenge would focus on the agency's data and analysis with the burden of proof belonging to the agency. For both risk assessment and cost-benefit analysis, the "state of the art" in estimating particular hard-to-measure risks or benefits (such as the value of a human life or an ecological system) is not sufficiently developed to demonstrate regulatory benefits with an accuracy that precludes judicial challenge. Moreover, a thoughtful judicial judgment would require a level of court expertise that can discern the validity of a particular analysis given the limitations of the technique and available data (Shenk 1995; Stevens 1995). In all, many onlookers, ranging from members of the environmental movement to experts skilled in performing cost-benefit analyses, opposed the proposed judicial review process as well as the bill's extension of a stringent cost-benefit test as a prerequisite to certifying each and every regulation with annual costs of $25 million or more.

After much debate during the early months of 1995, H.R. 1022 passed the House of Representatives (March 1) but was not brought to a vote in the Senate, and thus it did not become law. Nevertheless, the discussion serves to highlight some of the political interests that surround the use of cost-benefit analysis, as various parties (in this case, regulated industries and potential beneficiaries from the regulations) stand to gain or lose based on the results. More important, the experience demonstrates the political pressure that can arise in support of using the tool to supplant decision-maker judgment rather than as one source of information in a complex decision-making process. Such a stance establishes an economic criterion as the prerequisite to a given decision, perhaps at the expense of other laudable objectives (e.g., enhancing distributional equity, protecting human rights or nature's rights). In addition, the viewpoint attributes to the analysis an accuracy and reliability that is not warranted in those instances where appropriate valuation techniques are not yet sufficiently developed or data are unavailable or too costly to gather. Thus, caution is urged along with appreciation of what has become a highly sophisticated analytical technique—one that can provide useful economic assessment yet is no substitute for the decision maker's grappling with competing objectives and political interests in a complex real-world context.

CONCLUSION

The history of cost-benefit analysis has been one of growing application— across different fields, in a variety of countries and across a range of public policies, from infrastructure projects to programs to regulations. In addition, within the United States, the use of cost-benefit analysis has begun to expand to other levels of public decision making. For example, a number of states require the analysis to assess whether to offer economic incentive packages to induce corporations to establish in-state operations (Carlile 1994). Also noteworthy, environmental groups have begun to sponsor economic analyses for the environmental policies they support; one of many examples is an economic valuation study of the manatee partially funded by the Save the Manatee Club (Bendle and Bell 1995).

Likewise, private decision makers have found the tool valuable. For instance, as business expenditures have increased in response to expanding environmental regulations and the public's growing environmental consciousness, major corporations such as DuPont have begun to apply systematic techniques to assess the efficiency of alternative environmental investments they might pursue (Epstein 1994). Corporations can easily implement cost-benefit analyses as part of their decision methods to determine both a business decision's financial impact on the company and the broader social impact on customers or the surrounding community. Such analysis provides management with information that might show detrimental (or beneficial) social impacts in the long run that outweigh the short-term financial gains (or losses) and thus alter decisions based only on short-term profitability.

Such diverse applications suggest the usefulness of cost-benefit analysis as a decision-making tool. Moreover, it is a tool that developed in response to a practical decision-making need, specifically, how to assess and prioritize policy alternatives that generate benefits or costs not priced in markets. As such, it is one source of information in the decision-making process. Care must be exerted both in conducting and in interpreting a cost-benefit analysis to ensure appropriate use by the decision maker. The roles of the decision maker and analyst in shaping the analysis are considered in Chapter 2.

NOTES

1. Ironically, at this time the theoretical economics literature viewed cost-benefit analysis, along with its underlying theory ("welfare economics") and explicit value judgments, to be seriously flawed, with no prospect of future application. For a discussion of the theoretical issues, including a formal presentation of Scitovsky's "reversal paradox" discrediting the analysis, see Pearce and Nash (1981: 2–3) and Pearce (1983: 17, 20–23). The theoretical debate, which undoubtedly seemed highly abstract to applied practitioners, did not block the progress of applications. Indeed, the growing practice eventually inspired further development of the technique's theoretical foundation, and despite the paradox, welfare economics evolved to become a recognized field within economics.

2. The 1990 amendments allowed emissions trading between polluting plants, thereby introducing market incentives to encourage cost-effective pollution reduction as well as to stimulate private research and development of new low-cost, pollution-reducing technologies.

3. Executive Order No. 12044, 3 C.F.R 152 (1978); extended by presidential action, 45 *Federal Register* 44249 (1980).

4. Executive Order No. 12291, 46 *Federal Register* 13193 (1981).

5. HR 1022's text, in its original form as "Division D" of HR 9, is found on the Internet via ftp://ftp.loc.gov/pub/thomas/c104/h9.eh.txt.

Chapter 2

The Decision Maker, the Analyst and Cost-Benefit Analysis

INTRODUCTION

This chapter introduces the two main characters who work most closely with a cost-benefit analysis the decision maker who uses it as a tool in the decision-making process and the analyst who performs the analysis. The decision maker might be a government body, a political group, a committee or a sole individual. Likewise, the analyst may represent an entire agency, department, or work team or be one person. For convenience, this book refers in the singular to the decision maker and the analyst, as if she and he, respectively, are each one individual. It should be understood that the discussion applies if in reality multiple individuals assume either role.

The chapter considers the respective roles of the decision maker and analyst in shaping the cost-benefit analysis. While the decision maker is responsible for considering relevant information and making a final policy decision, it is the analyst's responsibility to perform an objective analysis and write a lucid, accessible and thorough report. Their interaction and cooperation are critical in ensuring that the final analysis is an appropriate and suitable tool that facilitates the decision-making process.

A DECISION-MAKING TOOL

As discussed in Chapter 1, cost-benefit analysis is a decision-making tool, designed to provide information and thereby aid the public decision maker when choosing between policy alternatives. As such, it does not displace political decision making, for it does not dictate the final decision. Rather, it is one input in the decision-making process. In the end, it is the decision-maker's responsibility to wrestle with difficult issues, weigh competing objectives and values and apply informed judgment to reach a final decision.

The public decision maker confronts numerous policy alternatives yet is constrained by finite budget resources. Choices must be made. Cost-benefit analysis offers a reasoned framework to help assess and prioritize alternative policies according to their relative efficiency. In particular, it measures individuals' preferences concerning the desirability (benefits) and burdens (costs) of a given policy alternative. Moreover, as a quantitative analysis, it assesses relevant data and mathematically deduces a policy's implications for society. Equally important, a properly conducted analysis explicitly states any and all assumptions, assesses uncertain policy consequences and carefully identifies and describes those policy effects that are not quantifiable. In these ways, the analysis facilitates decision-maker deliberation, providing useful information and illuminating issues for consideration.

INTERACTION: DECISION MAKER AND ANALYST

For an analysis to be conducted properly while also serving the decision-maker's information needs, it is important that the decision maker and the analyst interact cooperatively and productively at the beginning of the analytical process. In particular, close communication is required to resolve the key question of how rigorously the cost-benefit analysis should be performed. Before they confer, the decision maker must determine the analytical rigor she seeks as well as the budget available to finance the analysis. At one extreme, she might perform her own ''back-of-the-envelope'' assessment or request professional help in conducting a relatively informal weighing of the perceived benefits and costs to members of society. At the other end of the spectrum, she could ask for a highly sophisticated professional analysis that employs, as relevant, extensive surveys and valuation techniques applying multivariate statistical analysis.

With a level of professional analysis in mind, she is ready to consult the prospective analyst. In their exchange, the decision maker and analyst should consider the trade-offs among the following:

- desired thoroughness and accuracy of the analysis
- available budgetary resources
- allowable time frame for conducting the analysis
- readily available data
- feasibility and expense of gathering additional data
- feasibility of alternative valuation methods
- statistical sophistication and expense of any preferred valuation method

The analyst must find out the decision maker's reasons for requesting the analysis and, specifically, the information that the decision maker hopes to gain. Then, the analyst must assess the suitability of cost-benefit analysis for the decision maker's purposes and advise her accordingly.

It would be highly convenient if the analyst discovered that the decision maker's preferences and the requirements of the analysis are compatible. If not, then the analyst might decline the request to perform the analysis. (This may be no small decision if circumstances necessitate seeking alternative employment.) Or, instead, he might accept the assignment and confront the task of achieving an honorable compromise. If the latter, it is crucial that any adjustments compromising the analysis be carefully disclosed in the final report. For example, it may be a simple matter that particular benefits or costs receive extensive explanation and others are merely highlighted in the final report. If all benefits and costs are carefully valued and (correctly) included in the cost-benefit calculation, the analyst should simply explain the decision-maker's special interest in the details of designated benefits and costs. A more difficult situation occurs when, in compliance with the decision maker's preferences, the analyst excludes some policy effects from the analysis. Sassone and Schaffer advise,

> the analyst must flatly state in his report which areas have not been investigated, and also state his opinion as to whether such an investigation would affect the overall assessment of a project. In addition, he should state to what extent the choice of areas . . . was influenced by the decision-maker. In this way, the decision-maker may be accommodated without a sacrifice of CBA [cost-benefit analysis] integrity. (1978: 161)

Alternatively, the decision maker might prefer the analysis not be performed. The request for a cost-benefit assessment might stem from a government requirement, an administrative superior or external pressure imposed by policy advocates or adversaries. In such a case, interaction with the decision maker can be more difficult, and gaining decision-maker cooperation can be more challenging. Sugden and Williams write, "Because the analyst has some responsibility to principles over and above those held by the decision-maker, he may have to ask questions that the decision-maker would prefer not to answer, and which expose to debate conflicts of judgment and of interest that might otherwise comfortably have been concealed" (1978: 241). Furthermore, the analyst has an allegiance to the general society that the decision maker serves. As Sugden and Williams note, it might be argued that "the role of the analysis is to assist, not simply a decision-maker, but a decision-making process that has the assent of the community as a whole. The decision-maker is responsible for making a decision, according to his own lights, but he is responsible to the community. His right to decide stems from the consent of the community, expressed through the political system" (1978: 240–41). By upholding analytical standards, the analyst increases the decision-maker's accountability to society.

Once the analyst agrees to perform the analysis, and he and the decision maker concur as to the level of rigor (and associated details), there is another area of interaction. As is discussed in Parts II and III, there are a number of technical decisions where the analyst has some discretion; in each case, consultation with the decision maker is recommended. This dialogue can occur at the beginning of the process or at some point during the analysis.

OBJECTIVE ANALYSIS: THE ANALYST'S ROLE

As a tool of the social sciences, cost-benefit analysis combines systematic organization and assessment with information that is inherently subjective. Specifically, the analysis measures the subjective preferences of those individuals affected by a policy who perceive policy consequences as either beneficial or burdensome. In this respect, the analysis is political. In addition, the analytical technique itself embodies a number of value judgments concerning whose preferences count, how these are weighted and the role of income distribution in an assessment of efficiency. Moreover, although the analysis is an established method with decades of application experience, the current state of the art entails unresolved issues regarding a number of technical procedures, thereby allowing the analyst (or decision maker) to exert discretion. The analyst's choices when performing the analysis can thus introduce additional subjective influence.

It is critical for the analyst to assume the role of an objective third party who has no interest, one way or the other, in the analytical outcome. The analyst's responsibility is to conduct the analysis with professional objectivity and minimize inappropriate subjective influences. Specifically, in performing the analysis, the analyst must (1) minimize any biases or otherwise misleading influences reflected in the measurements of individuals' subjective preferences, (2) explicitly identify any value judgments embodied in the analysis and make transparent their implications for the outcome and (3) where analyst or decision-maker discretion is possible, choose an approach that minimizes either one's subjective influence and demonstrates the sensitivity of the analysis to alternative (subjective) choices. With respect to these ends, Parts II and III offer several recommendations to assist objective analysis.

THE ANALYST'S FINAL REPORT

When all is said and done, a cost-benefit analysis is designed to facilitate responsible decision making by providing information to the decision maker and, as relevant, the interested public. Accordingly, when writing a cost-benefit analysis, the analyst's goal is to keep the presentation simple yet informative for the decision maker as well as other interested readers. The analysis must be clear, readable and understandable. Just as important, the final report should provide enough details (including, for example, appending any survey instrument and collected raw data) to allow the results to be reproduced, if desired, by anyone scrutinizing the accuracy of the techniques. Unclear presentation renders the analysis unusable as a decision-making tool as well as inaccessible to interested parties.

Throughout the report, the analyst should make explicit each of the following:

* all assumptions made in the analysis
* all value judgments embodied in the cost-benefit technique
* any technical choice made when performing the analysis
* any biases or subjective influences that may affect the analytical outcome
* possible errors in analytical procedures or estimates

In each case, the analyst should indicate the implications for the study's estimates and conclusions. Where analyst or decision-maker discretion is involved, justification should be provided for the particular choice along with the associated advantages and disadvantages. Also, when writing the final report, the analyst should keep in mind the decision maker's objectives in considering the policy as well as the competing values and views that the policy proposal is likely to encounter. The report should explicitly highlight any aspects of the analysis that are relevant to these concerns. Finally, the analyst should assess the factors that are likely to cause the final estimate in the analysis to be a conservative one or an overestimate.

INSTITUTIONAL CAPTURE: THE NEED FOR ACCOUNTABILITY

The possibility is always present that either the decision maker or the analyst might influence the analysis and thus "capture" it for her or his own ends. Sometimes such *institutional capture* can be very subtle, to the point that many would not be able to distinguish the key characteristics that differentiate an objective analysis from one that has been purposefully directed. Several examples illustrating institutional capture are classic. First, the decision maker might require technical procedures that alter the analytical assessment of efficiency. For instance, President Nixon ordered the use of a relatively high discount rate for analyses of most federal projects; thus, some relatively efficient projects were determined to be inefficient. Many authors relate this requirement to Nixon's promise to reduce public expenditures. (An arbitrarily high discount rate establishes a hurdle that relatively few projects can pass.) Moreover, in response to Western states' interests, federal water projects were excluded from this stipulation; analyses for these projects were allowed to use a specified low discount rate. The dual rates altered the relative efficiency ranking of the projects, making water projects look more efficient and other projects less efficient than actually was the case. By instituting different discount rates for two separate categories of federal projects, Nixon effectively shaped all federal cost-benefit analyses produced during his administration.

Second, the decision maker might issue rules that alter the use of properly and objectively conducted analyses to achieve a separate agenda. Examples include President Reagan's 1981 executive order and the 1995 Congressional legislative efforts to require every new major regulation to meet a strict cost-benefit standard in order to receive consideration—a stringent test that the analytical tool, given the current state of the art, is not yet designed to meet. Indications are that the objective was to reduce the number of new regulations and the associated regulatory burdens on private businesses, at the expense of efficiency and rational decision making. (Note that the issue is not that the decision makers sought to achieve an objective different from efficiency—a perfectly legitimate option—but rather that they stretched the tool too far and subordinated the decision-making process to the cost-benefit calculation and assessment.)

Third, some analysts have been known to "capture" analyses. For example, agency analysts have reportedly adjusted analyses, perhaps by projecting generous benefits or excluding select costs from the cost-benefit calculation. They thereby made agency-sponsored policies look more efficient in order to be more competitive for funding from the decision maker.

To reduce the possibility of *institutional capture*, the main solution is to make the analysis accountable. Cost-benefit analysis must be subject to inspection by both the public and peers. It is therefore imperative that interested persons, especially those affected by government policies (or groups or individuals working on their behalf), become familiar with the technique. Chapter 3 emphasizes further the importance of learning the technical details of the analysis. It presents a few applications that illustrate how advocates and adversaries of an assessed policy might scrutinize an analysis. Through public and private debate, the raised questions and criticisms increase the accountability of the analysis and, in turn, the accountability of the analyst and decision maker.

Chapter 3

Policy Advocates and Adversaries: Scrutiny and Accountability

INTRODUCTION

This chapter presents a number of hypothetical though realistic applications to illustrate cost-benefit analysis in practice. None of the examples is complete in itself; however, together the sketches introduce many of the main procedures that comprise cost-benefit analysis. Moreover, the scenarios suggest the role played by interested parties (both policy advocates and adversaries) in scrutinizing analyses to ensure their accuracy. This scrutiny, along with the rigor of a properly conducted cost-benefit analysis, work together both to inform decision makers and to add accountability to the decision-making process.

Also, the examples highlight some of the technical details that the reader, whether prospective analyst, decision maker or interested party, should consider when preparing to undertake, interpret or critique a cost-benefit analysis. For those readers interested in turning directly to the particular book section that addresses a specific technical concept, the concept and relevant chapter number are indicated at the end of each illustration.

These short scenarios undoubtedly will raise additional questions in the reader's mind—which is perhaps a useful exercise in itself. With a questioning mind and sharpened focus, the reader can inspect an actual cost-benefit analysis while asking critically: What else does he or she want to know? What assumptions or other important details are not presented, whether purposefully or by oversight, that have important bearing on the analytical conclusions? Furthermore, it should be noted that these examples do not describe any single case in reality but, rather, are composite scenarios of many different cost-benefit applications.

SEVEN ILLUSTRATIVE APPLICATIONS

Parades

A major city government receives growing complaints from city drivers and local businesses about the frustration of traffic delays and detours as busy downtown streets are increasingly closed for parades at intermittent points throughout the week. With a political election imminent, and thus a brief time frame in which to respond to the growing clamor, the mayor seeks a rapid assessment of the social costs of parades. A policy analyst quickly determines the municipal government's expenditures during a recent parade for the hours spent by police controlling traffic and sanitation workers cleaning streets. He also approximates the value of passenger time lost during parade delays. Specifically, he estimates the number of affected cars and passengers from traffic study data, uses a working estimate of the typical time loss during the parade delay, then values this time with an average wage rate for the city. (For a real world application, see Tierney 1995.) He reports these calculations to the mayor, indicating that the total social cost imposed by the one parade is roughly $1 million. The mayor presents this argument at a press conference along with a statement that he is seriously considering regulating the number of parades. Parade sponsors immediately contact the mayor's office, arguing this reasoning ignores the contribution that parades make to enhancing a sense of community within the city as well as celebrating and strengthening the sponsoring groups' identities. At the next press conference, the mayor issues a statement indicating his commitment to finding alternative venues (entailing fewer social costs) to support various groups in the city.

This example suggests the merit of cost-benefit logic, even when performed informally using ''ballpark'' estimates, in helping the decision maker formulate policy. Moreover, the explicit assumptions, when presented openly to policy adversaries, facilitate effective opponent response, resulting in additional useful information being communicated to the decision maker.

Technical concepts:

• valuation of time, see *travel cost method* (Chapter 19)

Mass Transit

A small city proposes constructing a modern high-tech, fixed-rail mass transit system. It seeks federal funding for part of the very expensive capital construction costs. City planners survey a random sample of city residents, asking respondents to state the likely number of rides they would take per month and the maximum amount they would be willing to pay per trip if such a transit system was available. Using this information, the number of riders and the total value they receive from the transit trips are estimated. Anticipating city population growth, these figures are projected 100 years into the future. In addition, the city reports the expected increase in property values near the mass transit line as an indication of the many city residents who would benefit from the proposed transit system. Together, these provide what the city planners believe is a compelling case that the social benefits are greater than the costs of the transit system.

Upon reviewing the city's grant application, the federal funding agency raises some questions. The agency observes that the city planners simply add the projected riders' values over time, yet the common practice in economics is to discount future values. Appropriate discounting would lower the estimated benefits notably. The federal agency also questions the lengthy time period over which benefits are counted—a not uncommon practice that overstates the total benefits. In addition, whether the planners considered relative price changes and expected future inflation is unclear. As for the estimated increases in property values, the agency's analyst points out that in some situations such values can be relevant in assessing a policy's benefits. In this case, however, these values are merely price effects, not representing any increase in real output; furthermore, the property values' inclusion essentially doubly counts the benefits received by those property owners whose valuation of the transit system is reflected in their stated willingness to pay (gathered by the planners' survey). A federal analyst quickly performs a cost-benefit analysis that uses the city's data and takes into account these concerns as well as others. The analysis determines that the very costly mass transit system is not warranted by the projected social benefits for such a small city. Given the large number of cities competing for limited federal funds, the agency rejects the grant application.

Technical concepts:

- survey asking respondents to state their willingness to pay, see *contingent valuation method* (Chapter 18)
- discount future values, see *present value* (Chapter 9)
- time period under analysis, see *time horizon* (Chapter 13)
- relative price changes and expected future inflation, see *inflation: ex ante analysis* (Chapter 12)
- price effects, see *pecuniary effects* (Chapter 16)
- property values, see *hedonic pricing method* (Chapter 20)

New Health Vaccine

A medical researcher has created and tested a new vaccine, determining it to be both safe and effective for immunizing children to avoid a particular common illness. Based on the tests, he assesses the benefits and costs of vaccinating children in the United States. The main benefits are (1) the reduction in the more serious diseases that a child might develop after having this particular illness, (2) the savings to those parents who would be spared from the time spent staying home with their sick child and foregoing several day's wages and (3) the reduced medical expenditures for treating the illness. The estimated cost is the expense of administering the vaccine. His analysis calculates a benefit-cost ratio (B/C) of 2.5, indicating that for every dollar spent, the vaccine generates $2.50 in benefits. He submits his study for publication in a leading medical journal.

Upon reading the article, the journal editors raise several questions. As medical doctors, they express concerns that the risks of short-term side effects are not quantified, let alone valued as part of the costs. Also, any long-term effects of the vaccine are ignored in the cost-benefit assessment (for instance, how long will the child's immunity last?). They believe most practicing doctors would want to know the evidence on these matters before administering the vaccine. One of the editors who has economics training questions the very low discount rate employed in the analysis and wonders how far the B/C would fall if a reasonably higher discount rate were used. He also expresses regret that the medical researcher reports the B/C and not the net present value (NPV). He notes that there may be practical reasons why the medical community prefers the B/C; however, the NPV is less prone to subjective influence and thus is more reliable for comparing and ranking alternative medical procedures according to their relative efficiency.

Technical concepts:

- risk of short-term side effects, see *risk* (Chapter 14)
- high or low discount rate, see *discount rate* (Chapter 11)
- B/C or NPV, see *decision criteria* (Chapter 10)

Oil Spill Damages

After a major oil spill in a pristine coastal region, a government agency takes the oil company to court seeking payment of compensatory damages. A government analyst conducts an extensive analysis to estimate the damages caused by the spill. The economic value of the lost commercial fish catch is predicted using time-series analysis of relevant fish markets. Losses to recreational fishers, sun bathers and other visitors who enjoy the area's coastal scenery are estimated by applying the results of a survey performed the prior year that analyzed visitors' travel expenses to and from the coast. In addition, a survey asks individuals throughout the country, who might never visit the well-known coastal area, to indicate, hypothetically, how much they would be willing to pay to prevent similar damage from occurring in the future. All together, the analyst estimates the total damages imposed by the oil spill to be $3 billion.

The liable oil company challenges the accuracy of the analysis in statistically isolating the oil spill's effects from other environmental and socioeconomic factors that affected the coastal region's commercial fishing and visitation rates. The company also questions the reliability of the national survey that asks respondents who may never visit the site to answer a hypothetical valuation question; the corporation contends that such estimates should not be included as part of the assessed damages.

In contrast, upon examining the analyst's report, regional residents challenge the $3 billion estimate as too low. Representatives of the tourism industry are quick to point out that regional motels, restaurants and businesses lost millions of dollars in tourist expenditures, yet these are not included in the visitor survey estimates. Moreover, lost jobs in the tourism and fishing industries resulted in declining expenditures by the local population, leading to further contraction of the regional economy. The representatives, upon being informed that these values might not fit appropriately within the cost-benefit methodology, contend that, nevertheless, these losses should be measured and included in a supplementary analysis, for they rightfully belong with the assessed damages.

A national environmental group protests that the oil spill killed numerous forms of marine life, including some members of endangered species. They recognize the visitor and national survey estimates might include some human valuation of marine life (and thus these deaths), yet they emphasize that as the life of any sentient being has a priceless, intrinsic value, the losses to marine life are incalculable. They call for a substantially larger damage assessment, with the additional funds devoted to research and development of preventive technologies to ensure such a spill will never happen again.

Representatives of indigenous coastal populations report that their traditional way of life and subsistence consumption of marine life has been compromised by the oil spill. They express surprise that the report makes no mention of their loss. Furthermore, they emphasize that traditional economic valuation is not appropriate for measuring the lost value to their communities because the approach estimates value in monetary terms; their peoples' respect for the customary way of life far surpasses the relatively meager incomes they earn.

Technical concepts:

- time series analysis of commercial fish markets, see *market valuation* (Chapter 17)

- a survey eliciting hypothetical valuation responses for a site that respondents may never visit, see *non-use value* and the *contingent valuation method* (Chapters 16 and 18)

- analysis of travel expenses to visit a site, see *travel cost method* (Chapter 19)

- declining tourist and local expenditures, see the *expenditure method, secondary benefits* and *economic impact analysis* (Chapters 16 and 19)

- loss of marine life, see *defined society* and *nonhuman nature's rights* (Chapter 6)

• indigenous populations' values, see *human rights* (Chapter 4) and *ability to pay* (Chapter 8)

Substance Abuse Treatment Programs for Adolescents

A clinic providing in-patient and out-patient services for adolescents seeks both public and private funding in support of expanding the in-patient facility. In order to strengthen the case to be presented to grant-sponsoring agencies and donors, the Board of Directors considers hiring a consultant to estimate the social benefits and costs of such an expansion. In an initial meeting with the prospective analyst, the board offers to provide estimates of the construction and annual operating costs of the facility expansion. The analyst shares a draft outlining suggested procedures for benefits valuation. He requests access to clinic records documenting past treatments and patient follow-ups in order to project the likely success rate of the expanded in-patient services. The benefits valuation would then focus on the successful participants, defined as those who never resume substance abuse. He explains to the board that the guiding principle is to value the "incremental benefits" resulting from these participants' success. Specifically, he would need to determine the likely lifelong changes for a successful participant in comparison to a "baseline" (defined as the same individual continuing to abuse substances at some designated, expected rate). His preliminary research suggests that, compared to the baseline, a successful participant is likely to experience a changed probability of completing high school or college, engaging in crime, achieving high on-the-job productivity and dying prematurely. The analytical approach involves, first, estimating these changed probabilities and, second, quantifying and monetarily valuing the changed behavior's magnitude.

The analyst and the board discuss professional contacts and other sources of information to estimate the changed probabilities, and they explore alternative valuation techniques. One board member mentions the benefits to society of saving the worker productivity lost with premature death. The analyst responds that, yes, this is a benefit identified in the professional literature on substance abuse treatment; however, the principles of a cost-benefit analysis suggest that a more inclusive value of human life is a preferred measure. They agree to discuss these measures further after the research is in progress.

The analyst indicates that the analysis, once concluded, will yield estimated total values for the discounted benefits, costs and net benefits of the expanded facility. A corporate member of the board asks about determining a rate of return on the investment. The analyst responds that, technically, such an estimate can be measured. However, he expresses hesitancy about reporting it to prospective funding agencies, for it is less reliable than NPV in ranking the discounted net benefits of one proposal relative to another. The board and the analyst conclude the meeting with a discussion of the desired rigor and accuracy of the analysis as well as the size of the budget that might be approved for the analyst and his research expenditures.

Technical concepts:

- incremental benefits, see *"with and without" analysis* (Chapter 7)
- probability and magnitude of future events, see *risk* (Chapter 14)
- lost worker productivity due to premature death, see *human capital method* (Chapter 21)
- discounted net benefits (NPV), see *decision criteria* (Chapter 10)
- rate of return on investment, see *internal rate of return (IRR)* (Chapter 11)

Mandatory Alcohol Testing of Transportation Employees

A federal agency proposes mandatory alcohol tests, randomly administered, for transportation employees as one of its regulations promoting transportation safety. In support of the proposed regulation, the agency presents an analysis demonstrating that the benefits of reduced transport accidents, including reduced physical damage and saved human lives, outweigh the costs of alcohol testing (to be borne by the industry).

Industry representatives respond to the announcement with dismay, arguing that the government's study greatly underestimates the expenses they will incur and uses data that grossly overstates the number of alcohol-related commercial transport accidents in recent years. Moreover, an industry consultant questions the benefits valuation, observing that the study used a value of human life notably higher than the range of estimates generally accepted in the economics literature. Accordingly, the transportation industry sponsors a cost-benefit analysis that uses industry estimates of the required alcohol testing expenses, revised figures for alcohol-related accidents, and three estimates (high, medium and low) derived from the recent literature for the value of the saved lives. This analysis finds that the cost of mandatory testing outweighs the safety benefits for all three value-of-life estimates. The transport industry thus challenges the federal agency's proposed regulation.

Technical concepts:

- value of a saved life, see *value of human life* (Chapter 21)
- applying high, medium and low estimates for an uncertain value, see *uncertainty* and *sensitivity analysis* (Chapter 14)

Municipal Recycling

A municipality seeks to promote recycling among community residents and, specifically, considers establishing either drop-off centers located at strategic points in the community or a residential curbside pickup service. An analyst estimates the cost per pound of recycled materials for each of the two programs.

Comparing the two estimates, he concludes that the drop-off centers are the relatively cost-effective alternative.

An environmental citizens' group, committed to maximum recycling and thus to curbside pickup, questions the analysis. They note that public statements of the analyst's appraisal do not indicate whose costs are being measured; however, a close reading of the report reveals that the analyst considered only the costs to the municipality. This, of course, makes the small number of drop-off centers appear to be the more cost-effective option, for omitted from consideration are the sizable costs incurred by the households who must devote time and resources to transport their recyclable materials to the centers. In contrast, the convenience of a curbside pickup service would not only lower these social costs but also encourage substantially greater materials recycling. The group's spokesperson further adds that when choosing one of two alternative policies, the appropriate decision criterion is the incremental cost-effectiveness ratio, not the average (or per unit) ratio.

Technical concepts:

- comparing the non-monetary quantity effects with clearly identified policy costs, see *cost-effectiveness analysis* (Chapter 22)
- valuing household time and resources spent in transport, see *travel cost method* (Chapter 19)
- choosing one of alternative policies, see *mutually exclusive policies* and *incremental cost-effectiveness ratio* (Chapter 22)

CONCLUSION

The illustrative applications presented in this chapter, although few in number, suggest the versatility of cost-benefit analysis. It is a systematic approach that is relevant for assessing a variety of policies in a wide range of decision-making contexts. Moreover, not only does the analysis inform the decision maker, but its availability for open review also adds transparency to the decision-making process. By explicitly stating assumptions, comprehensively identifying policy effects and mathematically deducing consequences, the analysis provides a framework that facilitates substantive discourse between the decision maker and interested parties—those individuals directly affected by a given policy as well as other policy advocates and adversaries. Furthermore, scrutiny of specific applications increases the accountability of cost-benefit analysis and, in turn, the decision maker. In these ways, the analytical technique encourages responsible decision making.

This chapter suggests the importance of the prospective analyst, the decision maker and interested parties alike becoming familiar with the details of the cost-benefit technique. The core of the book therefore focuses on explaining the analytical approach. Specifically, Parts II and III describe step by step the various procedures that comprise cost-benefit analysis and alternative valuation methods, respectively. Each chapter presents principles guiding how a particular procedure should be performed in conformity with the theoretical economic foundation. Where subjective influences may introduce bias or otherwise be misleading, special attention is devoted to identifying techniques the analyst can apply to enhance the objectivity of the analysis.

Part II

How to Do Cost-Benefit Analysis

Chapter 4

Economics and Cost-Benefit Analysis

INTRODUCTION

What constitutes a proper cost-benefit analysis? Although a standard decision-making tool for policy makers, the technique (especially its procedural details) is often not fully understood. The recent regulatory reform debate in Congress revealed confusion among members of Congress, lobbyists and regulated businesses as well as among the general populace concerning the appropriate components of a cost-benefit analysis. Even the question of what is a benefit, seemingly so simple and self-evident, elicits different, sometimes conflicting responses. The answer, derived within an economic theoretic framework, is not commonly known by non-economists. Part II (chapters 4–15) clarifies how to do a cost-benefit analysis, presenting practical principles rooted in economic theoretic logic.

THE ROLE OF ECONOMICS

Economics has played an important role in the evolution of cost-benefit analysis. This is perhaps best illustrated by highlighting the historical development of the tool. The U.S. federal government, from its inception, pursued policies in the name of the public interest. In time, public decision makers sought to provide more detailed justification for their policy choices. Beginning in 1936 the federal government required demonstration of the extent to which the common good would be served by proposed policies. At that time, in the case of flood control projects, Congress declared that before approving public expenditures, the recommending agency should determine whether the benefits "to whomsoever they may accrue" would exceed costs.[1]

Numerous government agencies, thus required (or otherwise encouraged) to assess and demonstrate the worthiness of their projects, embarked on a quantitative analysis of project benefits and costs. Without commonly accepted analytical procedures, however, the agencies developed their own sometimes inconsistent and even incomplete analytical procedures. (Perhaps this was due entirely to the wide array of benefits and measurement issues entailed in analyzing different projects, or perhaps it also reflected the agencies' vested interests in promoting their respective projects.) Approaches proliferated especially in the areas of defining and estimating benefits and choosing decision criteria. The diverse practices meant the assessment of alternative projects was not consistent. Thus, systematic comparison of the benefits and costs for different projects was precluded.

Accordingly, beginning in the 1950s the federal government sought to standardize cost-benefit analysis techniques. In the academic arena, several economists (Eckstein 1958; Krutilla and Eckstein 1958; McKean 1958; Maass et al. 1962) began to identify and apply existing economic concepts to provide a comprehensive rationale and theoretic base for the analysis. This marked the beginnings of a burgeoning literature on the neoclassical welfare economic foundations for cost-benefit analysis.

Thus, in considering the historical development of the tool, we find that the federal practice of cost-benefit analysis emerged out of necessity. Political decision makers needed a method for systematically assessing alternative public projects. To enable consistency, the analysis developed as an economic tool with procedural steps based in the logic, values and assumptions of welfare economics.

STEP-BY-STEP PRINCIPLES

It is important for the decision maker, the analyst and the citizen to understand the economic theoretic foundation, for it provides the rationale guiding appropriate application of cost-benefit analysis to specific cases. Moreover, somewhat controversial ethical values are embodied in the analysis, and these derive from the theoretical base. In order to be fully cognizant of these values, the underlying economic concepts must be understood.

While economic concepts and values together provide a coherent framework for cost-benefit analysis, there are some ambiguities that preclude complete consistency, especially when the analysis is applied to evaluate diverse projects, programs and policies. Most notably, extensive theoretical discussions dispute the appropriate use of weights and discount rates. These disagreements in turn allow the decision maker or analyst some discretion in exerting subjective influence on the analysis. The nature of these disputes and resulting discretion must be understood by the decision maker, the analyst and the citizen alike, for only then can they ensure an analysis provides useful information as objectively as possible.

Part II presents principles for conducting a proper and objective cost-benefit analysis. Our approach is to take the reader step-by-step through the analytical procedures, providing examples where relevant to illustrate how to undertake each component of the analysis. Theoretical economic concepts, sometimes quite sophisticated, are explained as needed to understand the recommended practical steps and applications. For easy identification, the recommended principles are enumerated in each chapter and then summarized in Chapter 15. The reader may find it useful to consult Chapter 15 as a reference for comprehensive overview and to identify relevant chapters that cover particular concepts or procedures.

We also devote careful consideration to the subjective areas inherent within a cost-benefit analysis. Where relevant, the conflicting theoretical arguments in economics are surveyed. Numerous texts delve admirably into the theoretical details, and we gladly refer the reader to these. Our focus is confined to an overview of those theoretical arguments that are useful for a practitioner's understanding of this practical tool. Therefore, our primary goal is to develop reasoned recommendations as to how an objective analysis can be conducted in light of these disagreements. In addition, we address such hard-to-quantify parameters as subjective human preferences, controversial ethical values and uncertain scientific relationships. The practitioner, the decision maker and the citizen can thus see the effects of these "soft spots" on this otherwise relatively objective analysis. More important, we recommend a number of practical, simple, yet sound solutions to enhance the objectivity and accuracy of the analysis. Our intent is to make the reader aware of the subjective areas and their consequences. At the same time we focus on ways an analysis can be conducted to provide useful information to aid the decision-making process as well as to withstand conflicting scrutiny by competing political interests and special-interest groups.

COST-BENEFIT ANALYSIS DEFINED

The discussion so far has referred to cost-benefit analysis without defining its precise meaning. As the definition is rooted in neoclassical welfare economics, it seems appropriate to elaborate. Cost-benefit analysis can be defined as follows.

Cost-benefit analysis (CBA) is a useful approach to assess whether decisions or choices that affect the use of scarce resources promote efficiency. Considering a specific policy and relevant alternatives, the analysis involves systematic identification of policy consequences, followed by valuation of social benefits and costs and then application of the appropriate decision criterion.

Let's look at this definition more closely.

1. Cost-benefit analysis assesses "decisions or choices." It is a *decision-making tool* designed to provide information to aid decision makers as they confront choices when allocating society's scarce resources.

Box 4.1
Rational Decision Choice in Economic Theory

When neoclassical microeconomic theory analyzes the private sector, it seeks to explain the behavior of two decision makers: consumers and firms. Economic theory assumes both decision makers act *rationally*; in other words, each has a goal and, when making decisions, each considers alternatives, weighing the cost of pursuing any particular alternative with its contribution to achieving the goal. The rational decision maker will choose that alternative that best meets the goal given the cost. Thus, economic theory assumes the rational consumer seeks to purchase those goods and services that maximize consumer satisfaction (*total utility*) subject to the consumer's income and market prices. Likewise, the rational firm is assumed to maximize profits, pursuing those business decisions that will maximize the difference between product revenues (or sales) and production costs.

Economic theory makes similar assumptions when analyzing the public sector. The main difference is that the government is the key decision maker, choosing which public policies to pursue. As with the private consumer or firm, the government must make decisions that allocate society's resources in order to achieve specific goal(s). Given resource scarcity, the government cannot pursue every policy it might consider. Which one(s) should it pursue? In addressing this question, economic theory assumes the government's goal is to maximize society's welfare. Thus, theory defines a decision choice to be *rational* if the government weighs the benefits and costs to society of different policies and selects and pursues the one(s) that maximize social welfare. For any given policy, if the benefits outweigh the costs, that is, if society gains more than it loses, the rational choice is for the government to undertake the policy rather than *not* to undertake it. Those policies that provide the greatest gains to society (relative to costs) are said to be *efficient*.

---

2. While public and private decisions often seek to achieve any of a number of different objectives, cost-benefit analysis focuses on one particular goal, "efficiency." In welfare economics, a decision is said to promote *efficiency* if it increases social welfare. (For further discussion of efficiency and a related assumption, rational decision making, see Box 4.1.)

3. *Social welfare* is distinct from private welfare. Cost-benefit analysis is not the same as an analysis of public expenditures and revenues for a public policy decision. Nor is it the same as a financial or accounting analysis of revenues and costs for a business decision; these are *private* revenues and costs. Cost-benefit analysis instead assesses the "social" value of the effects of a public or private decision, attempting to allow for all gains and losses as viewed from the standpoint of all individuals within society. Such gains and losses are *social benefits and costs*.

4. The points developed so far lead to the following principle.

Principle 4.1. Given the focus on efficiency, cost-benefit analysis is relevant for those decisions (government or private) which (a) involve the use of scarce resources and (b) generate "good" and/or "bad" consequences for social welfare.

Thus, cost-benefit analysis is appropriate for many decision-making contexts. For instance, a government decision is generally expected to promote the public interest and thus increase social welfare. A cost-benefit analysis is applicable whenever such a decision entails a reallocation of resources. In addition, cost-benefit analysis can provide useful information regarding relevant private decisions. For example, a business may consider a policy decision with a social goal in mind or it may pursue a policy for private gain (e.g., earning revenues or profits) where the policy also has social consequences. In either case, a systematic assessment of the private policy's social benefits and costs may be of interest to the public decision maker. For instance, the government might consider the private policy as an alternative or even a complement to an existing or possible public policy (e.g., a hydroelectric dam project proposed by an electric utility company might be a substitute for a publicly funded dam suggested by a government agency). As other illustrations, the public decision maker might seek a social efficiency assessment when deciding whether or not to issue a permit allowing a proposed private activity or when establishing regulatory policy. While this book explicitly addresses the public decision maker, it should be apparent that cost-benefit analysis is relevant for the private decison maker as well with regard to these and other matters, whether concerning a private policy that generates social benefits or costs or a government policy that has ramifications for the private enterprise.

5. A cost-benefit analysis generally evaluates the efficiency of a "specific policy," with "policy" used here to refer to any of a wide range of decision choices, such as public or private projects (investments), programs, policies and regulations. These might include infrastructure and transport projects, water resource projects, environmental quality regulations, hazardous waste cleanup projects, manpower training programs, garbage collection or municipal recycling as well as numerous other policies.

6. When analyzing a specific policy, cost-benefit analysis involves several components. First is the "identification" of the policy's positive and negative social consequences. Comprehensively listing all social consequences can, by itself, provide substantial information and make a significant contribution to rational decision making. The analysis can be especially useful if it identifies any unintended social benefits or costs generated by a particular policy that might otherwise be overlooked in the decision-making process. Proper identification may require substantial knowledge outside the field of economics, for example, scientific information in the case of environmental or health care policies or social science information predicting human behavior in the case of, say, risk assessment. Second is the "valuation" in monetary units of as many as possible of these consequences as social benefits and costs. A number of valuation techniques have been developed for this purpose (and are considered in Part III). Third is the "application of the appropriate decision criterion" to weigh the social benefits and costs and assess the policy's efficiency. Those consequences that could not be valued are considered qualitatively.

7. Cost benefit analysis assesses a given policy that employs "scarce resources" and generates social benefits and costs among various individuals in society over time. *Scarce resources* are finite resources with alternative uses. A policy that utilizes scarce resources precludes the allocation of those resources to other purposes. Therefore, when analyzing a specific policy, it is important to evaluate its efficiency as compared to "relevant alternatives."

Usually, a single cost-benefit analysis assesses the efficiency of the following decision choices (or alternatives) simultaneously.

(a) *Policy vs. no policy.* Is it more efficient to pursue a policy or not to pursue that policy?

(b) *Policy vs. alternative private or public investments.* Is the policy more efficient than using resources in alternative private or public investments? (For example, in the case of a government policy, resources are essentially transferred from alternative private uses to public use. Will the social return from the public use be greater than the private return that would otherwise be generated by private investment?)

(c) *The policy's future social value vs. present consumption.* Will a greater return be realized by investing resources to generate social value in the future or, instead, by using the resources for consumption in the present? (In other words, does the future social value of a policy compensate for the foregone current consumption?)

Besides comparing these alternatives, cost-benefit analysis is generally applied to assess *several different policy options.* Sometimes it might be possible and reasonable with forethought to design a single cost-benefit analysis that analyzes two policies simultaneously. Instead of comparing a specific policy with no policy, as in (a), the analysis evaluates the efficiency of one policy relative to another. Other times, separate cost-benefit analyses are required, with each assessing one policy (vs. no policy). Because of the expense of undertaking several formal cost-benefit analyses, however, decision makers' needs are sometimes served by undertaking first an informal assessment of social benefits and costs for a number of alternative policies and then a formal, thorough cost-benefit analysis for the one policy option that appears most promising (from an efficiency standpoint).

EFFICIENCY VERSUS OTHER GOALS

While cost-benefit analysis assesses a policy's efficiency, often other goals are also of concern to the decision maker. It is important to appreciate the possible trade-offs between efficiency and these other objectives. This discussion elaborates further the definition of efficiency and then explores several trade-offs.

Efficiency

The concept of efficiency, the implicit value at the heart of welfare economics and cost-benefit analysis, has changed in meaning over time. Vilfredo Pareto in the late 1800s is credited with the first definition. His idea can be explained in the following context. If scarce resources are allocated to implement a particular policy, then the resulting resource allocation is judged in terms of whether it is superior (or *Pareto Optimal*) relative to the resource allocation that would exist without the policy. If at least one person's welfare improves while no one is hurt or if those who gain from the policy compensate those who lose so that no one is worse off, then pursuing the policy (as opposed to not pursuing it) is said to promote Pareto Optimality.

The obvious difficulty with this definition is that few policies in reality are without costs, and compensation of the losers is not automatic. Therefore, few policy options can be said to promote Pareto efficiency. In 1939, two economists, Kaldor and Hicks, worked separately on practical variations of the Pareto definition. What became known as the *Kaldor-Hicks criterion* for efficiency (or *potential Pareto Optimality*) requires only that those who gain from a policy be able to compensate those who lose, not that they actually do so. In simpler terms, efficiency is promoted when a policy generates greater benefits than costs to society (thus society as a whole gains in net), regardless of who receives the benefits, who bears the costs or whether the losers are compensated. This efficiency definition is at the core of cost-benefit analysis.

Principle 4.2. As a decision-making tool, cost-benefit analysis provides the decision maker with information assessing a particular policy's efficiency; however, efficiency is only one of several possible goals that the decision maker might consider worthwhile. Thus, the final decision on whether to pursue the policy is resolved by the decision maker, who must weigh the policy's relative efficiency with other competing objectives.

Principle 4.3. The analyst must conscientiously inform the decision maker of the practical implications of the cost-benefit framework's focus on efficiency and, as needed, identify relevant trade-offs between efficiency and other policy objectives.

Distributional Equity

By applying the Kaldor-Hicks criterion, cost-benefit analysis belongs to the school of welfare economics that views the efficiency of resource allocation as distinct from distributional equity. Whether the gainers compensate the losers is considered to be an issue of income redistribution, not efficiency. A policy may therefore promote potential Pareto Optimality (or efficiency) and be assessed by cost-benefit analysis as beneficial in net to society, while generating significant income inequities. Substantial losers may receive no compensation, or benefits (costs) may be distributed inequitably in society's judgment. Perhaps few benefits are provided to the poor while the wealthy gain substantially; such distributional impacts may be deemed desirable by some and unacceptable by others. It should not be surprising, therefore, that policies promoting efficiency sometimes encounter steep opposition for equity reasons.

Equity considerations extend beyond income to other distributional impacts. For example, since the early 1980s, a growing *environmental justice* movement has raised concerns as to whether racial minorities and low-income individuals are disproportionately exposed to environmental pollutants and hazardous materials (Bullard 1994). Cost-benefit analysis identifies who is impacted and attempts to measure the harmful exposure consequences, yet it treats all exposed individuals the same regardless of possible discrimination. In addition, in the final calculation, the negative exposure consequences can be offset, in essence hidden, by equivalent ''goods'' being provided to other members of society. Likewise, a policy assessed as promoting efficiency may threaten the economic viability and survival of small towns and rural communities, much to the dismay of local inhabitants who value the sense of community and place (Orr 1994: 151–71).

Decision makers often cannot ignore such distributional effects. Thus, they may face a difficult choice in deciding whether to pursue a policy that promises net gains to society overall while adversely affecting some individuals. A cost-benefit analysis cannot determine whether efficiency or equity is the more desirable objective. However, even when the decision makers have determined that equity is, without compromise, the foremost goal, a cost-benefit analysis offers useful information. By estimating the benefits and costs received by various individuals or groups, it can help decision makers assess the policy's distributional impacts as well as evaluate the efficiency-equity trade-off.

Sustainability

There is little consensus on the exact meaning of sustainability. Generally speaking, the concept concerns trade-offs between present and future generations. With the possibility of resource depletions, species extinctions and cumulative pollutants, actions in the present can significantly affect future generations. Is a policy that promotes efficiency (generating greater social benefits than costs over time) consistent with sustainability? In the simplest terms, it will depend on whether the future is adequately represented in the cost-benefit analysis. Four questions can be addressed. (1) Since future generations are not here to speak for themselves, how well do the preferences of the present generation reflect those of the future generation? (2) How does the analysis handle irreversible changes to *natural capital* (e.g., animal, plant and tree species, environmental quality)? A key area of contention in the sustainability debate is how much substitutability, if any, is possible among natural assets as well as between these assets and human-made capital (e.g., buildings, machinery). If there is no substitutability, as some argue, then any decline in natural capital threatens future sustainability. If some degree of substitution is possible, then an increased investment in one asset might offset (or mitigate) a decline in another asset. Should the decision maker recognize sustainability as an explicit goal, then such mitigation might be incorporated in a cost-benefit analysis, essentially placing a *sustainability constraint* on the efficiency analysis.[2] (3) How does the analysis account for uncertainty about long-term consequences? Is the unknown long run disregarded, so the analysis is assessing only short-run efficiency and thus ignoring long-term sustainability? (4) Should future dollar values count the same as present dollars or should they be discounted, as traditional economic analysis stipulates, and thus count less? These four considerations should be highlighted when assessing a policy that is likely to have important long-term effects on future generations. The analyst can thereby help the decision maker ascertain whether the assessment of efficiency adequately reflects the future's interests or, if not, the extent of the trade-off with sustainability.

Human Rights

Most commonly, the term "human rights" is used to refer to inviolable, fundamental rights. In moral philosophy, the *deontological* principle emphasizes the ethical duty to protect such rights. Thus, for examples, the right to liberty should not be violated, and the prevention of harm to humans is a moral obligation. Cost-benefit analysis, in contrast, incorporates a different moral principle, utilitarianism. According to the *utilitarian* ethic, "what is right is what will maximize what is good" for society (Beatley 1994: 24). Utilitarianism considers a policy to be morally correct (or right) if it does more good than bad. Accordingly, a policy may impose or allow harm as long as it generates greater benefits.

These two ethics suggest markedly different policy decisions. For example, cost-benefit analysis supports controlling pollution to the level where any further reduction yields greater control costs than benefits (reduced damages). A deontological perspective, however, invokes an ethical imperative to prevent the harm caused by pollution; how much pollution must be reduced depends on the right's status. To illustrate, suppose humans have a right to clean air. Then, as Lesser, Dodds and Zerbe indicate, the decision maker might draw one of two conclusions: (1) if the right to clean air is a fundamental human right, then zero pollution impacts should be allowed, or (2) if the right to clean air is secondary, derived from a fundamental human right not to be exposed to a health risk without consent, then pollution should be reduced to a designated safe level (1997: 201). Neither of these pollution levels is necessarily the same as the utilitarian-based (efficient) level.

Economic analysis offers little help to the decision maker in determining whether to apply the utilitarian or deontological ethic. Also, if the decision maker chooses the latter, perceiving a moral obligation to control pollution, then the cost-benefit trade-off is not relevant for her purposes. In such a case, however, the decision maker still has use for an analytical tool that assesses how to achieve the desired objective within the context of resource scarcity. *Cost-*

effectiveness analysis can accept as given the pollution level set by ethical imperative, evaluate alternative control methods and identify the least-cost method that achieves the stated pollution goal.

Nonhuman Nature's Rights

Much debate surrounds the question of whether (nonhuman) nature—and which of its components (e.g., higher-level animals, lower-level animals, trees, rocks)—has rights. For policy purposes, the issue parallels that of human rights, with a deontological perspective emphasizing humans' moral obligation to various components of nature and a utilitarian perspective weighing the benefits and costs of actions impacting (or preserving) nature. The deontological standard is evident in some U.S. federal legislation that considers nature preservation to be the foremost goal. For example, the Endangered Species Act protects the survival rights of individual species regardless of economic considerations. Again, cost-benefit analysis cannot determine which ethic is more appropriate, nor is it relevant for decision-making purposes if a moral obligation is deemed preeminent. In such a case, however, *cost-effectiveness analysis* can provide insight as to which scientifically recommended approach to preservation is least cost. In addition, if the utilitarian ethic is accepted by the decision maker, a distinction must be recognized. The measurement of benefits and costs is from a human perspective only, as nonhuman nature cannot express economic preferences. By weighing the benefits and costs that humans receive from nature preservation (or destruction), a cost-benefit analysis excludes nonhuman nature's intrinsic value as well as the instrumental value provided by components of nature that support other natural organisms (e.g., seagrass serving as habitat for the endangered manatee). This is a major source of criticism by many environmentalists. Thus, when a cost-benefit analysis is performed to assess the efficiency of a policy that affects nonhuman nature, the omission should be explicitly stated in the report, so that the decision maker can anticipate environmentalists' concerns.

NOTES

1. United States Flood Control Act of 1936.
2. A sustainability constraint can be expressed in (1) physical quantities (for example, a development project destroys one acre of wetlands and an "equivalent" acre is replanted elsewhere) or (2) monetary terms, with the value of environmental damage offset by an equivalent value of environmental improvements, either each year (the "strong form") or over time (the "weak form"). For a critique of these constraints, see Hanley and Spash (1993: 166–67).

Chapter 5

Economic Valuation of Individual Preferences

INTRODUCTION

Decision makers often consider a wide array of information when they are responsible for selecting policies. One source of information that may be useful is the marketplace. Here individuals express seemingly countless preferences while choosing between various goods and services. These economic preferences, also called *consumer demand*, reflect what people want or believe they need and are willing and able to purchase. Individuals convey this information in the market through the use of money, offering dollars in exchange for some good or service received. This exchange process permits economic valuation of their preferences. Furthermore, consumer willingness to pay for select goods and services represents not only what individuals prefer, but also how much they prefer specific goods and services over others. Ultimately, this market information can provide the decision maker with a detailed picture of who wants specific goods and services as well as the intensity of these preferences.

A cost-benefit analysis applies economic valuation to estimate a policy's social benefits and costs. How much do individuals prefer (or value) the social goal(s) a policy promises to achieve? How much do individuals value the resources allocated to implement the policy? These questions are answered by economic valuation of individual preferences. Cost-benefit analysis thus presumes that preferences expressed in the marketplace can provide valuable data for measuring social values and thereby inform the decision-making process.

The analytical foundation for both the economic valuation of individual preferences and cost-benefit analysis is a single theoretical economic concept, consumer surplus. This chapter defines the meaning of consumer surplus within the private marketplace and then explores the concept's extension to the valuation of social benefits and costs.

After investigating what is entailed in the economic valuation of individual preferences, the discussion considers a subject marked by some controversy, specifically, whether the economic expression of individual preferences provides relevant information for political decision makers. Some scholars believe that the political voting process provides more appropriate information. Distinguishing citizen from consumer preferences, these critics question the usefulness of the latter for influencing public decisions on behalf of society. Comparing consumer and citizen preferences, we affirm the use of both in the decision-making process. Individual preferences, whether expressed economically or politically, can give valuable information to the political decision maker.

CONSUMER SURPLUS AND NET BENEFITS

Consumer surplus provides the theoretical basis for valuing economic preferences for public (or private) policies that have social goals. As historical background, prior to the mid 1800s, it was generally accepted that the government should implement public projects for the common good or public interest, but there was no precise systematic quantification of the extent to which specific projects served the public interest. In 1844 the economics literature began making reference to "measuring the utility of public works" (Dupuit 1952). The analytical basis for such measurement derived from a concept that Alfred Marshall later termed "consumer surplus." (For a discussion of the value judgments embodied in this concept, see Box 5.1.)

Consumer surplus is often defined in the context of markets for private goods, where consumers pay a monetary price in return for a good or service that provides value (utility) to the consumer. To the extent that the value the consumer receives (and thus the maximum price the consumer would be *willing to pay*) is greater than the price actually paid, the consumer receives extra value, called *consumer surplus.*

Consumer surplus can be illustrated graphically, as shown in Figure 5.1. The market graph is for a private good, with price on the vertical axis and quantity of the good on the horizontal axis. The demand curve shows consumer willingness to pay for incremental quantities of the good. (The curve's negative slope indicates that for each additional unit of the good, consumers are willing to pay a lower and lower price.) Suppose $5 is the market price that consumers actually pay. Then, as shown in the graph, consumers would be willing to purchase a total of 10,000 units of the good. Note that while paying $5 per unit, most consumers are receiving value greater than $5. For example, for the two thousandth unit, a consumer is willing to pay $9, but only has to pay $5; thus, the consumer receives a surplus value of $4 from the purchase. Indeed, surplus value is generated for each incremental unit sold, except the last one. For the ten

---

Box 5.1
Consumer Surplus, Consumer Sovereignty and Income Distribution

Recognizing cost-benefit analysis derives from the theoretical concept of consumer surplus, two key precepts embodied in the technique can be identified.

1. Valuation of a policy is based on society's willingness to pay, and underlying this valuation approach is the assumption of *consumer sovereignty*, that is, the consumer knows what is best. In other words, the values of all individuals in society, rather than those of an elite group, specialized experts, government bureaucrats or elected officials, determine whether a policy has sufficient value to warrant being pursued.

2. An individual's valuation of the policy is limited by *ability to pay*. This is similar to the consumer in the market who determines the amount he or she is willing to pay for a particular good within the constraint of available household income. Since individuals have different income constraints, they have different abilities to pay. Thus, the analysis in effect accepts the existing income distribution as given.

The significance and controversial implications of these two precepts are addressed in Chapter 8. At this point, it is important to realize that because cost-benefit analysis derives from the concept of consumer surplus, the analysis entails those value judgments that are inherent in accepting consumer sovereignty and the existing income distribution.

---

thousandth unit, a consumer values the unit at $5, and this is exactly what he or she pays; the surplus value is zero. The surplus values for each of the 10,000 units sold can be added together to find the entire consumer surplus generated in this market. This is shown by the lined triangle in Figure 5.1.

The concept of consumer surplus can be extended to analyze decisions (public or private) entailing social benefits and costs. For example, if the government implements a particular policy, how much surplus value will be generated for society? This can be divided into two questions.

1. How much do different members of society value the policy? (i.e., how much would each member be willing to pay for the policy? Or, in other words, what *social benefits* (or utility) will society receive from policy implementation?)

2. How much does society actually pay for the policy? (i.e., what are the *social costs* in terms of resources used to provide the policy?)

Once these two questions are answered, the difference between social benefits and social costs can be calculated to find the surplus value generated by the policy. This surplus value is called the *net benefits to society*, where

$$\text{net benefits} = (\text{total benefits}) - (\text{total costs}). \tag{5.1}$$

Figure 5.1
Demand Curve and Consumer Surplus in a Private Market

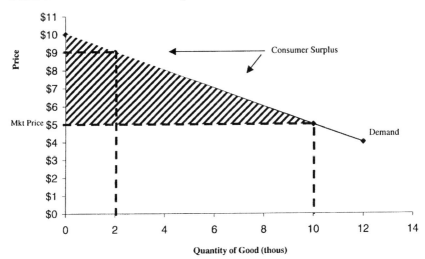

ECONOMIC VALUATION OF BENEFITS AND COSTS: WILLINGNESS TO PAY AND OPPORTUNITY COST

Consumer surplus provides the conceptual basis for the economic valuation of social benefits and costs. *Economic value* is the sum of individual preferences usually expressed in the marketplace; thus, economic valuation measures consumer willingness to pay.

Principle 5.1. Social benefits are valued by summing individuals' *willingness to pay* (WTP).

Principle 5.2. Social costs are valued by the *opportunity cost* of the allocated resources, defined as the foregone benefits of the resources' best alternative use. The foregone benefits, in turn, are valued by individuals' willingness to pay.

IDENTIFYING BENEFITS AND COSTS

The conceptualization of net benefits as reflecting both society's willingness to pay and the opportunity cost of resource allocation provides the guiding principles for identifying which policy consequences constitute social benefits and costs. It is noteworthy that these principles do not include all of the policy consequences that many individuals might perceive to be beneficial or costly. For instance, when assessing a government policy, some would consider as benefits the revenues, producer incomes or jobs the policy provides to a specific industry or firm. While perhaps desirable outcomes, these are not necessarily benefits to be incorporated into a cost-benefit analysis.

Consider an example for illustration. Suppose a public policy has been in effect for several years and has supported a larger fish population and in turn an increased commercial fish catch. It might be tempting to conclude the benefits of the policy are the increased incomes and employment of commercial fishers. Instead, however, cost-benefit analysis evaluates the commercial fishing consequences using equation 5.2.

The net benefits to society of the increased commercial fish catch   (5.2)

=	total benefits	−	total costs
=	(society's WTP for the increased fish catch)	−	(opportunity cost of additional resources used to increase the catch).

Concerning the benefits, society's willingness to pay for the increased fish catch reflects consumer demand for the additional fish. As for costs, the opportunity cost of the resources used to increase the fish catch represents the benefits foregone to society by not allocating the resources to their next best alternative use; these foregone benefits are also measured by consumer willingness to pay. Thus, the concept of willingness to pay underlies the valuation of both benefits and costs.

Part III (chapters 16–23) explores in detail several techniques for valuing benefits and costs. At this point in the discussion, it might be helpful to introduce a few basic steps for estimating willingness to pay. Let's begin with the example sketching a policy that increases the fish catch, where the fish are sold in a market.

WILLINGNESS TO PAY FOR MARKETED GOODS AND SERVICES

In estimating the benefits of the increased commercial catch of fish, what is entailed in measuring society's willingness to pay? Suppose the graph in Figure 5.1 presents consumer demand for the increased fish catch. Then, the curve shows consumer willingness to pay for the additional fish.

Total WTP = the area under the consumer demand curve,   (5.3)
from the origin to the actual quantity of output.

The analyst's task is to estimate this area. Suppose, using the numbers in the graph, the quantity of additional fish caught and marketed is 10,000, and the dock-side price[1] per fish is $5. In this case, what is the dollar value of the consumers' Total WTP? Looking at the graph, it is the sum of the area of the rectangle, market price times quantity, which is $50,000 ($5*10,000), plus the area of the lined triangle above the market price, $25,000 (1/2*[$10 −

$5]*10,000). Thus, in this simple example, consumers are WTP a total of $75,000 for the additional 10,000 fish caught as a result of the policy.

Let's think about this in general terms. For any private good that is sold in a market, the consumers' total willingness to pay is the sum of two areas: (a) the rectangle and (b) the triangle.

(a) The rectangle represents the market price times quantity (PQ). Perhaps the reader is thinking that this is *total revenue*. It is. Thus, the commercial fishers' revenues from the additional fish caught may be useful information to collect. But be aware that the goal is to estimate the total value consumers are willing to pay for the fish. It just so happens that, mathematically, *consumer expenditures* for the fish are equivalent to the commercial fisher revenues. (Note that any increase in the number of commercial fishers, or increased employment, is not a consideration.)

(b) Actual consumer expenditures (or total revenues) by themselves do not fully reflect consumer willingness to pay. Also to be included is the triangle depicting *consumer surplus*. Remember this is the surplus payment over and above the market price that consumers would be willing to pay, if required, to purchase the fish. It is part of the value society receives from consuming the fish. Thus,

$$\text{Total WTP} = \text{consumers' total expenditures} + \text{consumer surplus} \qquad (5.4)$$

$$= \text{firms' total revenue} \qquad + \text{consumer surplus.} \qquad (5.5)$$

In practice, the estimation of consumer expenditures (or fisher revenues) may seem fairly straightforward. But, the reader might ask: How is consumer surplus measured? This is discussed in greater depth in Chapter 17. For now, note that when a policy impacts a private good sold in a market, the analyst ideally estimates both consumer demand for the good and the area under the demand curve.

Suppose, however, the analyst's budget and time frame for undertaking the analysis preclude such sophisticated estimation. Then, the analyst may (at best) be able to quantify only consumer expenditures (or total revenues). Keep in mind that such a calculation provides a *conservative estimate* of consumer (and thus society's) willingness to pay. The analyst should state this in the written report and, when drawing conclusions at the end of the analysis, should highlight the implications of using this conservative estimate for consumer willingness to pay.

WILLINGNESS TO PAY FOR NONMARKETED GOODS AND SERVICES

It should be emphasized that the discussion so far focuses on commercial fish, which are sold, and thus priced, in a market. However, in many instances cost-benefit analysis is concerned with goods and services (e.g., environmental attributes, good health, etc.) that are not sold in markets. To quantify the benefits and costs, economic valuation again applies the marketplace philosophy of measuring consumer willingness to pay. Economists have developed several valuation methods for estimating the willingness to pay for nonmarketed goods and services.

A number of valuation techniques examine consumer choice and behavior in *surrogate markets*, that is, markets that are somehow related to the nonmarketed good or service to be valued and thus provide a measurement of individual preferences for the nonmarketed item. For example, in valuing water quality (for which there is no direct market), one approach is to analyze property values. Values in a well-established property market can reflect the perceived benefits (or costs) of water quality. The value of higher water quality can be inferred, using appropriate techniques, by comparing the values of different properties that are adjacent to water bodies with differing water qualities. For another example, human life is not generally bought and sold directly on a market. However, the value of a human life can be inferred from numerous markets where consumers are willing to pay a higher price for a safer design of a product compared to a less safe (more risky) model. Estimates of the price differential along with the reduced risk can, again applying appropriate techniques, be used to extrapolate an individual's willingness to change behavior and pay for a greater chance of a longer life. For a final example, in valuing beach preservation, one approach is to estimate the travel and time costs incurred by beach-goers traveling to and from the preserved beach. The relationship between these travel costs and the beach visitation rates can enable estimation of the visitors' valuation.

At this point, it seems reasonable to express some caution. Care is needed in defining surrogate markets. A common mistake is to consider expenditures on any and all related goods or services automatically to be appropriate surrogates for the good or service in question. This is not necessarily the case. For example, in valuing a family's willingness to pay for improved water quality that enables an enjoyable day of water skiing, a faulty analysis might include the purchase price of the skis (owned by the family), the expenditures on lunch and snacks at the waterfront snack bar facility and the like. We refer the interested reader to Part III, which identifies a number of appropriate surrogate markets and addresses the related valuation techniques.

Besides surrogate markets, another approach is to create *hypothetical markets*. In other words, individuals can be asked to hypothesize how much they would be willing to pay for, say, improved water quality if a market for water quality did exist. This technique, known as *contingent valuation*, attempts to simulate the setting and mechanisms of a real market in order to measure consumer willingness to pay. As we will see in Part III, this technique has been especially useful in estimating individual preferences for such hard-to-value attributes as preserving endangered species and habitat.

ECONOMIC VERSUS POLITICAL EXPRESSION OF INDIVIDUAL PREFERENCES

Political decision makers often wish to consider individual preferences when making decisions. They generally want to know whether individuals support one decision over another, and if so, by how much. In a democracy, individuals have the opportunity to reveal preferences through the political process. At the same time, the economic valuation embodied in cost-benefit analysis considers another set of revealed preferences, specifically, those expressed by consumers in the marketplace. Implicit in the analysis is that these economic preferences are also relevant for decision makers who seek to gauge the tastes and choices of the individuals constituting society.

In comparing economic with political preferences, it should be noted that the former provide additional information. Willingness to pay and the resulting economic value show not only individual preferences but also, since they are expressed in monetary terms, the intensity of individual preferences. (How much more are individuals willing to pay for one good over another?) Economic value is therefore a cardinal measure. In contrast, the preferences revealed through the political voting process are ordinal, simply indicating individual preferences (a YES or NO vote), but not the intensity of each vote (the strength of the YES or NO).

Nonetheless, some believe that the overall political process, which includes elections, lobbying and at times public consultation, provides the relevant measure of individual preferences and should be used in place of willingness to pay and cost-benefit analysis. For instance, in making this argument, Sagoff refers to

two rather abstract social roles we all play, namely, the role of citizen and the role of consumer. As a *citizen*, I am concerned with the public interest, rather than my own interest; with the good of the community, rather than simply the well-being of my family. . . .

In my role as a *consumer* . . . I concern myself with personal or self-regarding wants and interests; I pursue the goals I have as an individual. I put aside the community-regarding values I take seriously as a citizen, and I look out for Number One instead. (1988: 8; emphasis in original)

Sagoff thus "contend[s] that social regulation should reflect the community-regarding values we express through the political process and not simply or primarily the self-regarding preferences we seek to satisfy in markets" (1988: 8).

As Pearce (1983: 4) has noted, criticisms such as these seem to embody the concern that the behavior and preferences expressed in markets (and thus cost-benefit analysis) do not necessarily indicate what is morally correct. And indeed this is the case. Market decisions reflect actual consumer preferences, trade-offs and behavior; in other words, they reflect what is. They do not indicate what is right or wrong, nor do they identify what individuals believe ought to be. It is up to the political process to indicate the moral values that must be considered for social decisions. However, Sagoff and other critics go so far as to say that market transactions that are pursuant to individual wants do not, indeed cannot, generate any appropriate guidance for political decision making and thus should not be considered by decision makers. This last seems illogical and extreme.

Accepting Sagoff's distinction between consumer and citizen preferences, we believe the decision-making process should consider both. Indeed, in a democracy the use of cost-benefit analysis within the public decision-making process ultimately means both sets of preferences are likely to be taken into account; elected decision makers, to be successful, must generally consider political votes and lobbying in addition to economic willingness to pay. The use of cost-benefit analysis certainly should not preempt the political process or automatically override citizen preferences.

Hanley and Spash argue, furthermore, that leaving resource allocation decisions entirely to the political realm, with no economic assessment, compromises the decision-making process. They suggest there is little reason to expect that political decisions will automatically represent the interests of society.

Not only is there potential for self-serving action here (so that bureaucrats act selfishly rather than in the public interest), but there is a danger that individuals will lose all control over the process, except in their capability to organize as a lobby group, and in the occasional, and very indirect, way of an election every four or five years. Therefore CBA might, to a degree, be considered to preserve the democratic alternative. (1993: 270–71)

Moreover, elected bureaucrats must employ some method to make decisions. As Hanley and Spash note, ''How do the elected bureaucrats make their day-to-day decisions? If not through CBA, then either through some other process, which may be a setdown methodology such as Environmental Impact Assessment (EIA) or through rules of thumb'' (1993: 270). They then write, ''none of the alternatives to CBA is problem-free whilst many are less comprehensive'' (1993: 272), and thus they recommend the use of cost-benefit analysis in the decision-making process.

Pearce likewise reminds us that the marketplace provides substantially greater information than does the political process. He writes, ''markets are the only contexts in which individuals express millions of preferences daily. The political system does not begin to compare. We would have to have endless referendums and elections to get remotely near the complexity of the marketplace'' (1983: 5).

It seems obvious in our minds that the public decision maker needs to be as informed as possible about citizen and consumer preferences concerning specific decisions. Both economic assessment as well as the various political processes (e.g., voting, lobbying, etc.) offer advantages, and both should be consulted to gather the greatest amount of information concerning individual preferences.

MONEY AS A UNIT OF MEASUREMENT

An additional criticism levied against cost-benefit analysis concerns its use of monetary valuation. Schumacher, for example, argued that ''to press noneconomic values into the framework of the economic calculus'' purports ''that money is the highest of all values'' (1975: 43–44). However, in actuality, money provides a common unit of measurement that enables comparisons of diverse policy alternatives and their consequences. The measuring unit does not have to be money; it can be whatever is the common medium of exchange within a given society, whether it be clamshells, stones, or another valued item. It just so happens that in our society, as well as in other advanced societies, money has long been used for exchange.

Moreover, the field of economics does not purport that money itself has value. Rather, money has importance because it serves as a medium of exchange; and the medium of exchange, whatever it may be, provides information. It measures individual preferences expressed in the context of making realistic (actual) trade-offs in the marketplace. The consumer with finite resources (in this case, monetary income) must make choices. How does the consumer allocate the finite income between a variety of goods and services? How valuable is one particular good relative to the others? The consumer's willingness to pay for the good is an indication. The monetary measurement conveys useful information to the extent that the trade-off reflects meaningful choices for the consumer. Therefore, money provides a convenient unit of measurement for valuing goods and services, one which reflects the demonstrated preferences of consumers in the context of finite income and many possible choices.

NOTE

1. The dock-side (or ex-vessel) price is the appropriate price to use in the analysis, for it reflects consumer willingness to pay for the fish. This price is distinct from retail fish prices at inland markets. At a retail market, consumers generally pay a higher price, one that covers the value of the fish, expenses by a transporter hauling the fish to the market and expenses by the merchant for packaging and marketing. This higher retail price reflects consumer willingness to pay for such items as convenient location to purchase fish, useful packaging, and the like, in addition to the consumer's valuation of the fish by itself. The cost-benefit analysis in this example seeks to analyze the willingness to pay only for the fish.

Chapter 6

Who Is Society?

DEFINING SOCIETY

In order to identify all benefits and costs to society, the analyst needs to define precisely whose preferences count, in other words, who has *standing*. The individuals who have standing constitute the "society" for the analysis.

Principle 6.1. The analyst should define *society* as including all persons who benefit or incur a cost from the policy under consideration.

Thus, the analyst should not limit the focus only to those persons living in a designated country, state or town or attending a particular college or employed by a given firm. All persons who are affected by the policy, regardless of residence or location, should be included.

In practice, however, analyses of federal policies tend to consider the relevant society to be U.S. citizens or residents; analyses of state policies may focus on state residents; and so on. The obvious rationale is that the politicians and government agencies that make policy decisions have to answer to voters; accordingly, they are often primarily interested in the benefits and costs to their constituents. At the same time, given the growing number of policy effects that spill across political jurisdictions, with some having global consequences, it is important for the analyses to become increasingly inclusive. In addition, within a given political jurisdiction, noncitizens and illegal aliens may not have voting rights or legal standing, yet by definition, if affected by a policy, they have standing in a cost-benefit analysis. Of course, if the decision maker wishes for society to be defined narrowly, then the analyst has little choice (if desiring continued employment!). In such a case, whenever the analyst finds a particular policy has *spillovers*, that is, effects on persons outside the narrowly defined society, then he should bring these to the decision-maker's attention, preferably in a separate section of the report.

Principle 6.2. If the decision maker stipulates a narrow society for the net benefits estimation, then in a separate discussion the analyst should identify and quantify the spillovers and, ideally, note how the inclusion of spillover benefits and costs would affect the calculated net benefits.

Defining society as including everyone who is affected by a policy, in many cases, is fairly straightforward. However, occasionally an analysis encounters "socially unacceptable preferences" and the analyst's judgment is required. For example, it is doubtful that an individual's preference for engaging in criminal activity, such as theft, warrants inclusion when analyzing a crime-reducing policy. A different, perhaps less clear, example concerns a policy affecting another culture. Should preferences that are deemed socially unacceptable by either that culture or the analyst's own culture be counted? (Boardman et al. 1996: 44). The analyst's sensitivity and attention to such issues is important.

FUTURE GENERATIONS

Principle 6.3. Theoretically, future persons have standing in cost-benefit analysis; their preferences are ideally reflected in future benefits and costs. Empirically, however, the analysis can measure directly only the preferences of the present (or past) generations. The extent to which these are likely to reflect future preferences must be considered.

For those policies that have far-reaching impacts into the future, the inability to ask future generations for their preferences becomes a significant concern. At best, the analysis assumes present and future preferences are identical; this assumption is perhaps reasonable if the future impacts already affect people today (Boardman et al. 1996: 45). In addition, there is some reason to believe that the present generation's preferences include a *bequest value*, which is the value individuals receive today from preserving resource options for their descendants and future generations (Pearce and Turner 1990: 131). To some degree, then, the well-being of future generations is included in the analysis. However, it is not clear that today's bequest values fully reflect the future's interests. Thus, the analyst must take special care when quantifying future policy impacts.

NONHUMAN NATURE

Principle 6.4. Cost-benefit analysis is *anthropocentric*, recognizing only humans in the defined society; nonhuman nature does not have standing. Therefore, only those values of nonhuman nature beheld by humans are included.

The exclusion of nonhuman nature from having standing in a cost-benefit analysis can have significant implications for decision making, especially for policies that affect environmental quality or natural resources. The ramifications can be appreciated by identifying which values carried by nonhuman nature are (and which are not) reflected in economic values.

Philosophers distinguish between three types of value for a natural being (object or event). The first two, instrumental and inherent values, require some other, external being to behold the natural object as having value. *Instrumental value* is generated by the use of a natural object to satisfy another being; the object thereby serves as a means to enhance another's welfare. Thus, for example, fish caught to feed humans or a forest harvested to produce wood or other forest products for human consumption holds instrumental value (Armstrong and Botzler 1993: 53). *Inherent value*[1] is created when a beholder feels affection, sympathy or appreciation for a natural object or event, thus valuing it *for itself* (Callicott 1993). An example might be a human valuing a tropical rain forest for its natural beauty. Worth noting is that inherent value requires the existence of a beholder, but the latter need not be physically present at the area to value it (Armstrong and Botzler 1993: 53). Thus, a beholder miles away may treasure a rain forest's beauty and existence, and the forest is said to have inherent value.

The third value, intrinsic value, does not reflect any other, external being's preferences. *Intrinsic value* is the value of a natural object in itself. Intrinsic value is the value of the *holder*,[2] separate from any existence of a beholder (Armstrong and Botzler 1993: 53; Rolston 1993: 64). As Norse explains, "when an organism acquires food, defends itself, or reproduces, it is protecting something of value, its self and thus its genes. People who think, 'Kelps and crabs don't care, so why should I?' should recognize that they act very much as if they *do* care" (1993: 35; emphasis in original). As living beings, they are holders of value.[3]

When analyzing nonhuman nature, which of these three values are included in economic value? *Anthropocentric* economic valuation reflects individual *human* preferences and at most can incorporate how much individual humans value other natural beings. Other beings' preferences are thereby omitted. Thus, the intrinsic value of nonhuman nature is automatically excluded. As for nonhuman nature's instrumental and inherent values, the concept of economic value has evolved over time. Since the days of Aldo Leopold's "Land Ethic" (1949), when economic value was often considered synonymous with commercial value, the term's definition has broadened considerably. For example, the use of a wooded area for such noncommercial activities as camping, reflective walks, photography and bird watching provides instrumental value for humans. A number of economic techniques have developed to measure individual (human) willingness to pay for such *use values*. Still excluded from such measurements, however, are those instrumental values that increase the welfare of nonhuman beings, such as the woods providing food and habitat for birds. (Human valuation of the woods' contribution to the birds' welfare can potentially be included in the analysis, but the birds' valuation cannot!) Economic valuation has also expanded to recognize that humans do feel affection, sympathy or appreciation for other beings independent of any current or future use. Such human-based inherent value is reflected in a willingness-to-pay concept called *non-use value* (also called passive use or existence value).[4] Thus, theoretically, economic valuation can include any instrumental and inherent values that satisfy human welfare. In sum,

$$\begin{matrix} \text{economic value} \\ \text{of nonhuman nature} \end{matrix} \quad = \quad \begin{matrix} \text{human-beheld} \\ \text{instrumental value} \end{matrix} \quad + \quad \begin{matrix} \text{human-beheld} \\ \text{inherent value.} \end{matrix} \qquad (6.1)$$

Economic value, therefore, does not include nonhuman nature's preferences concerning policy consequences. In that respect, economic valuation falls short of Aldo Leopold's call for a "land ethic" that recognizes the "biotic right" of other species to exist (1949). Many environmentalists, believing that intrinsic values should not be ignored, seriously question whether cost-benefit analysis is an appropriate basis for determining environmental policy. We emphasize that cost-benefit analysis is a decision-making tool and, as such, is one source of information, not intended to be the sole basis for making a decision. If the decision maker determines nonhuman nature's rights are preeminent, then, indeed, cost-benefit analysis is not relevant. In that case, *cost-effectiveness analysis* (which can accept as given the chosen preservation goal and identify the lowest-cost method for achieving that objective) would be a more useful economic analysis. If, instead, nonhuman nature's values are to be considered along with human preferences, then the decision-making task is (somehow) to weigh the excluded values of nature with the human-based efficiency assessment provided by cost-benefit analysis. (Also, other objectives might need deliberation as well.) To go so far as to prohibit cost-benefit analysis from providing input to the decision-making process is to choose to ignore valuable information concerning human preferences—an ironic, if not questionable, approach to human decision making. Admittedly, if cost-benefit analysis is allowed, there is a risk that decision makers might overemphasize quantifiable human preferences and neglect the unmeasurable values of nonhuman nature. At the same time, given the historical tendency for decision making to be swayed by commercial development interests, cost-benefit analysis offers the prospect of systematically bringing human preferences for preserving nature into the decision-making process.

NOTES

1. The term *inherent value*, although not used by Callicott, is used here in accordance with Armstrong and Botzler (1993: 53).

2. Similar to Leopold (1949), Rolston (1993) indicates that the "holder" might be an entire ecosystem, not just an individual being.

3. While some writers (for example, Hare 1987) reason that only sentient beings can have intrinsic value, others extend intrinsic value to nonsentient beings, such as an in-animate planetary system (Rolston 1993: 62).

4. Some writers suggest that non-use or existence values may reflect (at least partially) the intrinsic rights of other beings, for willingness to pay might measure human respect for nonhuman beings (Pearce and Turner 1990: 22, 27, 130, 136). As Pearce and Turner indicate, perhaps in these existence values humans are "voicing those rights because the beings in question cannot do so" (1990: 136). We note, however, that such valuation is expressed by humans as beholders (Ragland 1993: 84), and the stated sum reflects human satisfaction in recognizing the other's right. This amount may have little relation to the valuation held by the other being—if indeed the being could express its preferences in the context of finite monetary income! Such valuation is therefore more appropriately considered inherent value.

Chapter 7

"With and Without" Analysis

INCREMENTAL BENEFITS AND COSTS

The benefits and costs that are included in a cost-benefit analysis are *incremental*; they arise *with* the policy, compared to *without* the policy. In order to identify the incremental benefits and costs, the analyst must explicitly detail what would happen if the policy was *not* pursued. This without-policy scenario is called a *baseline scenario*. Next, the analyst must identify exactly how policy implementation changes the baseline scenario. What "good" changes and what "bad" changes result? These changes constitute the incremental benefits and costs arising from the policy. Thus,

incremental benefits = (7.1)
     (benefits with the policy) − (benefits without the policy);

incremental costs = (7.2)
     (costs with the policy) − (costs without the policy).

Principle 7.1. Cost-benefit analysis is a *"with and without"* analysis. The analyst should first develop the baseline scenario (i.e., what would happen without the policy) and then identify and calculate incremental benefits and costs by comparing consequences "with" the policy to those "without" the policy.

"WITH AND WITHOUT" AS DISTINCT FROM "BEFORE AND AFTER"

Be careful. This "with and without" approach is not the same as comparing the situation "before" and "after" the policy (Eckstein 1958: 51–52). A before-

Figure 7.1
Incremental Benefits of Organic Tomato Farming, Assuming Annual Output
Increases 10% "With" and 6% "Without" Project

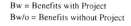

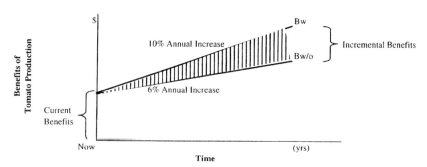

and-after comparison fails to account for changes that might occur without the policy. To illustrate the distinction, suppose a farmer currently uses petrochemical fertilizers and pesticides to grow tomatoes and is considering switching to organic farming methods. Also assume that with organic farming, tomato output is expected to increase 10% each year. A "before and after" approach estimates the benefits of the switch to be the 10% increase in tomato output each year. The "with and without" approach takes another perspective, one that can result in a distinctly different estimation of organic farming's benefits.

Two steps are involved. First, the analyst constructs the baseline scenario sketching what would happen without organic farming. In this example, the farmer would continue to use petrochemical fertilizers and pesticides to grow tomatoes. Suppose these are expected to increase tomato output by 6% per year. Second, the analyst identifies how the proposed new farming methods will alter the baseline scenario. Here, if the farmer switches to organic methods, the anticipated increase in tomato output is 10% per year. This is a 4% incremental annual increase over and above what the farmer would have experienced without the switch. Thus, the *incremental benefits* of organic farming are equal to the value of the annual 4% increase in tomato output, compounded annually, resulting from organic farming compared to continued use of petrochemical inputs.

It may be helpful to illustrate these incremental benefits graphically. Figure 7.1 presents the incremental benefits over time. The top line represents the benefits with organic farming (B_w) and shows the dollar value assuming a 10% annual increase in tomatoes. The lower line shows the benefits without organic farming ($B_{w/o}$) and reflects a 6% annual increase in tomatoes. The vertical distance between the two lines ($B_w - B_{w/o}$) represents the incremental benefits for each time period.

For another example, suppose the same tomato farmer is again considering switching from using petrochemical fertilizers and pesticides to organic farming methods. However, in this case, it is anticipated that the farmer's continued use of the petrochemical inputs would result in soil erosion and, in turn, a loss in tomato output of 5% annually. Organic farming methods are being considered for adoption because they promise to maintain the soil's quality and thus sustain current tomato output levels (i.e., 0% change annually). A "before and after" approach would identify zero benefits as resulting from the adoption of organic farming methods, since output would be no greater (or less) than before their adoption. In contrast, a "with and without" approach recognizes the benefits of switching to organic farming methods as avoiding the annual 5% loss in tomato yields. Again, the "with and without" approach is illustrated graphically in Figure 7.2, with the vertical distance between the two lines, B_w and $B_{w/o}$, showing the incremental benefits expected to arise each year from the proposed organic farming.

Likewise, for each case, the *incremental costs* of adopting organic farming methods relative to using petrochemical inputs need to be estimated. Suppose, for example, that the petrochemical input costs are projected to be $50,000 annually in constant 1995 dollars, while organic inputs are an estimated $60,000 annually in constant 1995 dollars. Then, the incremental costs of adopting organic farming methods would be the difference, that is, $10,000 annually in constant 1995 dollars (represented by the vertical distance between the with- and without-project cost lines in Figure 7.3).

IDENTIFYING DATA TO COLLECT FOR INCREMENTAL BENEFITS AND COSTS

Since cost-benefit analysis is a "with and without" analysis that assesses incremental benefits and costs, careful thought must be given to identifying which data to collect. Before gathering data, the analyst must conceptualize the analyzed policy in terms of its incremental effects. Then, the analyst has a possible choice: he must consider whether to collect separate data for each of the with-policy and baseline scenarios (and then calculate the incremental differences) or, instead, to collect data directly measuring the incremental effects of the policy.

To illustrate the first option, take the case of the farmer who is considering switching from petrochemical inputs (where he can anticipate a 6% annual increase in tomatoes) to organic farming methods (expecting a 10% annual increase). Besides these quantity projections, another piece of information is needed: the current value of the tomato crop using petrochemical inputs. Then, with an assumption about future tomato prices, both the with–organic farming and without–organic farming benefits can be projected separately. Suppose the tomato crop is currently (in 1995) selling for $100,000 and it is reasonable to believe the real tomato price will remain constant for the foreseeable future.

Figure 7.2
**Incremental Benefits of Organic Tomato Farming, Assuming Annual Output
Decreases 0% "With" and 5% "Without" Project**

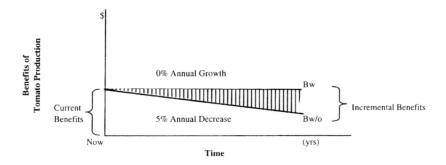

Since a switch to organic farming methods will increase output 10% each year,
the tomato crop will increase in value in respective years from $100,000 to
$110,000, then $121,000, and so on, in constant 1995 dollars. Projections for
five years are shown in column 1 in Table 7.1. Suppose instead the farmer
continues to use petrochemical fertilizers and pesticides (which is the baseline
scenario). It is expected the tomato output will increase by 6% each year, yielding $106,000, $112,360, and so on, respectively, in constant 1995 dollars (as
shown in column 2). Having projected the data for both the with-policy and
without-policy scenarios, the analyst can calculate the *incremental benefits* using
equation 7.1. Thus, as shown in column 3, the incremental benefits of switching
to organic farming methods begin in the first year at $4,000 ($110,000 −
$106,000) and increase in the years thereafter to $8,640, and then $13,998, and
so on, in constant 1995 dollars.

In this case, it is easier to project benefits separately for organic farming and
petrochemical farming and then calculate the incremental benefits of organic
farming. However, in other cases, collecting (or projecting) data that measure
directly the incremental benefits or costs may save the analyst some effort. For
example, suppose that when the analyst interviews the farmer, the latter is reluctant to reveal current expenses for petrochemical inputs (a matter of business
confidentiality), but the farmer volunteers that switching to organic farming
methods would increase annual farming costs by $10,000 in 1995 dollars. This
is exactly the information that the analyst needs: the incremental costs of switching to organic farming methods. No additional calculations are needed for these
costs.

Or, instead, the farmer might be forthcoming about the petrochemical farming
costs. For example, as presented in Figure 7.3, the farmer might reveal petro-

Figure 7.3
Incremental Costs of Organic Tomato Farming

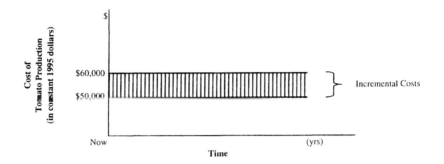

chemical farming costs to be $50,000 and organic farming costs to be $60,000 in 1995 dollars. In this case the analyst can, if he chooses, devise a spreadsheet of estimates (as in Table 7.2) showing both the with-organic farming and baseline scenario costs, along with the calculated incremental costs.

As suggested with this example, thinking in terms of *incremental* benefits and costs may save the analyst some data-gathering and calculation effort. This is especially true in specific cases. For example, a student analyzed the social benefits and costs of establishing a private pyrolysis plant to recycle tires—a project that would replace the existing practice of disposing tires at a county landfill. The analyst identified the need to estimate the difference in costs society would incur by delivering the tires to the location of the pyrolysis plant as opposed to the landfill. The analyst was all set to make two calculations (i.e., with the pyrolysis project and without the project), when research revealed that the most likely location for the pyrolysis plant was on the landfill's property. By thinking in terms of incremental costs, the analyst could quickly determine that the tires would travel from all over the county to, in effect, the same location. Thus, there was no difference in these costs with or without the project. Hours could have been spent calculating the expense of transporting the tires from all over the county to each location, but, by thinking in incremental terms, the student recognized these incremental costs were zero and saved the effort. Even when the incremental costs (or benefits) are not zero, the analyst may be able to save time and energy collecting data directly measuring the incremental change rather than collecting separate data for each of the with- and without-policy scenarios.

Mathematically, it makes no difference which approach the analyst takes. Thus, it is the analyst's choice, and one that should be kept in mind when identifying the data to collect for the analysis.

Table 7.1
With-policy, Without-policy and Incremental Benefits of Organic Farming (in
constant 1995 dollars)

Year	(1) Benefits with Organic Farming	(2) Benefits without Organic Farming	(3) Incremental Benefits
1996	110,000	106,000	4,000
1997	121,000	112,360	8,640
1998	133,100	119,102	13,998
1999	146,410	126,248	20,162
2000	161,051	133,823	27,228

Principle 7.2. The use of incremental benefits and costs provides the analyst with a choice when gathering data. The analyst might collect separate data for each of the with-policy and baseline scenarios (and then calculate the incremental differences) or instead, collect data directly measuring the incremental effects. Either approach yields the same final mathematical calculation. Therefore, the decision depends on data availability, ease of data collection and whether there is a practical reason for the analyst to present particular data in the report.

When should each approach be used? (1) Collect data directly measuring incremental benefits or costs when either of the following holds.

- Data are available only for the incremental effects.
- Data are available for each scenario, but it is easier to collect data directly measuring the incremental changes.

(2) Collect data measuring the with-policy and baseline scenarios separately under either of the following circumstances.

- It is easier to collect data for each scenario and then calculate the incremental change.
- The analyst has reason to track and explicitly report the with-policy benefits and costs as separate from those for the baseline scenario.

BASELINE SCENARIO

The importance of the baseline scenario should not be underemphasized, for its specification helps define a policy's incremental benefits and costs. Indeed, identifying the without-policy scenario during the early stages of planning the analysis can be critical in determining exactly which data must be collected. An

Table 7.2
With-policy, Without-policy and Incremental Costs of Organic Farming (in constant 1995 dollars)

Year	Costs with Organic Farming	Costs without Organic Farming	Incremental Costs
1996	60,000	50,000	10,000
1997	60,000	50,000	10,000
1998	60,000	50,000	10,000
1999	60,000	50,000	10,000
2000	60,000	50,000	10,000

example may help to illustrate. Suppose a landowner (an individual or a firm) considers setting aside some "idle" land as a nature preserve, including replacing the exotic plant species currently growing on the land with native plant species and perhaps making other "natural" enhancements. Among the questions to be answered when analyzing this decision is: What are the land costs of pursuing this project? If the decision maker was going to buy the land from someone else in order to establish the nature preserve, then the costs would be obvious: the land's purchase price. However, since the land is already owned by the decision maker, then what is the cost of deciding to allocate it to create a nature preserve? Is the cost automatically zero? Not necessarily. The relevant concept is *opportunity cost*; by preserving the land, what is foregone? If the land is not allocated for preservation, then what will be its next best use? In other words, what is the baseline scenario?

Several possible baseline scenarios and their implications for estimating the land costs are enumerated here:

• Without the nature preserve, the owner might otherwise sell (or lease) the land to someone else. Thus, the selling (or rental) price the owner would likely receive is the relevant cost for the decision to use the land for a nature preserve.

• The owner might otherwise develop the land for some economically productive use, such as farming, housing or resort development. In this case, society's valuation of the land's contribution to the foregone use or development is the cost of allocating the land to the nature preserve.

• The owner might otherwise plan not to use the land at all, allowing it to persist in its current "idle" state with exotic habitat. If no social value is generated by this option, then the cost of allocating the land to the nature preserve is indeed zero. If, however, society values the "idle" land, this foregone value is the land cost entailed in establishing the nature preserve.

Box 7.1
Opportunity Cost of Prison Labor

A student undertook a cost-benefit analysis evaluating a privately operated prison enterprise that provided commercial printing services using, among other inputs, prison labor. What is the social cost of prison labor? The prison industry incurred financial expenditures in paying wages to the prison workers. Do these wages represent a social cost? Not necessarily. In the specific case being analyzed, no alternative employment opportunities existed whereby the prisoners could generate other productive value. Thus, if not employed in this capacity, the prison labor would have remained idle. This meant the opportunity cost of prison labor was zero. This point is mirrored by Sassone and Schaffer when they state, "Labor that would *otherwise* be unemployed should be valued at a zero social cost when employed in the project— in spite of the fact that labor has a dollar cost" (1978: 69–70; emphasis in original). Recognizing that the financial wage payments were really income redistribution from the firm to the hired prisoners (rather than a value reflecting the prisoners' best alternative use), the student correctly valued the social cost of the prison labor at its opportunity cost, zero (Staman 1992: 10).

Obviously, there are numerous other possibilities for this hypothetical example. The ones listed illustrate the importance of precisely specifying the baseline scenario in order to determine the specific policy cost data to be gathered. Box 7.1 provides a different example demonstrating how specification of the baseline scenario determines the opportunity cost of prison labor. Likewise, similar examples could be presented indicating the role of the baseline scenario in identifying relevant incremental policy benefits.

Chapter 8

Aggregate Benefits and Costs

TRADITIONAL COST-BENEFIT ANALYSIS

Principle 8.1. The analyst adds (aggregates) all policy benefits received and aggregates all policy costs incurred by everyone in society within each time period.

The traditional cost-benefit analysis adds all of the (incremental) policy benefits received by each and every member of society within each time period, and then likewise adds the (incremental) policy costs incurred by all. (From this point on, the discussion will use "benefits" to refer to "incremental benefits" and "costs" to refer to "incremental costs" unless otherwise noted.) Once aggregated, the benefits and costs can then be compared to determine whether the allocation of resources to implement the policy, rather than assessed alternatives, promotes efficiency.

Although the basic principle of adding dollars within each time period may be fairly straightforward, two caveats must be addressed. The first recognizes that simply adding dollar benefits for different members of society entails the implicit value judgment that everyone in society is equal in the sense that a \$1 benefit to one person is treated as identical to a \$1 benefit to someone else. The same with costs. Likewise, an extension of the \$1 = \$1 principle is that cost-benefit analysis does not differentiate between the winners and losers under the proposed policy. A \$1 gain to one person exactly offsets a \$1 cost incurred by another. Who exactly reaps benefits and who incurs costs is, in effect, ignored in the quantification. Thus, whether the benefits or costs go to poor individuals, wealthy individuals, particular regional areas or members of specific ethnic, gender, religious, political or occupation groups is extraneous in the calculation of net benefits. In this manner, cost-benefit analysis disregards distributional impacts.

At the same time, decision makers are often interested in a policy's distributional implications.[1] Suppose that during assessment the analyst discovers the policy has significant consequences for identifiable groups. It is consistent with the traditional approach for the analyst to bring these distributional consequences to the attention of the decision maker (McKean 1958: 206–8, 240–43). This is no small task, however, as the data requirements can be considerable to identify a policy's beneficiaries and losers as well as to determine the size of the distributional effect for each group.

Principle 8.2. When a policy has important implications for distinct groups, the analyst should, where reasonable and practical, include a separate statement detailing how policy benefits, costs and net benefits are distributed among members of society. The decision maker can then weigh any adverse (or desirable) distributional consequences with the efficiency assessment of the policy's overall net benefits.

The second caveat to aggregating benefits and costs is that different individuals do not have the same *ability to pay*, as income is distributed unequally. Thus, the individual economic preferences expressed for a particular good or service are constrained by finite income. For instance, the urban poor, although perhaps feeling very strongly about air quality, may not be willing to pay very much for air quality improvements because family income is limited. Thus, the strength of the poor's preference (or ''vote'') for such improvements is understated (relative to that of the wealthy) in a cost-benefit analysis. By aggregating dollar values, the analysis in effect accepts the existing income distribution as given. Keeping this in mind, when a policy has important effects that are valued by individuals with greatly differing incomes, the analyst should explicitly state implications of the poor's limited ability to pay in the report for the decision maker.

In this respect, one advantage of the political process becomes apparent. The one person–one vote system treats every individual's preferences equally, with wealthy and poor individuals alike each receiving one vote. (In contrast, lobbying is similar to the economic valuation of preferences in that it requires monetary expenditure. It is therefore a vehicle most often used by the wealthy, who have the greater ability to pay to express political preferences. Thus, lobbying too can underrepresent the poor's preferences.)

Principle 8.3. When a policy's effects are valued by individuals with greatly differing incomes, or abilities to pay, the analyst should include a separate, detailed statement showing the valuation by various income groups. Also, the analyst should state explicitly that the strength of low-income individuals' preferences is underrepresented in the analysis. The decision maker can then consider this information along with the policy's calculated net benefits.

MODERN TECHNIQUE OF DISTRIBUTIONAL WEIGHTS

Although we recommend the traditional approach to cost-benefit analysis (accompanied by a statement of distributional effects or income groups' valuations), in recent years another approach has evolved. It entails the application of *distributional weights* within the net benefits calculation. To illustrate, if a policy provides net benefits to members of different income groups, the decision maker might view a $1 net benefit received by the poor as more important than a $1 net benefit to the wealthy. (This might reflect the decision maker's political goal to provide benefits to the poor or, perhaps, the decision maker's recognition that cost-benefit analysis understates the preference strengths of the poor relative to the wealthy.) Weights (w) can be assigned to different groups' net benefits to reflect the decision maker's prioritization and ranking of the identifiable groups. The NPV can then be calculated as the weighted sum of each group's discounted net benefits (npv). Thus, for n groups,

$$NPV = w_1{}^*npv_1 + w_2{}^*npv_2 + w_3{}^*npv_3 + \ldots + w_n{}^*npv_n. \qquad (8.1)$$

Suppose, for instance, society is divided into three groups based on income. Each group's npv is calculated; for a simple math example, assume each would receive the same discounted net benefits, $100,000. A traditional cost-benefit analysis counts everyone equally (implicitly, each group's weight is 1), yielding an NPV of $300,000. This NPV is then used to assess the policy's efficiency. Suppose, however, redistributing income to low- and middle-income families is deemed desirable. The practice of distributional weighting assigns different weights to the income groups. If the low-income group is given a weight of 2, the middle-income group a weight of 1.5 and the high-income group a weight of 1, then the calculated NPV is $450,000. This NPV combines both efficiency and equity goals in one calculation, expressing them in common, comparable units, which, it is argued, can exhibit their trade-off. Essentially the approach requires the decision maker to indicate the desired rate at which "to sacrifice efficiency for redistribution" and then formulates and assesses policies to "maximize a weighted sum of redistribution and efficiency" (Marglin 1962: 79).

The practice of using unequal weights is highly controversial. The pragmatic question immediately arises of what the proper weights should be.[2] Is a $1 value to one group worth 1.5, two, three or four times the same $1 value for another group? The economics literature suggests a number of approaches for determining specific weights. Several are highlighted to illustrate the diversity.

1. Perhaps the simplest approach recognizes the income constraints on low-income individuals' valuations and seeks to calibrate each individual's valuation to reflect "what each person *would* vote if their incomes were equalised" (Pearce 1983: 64; emphasis in original). For each income group i, each member's valuation is multiplied with the weight,

$$w_i = (MnY/MnY_i)^b,$$ (8.2)

where *MnY* is the mean income for all individuals, *MnY_i* is the mean income for group *i*, and *b* is the income elasticity of demand for the resource, good or service being valued (65–66). The ratio of incomes results in weights that increase the valuations of low-income individuals while lowering the high-income valuations. The income elasticity quantifies how individual expenditures (or valuations) for a particular good change as income increases. An empirical challenge in using this equation is that the elasticity specific to the case is often not known.

2. Weights might incorporate society's preference for providing net resource benefits to individuals at one income level relative to another. The concept, the elasticity of marginal social utility of income, η, explicitly recognizes that society may place different values on a $1 net benefit received by, say, a low-income individual and that received by a high-income individual. The greater is positive η, the larger the value society receives when net benefits accrue to individuals with low incomes.[3] For each income level Y_i, the respective weight is calculated as

$$w_i = (Y_i/MdnY)^{-\eta},$$ (8.3)

where *MdnY* is the median[4] income for the population. Since η is unknown, it is suggested that alternative values for η can be plugged into the equation, and the decision maker can choose the preferred value (Feldstein 1974). An empirical challenge for both this and the prior approach is that besides ascertaining the size distributional effects and identifying the beneficiaries and losers for a policy, the analyst must find the income levels of these individuals. This can be a daunting data collection task, although Dinwiddy and Teal suggest that in some cases a "rough and ready," "broad-brush approach" using available income data might be sufficient (1996: 72). Also, Brent notes that the equation estimates weights for all income levels, yet it is likely that society is notably less concerned about redistribution among middle-income individuals than from the high to the low incomes (1996: 248–49).

3. A different method[5] is to impute the distributional weights implicit in past government expenditure decisions and then to adjust these revealed weights as needed for use in the analysis. The fundamental idea of this approach, as introduced by Weisbrod, is to analyze past government decisions that selected some policies that were less efficient than considered alternatives. Given the policies' distributional implications, simultaneous equations are used to determine what the weights must have been for less efficient policies to have been preferred (1968). Brent defends the usefulness of revealed distributional weights, noting that these can aid the decision maker by associating particular weight numbers with a past policy's distributional consequences. If the decision maker considers the past consequences to have been acceptable, then the same values can be

used as weights in a particular analysis; if unacceptable, the weights can be appropriately increased or lowered to reflect the desired effects (1996: 250). An advantage of this approach is that as the weights are not attached to income levels, the latter need not be measured for individuals affected by the policy. At the same time, Haveman indicates that the estimated weights vary with the number of policies included in the model and thus contends that all of a particular government's expenditures should be considered, which in turn would make the entire model unwieldy (1968: 210–11). Moreover, the assumption that the selected policies' actual distributional consequences accurately reflected what the historical decision maker had intended is open to question (Pearce 1983: 69). Another difficulty is the presumption that past government decisions had only two objectives, efficiency and equity, for the weights attribute the entire basis for an inefficient decision to distributional considerations (Haveman 1968: 211; Mack 1968: 219). Accordingly, some economists have sought to develop more sophisticated estimation procedures; for instance, Brent discusses a formula that also takes into account political objectives that might have influenced the decisions (1996: 251–52).

4. Another technique, suggested by Eckstein (1961: 448), imputes weights from marginal income tax rates. According to this approach, a progressive system that imposes higher tax rates on high-income than on low-income individuals reveals the government's preference for the poor to receive income gains. The inverses of the marginal rates are then used to derive distributional weights for income levels. A problem is that income tax rates reflect considerations other than equity, such as economic growth, price stability and full employment; in addition, if other (non-income) taxes have been set to achieve equity goals, then their incidence should also be incorporated to estimate the distributional weights (Pearce 1983: 70).

5. Squire and van der Tak have recommended an approach to the World Bank that has particular relevance when evaluating projects in less developed countries. They argue that when a country's savings and investment are insufficient, yielding low economic growth, then two distributional effects should be weighted. First, attach a greater weight to income that generates savings (investment) rather than current consumption; second, assign larger weights to the current consumption benefits for low-income relative to high-income individuals. In this manner, the analysis explicitly incorporates the trade-off between economic growth (i.e., future consumption) and low-income individuals' current consumption benefits. Squire and van der Tak (1975) and Ray (1984: 102–25) detail how to calculate and incorporate such weights within "shadow prices" in determining net benefits.

Despite these and other efforts to develop a logical basis for specifying appropriate unequal weights, no single approach has received general support in the literature. The choice thus remains open as to which procedure to use. In addition, the information required to compute a particular set of weights is extensive, and in most cases available data are insufficient to specify the suggested formulas with reasonable accuracy. Furthermore, weights must be applied consistently in all analyses to enable policy comparison. For these reasons, we believe the use of unequal weights invites subjective influence within the analysis, for the benefits and costs can be adjusted simply by the selection of specific weights. Any desired outcome (from highly positive to extremely negative net benefits) can be obtained.

In our minds, the traditional approach is the most pragmatic in providing useful information to the decision maker. Rather than integrating efficiency and equity goals in a single computation, it provides a calculated assessment of efficiency complemented, where reasonable and practical, by a separate detailed listing indicating the distributional effects for select groups. The decision maker can then consider these assessments and weigh the trade-offs between efficiency and equity goals, along with other criteria pertinent to the decision.

If additional information is sought, an intermediate approach suggested by Gramlich might be applied under select circumstances. Specifically, if society can be meaningfully divided into two groups according to distributive criteria, then *internal weights* might be calculated. For example, if the high-income group's net benefits are weighted with 1, this technique finds how high the weight for the low-income group's net benefits would need to be in order for the overall NPV to "break even" at 0. The two weights are then presented to the decision maker for her to assess whether the break-even weight for the low-income group is too high to justify the policy (1981: 122). For an illustrative example, see Boardman et al. (1996: 421–23).

Alternatively, a *distributional constraint* might be imposed on the cost-benefit analysis. For example, if the decision maker can specify the minimum net benefits that an acceptable policy must provide to designated group(s), then the analyst's task is to consider those policies that meet this constraint and assess which one(s) maximize net benefits (Marglin 1962: 70–78). Howe emphasizes the importance of performing a *selective sensitivity analysis* to assess the "reasonableness" of any constraints, first altering a constraint by plausible amounts to see how net benefits change and then, if there is more than one constraint, finding the trade-offs between them by altering the constraints in various ways while keeping net benefits constant (1971: 32–33).

A different option is possible if the primary purpose of the policy is to redistribute income. In such a case, a *cost-effectiveness analysis* might be performed to identify the policy that achieves the desired redistribution at the lowest cost (Gramlich 1981: 123–33).

If the decision maker wishes unequal weights to be assigned in the net benefits calculation, then ideally she should select the size of the weights. It seems highly inappropriate to us for the analyst on his own to decide to assign a specific set of unequal weights, as this compromises the "objective" position of the analyst in undertaking the analysis. As discussed in Part I, the analyst serves as an "objective" third party between the analysis and the decision maker. In making decisions about weighting benefits and costs unequally, the analyst effectively moves to a position of subjectively influencing the analysis; as a result, he may incorporate a view that is not consistent with either that of the decision maker or an objective analysis. If, however, the analyst does deem the use of unequal weights to be worthwhile, he should discuss the options with the decision maker, for the specific weights chosen should be subject to her discretion. Then, in the written report presenting the final analysis, the analyst should explicitly indicate the selected weights and their implications for the net benefits calculation.

Principle 8.4. We do not recommend the use of distributional weights within a cost-benefit analysis, because specific unequal weights can be subjectively chosen to influence the results. However, if a decision maker requests or approves that benefits and costs be unequally weighted, then the analyst should explicitly state which weights are selected and present justification for the specific choice. Also, in order to demonstrate the implications of using distributional weights, the analyst should calculate the net benefits without unequal weights. Even better, the analyst should undertake a *selective sensitivity analysis*, first calculating the unweighted net benefits and then assigning several different sets of weights and examining the weights' effects on the net benefits calculation. In any of these cases, a detailed listing of the distribution of benefits, costs and/or net benefits should also be reported for the decision maker's perusal.

CONSUMER SOVEREIGNTY VERSUS EXPERT OPINIONS

Questions have been raised as to whether expert opinions should receive greater weight in the analysis. Underlying the valuation approach in cost-benefit analysis is the assumption of *consumer sovereignty*, that is, the precept that the consumer knows what is best. In other words, the values of all individuals in society, rather than those of an elite or of government bureaucrats or politicians, should determine whether a policy generates sufficient value to warrant implementation. Economic theory also assumes *perfect information*, that is, the individual is fully informed. The economic valuation of individual preferences, which is the foundation of cost-benefit analysis, has been criticized by some who question the assessment of policies using the views or preferences of ill-informed individuals. The presumption of consumer sovereignty is especially scrutinized when considering policies that impact (for better or worse) complex ecological systems. Realizing that the average citizen is not fully informed about the intricate relationships between specific marine habitat and fish species, for example, some critics propose that in such cases the analysis should give expert and specialist opinions greater weight than the preferences of the general public.

Although aware of the limitations, we again affirm the traditional approach of cost-benefit analysis, which aggregates individual preferences. Since the analysis and decision maker are considering policies that have social consequences, the views of the public must be taken into account irrespective of the perceived level of ignorance. Indeed, we note that economic valuation is similar to political voting in this regard; both involve the expression of individual preferences regardless of how well informed the individual may be. And both provide valuable information to the decision maker, for they reflect what is actually the case; they represent individual preferences given the level of information and understanding that individuals actually have. In addition, remember that cost-benefit analysis is one (and only one) source of information. Expert and specialist opinions, expressed in other forums or reports, should also be considered by the decision maker who in the end gives the final (subjective) weight to all information received.

Principle 8.5. Rather than choosing in the cost-benefit analysis to weight expert and specialist preferences more heavily than the preferences of the less-informed public, we again affirm the traditional approach whereby the preferences of all individuals, whether they have expertise or not, are simply aggregated. Although individuals may not be fully informed, their preferences provide important information to the decision maker. It is imperative that the decision maker also consider expert and specialist views expressed in other arenas or analyses, and then subjectively weigh all information received.

NOTES

1. For instance, an EPA-appointed Environmental Equity Workgroup has recommended that cost-benefit analyses for prospective major environmental regulations include "where appropriate" a "population distribution analysis," assessing the reduced risks for different groups, defined by gender, age, income or race (EPA 1992: 10, 28).

2. The literature presents a number of arguments, some highly theoretical, against using distributional weights. Among these are (1) acceptance of the Kaldor-Hicks assumption that the marginal utility of income is constant and (2) trust in the tax system to address all distributional equity issues. Counter to the first claim, in actuality, individuals with high incomes are believed to receive a smaller increase in utility from an additional dollar of income than do individuals with low incomes. This *diminishing marginal utility of income* suggests a greater weight should be applied to an increase in income for the poor than for the rich. As for the second contention, given the many factors (e.g., political realities, multiple goals, administrative costs) that shape fiscal policies, assigning distributional goals to be the responsibility of the tax system is likely to be insufficient. We therefore find these and other anti-weight arguments less than compelling. Thus, our cautions about the use of unequal weights are entirely pragmatic. For careful presentations of various arguments against using distributional weights, along with reasoned counterarguments, we refer the interested reader to Brent (1996: 242–43), Tresch (1981: 542–44) and Pearce (1971: 27, 61–64).

3. η is sometimes referred to as the "inequality aversion parameter" or "equity parameter."

4. Given a skewed income distribution, a common practice is to measure average income with the median value.

5. Sometimes called the "imputation" or "preference revelation" method.

Chapter 9

Present Value of Benefits and Costs Distributed over Time

DISCOUNT FUTURE VALUES TO THE PRESENT

Once the analyst has aggregated all policy benefits within each time period, the values must be summed over the policy's time horizon. The same is true for policy costs. Generally speaking, benefits and costs tend to be distributed over several time periods (often years, although sometimes over several months). In order to be able to add the dollar values over the time frame of the analysis, the benefit and cost streams must be *discounted* to obtain *present values*.

Discounting is necessary because $1 today does not have the same value as $1 in the future. (This is the case regardless of whether there is inflation. Indeed, in the example that follows, assume prices, and thus the purchasing power of a dollar, are held constant.) A dollar received today is worth more than a dollar received in five years. Why? There are two reasons. First, a dollar today can be invested and generate a yield or return; then the next year *$1 + yield* can be reinvested to generate a second return, and so on, so that in five years time the holder of the dollar will have $1 plus five years compounded interest. That is worth more than receiving $1 in five years. Second, a dollar today can be spent on current consumption. Numerous market behaviors indicate that individuals prefer to receive satisfaction today rather than in the future; in other words, individuals are said to exhibit a *positive time preference*. A common example is consumer credit, where individuals are willing to pay interest to enjoy consumption of goods sooner instead of later.

Thus, when policy benefits and costs are distributed over different time periods, each dollar represents a different amount depending on when it is incurred. It is therefore necessary to convert all of these dollar values to a common unit of measurement. The usual practice is to discount the future benefits and costs

Table 9.1
Project Benefits and Costs over Time

	Year	Benefits ($)	Costs ($)
Dec. 31, 1995	0	0	5,000
1996	1	1,000	100
1997	2	2,000	100
1998	3	3,000	100

to values in the *present*, defined as the date resources are first committed to the policy.

Principle 9.1. In order to add dollars over time, future dollar values are discounted to obtain present values.

PRESENT VALUE CALCULATION

When undertaking an analysis, any of a number of computer spreadsheets (e.g., Excel, Lotus 1-2-3, PlanPerfect) will calculate the present value of the benefit and cost estimates. Thus, the analyst need not work directly with the calculation formula. However, in order to understand exactly what is meant by discounting and present value, a numerical example using the calculation formula is presented.

Suppose a government agency considers a project with a time horizon of three years. The public project has initial construction costs ($5,000); these are assumed to occur at the beginning of the project in the "present," defined by the analyst as the beginning of 1996 (at midnight, December 31, 1995). On January 1, 1996, the project is thus ready to start operation. Thereafter, relatively low operating costs (approximately $100 annually) are anticipated for the three years, 1996 through 1998. As with many public projects, yearly benefits tend to be distributed more evenly, perhaps growing over time; here, estimated benefits increase from $1,000 in 1996 to $3,000 in the third year, 1998. Table 9.1 presents the benefit and cost streams over the public project's time horizon.

If the dollar values could simply be added, it would appear that the total benefits are $6,000 and total costs are $5,300, over the project's horizon. However, the timing of the specific benefits and costs cannot be ignored. The sum of $1,000, $2,000 and $3,000 during successive years does not equal $6,000 in the present. Nor does $5,000 in the present plus $100 in successive years equal a present value of $5,300. Each time period's dollar amounts must be converted to their present value before they are added.

Let's begin by calculating the present value of benefits (PVB). As can be seen in Table 9.1, no benefits are received during the present, as the project is under construction and has not begun operation. However, by the end of the first year, project benefits have begun to arise. To discount the benefits in year 1 to the present, the following equation is used:

$$PV = \frac{B_1}{(1 + d),} \tag{9.1}$$

where PV is the present value, B_1 is the incremental benefits in year 1 and d is the discount rate. Suppose d is 10%, then PV is $1,000/(1 + .10) or $909.09. Thus, $1,000 at the end of the first year is equal to $909.09 value in the present.

To understand equation 9.1, turn the numbers around. If today $909.09 is invested at an interest rate of 10%, then at the end of the year the investor would have $1,000. To verify, the dollar amount at the end of one year is calculated as $909.09 + (.10)($909.09), or $1,000 (with rounding). In general, this equation is ($909.09)(1 + d), or

$$PV(1 + d) = B_1. \tag{9.2}$$

Equation 9.2 can be rearranged to obtain the present value equation 9.1.

In year 2, $2,000 is generated in benefits. To discount these benefits to the present, the following equation is used:

$$PV = \frac{B_2}{(1 + d)^2,} \tag{9.3}$$

where PV is the present value, B_2 is the incremental benefits in year 2 and d is the discount rate. Substituting for d and B_2 yields a PV of $1,652.89, or $2,000/$(1 + .10)^2$. Thus, $2,000 at the end of the second year equals $1,652.89 in present value terms. Reversing the numbers, if today $1,652.89 is invested at an interest rate of 10%, then at the end of one year, the investor would hold ($1,652.89)(1 + d). If this amount is reinvested, then by the end of the second year, it would multiply by $(1 + d)$, yielding the investor $2,000 (with rounding). In general terms, this equation is:

$$(PV)(1 + d)^2 = B_2, \tag{9.4}$$

which can be rearranged to obtain the present value equation 9.3.

The present value calculation for the benefits in the third year follows a similar pattern. The general formula for the present value of benefits (PVB) is presented as equation 9.5.

$$PVB = \sum_{t=0}^{T} \frac{B_t}{(1 + d)^t},$$ (9.5)

where B_t is the incremental benefits in time t, d is the discount rate and T is the time horizon of the analysis. For the project example, the present value of benefits is calculated as follows.

$$PVB = \frac{B_0}{(1 + d)^0} + \frac{B_1}{(1 + d)} + \frac{B_2}{(1 + d)^2} + \frac{B_3}{(1 + d)^3}$$
$$= \$0 \qquad + \$909.09 + \$1,652.89 + \$2,253.94$$
$$= \$4,815.92.$$

Likewise, the project costs over time must be discounted to the present value. The general formula for the present value of costs (PVC) is shown in equation 9.6

$$PVC = \sum_{t=0}^{T} \frac{C_t}{(1 + d)^t},$$ (9.6)

where C_t is the incremental costs in time t, d is the discount rate and T is the time horizon. For the specific project examined here, the present value of costs is calculated as follows. (Note that the \$5,000 construction costs are already in present value terms, as these occur during the present, year 0, and thus are not discounted.)

$$PVC = \frac{C_0}{(1 + d)^0} + \frac{C_1}{(1 + d)} + \frac{C_2}{(1 + d)^2} + \frac{C_3}{(1 + d)^3}$$
$$= 5,000 \qquad + \$90.91 \quad + \$82.64 \quad + \$75.13$$
$$= \$5,248.68.$$

For this particular project, discounting makes a difference. Instead of comparing \$6,000 benefits with \$5,300 costs, the analyst compares the PVB (\$4,815.92) with the PVC (\$5,248.68); and in this case, PVB is less than PVC! As a caution, be aware that an economic analysis will never add the stream of benefits and costs without discounting. Thus, the reference to the \$6,000 benefits and \$5,300 costs is for illustration purposes only. An actual cost-benefit analysis should not report the simple summation of benefits or costs over the time horizon. Always discount to the present value before adding dollar values over time!

Naturally, in some instances, the decision maker or other policy stakeholders may want to know the simple sum of financial costs or revenues over time, perhaps to anticipate the expected future budgetary impact. If such is the case, the analyst should of course report the relevant sum. However, as a general rule, the analyst should not do so without a compelling reason.

Principle 9.2. In economic analysis, dollar values incurred over time are not to be added together without discounting. *Always* discount to the present value. However, if there is some compelling reason for reporting the simple sum of benefits or costs over time, the reported sum should be kept separate from the economic analysis and should be interpreted and explained within the context of the compelling reason.

APPROXIMATION ERROR IN PV CALCULATION

It must be noted that in the present value calculations performed here, an approximation is made that entails some degree of error. For example, consider the benefits and costs incurred during the first year. In discounting them to the present by the full 10%, the analysis in effect assumes the values are incurred in their entirety on the *last day of the year* (rather than being spread over various dates within the year). In contrast, the assumption that all of the construction costs occur in the present (year 0) essentially assumes they transpire in an instant right at the very beginning of the project's time horizon and thus warrant no discounting whatsoever. Each of these assumptions introduces some error into the analysis.

Such error underscores the importance of carefully selecting the time distribution of benefits and costs for the policy being analyzed. Exactly which benefits and costs occur in the present (year 0) as opposed to year 1, and so on? Suppose for the public project analyzed in the example that the $5,000 construction costs were actually incurred over a two-week period, January 1 through 14, 1996, with the project ready to begin operation on January 15, 1996. In Table 9.1, the analyst assumes the two-week expenditures were all incurred instantaneously at midnight December 31, 1995. Such a scenario is not uncommon, because it makes working with the numbers convenient. It is only one of several possibilities, however.

Alternatively, the analyst might assume the construction costs occurred during the first year. In actuality, that is when they were incurred, yet the present value equation would view these costs as occurring on the last day of the year, December 31, 1996, and discount them over the full twelve-month period. Since these expenses took place so early in the year, such an assumption would yield greater error than assigning the construction costs to year 0.

Another option is to use monthly data along with a monthly discount rate. These reflect more closely the actual timing of all of the benefits and costs, and monthly discounting treats each as occuring on the last day of the respective month. Less error is involved than when using annual data. At the same time, data collection costs increase. Gathering weekly data would increase the accuracy even further but still entail some error. Error is unavoidable unless the analyst discounts daily (which requires the formidable task of keeping track of daily benefits and costs).

Principle 9.3. Be cognizant that present value calculations entail some error and that the analyst can affect the size of the error by carefully selecting the time distribution of policy benefits and costs for analysis. Efficiency dictates that when considering ways to reduce the error, the analyst should weigh the benefits gained from more precise data with the costs of detailed data collection and manipulation.

In the analysis, the analyst should be careful to explain to the reader that an error is entailed in the present value calculation.

Principle 9.4. The analyst should explicitly indicate in the report that (1) the present value calculation assumes that all benefits and costs accrue on the last day of each time period and (2) this assumption does allow some error but greatly increases the ease of computation.

DEFINING THE PRESENT

We define the *present* as the date when resources are first committed to the policy. Our rationale is that as at this point in time, resources could be used elsewhere, therefore opportunity costs are being incurred. From the point of view of the decision maker and, more important, society, the question to be analyzed is the following: What are the social benefits and costs that result from devoting resources toward the policy rather than pursuing the next best alternative? Accordingly, it seems most appropriate to define the ''present'' as that date when resources are first committed to the policy and thus first denied to the best alternative use.

Principle 9.5. Define the *present*, that is, the beginning of the policy, as that date when policy resources are first committed and begin to generate opportunity cost.

There are times, however, when an analyst might choose to define the present (year 0) as the commencement of the policy's operation, with capital or start-up costs being incurred prior to that time. Such costs, therefore, must be ''grossed up'' to their value at the ''present.'' The calculation formula for ''grossing up'' past expenses to the present value of costs (PVC) is:

$$\text{PVC} = \sum_{t=0}^{-K} C_{-t}(1 + d)^t, \tag{9.7}$$

where C_{-t} is the incremental costs in time t preceding the present, d is the discount rate and $-K$ is the total number of time periods prior to the present.

In defining the present as the commencement of the policy's operation rather than the initial commitment of resources toward the policy, there are at least two issues. First, which arrangement is easiest to compute mathematically? Second, which arrangement generates the smaller calculation error?

An example illustrating both issues is as follows. A student assessed the social costs resulting from a mother giving birth to a substance-dependent baby. A particular problem arose when defining the "present." Is it the date of conception or the date of birth? Social costs are incurred shortly after conception when the mother does (or does not) seek appropriate prenatal care, and medical resources are (or are not) properly committed. This would seem to indicate the "present" is the moment of conception. However, a question arises because gestation and the related medical and prenatal expenses extend over nine months. At the same time, the social costs for the child after birth are compiled on an annual basis. There are two main alternatives for the analyst to consider. First, treat the point of conception as the "present." The difficulty is that the first year of the analysis would include nine months of gestation and three months of the infant's life. Thus, the annual data must be divided into quarterly data. This entails several data calculations and can generate error. Is it accurate to divide annual data evenly across quarters? Are the social costs incurred evenly throughout a given year? If not, an error will be incurred. The second option is to treat the time of birth as the "present" and "gross up" the nine months of prenatal expenses to the time of birth. This also causes error, but as the student's research indicated the costs during pregnancy were minimal, the error would be small. For ease of computation, as well as to avoid the arbitrary division of annual data, the student chose the latter option, defining the "present" as the time of birth and "grossing up" the prenatal expenses (Lynch 1991).

Chapter 10

Decision Criteria

INTRODUCTION

Once policy benefits and costs, respectively, are aggregated within each time period, the future values are discounted to their present values. The analyst must then determine the appropriate decision criterion for comparing the discounted benefits and costs to assess the policy's efficiency.

Principle 10.1. To assess the efficiency of alternative policy options, the analyst should:

- identify the type of decision the decision maker seeks to make, and
- apply the corresponding decision criterion.

Three general decision types can be distinguished.

1. The decision maker might be considering one (and only one) policy, trying to decide whether to pursue it. Remember that cost-benefit analysis evaluates alternatives. What are the alternatives concerning the one policy under consideration? To implement it *or* not to implement it.

2. The decision maker might consider several alternative (mutually exclusive) policies in order to determine which one (if any) to implement.

3. The decision maker might consider several policies (not mutually exclusive) with plans of pursuing a *subset*.

Upon determining the decision type, the analyst should select the appropriate decision criterion. Errors in choosing a criterion have not been uncommon, especially in some of the earlier cost-benefit analyses. If the analyst selects the wrong criterion, an incorrect conclusion may be drawn from the analysis, thereby misinforming the decision maker. This discussion explores the appropriate criterion corresponding to each of the three general decision types. Overall, we recommend net present value as the preferred criterion to identify the specific policy or, where relevant, policy combination that promotes efficiency.

DECISION TYPES AND NET PRESENT VALUE

1. One Policy: Implement or Not?

According to the Kaldor-Hicks criterion, a single policy promotes efficiency if the social benefits outweigh the social costs. Thus, the appropriate criterion for assessing one policy's efficiency is whether the *net present value* (NPV) is positive. NPV is the *present value of incremental net benefits* generated throughout the policy time horizon. If the PV of Benefits (PVB) outweighs the PV of Costs (PVC), then net benefits are positive (NPV > 0) and from society's perspective, pursuing the policy promotes greater efficiency than not pursuing it.

• For the *decision*: whether or not to implement one policy, the appropriate *decision criterion* is: policy implementation promotes efficiency if NPV = PVB − PVC > 0.

Mathematically, NPV can be calculated as follows.

$$NPV = PVB - PVC = \sum_{t=0}^{T} \frac{B_t}{(1 + d)^t} - \sum_{t=0}^{T} \frac{C_t}{(1 + d)^t} \tag{10.1}$$

$$= \sum_{t=0}^{T} \frac{B_t - C_t}{(1 + d)^t}, \tag{10.2}$$

where B_t and C_t are incremental benefits and costs, respectively, in time t, d is the discount rate and T is the time horizon of the analysis.

2. Mutually Exclusive Policies: Choose One

Policies are *mutually exclusive* when the acceptance of one precludes the acceptance of the others. For example, several policies may perform the same function, such as building a new highway or a rail transit system to expand city transport capacity or, as another illustration, applying alternative medicines to cure a particular illness, where in either example only one option is to be chosen. Also mutually exclusive are policies that occupy or affect the same site, such as building a coastal marina or, instead, preserving the proposed coastal site. Another example is constructing a particular project, such as a hydroelectric dam, at one of several locations. In each of these cases, the decision to pursue one policy option precludes the others.

Single policies promote efficiency if NPV > 0. When assessing mutually exclusive policies, if two or more policies under consideration have positive NPVs, then which one is most efficient? According to the *fundamental rule*, derived from the Kaldor-Hicks criterion, "select the alternative that produces the greatest net benefit" (Stokey and Zeckhauser 1978: 137). Thus, the most efficient policy is the one with the maximum NPV.[1]

• For the *decision*: choose one of several mutually exclusive policies, the appropriate *decision criterion* is: the most efficient policy maximizes NPV.

A wide variety of policy decisions can be analyzed as mutually exclusive choices. When determining the optimal scale of a policy, for instance, each alternative scale can be assessed, and the one that yields the maximum NPV is the most efficient. Likewise, in deciding the optimal date to begin a policy (say, for example, that an initial project capacity is large and requires expensive investment while demand is expected to grow to match the capacity at some future date), NPVs can be calculated assuming different starting dates and then compared. As another illustration, alternative designs of multipurpose projects can be assessed as mutually exclusive options. For instance, one design, including a hydroelectric dam and reservoir, can be compared with the same dam and reservoir plus an irrigation system. If the NPV for the latter is the greater of the two, then adding irrigation as an additional project objective promotes efficiency.

3. Several Policies: Choose a Subset

For this type of decision, Stokey and Zeckhauser's "fundamental rule" can again be applied. However, the appropriate criterion varies depending on two characteristics: whether the policy options are dependent or independent and whether there is a budget constraint.

3a. Dependent policies. A policy is *dependent* on others if its net benefits change should any of the other policies be implemented or if its net benefits change with the scale of these other policies (Sassone and Schaffer 1978: 25). In order to see the implications of policy interdependence for the appropriate decision criterion, an example is presented. Suppose a regional planning council is deciding how many bridges (if any) to build spanning a bay that separates two cities. Three different bridge sites are considered, with the possibility that any subset of these sites might be selected for construction. In this case, the value of the benefits provided by each bridge site is dependent on whether the other bridge(s) are built. To see why, consider some of the benefits a bridge provides society. In the bay area, without any bridge, individuals traveling by car between the two cities have to travel on land the long way around the bay. Thus, the bridge benefits these individuals by reducing their travel time and

Table 10.1
Net Benefits of Alternative Bridge Sites: Dependent Projects (in millions of dollars)

(1) Possible Bridge Combinations	(2) Present Value Benefits	(3) Present Value Costs	(4) Net Present Value
A	200	100	100
B	250	100	150
C	210	100	110
A, B	370	200	170
A, C	350	200	150
B, C	300	200	100
A, B, C	380	300	80

expense per trip. Another benefit is the increased utility provided to these and other individuals who choose to take additional trips—trips not otherwise taken without the convenience of a bridge. The value of both of these benefits for a particular bridge varies depending on whether other bridge(s) are constructed. If only one bridge (A) is built, then individuals living or working in a fairly broad area might be likely to travel across the bridge (rather than taking an on-land, around-the-bay route). However, if a second bridge (B) is also built, some individuals will choose to use Bridge B rather than A; thus the benefits provided by Bridge A are less.[2] Bridge A's benefits are even lower if a third bridge (C) is also built, as the latter will satisfy some of the traffic that otherwise would use Bridge A.[3]

Dependent policies, without any budget constraint. Besides considering the dependence of the bridges, also important is whether the decision maker faces a *budget constraint* that limits the options that can be considered. Assume there is no such constraint; in other words, suppose the decision maker has available or can borrow sufficient funds to finance any possible combination of the three bridges. If such is the case, all possible bridge combinations should be considered in the analysis.

Both the dependence of the bridges and the lack of budget constraint are taken into consideration by the hypothetical numbers presented in Table 10.1. Column 1 lists all possible combinations (any one, any two or all three bridges) that the decision maker might consider building. The numbers in column 2 demonstrate the dependence between policy benefits. Suppose the present value of the benefits from building one bridge is $200 million for Bridge A or $250 million for only Bridge B. The option of building both bridges A and B together is not the simple sum of these amounts (although that would be the case if the projects were independent). Rather, the benefits generated by either bridge when combined (say, $170 million and $200 million for bridges A and B, respectively) are less than those for each bridge by itself; in sum, the two bridges together provide only an estimated $370 million benefits in present value terms. Other values in column 2 concern the option of building Bridge C; these values follow a similar pattern, reflecting the dependence of the policy's benefits on other bridge(s) construction. For the option of building all three bridges together, the benefits from each individual bridge become even less (perhaps $150, $140 and $90 million for Bridges A, B and C, respectively), summing to a total of $380 million in present value terms.

In column 3, it is assumed that whether one, two or three bridges are constructed, the cost per bridge does not vary; in other words, each bridge's costs are not dependent on the construction of the other bridges. Also, for simplicity, it is supposed that the costs of constructing and maintaining each bridge are identical, equal to $100 million per bridge in present value terms.

In order to decide which combination of bridges most efficiently serves society's interests, the appropriate criterion is to select the combination that maximizes NPV. (Note that listing all possible combinations essentially converts the decision to choosing one of several mutually exclusive combinations.) Column 4 in Table 10.1 presents the NPV for each bridge combination. NPV is calculated as *PVB* − *PVC*, or column 2 − column 3 in Table 10.1. As can be seen, the combination of the two bridges A and B generates the highest NPV, at $170 million.

- For the *decision*: choose a subset of several dependent policies with no budget constraint, the appropriate *decision criterion* is: identify all possible combinations of policies, and the most efficient combination is the one with maximum NPV.

Be aware that this criterion can become cumbersome if numerous policies are compared. The three bridges considered in the example requires a list of seven combinations. Five bridges would result in 25 possible combinations. However, considering all possible combinations is the only way to take into account the policies' interdependence when weighing policy alternatives.

Dependent policies, with budget constraint. Suppose the decision maker has limited funds and cannot (or is reluctant to) borrow sufficient funds to cover the total initial costs;[4] the budget then constrains the policy options that can feasibly be financed. In particular, for the example of the bay bridges, assume that a maximum budget of $250 million (in present value terms) can be allocated to cover costs. In that case, one combination, building all three bridges, with an estimated PVC of $300 million, would not be affordable. The decision maker thus omits that option from Table 10.1 and considers only the financially feasible bridge combinations. Given the NPV estimates in this particular example, the rational decision remains the same as without the budget constraint: construct bridges A and B.

- For the *decision*: choose a subset of several dependent policies with a budget constraint, the appropriate *decision criterion* is: identify all affordable combinations of policies, and the most efficient combination is the one with maximum NPV.

3b. Independent policies. When identifying a subset of several policies, it is possible the policies are *independent*. This means the policies are neither mutually exclusive nor dependent. The choice of one policy does not necessarily preclude acceptance of any of the others, and one policy's net benefits do not vary with the implementation of any other policies under consideration (Bierman and Smidt 1988: 64). For example, suppose a municipality is considering undertaking any (or all) of the following five projects: new police equipment, inner-city renovation, water reservoir, mass transit system and computerized tracking of garbage trucks. As there is no technical reason why all five projects cannot be implemented, choosing one does not preclude also choosing the others. Also, the construction of the mass transit system (or any of the other projects) will not affect the benefits and costs of providing, say, a water reservoir; and the same can be said for any of the projects. These five projects are independent.

Independent policies, without budget constraint. Suppose the decision is not constrained by the available budget, then all five projects can be considered. In order to assess which projects warrant financing from an efficiency perspective, the NPVs for each project should be estimated. The NPV (as well as the PV of benefits, future annual costs and initial capital costs) for each project is presented in Table 10.2. (Since each project's NPV remains the same regardless of whether any other projects are pursued, it is not necessary to list all possible project combinations.)

As can be seen in column 4 of Table 10.2, the computerized tracking system's NPV is negative; as the estimated costs exceed the benefits, this project does not promote efficiency and is removed from further consideration in this discussion. The NPVs for the other four projects are positive. Since there is no budget constraint, society would benefit (in net) from all four of these projects being implemented.

- For the *decision*: choose a subset of several independent policies with no budget constraint, the appropriate *decision criterion* is: efficiency is promoted by all policies with NPV > 0.

Independent policies, with budget constraint. Suppose the municipality that is considering the five projects faces an initial capital budget constraint of $50 million, in present value terms. According to the NPVs, the mass transit system

Table 10.2
NPV and B/C for Independent Projects

Projects	(1) PV Benefits ($ mils)	(2) PV Annual Costs ($ mils)	(3) PV Capital Cost ($ mils)	(4) NPV[a] ($ mils)	(5) B/C[b]
Police equipment	17	2	5	10	3.0
Inner city renovation	67	7	25	35	2.4
Reservoir	45	5	20	20	2.0
Mass transit	100	10	50	40	1.8
Computerized tracking	1	0	2	-1	0.5

[a]Calculated as (PV benefits) − (PV annual costs) − (PV capital cost) or columns (1) − (2) − (3).
[b]Calculated as (PV benefits − PV annual costs)/(PV capital cost) or columns [(1) − (2)]/(3).

generates the largest net benefits of any of the individual projects; thus, it is the one that most promotes efficiency. Since its capital cost, $50 million, exhausts the municipality's budget, no other project can be built. However, let's look more closely at this assessment. Does building the mass transit system maximize the total net benefits achievable with the budget? The decision to undertake the mass transit system will generate $40 million in NPV. Is there any other possible combination of projects that is affordable with the $50 million budget and will create an NPV greater than $40 million? Looking at column 3 in Table 10.2, $50 million would pay the initial capital costs for three other projects (police equipment, inner-city renovation and water reservoir) and, referring to column 4, together these generate a combined NPV of $65 million. Thus, for a decision considering several independent projects with a budget constraint, the individual project NPV does not guarantee accurate guidance concerning which projects provide the greatest net benefits to society.

When considering this type of decision, a different measure, the *benefit-cost ratio* (B/C), is sometimes used to rank the project options. In its simplest form, the benefit-cost ratio is calculated using the same PV of benefits and costs as the NPV; however, division, and not subtraction, is employed. Mathematically, the simple benefit-cost ratio is calculated as follows:

$$B/C = \frac{PVB}{PVC} = \sum_{t=0}^{T} \frac{\dfrac{B_t}{(1 + d)^t}}{\dfrac{C_t}{(1 + d)^t}} \qquad (10.3)$$

A project is said to promote efficiency if the benefits outweigh the costs (PVB > PVC); in such a case, the calculated benefit-cost ratio is greater than 1. The more the benefits exceed the costs, the larger is the ratio's value.

For a decision involving a constrained capital budget, it is more appropriate to use equation 10.4 to calculate the benefit-cost ratio.

$$B/C = \frac{PVB - PV \text{ Annual Costs}}{PV \text{ Initial Capital Costs,}} \qquad (10.4)$$

where the initial capital costs are incurred in a single period, presumably either the present (C_0) or in the first year (C_1)—if the latter, the costs are discounted to present value as $C_1/(1 + d)$. Benefit-cost ratios for each of the five projects, calculated with equation 10.4, are shown in the final column of Table 10.2. To assess a single project's efficiency, the B/C is compared with 1. If the ratio is greater than 1, then the PV of annual net benefits (benefits minus annual costs) is greater than the initial capital costs, and pursuing the project (compared to no project) promotes efficiency. As might be anticipated, the B/C for the computerized tracking system is less than 1, while the B/C for each of the other four projects is greater than 1.

With a finite budget, the four projects warrant further consideration. The calculated benefit-cost ratios (shown in column 5 of Table 10.2) estimate the discounted annual net benefits per discounted dollar of capital costs. Thus, for example, the B/C of 3 for the police equipment indicates that for each $1 initially invested in the equipment, $3 of future net benefits will be generated, in present value terms. Likewise, for inner-city renovation, water reservoir and mass transit, each discounted dollar in the initial capital expenditure is expected to yield $2.40, $2 and $1.80, respectively, in discounted net benefits. Ranking the four projects according to the B/C yields a different ordering than obtained with the individual project NPV. As can be seen in Table 10.2, the B/C ranks highest the three projects—police equipment, city renovation and reservoir—that together yield the greatest combined NPV ($65 million) for a $50 million budget.

Why does the B/C outperform the individual project NPV in this instance? When there is no budget constraint, the NPV ranking guarantees that the independent projects yielding the highest NPV are the top priorities. When there is a budget constraint, the focus changes; critical is how to allocate, in this case, the discounted $50 million budget to achieve the maximum NPV. The NPV criterion chooses individual projects yielding the greatest net benefits; however, it does not take into account the size of costs and hence the extent to which a project may spend the budget. The criterion thus selects the mass transit system that generates the greatest net benefits (discounted $40 million) of any single project, yet expends a great deal of money to do so. For every discounted dollar initially invested in the mass transit system, only $1.80 in discounted net benefits results. The B/C ranking, in contrast, identifies those individual projects that yield the greatest net benefit per investment dollar spent; in effect, it seeks to maximize the net benefits provided by a finite budget.

This is the classic reason why some authors recommend use of the B/C to rank independent projects given a budget contraint. The B/C is not consistently the best guide, however. To illustrate, suppose the budget increases to $75 million in present value terms. A difficulty is encountered if, as is assumed, the projects cannot be adjusted to a larger or smaller size to fit the budget (in other words, the projects are *indivisible* or "lumpy"), for in this case, the ranking of projects by B/C does not spend the budget exactly.[5] The top three projects entail a capital cost of $50 million, and adding the fourth-ranked transit system requires another $50 million, overspending the $75 million budget. Is there any other affordable combination of projects that generates a combined NPV greater than the $65 million attained by the top three? Looking at Table 10.2, there are two combinations: (1) police equipment, reservoir and transit system, yielding a combined NPV of $70 million, and (2) city renovation and transit system, $75 million. The second is thus the most efficient combination. Note that the two projects, city renovation and transit, are ranked second and fourth, respectively, by the B/C criterion.

These two examples illustrate that neither criterion, the individual project NPVs nor B/Cs, consistently indicates the more efficient policies for a constrained budget. In both cases the procedure that does dependably identify the most efficient budget expenditure is to consider all affordable project combinations and find the one with maximum NPV.

Concern has been expressed that for a large number of independent projects, this approach results in an unwieldy number of possible combinations. However, the list can be reduced by following three steps. First, use a preliminary B/C ranking to identify possible priority projects. Second, add to the list the high-NPV projects. (Note that while the B/C correctly specified the priority projects in the first example, in the second example the combination identified as most efficient consists of the projects ranked first and second by their individual NPVs.) Third, group these projects into combinations, where each group spends a high percentage of the budget. These three steps should notably reduce the number of project combinations under consideration. Then, rank these project groups according to their combined NPVs to identify the most efficient allocation of a constrained budget.

Once the most efficient combination is identified, the analyst should recognize that in some cases the project B/Cs may provide useful supplementary information. For instance, in the second example with the $75 million budget, the police equipment was not a part of the most efficient combination, yet it had the highest B/C. In that case, an additional $5 million in capital expenditures would yield three times itself in net benefits. This is useful information for the decision maker, who might consider increasing the current budget a relatively small amount to afford this project. The project with the third highest B/C was also excluded, and the decision maker may wish to consider expanding the budget to pay for this project as well. If not, the information highlights promising projects for future budgets. The decision maker might also decide to disregard the combined NPV ranking and invest in the top three B/C-ranked projects, spending only part of the budget and saving the rest for a future budget expenditure. This is not the most efficient use of the constrained budget, but it may certainly be within the decision maker's prerogative. Thus, we recommend the analyst also report and interpret carefully the project B/Cs as supplementary information.

- For the *decision*: choose a subset of several independent policies with a budget constraint, the appropriate *decision criterion* is: identify all affordable combinations of policies, and the most efficient combination is the one with maximum NPV; in addition, ranking individual policies by B/C can provide supplementary information.

Summary: Decision Types and Criteria

A summary of the different types of decisions and the appropriate criterion for each is presented in Table 10.3. As can be seen in the last column, the individual or combined NPV is generally the recommended criterion for evaluating the efficiency of policy alternatives. For one, and only one, type of decision (the one considering several independent policies with a budget constraint) is the B/C recommended, and in that case to provide supplementary information. This is a crucial point to emphasize, for especially in the earlier years, the B/C was widely used as the decision criterion for assessing project efficiency, especially in the area of water resource projects. (The Federal Bureau of Reclamation, most notably, received criticism for this practice.) Indeed, even today occasional texts when overviewing cost-benefit analysis refer only to the B/C. Yet, the NPV is the preferred criterion.

THE BENEFIT-COST RATIO: FURTHER CONSIDERATIONS

Why not recommend presenting the benefit-cost ratio as supplementary information for all policy decisions? At first glance it may appear desirable to do so; however, two difficulties limit the usefulness of the B/C. The first concerns the varying classification of benefits and costs and the second, the ranking of policies with different size costs (or scales).

The B/C is sensitive to how particular policy consequences are categorized, for what is classified as a positive or negative benefit goes into the numerator while a positive or negative cost is included in the denominator. Numerous

Table 10.3
Summary: Decision Types and Criteria

Type of Decision	Decision Criterion
1. One policy: implement?	NPV > 0
2. Mutually exclusive policies: choose one	Maximum NPV
3. Several policies: choose a subset	
a. Dependent policies	
i. No budget constraint	Find possible combinations, maximum NPV
ii. Budget constraint	Find affordable combinations, maximum NPV
b. Independent policies	
i. No budget constraint	All policies with NPV > 0
ii. Budget constraint	Find affordable combinations, maximum NPV; rank by B/C for supplementary information

versions of B/C, with different classifications, have been used. For instance, the simple B/C, presented in equation 10.3, may be straightforward, yet its calculation can vary. To illustrate, suppose a policy will reduce environmental damage. Is this a positive benefit or a reduction in the damage costs otherwise imposed on society? The choice affects the ratio. Suppose the B/C for the other policy benefits and costs (excluding the damage reduction) is PVB/PVC = $4 million/$3 million. Next, incorporate the estimated value of the reduced environmental damage (say, $2 million). If treated as a positive benefit, then it is added to the policy benefits, and the B/C is $(4 + 2) million/$3 million, or a ratio of 2. However, if viewed as a reduced cost, the reduced damage is subtracted from the policy costs, so the B/C is $4 million/$(3 − 2) million, or 4. In either case, the B/C is greater than 1, so the policy is assessed as promoting efficiency. However, if compared with other policies, its relative ranking could be impacted, in turn affecting the likelihood of implementation. In contrast, the NPV calculation does not vary whether the reduced damage is treated as a positive benefit, $(4 + 2) million − $3 million, or as a reduced cost, $4 million − $(3 − 2) million. In either case the NPV is $3 million.

Other versions of B/C can be obtained by altering the benefit and cost classification. The B/C presented in equation 10.4 calculates the discounted net annual benefits per initial capital dollar expenditure. Future annual costs are treated as negative benefits and subtracted in the numerator, thereby affecting the value of the B/C. An alternative B/C, employed in some U.S. government analyses, is

$$\text{B/C} = \frac{\text{PVB} - \text{PV Other Costs}}{\text{PV IOM Costs}} \qquad (10.5)$$

where IOM costs are investment, operation and maintenance costs. Thus, all government costs are in the denominator, while other costs are incorporated as negative benefits in the numerator. The resulting ratio estimates discounted net benefits per discounted dollar of government expenditure. Another calculation formula,

$$\text{net B/C} = \frac{\text{PVB} - \text{PVC}}{\text{PVC}} = \frac{\text{NPV}}{\text{PVC}} \qquad (10.6)$$

is occasionally used in cost-benefit analyses. The net B/C is usually expressed as a percentage, showing net benefits as a percentage of costs. (This ratio is compared with 0 to assess a policy's efficiency.) Policy consequences classified as benefits appear in the numerator, while costs appear in both the numerator and the denominator; thus varying classifications as to whether a particular consequence is a positive benefit or a negative cost lead to different net B/Cs.

What are the implications of the many ratios for analyzing decisions? At the very least, when evaluating several policies, the analyst should use the same version of B/C. Still, even consistent use of one B/C formula as opposed to another can rank a group of policies in varying order. As for assessing a single policy's efficiency, different classifications do not alter whether a B/C calculated for a particular policy is greater or less than 1 (or 0, in the case of the net B/C). Thus, some analysts consider the B/C to be equivalent to the NPV in single policy evaluation. Nonetheless, we do not recommend calculation of the B/C because the value is sensitive to classification, and the magnitude of B/C has meaning—the larger it is, the more efficient the policy appears. The ability to categorize benefits and costs and thereby to increase or decrease the B/C allows subjective influence. Straightforward calculation of the NPV avoids this difficulty.

The second issue is that when policies have different size costs (or scales), B/C and NPV can result in disparate rankings. In the case of independent policies with a budget constraint, the B/C is therefore able to provide additional insights. However, when analyzing mutually exclusive policies, use of the B/C can result in selecting a less efficient policy. Let's look at a decision where three alternative policies are under consideration and only one is to be implemented.

Table 10.4
Mutually Exclusive Policies: NPV, B/C and Incremental B/C

Policy	PVB ($ mils)	PVC ($ mils)	NPV ($ mils)	B/C
X	4	1	3	4.0
Y	10	5	5	2.0
Z	12	10	2	1.2

Incremental Policy	PVB ($ mils)	PVC ($ mils)	Incremental B/C
Y-X	6	4	1.5
Z-Y	2	5	0.4

Table 10.4 presents the policies' PV of benefits and costs and the calculated NPVs and simple B/Cs. As can be seen, if the B/C is the criterion used, the decision designated as most efficient is to pursue policy X. In present value terms, policy X provides the greatest benefits per dollar spent ($4 as opposed to $2 or $1.20 for policies Y and Z, respectively). However, policy X is so small, entailing such low costs ($1 million, discounted), the net benefits remain small ($3 million, discounted). Policy Y, in contrast, requires a larger expenditure ($5 million, discounted) but yields the greater net benefits ($5 million, discounted); policy Y is identified by the NPV criterion as most efficient. In this case, the B/C, because it focuses on benefits per dollar spent rather than the total net benefits generated, suggests an inefficient choice. It recommends selection of a policy yielding less than the maximum net benefits for society.

It is possible, however, to adjust the B/C calculation to select the most efficient alternative among mutually exclusive policies. The computational procedure involves several steps. Rank the alternatives in order from least to highest cost. Start at the top of the list with the least cost alternative, and find the incremental benefit and incremental cost of the next costly alternative compared to the least cost policy. In ratio form, this benefit and cost yields what is called an *incremental B/C*. If the incremental B/C is greater than 1, then the more costly alternative generates sufficient incremental benefits to warrant the extra cost; it promotes efficiency compared to the least cost policy. If less than 1, then the least cost policy is the more efficient. Begin the steps again, comparing the more efficient of the two policies with the next costly alternative on the list, and so on, continuing to compare alternatives in the order of increasing cost.

To illustrate, the three policies, X, Y and Z, are listed in Table 10.4 in the appropriate order. The incremental difference between the first two, $Y - X$, has an incremental benefit of $6 (= $10 − $4) million and incremental cost of $4

(= \$5 − \$1) million, both discounted. The incremental B/C, 6/4, is thus greater than 1 and correctly identifies policy Y as more efficient than X. Policy Y is then compared with the next costly policy, Z. The incremental policy, $Z − Y$, has a B/C of 0.4. Since the ratio is less than 1, the less costly policy Y is appropriately selected, emerging as the most efficient of the three policies.

When comparing mutually exclusive policies, the incremental B/C can provide results as accurate as the NPV. At the same time, the pairwise comparisons can become quite tedious when there are several policy alternatives. Also, the incremental B/C remains sensitive to how benefits and costs are classified. Thus, the NPV offers greater consistency and easier calculation and, in our minds, is the preferred criterion.

For these reasons, we conclude the NPV criterion has the greater general applicability and is the superior criterion to use in a cost-benefit analysis. It may seem reasonable to present the policy B/C as supplementary information. However, only for decisions concerning independent policies with a budget constraint is it really useful to do so. In other cases, the B/C either provides an incorrect appraisal of efficiency or, along with the incremental B/C, repeats the NPV's assessment while potentially confusing matters with the variable classification of benefits and costs. Thus, we suggest caution and generally discourage reporting the B/C as additional information for most decision types.[6]

Principle 10.2. For all decision choices, the NPV is preferred in identifying which policy or policy combination promotes efficiency. In one situation only, where the decision is to choose a subset of several independent policies with a budget constraint, is the B/C recommended for supplementary information. An analysis that does not use the appropriate criterion risks mistakenly identifying a relatively inefficient policy option as the one most efficient.

OTHER DECISION CRITERIA

A number of other criteria have been used to assess policy efficiency. Perhaps most popular, yet generally discouraged in the literature, is the internal rate of return (IRR). Discussion of the IRR is postponed until discount rate selection is considered in Chapter 11. Two other criteria are consistent with the NPV, yielding equivalent assessments of efficiency. First, instead of discounting future values to the present, each time period's net benefits can be compounded forward to a specified future date (usually the end of the time horizon, T) to obtain the *net terminal value (NTV)*. Mathematically,

$$NTV = \sum_{t=0}^{T} (B_t − C_t) * (1 + d)^{T − t}. \tag{10.7}$$

While NTV can be applied, the conventional practice is to calculate NPV. Second, benefits and costs can be *annualized*, converted to an equivalent stream of equal annual values, by dividing by an "annuity factor." This technique is sometimes applied for capital-intensive projects with initial capital costs and constant annual operating costs and benefits. In this instance, *amortization* converts the initial capital costs to annualized costs; these can then be added to annual operating expenses and compared with annual benefits to assess efficiency. If the equivalent annual net benefit (EANB) is greater than 0 (which will be the case if NPV > 0), then the project promotes efficiency. Such a practice can be convenient if the decision maker usually considers annual costs rather than present values. Alternatively, the NPV can be calculated and then annualized to obtain the EANB. Indeed, some adjustment in the NPV calculation is usually required when comparing policies with differing time horizons, and this is one approach. Accordingly, calculation of the EANB is presented in Chapter 13's discussion of time horizons.

EFFICIENCY-PROMOTING DECISION CRITERIA: ONE PIECE OF INFORMATION

This chapter explores a number of decision criteria, each of which recommends specific policy decision(s). It must be kept in mind, however, that each criterion seeks to achieve only one of many possible goals, specifically, to promote efficiency. The intention is not to suggest that a cost-benefit analysis by itself should be the sole consideration for any particular policy decision. Rather, we emphasize that in identifying which policy decision(s) promote efficiency, cost-benefit analysis can provide useful information to the decision maker. However, this is only one piece of information, and efficiency is only one of several possible goals that the decision maker might consider. Once again we underscore the decision-making process in which all relevant information and alternative, perhaps conflicting, goals are considered by the decision maker, who then selects the final criteria by which to make the decision. Thus, in the end, the decision maker determines whether or not to pursue policies that promote efficiency.

Principle 10.3. Cost-benefit analysis identifies those policy alternative(s) that promote efficiency. As efficiency is only one of several possible goals that might be considered by the decision maker, it is not the intent of the analysis to dictate the final decision. Rather, the goal is to provide information that enables the decision maker to make a more rational decision, if desired, and to be aware of trade-offs when pursuing other goals.

DOES THE DECISION CRITERION YIELD DYNAMIC EFFICIENCY? (ARE ALL RELEVANT POLICY ALTERNATIVES CONSIDERED?)

The appropriate criterion for each type of decision indicates which policy or policy combination, among the alternatives considered, most promotes efficiency. Does this mean the designated option is efficient? Efficiency (really, what economists call *dynamic efficiency*) is achieved by the particular allocation of resources that *maximizes* the present value of net benefits. The word "maximize" is emphasized because efficiency assumes there is no other resource allocation that can generate a greater increase in net benefits. Thus, whether the appropriate decision criterion yields dynamic efficiency depends on whether there is any other more efficient policy that might be pursued.

For this reason, it is important for the analyst and decision maker to consider all relevant alternatives. Because of the expense of performing several formal cost-benefit analyses, it is not uncommon for the analyst to assess informally the benefits and costs for a number of alternative policies and then to undertake formal, thorough cost-benefit analyses for only those policy option(s) that appear most efficient. The final report should indicate the alternatives that are appraised but ruled out by informal assessments. If indeed all relevant alternatives have been considered, the policy option or combination selected by the decision criterion maximizes net benefits and is dynamically efficient. If not, then the criterion identifies the relatively efficient decision for the alternatives under consideration but does not guarantee dynamic efficiency.

Principle 10.4. It is important for the analyst and decision maker to identify and appraise all relevant alternatives. Even the most accurate, detailed cost-benefit analysis is going to be of limited value if promising alternative policies are ignored. The appropriate decision criterion indicates which policy option(s) among the ones evaluated most promote efficiency. Only if all relevant alternatives are adequately assessed does the criterion identify the efficient (or dynamically efficient) decision.

NOTES

1. For a given set of policies, the particular policy with the maximum NPV might vary for different discount rates. Chapter 11 on discount rate selection recommends selective sensitivity analysis to determine whether the NPV ranking changes.

2. It is possible for dependent policies to increase each other's net benefits, as would be the case, for example, with decisions to build an amusement park and to construct a highway passing near the park site.

3. In this example, each bridge's scale is taken as given. Note that a more complex example could show that the net benefits of one bridge varies with the scale (number of lanes) of another bridge. For instance, Bridge A yields lower net benefits if Bridge B is built with four, rather than two, lanes.

4. The discussion assumes the budget is limited for a single period, usually for construction or start-up costs. If the budget constrains expenditures for more than one period, programming models are generally required to identify the optimal decisions.

5. If some projects are divisible, estimates should be performed for other relevant project scales and then the same assessment procedure followed to determine the most efficient combination.

6. One reason this text calls the analysis "cost-benefit" rather than "benefit-cost" analysis is to avoid the automatic assumption that the analysis involves a benefit-cost ratio.

Chapter 11

Discount Rate

INTRODUCTION

Discount rate selection engenders extensive disagreement among theorists and practitioners alike. Two rationales for discounting have been actively debated with no consensus as to which is best. Adding further confusion is the multitude of possible rates that might be selected using either rationale. Should the discount rate represent a return on private investments? These range from corporate bond rates to bank interest rates to project returns; such private returns are usually short-term, high rates, including a risk premium and tax payments. Or, should the discount rate be the relatively low yield on a riskless, long-term government bond? Furthermore, should any of these market rates be adjusted to represent social values? Maybe instead a synthetic rate, a weighted average of private and public rates, is an appropriate "compromise." Still another option applies a theoretically specified formula to estimate a discount rate reflecting social preferences—a sophisticated approach yet one that entails approximate, even arbitrary, estimates of economic variables.

The choice of a specific discount rate can profoundly affect the outcome of an analysis. The rate's size (high or low) influences the calculation of the discounted decision criterion (NPV) and can lead to distinctly different conclusions about the policy's efficiency. In selecting a rate, consideration must thus be given to the practical implications.

In recent years questions have been raised by critics challenging the very practice of discounting in light of environmental concerns and intergenerational rights. The specific discount rate selected has mixed implications for improving environmental quality and preserving natural resources. Also, it includes assumptions about the current generation's ethical and moral obligations to future generations. Nevertheless, neoclassical economics continues to support discounting as a proper technique that appropriately reflects individual preferences and behavior.

This chapter explores the issues that are relevant to selecting a discount rate. With no resolution to the theoretical debate in sight, the choice can be easily influenced by analyst or decision-maker subjectivity. In some instances a government agency stipulates a particular rate, thereby preempting others' discretion, yet the chosen rate still affects the analysis. Accordingly, the conceptual rationales and practical implications for selecting specific rates need to be understood by the analyst, decision maker and interested parties alike. This chapter considers the options and recommends that a selective sensitivity analysis be performed in order to enhance analytical objectivity and provide greater information to the decision-making process.

In addition, related to the discount rate concept is the internal rate of return (IRR), which is sometimes used as a decision criterion. Reasons for the IRR's popularity as well as difficulties encountered in its application are addressed. The discussion reaffirms the NPV as the preferred criterion.

SELECTING A DISCOUNT RATE: CONCEPTUAL RATIONALES AND PRACTICAL CONSIDERATIONS

The practice of discounting derives from individual preferences as revealed in investment and consumption decisions. (Remember the discounted value of a future dollar is unrelated to inflation, so for the purposes of this chapter's discussion, assume inflation does not exist.) Relevant to a cost-benefit analysis is the *social rate of discount*. Two conceptual reasons justify discounting future social benefits and costs to the present value.

- In pursuing a policy, funds are diverted from an alternative investment so that society foregoes a return; the policy's future values should thus be discounted at a rate representing the *social opportunity cost of capital*.

- As society prefers present over future consumption, the policy's future values should be discounted with the *social time preference rate*.

In theoretically perfect capital markets, the rates reflecting each of these concepts are identical to the market rate of interest. In the real world, however, such market distortions as corporate and individual income taxes cause these rates to diverge from each other as well as the market rate. A choice must be made as to which rate to employ.

An extensive literature has evolved, expressing considerable disagreement as to the preferred rate. Each conceptual rationale has its adherents, and in actual analyses the selection practice varies widely. This chapter takes a pragmatic approach and considers three categories of discount rates. These are: (1) the rate of return from the best alternative investment, (2) the cost of borrowing funds, and (3) the social rate of time preference. For each category, the discussion presents the relevant conceptual reason as well as practical considerations for selecting a specific discount rate.

1. Rate of Return from the Best Alternative Investment

The discount rate might be chosen to reflect the pretax rate of return otherwise generated if equivalent resources are allocated to the best alternative investment.

(a) Conceptual rationale. Employing an alternative rate of return as a discount rate recognizes that capital funds have a social opportunity cost. According to this reasoning, discounting future values is warranted because society values an investment dollar in the present more than a dollar in the future, for a dollar today can be invested and generate a greater future value. By investing in a particular policy, society foregoes earning a future return on an alternative investment. Would the policy's net benefits be greater than the foregone return? This question can be answered when the selected discount rate is the best alternative rate of return. In this case, if the analysis generates a positive NPV, allocating scarce resources to pursue the policy is assessed as more efficient than the relevant alternative investment.

When evaluating a private policy, the analyst generally uses a rate of return for other project or portfolio investments in the private sector, although for some risk-averse private investors with limited opportunities, the yield on government bonds or Treasury bills might be a realistic alternative. The analysis then determines whether pursuing the policy is more efficient than the relevant alternative private investment or, if reasonable, an appropriate government security.

In the case of a government policy, it is often argued that resources are essentially transferred from alternative private uses to public use. The question arises: Is the social return from the public use greater than the return otherwise generated by private investment? In other words, is the public allocation of resources more efficient than the private use? Discounting with a private rate of return when analyzing the public policy provides an answer (Baumol 1968). Some writers believe, however, that use of a private return is appropriate only if the funds would actually be used in the private sector should the government policy not be pursued. For example, Boardman and associates suggest that if, instead, the resources would otherwise be allocated to another public investment, the foregone public return is the appropriate discount rate (1996: 170). Zerbe and Dively offer a more stringent requirement, recommending use of a private rate only when deciding whether the government or a private firm should undertake a particular policy (1994: 281). We emphasize that the analyst or decision maker must decide which approach seems logical for the analysis. Key is to recognize that selection of a specific rate of return determines the investment alternatives being compared, and the results of the analysis must be interpreted accordingly.

Principle 11.1. Discounting might be performed using the pretax rate of return from the best alternative investment. The cost-benefit analysis thus assesses the decision to devote resources to a particular policy rather than to an alternative investment in the private or public sector. Efficiency is evaluated in terms of whether the policy's net benefits are greater than the foregone investment return.

(b) Practical considerations in selecting a specific rate. Literally thousands of private rates of return and public security yields exist in domestic and international financial markets. When selecting a discount rate that represents the return from the best alternative, the analyst must identify which investments represent realistic alternatives for the decision maker and how the funds would be used if the policy were not pursued. Even then, the analyst often faces a number of choices.

To identify the most suitable discount rate, several considerations warrant attention. First, the before-tax rate of return is appropriate when measuring the social opportunity cost of capital. The return prior to taxation represents the full value the investment would generate for society; this includes the private investor's after-tax return and the taxes (viewed in economic analysis as a redistribution of income) paid to the government to serve society.

Second, the foregone investment is assumed to be the best alternative for the last unit of investment in the economy—in other words, that investment that at the margin is not being undertaken in order to pursue the assessed policy. Ideally, the expected pretax return specific to that marginal investment should be estimated. Sometimes, however, an average pretax return is calculated for several current or historical rates of return and then used as the estimated return for the marginal project. Some caution is suggested, as basic economic principles indicate that the average may overstate the marginal return. This underscores the care needed in determining the likely return specific to the foregone investment.

Third, in order to ascertain a particular rate of return's suitability for discounting a policy's future values, the analyst should be cognizant of such characteristics as risk, duration and periodic fluctuations or trends. Generally speaking, risky investments generate higher returns than low-risk investments. Thus, the riskiness of the policy alternatives a decision maker is likely to consider is pertinent in selecting a discount rate. For instance, when assessing low-risk public projects, the return from an alternative high-risk private investment includes a risk premium that is not applicable. Likewise, the asset's duration (or time period to achieve maturity) requires thought, as long-term rates of return tend to be lower than short-term rates. Also, many rates change over time. Short-term rates are often subject to cyclical fluctuations, while changes in long-term rates reflect long-run trends. The analyst should consider whether the fluctuations or trends reflected in a rate are appropriate for the policy time horizon.

2. Cost of Borrowing Funds

The discount rate might be selected to reflect the cost of borrowing.

(a) Conceptual rationale. In those cases where funds are borrowed in order to finance the policy, a key question becomes: Will the policy generate a sufficient return to more than cover the expense of borrowing? By discounting with a rate representing borrowing costs, the analyst can answer this question.

The rationale for discounting with borrowing costs relates to the social opportunity cost of capital. Borrowing charges reflect the return likely to be earned by some other purpose to which the lender might lend the funds. In effect, this approach recognizes that society foregoes an alternative investment return. We distinguish the two discount rate categories, alternative returns and borrowing costs, for pragmatic reasons. In a world of imperfect capital markets, each can identify different discount rates that the analyst might consider using in the analysis.

Principle 11.2. If relevant, discounting might be performed with a rate measuring the cost of borrowing. The cost-benefit analysis then assesses whether a particular policy generates sufficient returns to cover the borrowing costs and thus determines whether borrowing the resources to pursue the policy promotes efficiency.

(b) Practical considerations in selecting a specific rate. A wide range of borrowing rates is available. Treasury bond and other government security yields represent the cost to the government of borrowing funds from the private sector. Private borrowing expenses include interest rates on bank loans, yields promised with a new issue of corporate equities, and the like. For the analysis, the choice is usually determined by the specific borrowing arrangement. Use of the actual borrowing rate is thus quite practical. However, the analyst should be aware that if unduly influenced by macroeconomic policy, the borrowing rate is not an accurate indicator of social opportunity cost.

When analyzing a policy still in the proposal stage, where the source of financing is not yet known, the analyst can identify realistic borrowing options. The scope of the defined society can help determine whether the relevant borrowing rate is a regional, national or world market rate. For government borrowing, obvious considerations are whether the federal, state, county or local government will finance the policy. Also, the interest rate should correspond to a financing instrument with a life fitting the policy time horizon. For instance, if a federal government policy will be financed for ten years, the yield on a ten-year government security is most appropriate.

3. Social Rate of Time Preference

The discount rate might be chosen to reflect the *social rate of time preference;* this is the rate at which society as a whole is willing to trade present consumption for future consumption.

(a) Conceptual rationale. Before examining the meaning of the social rate, let's first consider the *individual time preference rate.* Market behavior provides evidence that the individual as consumer exhibits a *positive time preference,* that is, he or she values the present more than the future. This is suggested by a number of common examples. For instance, in order for the typical individual to forego consumption today and save money, the individual must be paid interest—essentially a reward for postponing consumption until a later date. The after-tax market interest rate thus measures the individual time preference rate; it reflects the rate of compensation required to offset the individual's preference for receiving consumption benefits in the present compared to the future. Likewise, widespread consumer debt through credit cards and consumer loans indicates many individuals are willing to pay interest in order to be able to consume sooner rather than later. How much is an individual willing to pay in interest in order to consume now? The answer is an indication of the strength of the individual's time preference. The greater the additional dollars, the more he or she prefers present consumption over future consumption.

Of interest for a cost-benefit analysis is society's time preference. Compared to the individual, does society (an aggregation of individuals) exhibit a preference for the present over the future? Economists believe the answer is yes; society has a positive time preference but its rate is different than that of the individual (Marglin 1963a). Hanley and Spash distinguish three reasons in the literature that argue the social rate is lower. First, a current individual's decision to save provides future benefits not only to that individual and immediate heirs but also externally to others. Society, representing the aggregate of future beneficiaries, values the external benefits and would choose to save more than would the sum of individuals making independent savings decisions. Second, as citizens, current individuals value the future more, and thus have a lower time preference, than they do as consumers. Third, the preferences of the future generation are not included in present-day market decisions. According to the "super-responsibility" argument, society has a collective obligation to ensure the welfare of both present and future generations and, consequently, prefers present (relative to future) benefits at a lower rate than current individuals (1993: 129–30). These three reasons each imply that the social time preference rate is less than the individual time preference rate. Society therefore discounts future values at a rate lower than the market rates reflecting individual decisions.

Cost-benefit analysis can be interpreted from the perspective of society's time preference. The decision to allocate resources to a particular policy means a stream of social values is generated into the future, while society foregoes using the resources for consumption in the present. Are the policy's future social values large enough to compensate for the foregone present consumption? Discounting with the social time preference rate enables an answer. If the analysis generates a positive NPV, then the policy is said to be more efficient than devoting equivalent resources to present consumption.

Principle 11.3. The discount rate might be selected to reflect the social rate of time preference, that is, society's preference for present relative to future consumption. The analysis thus assesses efficiency by determining whether the policy's future stream of social values is greater than the value society foregoes by not using the resources for present consumption.

(b) Practical considerations in selecting a specific rate. In theoretical economics, the social rate of time preference is often presented as an ideal discount rate. Since *consumer sovereignty* is a fundamental concept in cost-benefit analysis, a discount rate reflecting society's time preference for consumption seems highly appropriate, even superior in the eyes of proponents.

From a pragmatic standpoint, however, the analyst encounters a difficulty. Unlike individual time preferences, social time preference rates are not observed in the markets. An avenue does not exist by which all individuals who receive social benefits and bear social costs are able to communicate their time preferences to the decision maker. This imposes a practical limitation on the search for the precise social rate of time preference.

The economics literature, however, has specified the rate theoretically. The most frequently used formula recognizes two components of social time preference. The first is the "pure rate of time preference" *(Pref)* and is simply society's utility (or preference) for consumption now rather than in the future. The second anticipates rising per capita incomes enabling society to consume more in the future. According to basic economic principles, increased increments in consumption are subject to diminishing marginal utility, thus additional consumption in the higher-income future is valued less than in the present. In mathematical terms, the social time preference rate (STPR) is defined as follows.

$$STPR = Pref + MUC * Cons, \tag{11.1}$$

where *MUC* is the elasticity of the marginal utility of consumption and measures the rate of diminishing marginal utility, and *Cons* is the expected growth rate in per capita consumption. A number of studies have used equation 11.1 to calculate STPR; however, values for *Pref* and *MUC* are arbitrary or subject to dispute. Thus, although the theoretical foundation may be appealing, the rate itself is not quantified with confidence.

Nonetheless, there is general agreement in the economics literature that the social rate of time preference is less than the individual time preference rates observed in markets. Less clear is which market rates provide the upper bound or how far below these rates is the social time preference rate. A common practice is to employ the yield on long-term government bonds, ideally with a maturity equal to the policy time horizon, to approximate the social rate. Also, the after-tax yield is preferred, recognizing that individual savers express time preference in terms of the return they receive after taxes. Although there is no consensus as to the exact value, conceptual knowledge of the social time preference rate underscores the importance of considering a low discount rate—one that gives greater weight to the future than do many market rates.

Conclusion

To summarize, the discussion has considered two conceptual rationales for discounting—each with differing implications for selecting a specific discount rate. Based on the concept of social opportunity cost of capital, the analyst might use the rate of return on the best alternative investment or the cost of borrowing. Any of a number of relevant private market rates or government security yields might be preferred. Depending on the specific options available to the decision maker, the chosen rates can be quite high or relatively low. In contrast, acceptance of the social time preference rate as the rationale for discounting, although not indicating a particular rate, suggests the selection of a low discount rate.

Recognizing validity in both rationales, some economists have proposed a *synthetic discount rate* for analyzing government policies. For a review of several rates see Markandya and Pearce (1988: 9–25). Most frequently discussed elsewhere in the literature is the *weighted average* proposed by Harberger (1976). The underlying principle is that in pursuing a government policy, some funds may be diverted from an alternative investment while others are taken from consumption and, accordingly, the discount rate appropriate to each source of funds is to be applied. Those government expenditures that displace private investment are to be discounted with the social opportunity cost of capital (SOC), while those that displace consumption are discounted at the STPR. Harberger's rate is thus the weighted average of SOC and STPR, where the weights are the proportion of funds displacing private investment (*inv*) and consumption (*1 − inv*), respectively. The Harberger discount rate, d_{wa}, a weighted average, is calculated as

$$d_{wa} = (inv) * SOC + (1 - inv) * STPR. \qquad (11.2)$$

Although sometimes applied, the weighted average is subject to several criticisms. On the one hand, there is disagreement as to how much government expenditures "crowd out" private investment, if at all, and thus little consensus as to the appropriate size weights. On the other hand, some challenges suggest the weighted average is not sufficiently inclusive; while considering costs, it does not distinguish whether benefits are consumed or reinvested. Such arguments generally consider an alternative approach, the shadow price of capital, to be theoretically correct. Occasionally confused with synthetic discount rates, the shadow price of capital involves an adjustment in benefits and costs, not the discount rate, to reflect a policy's effects on consumption and investment flows (see Box 11.1).

In all, despite decades of debate, there remains no consensus as to the appropriate rationale for choosing a discount rate. A wide range of theoretically pos-

Box 11.1
Shadow Price of Capital

The shadow price of capital method, initiated by Marglin (1963b) and developed by Bradford (1975), is similar to the Harberger rate in its reasoning that the use of resources to pursue a government policy may displace private consumption or investment, where the latter in turn would have generated future consumption and reinvestment streams. Thus, a government policy imposes an additional cost if private investment, rather than consumption, is foregone. The approach also recognizes that the policy benefits likewise may be consumed or, if in cash form, may lead to increased private investment that then contributes to greater future consumption and reinvestment. When analyzing government policies, therefore, the displaced and increased private investments deriving from costs and benefits, respectively, are adjusted to their consumption equivalents. Specifically, the changes in private investment are multiplied by the *shadow price of capital*, which is the present value of the stream of consumption resulting from $1 of private investment. With this adjustment, the benefit and cost streams are expressed entirely in consumption units. These are then discounted using the rate that measures society's time preference for consumption, the social time preference rate. We refer the interested reader to Lind (1982a: 39–55) for a detailed exposition.

While the current literature generally favors use of the shadow price of capital approach on theoretical grounds, several challenges are encountered in application. The following information is needed to calculate the shadow price of capital (SPC): the rate of return (net of depreciation) on private investment (i), consumer propensity to save or rate of reinvestment (s), and STPR. The formula is

$$\text{SPC} = \frac{(1 - s)i}{(\text{STPR} - si).} \tag{11.3}$$

For a mathematical derivation, see Zerbe and Dively (1994: 281–83). Estimation of the values in the equation is difficult. For empirical examples, providing attention to the challenges, see Lind (1982a: 77–87), Lyon (1990: S30–S44) and Boardman and associates (1996: 171–73).

Once the SPC is calculated, the proportions of costs and benefits that respectively displace or generate investment (*inv*) and consumption (*1 − inv*) must be determined. A simplistic rule of thumb says funds raised through taxation preclude consumption, while government borrowing diverts resources from private investment. Yet, taxes in reality have different effects, and Lind (1990) argues that elastic international capital mobility reduces government "crowding out" of domestic private investment to negligible amounts. Likewise, while cash benefits are potentially investable, these could be spent on consumption. How much will be spent depends on the marginal propensities to consume and invest. Economy-wide estimates for these measures are generally available, although Tresch questions their relevance in the case of specific policy benefits (1981: 492). If reasonable values for *inv* and *1 − inv* can be obtained, the benefit and cost streams are each adjusted using SPC. For example, costs in year t (C_t) are converted to adjusted costs ($AdjC_t$) as follows:

(continued)

Box 11.1 (continued)

AdjC$_t$ = C$_t$[inv * SPC + (1 − inv)].   (11.4)

Benefits are adjusted in a similar manner to *AdjB$_t$*. The adjusted net benefits, *AdjB$_t$* − C$_t$, are then discounted over the time horizon with the SRTP (Zerbe and Dively 1994: 283–84).

Given the information required when applying the shadow price of capital method, it is not surprising that, in practice, analyses generally do not distinguish the investment and consumption components of benefits and costs. Rather, the common procedure is to discount unadjusted benefit and cost streams using a discount rate reflecting one of two rationales: either social opportunity cost or time preference.

---

sible discount rates are therefore available for selection. From a pragmatic perspective, the question is: What difference does the choice make for the analysis? To answer this question, the discussion addresses the practical implications of selecting a high or a low discount rate.

IMPLICATIONS OF HIGH OR LOW DISCOUNT RATE

The selection of a particular discount rate can be very important in a cost-benefit analysis, for the discount rate has the power to reduce sizable future benefits and costs to very small present values. This power can skew the analysis in one direction or the other through its effect on the magnitude of the NPV (or B/C ratio). Accordingly, the analyst must be cognizant of the discount rate's influence in order to ensure an objective analysis.

The power of the discount rate is derived from its location in the denominator of the PV calculation. The equation for NPV is reproduced for convenience.

$$NPV = \sum_{t=0}^{T} \frac{B_t - C_t}{(1 + d)^t}.$$ (11.5)

where $B_t - C_t$ is the incremental net benefits in time t, d is the discount rate and T is the time horizon. As can be seen in the equation, the *higher* the discount rate, d, then the greater the denominator and therefore the *lower* the PV of net benefits, NPV. The effect is magnified because $(1 + d)$ is raised to the t power and thus grows exponentially as t (the number of time periods) increases. The discussion explores the quantitative impact on, first, future benefits and costs, and then NPV.

The Discount Rate's Impact on Future Benefits and Costs

The *Rule of 72* reveals that a discount rate of 7.2% reduces future benefits and costs by half over a ten-year period. For example, a $100 benefit (cost) in year 10, if discounted at a rate of 7.2%, is $49.89 in present value. Likewise, a

Table 11.1
Discount Factors

Year	d = 5%	d = 7%	d = 10%	d = 12%	d = 15%
5	.7835	.7130	.6209	.5674	.4972
10	.6139	.5083	.3855	.3220	.2472
15	.4810	.3624	.2394	.1827	.1229
20	.3769	.2584	.1486	.1037	.0611
25	.2953	.1842	.0923	.0588	.0304
50	.0872	.0339	.0085	.0035	.0009
60	.0535	.0173	.0033	.0011	.0002
75	.0258	.0063	.0008	.0002	.0000
100	.0076	.0012	.0001	.0000	.0000

$500 benefit (cost) in the tenth year has a present value of approximately half, or $249.47. In addition, suppose the discount rate is doubled to 14.4%. This reduces the present value again by half over the same ten years. For example, $100 in the tenth year, discounted at 14.4%, is $26.05, and $500 becomes $130.23. These present values are just over one-fourth of the respective future values (or half of the present values at 7.2%). Obviously, the effect of the discount rate in reducing the value of future benefits and costs can be quite large.

As a second way to see the power of the discount rate, consider discount factors. A *discount factor* is the fraction, $1/(1 + d)^t$, that is multiplied by each benefit and cost to obtain the PV (see equation 11.5). Several discount factors are presented in Table 11.1. For example, the discount factor for year 5 with a discount rate of 10% is 0.6209. This means that a $1,000 benefit occurring in year 5, if discounted at 10%, is reduced to a present value of (0.6209 * $1,000) or $620.90.

As can be seen in Table 11.1, all of the discount factors have a value less than 1. Thus, any future benefit or cost that is discounted with a positive discount rate is reduced. The size of the reduction is directly dependent on the magnitude of the rate (d) and number of time periods (t) over which the values are discounted. For example, a $1 million benefit occurring in year 5 would be equal to anywhere from $783,500 to $497,200 in present value terms at discount rates ranging from 5% to 15%, respectively. The same $1 million benefit, if it occurs in year 20, decreases to a present value ranging from $376,900 to $61,100, and if in year 60, from $53,500 to $200 (at discount rates of 5% to 15%, respectively).

Table 11.2
Two Policies' Annual Net Benefits and NPVs

	Net Benefits ($)	
Year	Policy A	Policy B
0	-10,000	-10,000
1	2,000	0
2	4,000	0
3	6,000	12,600

	NPV ($)	
Discount Rate (%)	Policy A	Policy B
1%	1,724.92	2,229.44
8%	44.20	2.29
15%	-1,291.20	-1,715.30

To illustrate the dramatic effect a discount rate can have on a cost (or benefit) that occurs far into the future, consider a third example. Suppose highly toxic wastes are placed in long-term storage containers. The containers are deemed "safe," with a small but positive probability of an accidental leak occurring during the containers' lifetimes. For the sake of this example, suppose it is certain that a leak will occur in precisely 470 years. This is a considerable length of time, indeed, far beyond the typical time frame of a political decision maker. However, assume some individuals today express concern for the welfare of the future generation more than four centuries hence, when the leak occurs. Suppose experts estimate the damages will be $20 billion dollars (in constant 1998 dollars) at that time. A cost-benefit analysis confronts the decision maker with the present value of that cost. If the $20 billion cost is discounted at a rate of only 5% over 470 years, the present value equals $2.20 (yes, this reads "two dollars and twenty cents"!). The substantial cost for a future generation is only a negligible component of a cost-benefit calculation.

Discount Rate's Impact on NPV

Table 11.2 presents the net benefits over time for two policies. Focusing first on policy A, during the present (year 0), the net benefit is negative, as the policy requires some initial start-up or construction costs. Thereafter, annual net benefits become positive and increase through year 3.

Suppose in order to calculate policy A's NPV, the analyst discounts the net benefits at three different discount rates. As can be seen in Table 11.2, as the magnitude of the discount rate increases from 1% to 15%, the NPV decreases. Moreover, as the discount rate increases above 8%, the NPV becomes negative.

Principle 11.4. For a given policy, the higher the discount rate used in the analysis, then (a) the lower the NPV, and (b) in some cases an otherwise positive NPV may become negative.

Suppose policy A is compared with a second policy, B. The net benefits of policy B are also included in Table 11.2. As shown, policy B requires some initial construction or start-up costs ($10,000) and then generates zero net benefits until year 3, when benefits outweigh costs by $12,600.

The NPVs for the two policies, calculated using three discount rates, can be compared. Referring to Table 11.2, the impact of the rates on the policies' respective net benefits is twofold. First, with the lower rates, 1% and 8%, the NPVs of both policies are positive; however, when discounting with the high rate, 15%, both NPVs are negative. Thus, the NPVs are highly sensitive to the choice of discount rate. Second, the policies' NPV rankings vary with the discount rates. At the low rate, 1%, policy B has a higher NPV than policy A, while at the middle rate, 8%, policy A has the higher NPV.

The discount rate, or *crossover rate*, at which the two policies' NPVs are equal can be determined. In this case, at the discount rate of 7.3644%, both policy NPVs are $180.98. The crossover rate calculation involves two steps. First, for each year, take the difference between the policies' net benefits:

Year	0	1	2	3
A − B's Net Benefits	0	$2,000	$4,000	− $6,600.

Second, find the rate that discounts these differences to zero. (The reader can confirm that the present value of this "differences" net benefit stream is zero at a discount rate of 7.3644%.)

Figure 11.1 presents the two policies' *NPV profiles*. Each profile shows the relationship between the discount rate and the respective policy's NPV. As can be seen, for discount rates less than 7.3644%, the dotted line (NPV for policy B) is greater than the solid diamond-point line (NPV for policy A). At the crossover rate, the two profile curves intersect. Then, for rates above 7.3644%, policy A's NPV (the solid line) is the greater.

Figure 11.1
NPV Profiles for Two Policies

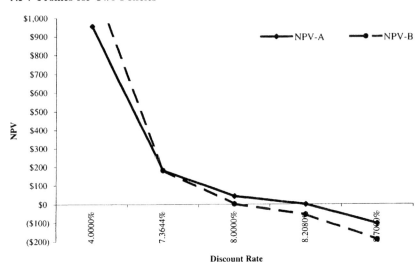

Principle 11.5. In comparing two or more policies, the selection of the discount rate can affect the policies' relative NPV ranking, thus changing which policy is identified as more efficient.

Why do specific discount rates determine a different policy to be more efficient? In Table 11.2 note the spread of benefits and costs over the two policies' respective time horizons. Compared to policy A, B generates larger net benefits in later years. Remember the structure of the present value equation (11.5) with both time period t and the discount rate in the denominator. As the number of time periods t rises, the discount rate's power increases exponentially, resulting in greatly reduced future values. Large discount rates decrease future values even more. Therefore, a high discount rate penalizes the larger future net benefits of policy B, causing B's NPV to fall below that for policy A.

Using the same logic, consider how the occurrence of large start-up or construction costs in the initial year (rather than later) reduces a policy's NPV. Costs incurred in the present ($t = 0$) are *not* discounted and thus lower the NPV to the full extent possible. If instead the policy incurs these same costs during a later year, discounting decreases the costs' present value, thereby allowing the NPV to remain higher. The greater the discount rate, the more the present value of future costs is reduced. Thus, when comparing two policies, high discount rates favor policies with future costs and thereby penalize policies with large initial start-up costs.

Principle 11.6. When comparing two or more policies, high discount rates penalize policies with large future benefits and large initial construction or start-up costs.

The example in Table 11.2 illustrates that the selected discount rate can have a profound effect in determining which policy promotes efficiency. Care must thus be exerted when selecting the discount rate. As one consideration, when analyzing two different policies for comparison purposes, the analyst should employ the same discount rate. Thus, if policy A is discounted at 8%, then policy B should also be discounted at 8%. To do otherwise, for example, to analyze policy A using a discount rate of 8% and policy B using 1%, is arbitrary and provides bias. Using the same discount rate essentially allows the decision maker to evaluate the respective policies with a common yardstick.

Principle 11.7. When analyzing two or more policies for comparison purposes, the analyst should use the same discount rate.

Another recommended practice, performing a selective sensitivity analysis for the discount rate, also greatly enhances the objectivity of the cost-benefit analysis.

SELECTIVE SENSITIVITY ANALYSIS

With no consensus as to the theoretically superior discount rate, yet recognizing a rate's potential power in calculating the NPV, the selection of a discount rate becomes a critical decision—one that can easily enable subjective influence by the analyst or decision maker and that in turn may be subjected to scrutiny from interested parties. To provide objectivity, a *selective sensitivity analysis* should be performed for the discount rate, where the analyst determines the sensitivity of the NPV to three alternate rates. The following steps are involved.

1. A moderate (middle-value) discount rate is selected according to a conceptual rationale that seems logical to the analyst and decision maker, and the NPV is calculated.
2. The analyst selects plausible high and low discount rates, which may reflect the same or different conceptual rationales, and computes the NPV with each.
3. All three NPVs for the policy are reported and interpreted.

In explaining the results, the variation in the NPVs shows their sensitivity to the choice of discount rate. In the report, the analyst should explicitly consider the impact of the high and low discount rates. Did the different discount rates have a sizable impact on the NPV calculation? Did they alter the conclusion concerning whether the policy promotes efficiency? If a policy's NPV is positive over a wide range of plausible discount rates, it is more reasonable to conclude that the policy promotes efficiency than if otherwise. Referring again to Table 11.2, the analyst can conclude that, for both policies A and B, the respective NPVs are highly sensitive to the choice of discount rate and that each policy promotes efficiency only if the discount rate is approximately 8% or less. Moreover, if more than one policy is being evaluated, the analyst should address whether the rates alter their relative ranking (as it does in Table 11.2), suggesting that sometimes one and sometimes another policy promotes efficiency. If the ranking does change, the crossover rate can be reported for the decision maker's consideration.

Principle 11.8. To enhance analytical objectivity and provide greater information to the decision maker, the analyst should conduct a selective sensitivity analysis for the discount rate. Three carefully selected discount rates should be applied in separate present value calculations; the resulting NPVs can then be compared to assess their sensitivity to the choice of discount rate.

The use of the range of discount rates provides greater information to the decision maker, thereby improving the quality of the decision-making process. Moreover, interested parties may not always agree with any single chosen discount rate and thus may (appropriately) challenge the analysis. Well-chosen high and low discount rates, along with an interpretation of the sensitivity of the NPV to the discount rate, can enable the analysis and its conclusions to withstand the scrutiny. Accordingly, the objectivity of the cost-benefit analysis is increased. (For a discussion of the U.S. federal government's practice in selecting discount rates, see Box 11.2 near the chapter's conclusion.)

DISCOUNTING AND ENVIRONMENTAL AND NATURAL RESOURCES

In recent years, a great deal of controversy has surrounded the practice of discounting in cost-benefit analyses. Members of the environmental movement in particular are quick to point to the discount rate's power, noting that the higher the discount rate, the lower the weight attributed to future environmental benefits and costs. Thus, when a policy has long-term environmental consequences, some environmentalists argue for application of a lower discount rate, most frequently appealing for a zero discount rate.

An examination of the full consequences of the discount rate for policies that affect the environment or natural resources is less clear, however. A high (rather than low) discount rate leads to assessments that sometimes hinder and other times enhance environmental resource protection. Specifically, selection of a high discount rate has the following effects.

- Future environmental and natural resource benefits are reduced in value. Thus, policies promoting sustained improvements in environmental quality and preservation of natural resources are appraised as less efficient. Likewise, assessments of management policies for renewable and depletable natural resources find the resources' rapid exploitation in the short term to be more efficient, for little appears to be gained from ensuring long-term availability of these resources.

- Long-run environmental damages are reduced in magnitude and therefore more likely to be disregarded in the decision-making process. Moreover, almost any positive discount rate results in insignificant present values for future catastrophic losses.

- The future commercial and social benefits of development projects in environmentally sensitive areas are reduced. Thus, the preservation of these areas is assessed as more efficient.

- The net benefits of all kinds of policies that employ investment resources are reduced. Thus, these policies are more likely to be considered inefficient, in turn discouraging the use of both renewable and depletable natural resources. (Pearce, Markandya and Barbier 1989: 135–37, 144; OECD 1994: 195, 199–200)

These examples illustrate that the consistent application of high discount rates has conflicting implications for environmental quality and natural resource preservation. As Pearce, Markandya and Barbier conclude, this "reduces considerably the force of arguments to the effect that conventionally determined discount rates should be lowered (or raised, depending on the view taken) to accommodate environmental considerations" (1989: 138).

DISCOUNTING AND INTERGENERATIONAL RIGHTS

Also engendering much debate is the discount rate's implications for the benefits received and costs incurred by future generations. By reducing these values, the interests of future generations are given less weight in the efficiency assessment. For this reason, some critics believe that discounting violates the rights of future generations.

The discount rate's weighting of future generations' interests and rights can engender much ethical debate. Nonetheless, neoclassical economics provides the conceptual framework for performing the analysis. It establishes the logic and values underlying the principles of cost-benefit analysis, which includes endorsing the practice of discounting. As presented in this chapter, according to economic reasoning, discounting reflects the preferences exhibited by individual and societal behavior. In considering the future relative to the present, both individuals and society tend to discount, where this discounting reflects either a positive time preference or the opportunity cost of foregoing alternative rates of return. In the terminology of neoclassical economics, discounting thus promotes *intergenerational efficiency*. From this line of reasoning, a decision *not* to discount future values, or to discount them at a rate chosen to reflect society's moral obligation to future generations as perceived by someone (the analyst, decision maker or particular interested parties), introduces subjective bias into the analysis. Such a practice weights the future in a way that does not reflect observed human behavior and social preferences. Recognizing the power of the discount rate, however, some economists recommend a low discount rate (which is consistent with the argument that society has a positive, but low, time preference rate).

If, however, contrary to economic reasoning, the analyst were to select the discount rate based on the decision maker's or a specific interested party's perceived notion as to the present society's moral obligation to future generations, then four options exist. These include the following:

- Set d at infinity, recognizing no moral obligation to the future, and thus not considering any future effects of current actions.
- Set d to be positive, recognizing a moral obligation but considering the future to be less important than the present.
- Set d at 0, recognizing a moral obligation and considering the future as equivalent to the present.
- Set d to be negative, recognizing a moral obligation and considering the future to be more important than the present. (Hanley and Spash 1993: 131–32)

In the end, we wish to emphasize that cost-benefit analysis is an economic analysis that employs discounting in accordance with economic principles. Therefore, we affirm the practice of the analyst performing a selective sensitivity analysis, in which three discount rates are chosen using the conceptual rationales presented in an earlier section. However, suppose the values of the decision maker or particular interested parties embrace ethical or environmental concerns for future generations that suggest a different discount rate should be considered. In actuality, the most commonly cited is a zero discount rate. In this case, we believe an objective analysis would employ a zero discount rate as a fourth rate.

Principle 11.9. Suppose that, for a particular policy, the decision maker or interested parties hold ethical or environmental concerns that suggest the future should be assigned the same weight as the present. The analyst can address their concerns, while simultaneously enhancing the objectivity of the analysis, by using a zero discount rate as a fourth rate in the selective sensitivity analysis.

INTERNAL RATE OF RETURN: AN ALTERNATIVE DECISION CRITERION?

The *internal rate of return (IRR)* is the discount rate that equates PVB with PVC so that NPV is 0. The following equation, substituting IRR for discount rate d and setting NPV to zero, is solved to calculate IRR.

$$\sum_{t=0}^{T} \frac{B_t - C_t}{(1 + IRR)^t} = 0. \tag{11.6}$$

Given the familiar concept of an investment yielding a rate of return, the IRR has been a popular decision criterion, especially among private managers, who often find it intuitively attractive to compare the IRR with alternative rates of return. The IRR can be interpreted as a "break-even" discount rate and is compared with the discount rate, d, to assess a policy's efficiency. As long as the IRR is greater than d, then the NPV discounted at rate d is positive. Thus, a high IRR generally suggests that a policy promotes efficiency.

Difficulties may be encountered in applying the IRR, however, depending on the policy's net benefit stream. A conventional stream involves a negative net benefit during the initial time period(s), followed by positive net benefits for each period thereafter. Mathematically, the net benefit sign reverses once from negative to positive, and thus a unique IRR can be calculated for the stream. In contrast, if the stream involves more than one sign reversal, the possibility of multiple IRRs exists, in which case the efficiency assessment is inconclusive. Practically speaking, most policy streams are conventional; and if a negative net benefit occurs in a future year, perhaps because of a capital replacement expenditure, it must be sizable to result in an additional IRR. Some policies, however, do involve large expenses in later years, such as building renovation, resource exploration and recovery, abandonment costs, environmental recovery costs and the like; these may give rise to multiple IRRs.

Moreover, the mathematical solution to equation 11.6 is found by trial and error. Fortunately, modern-day financial calculators and software packages are programmed to perform the calculation. However, when multiple IRRs exist, many packages simply report the first IRR found and do not indicate that multiple IRRs can solve the equation. Thus, the analyst must beware when analyzing a policy with an unconventional net benefit stream, for there might be multiple IRRs, rendering the obtained IRR uninterpretable.

A claimed advantage of the IRR is that it avoids the difficulty of designating a specific value for the discount rate, d. Indeed, if the IRR is 35%, for example, one feels safe in saying no d is likely to be as high; thus the policy promotes efficiency. However, for lower IRRs, assessment requires comparison with a stipulated d.

When comparing two mutually exclusive policies, the IRR is less reliable than the NPV. For example, consider policies A and B in Table 11.2. Suppose these are mutually exclusive and only one is to be chosen. As shown in Figure 11.1, the NPV becomes zero for policy A (the solid diamond-point line) at a discount rate of 8.208% and for B (the dotted line) at 8% (actually 8.008%). These are thus the respective policy IRRs, so the IRR for A is slightly higher than that for B, suggesting A is the more efficient policy. However, as indicated by the NPV sensitivity analysis, while A is the more efficient policy for discount rates above the crossover rate of 7.3644%, B is the more efficient policy for lower rates. Thus, the IRR ranking can be misleading.

An alternative, the *incremental IRR*, is sometimes applied. Policies are ranked in order of increasing cost. Beginning with the least cost policy, the incremental differences in benefits and costs required to switch to the next costly policy are found and the IRR for these increments is computed. If this incremental IRR is greater (less) than d, the more (less) costly policy promotes the greater efficiency. The more efficient of the two policies is then compared with the next

Box 11.2
U.S. Federal Government Practice in Selecting Discount Rates

Given the discount rate's power in influencing the assessed efficiency of specific policies, the federal government's selection of discount rates has received much scrutiny. Of particular concern are two discount rate practices that the Nixon administration prescribed in the early 1970s for federal agency cost-benefit analyses.

1. Beginning in 1972 the Office of Management and Budget (OMB) required all government agencies to use the same discount rate, a real rate of 10%. In effect, the government embraced the conceptual principle of selecting a discount rate equal to the alternative rate of return on private investment (before taxes and after adjusting for inflation). This particular rate, however, sparked numerous complaints that it was much too high, unfairly penalizing desirable government policies. Twenty years passed before the OMB in 1992 established a new lower rate, specifying a real discount rate of 7% for federal analyses (OMB 1992).

2. In fiscal year 1974, a second decision required that a different, lower discount rate be applied for capital-intensive, water-resource projects with long time horizons (such as dams and canal systems). This policy remains in effect today. Each year (by July 1), the U.S. Water Resources Council estimates the federal government's average long-term borrowing costs, to determine the discount rate to be used by federal agencies during the coming fiscal year for analyzing water-related projects.

These two discount rate policies offer the advantage of providing some consistency among federal government cost-benefit analyses. Indeed, prior to these stipulations, agencies submitted analyses using widely varying discount rates—a practice that hindered the decision maker's ability to compare the relative efficiency of different policy proposals. At the same time, both prescriptions violate the principles of cost-benefit analysis. First, there is no reason to believe that either a 10% or a 7% real rate always reflects the foregone alternative return on private investment; thus, the analyses do not necessarily identify the efficient policy decisions. Second, the federal government's prescription of a different discount rate for analyzing capital-intensive water projects violates the conditions for efficient resource allocation. Federal water projects appear relatively more efficient, and other policy alternatives less efficient, than is actually the case. Moreover, the government allows some flexibility, as an agency analyst may use a different discount rate for any specific policy with demonstrated reason. If done properly, this can enable a more accurate assessment of a particular policy's efficiency, yet it complicates the decision maker's comparison of different policies' relative efficiency.

All together, the federal government's practices demonstrate some of the practical difficulties encountered in selecting a discount rate. The particular prescriptions of the Nixon administration appear to be a response not only to economic principles but also to the political context. Specifically, a high discount rate facilitated the administration's objective of reducing government spending. The special discount rate for federal water projects recognized the penalty imposed by a high discount rate on large capital start-up costs and long-term future annual benefits. The authorized low discount rate also catered to the political interests of the Western states, which sought extensive water projects to enhance regional development (Lind 1982b: 5–8). Both of these are instances of *institutional capture*. Furthermore, the mandated procedures

(continued)

Box 11.2 (continued)

illustrate the trade-off between requiring use of one rate to facilitate policy comparisons and allowing a flexible rate to reflect accurately an appropriate conceptual rationale. The experience, all told, underscores the importance of employing *selective
sensitivity analysis* for the discount rate. By determining the effect of alternative
discount rates on each policy's calculated decision criterion, this technique facilitates
a comprehensive assessment of policy efficiency.

policy on the list, and so on, in order of increased policy costs. This procedure
is as reliable as the NPV, yet the pairwise comparisons entail more complex
calculations, while the NPV with sensitivity analysis provides the greater information. Thus, NPV is the recommended decision criterion.

CONCLUSION

After considering the numerous possibilities available to the analyst, it should
be apparent that, in an actual cost-benefit analysis, the selected discount rate is
likely to receive much scrutiny. Many questions may come from critics who
oppose the chosen conceptual rationale (economic principle) or from others who
argue that for a given rationale, a higher or lower discount rate is appropriate.
These concerns may reflect a conviction of the superiority of particular technical
elements or a vested interest in the outcome of the analysis. Accordingly, we
believe it is in the best interests of the analyst and decision maker to perform
a selective sensitivity analysis. Within the sensitivity analysis, the analyst can
choose the moderate, high and low rates to reflect different conceptual rationales
(or alternative values for a single rationale) and thereby enhance the ability of
the analysis to withstand scrutiny from vested interests or other critics. In instances where concerns are likely to be expressed on behalf of environmental
resources or future generations, with the claim that the appropriate discount rate
should be zero, the analyst might employ a zero discount rate as a fourth rate.
These practices increase the objectivity of the analysis by demonstrating the
decision criterion's sensitivity to the discount rate.

In some instances, the decision maker may indicate a specific rate to employ.
The analyst, for all appearances, is relieved of the burden of choosing the discount rate. Nonetheless, the analyst must not accept the exogenous rate without
question. If the analyst can honestly suggest a more practical or applicable rate,
he should consult with the decision maker to agree upon the best rate(s).

Chapter 12

Inflation

INTRODUCTION

The monetary values assigned to a policy's benefits and costs must be considered in the context of what is generally happening with other prices. Suppose a resource cost was $100 last year and $105 this year (a 5% increase). Over this same time period, other prices also rose; in other words, there was general price inflation. The resource's expense may therefore have increased faster, slower or at the same rate as inflation; its real cost may or may not have changed. Accordingly, an economic analysis is careful to account for inflationary changes. Appropriate methods for treating inflation[1] in a cost-benefit analysis are explored in this chapter.

To define some basic terms, *inflation* is an increase in the general price level of goods and services; it represents a reduction in a dollar's purchasing power. A *nominal price* is a price expressed in *current dollars*; in other words, the price has not been adjusted for inflation. The prices that individuals pay or observe in the market, such as the $100 and $105 in the example, are nominal. Each is measured in dollars, with purchasing power "current" to the respective price's year. A *real price* has been adjusted for inflation. Such a price is expressed in dollars with a constant purchasing power, that is, in *constant dollars*.

Principle 12.1 The use of monetary values requires careful consideration and possible adjustment for inflation. Adjusting for inflation is sometimes confused with discounting to present value. To clarify, inflationary adjustments acknowledge the declining purchasing power of the dollar as the general price level increases over time. Discounting reflects a dollar's greater value in the present than in the future, due to one of the following: the present dollar's ability to earn a return from alternative investments, society's preference for present consumption or the future repayment of borrowing costs.

NOMINAL OR REAL VALUES?

When presenting the data, the analyst has a choice between expressing the benefits and costs in nominal prices (i.e., current dollars) or real prices (i.e., constant dollars). Either can be chosen without influencing the outcome of the analysis if consistently applied to all benefits, costs and discount rates.

Principle 12.2. The analyst can express benefits and costs either all in nominal prices (i.e., current dollars) or all in real prices (i.e., constant dollars), as long as the discount rate is expressed the same way. Specifically, use of nominal benefits and costs requires a *nominal discount rate*. If, instead, the benefits and costs are real, then a *real discount rate* adjusted for inflation must be employed.

Since the choice has no effect on the outcome of the analysis, what are the practical considerations in deciding whether to express values in nominal or real terms? Cost-benefit analyses often use real values, especially when assessing future policies, for two main reasons. First, economic analysis is interested in relative (real) price changes; the use of real prices makes it easier to see either relative price changes or, if relative prices remain constant, quantity changes over time. (As nominal prices, in contrast, increase with inflation, these other changes are not explicitly apparent.) Second, the number of computations needed to make inflation adjustments is often a concern. To analyze future policies, fewer calculations are usually required when working with real values, particularly when real prices remain constant over time. In the case of historical policies, in contrast, the number of computations can vary depending on the form of the available data; for example, if most data are nominal, then working with nominal figures entails fewer adjustments and thus might be preferred.

Another consideration, however, is that performing a cost-benefit analysis in real prices does not show the decision maker the actual dollar values incurred in each year. Such information might be of particular interest for planning future annual budgets or investments. For this reason, the analyst might choose to perform the entire analysis using nominal values. (Another possibility would be to display the yearly budget or investment expenditures in nominal prices in a separate table in the report, while conducting the analysis in real values. Of course, this will increase the number of required calculations!)

Whether choosing to work with nominal or real values, the analyst must be diligent when collecting data, keeping careful track of whether the monetary values are expressed in current or constant dollars (and for which year) and whether the selected discount rates are nominal or real. Likewise, when reporting dollar values or discount rates, the analyst must thoroughly indicate the pertinent information for the collected data as well as any inflationary adjustments or price projections made for the analysis.

CHOICE OF INFLATION MEASURE

Inflation can be expressed numerically in one of two forms, using either a price index or an inflation rate. An (annual) *price index* is created by assigning the index number 100 to the general level of prices in an arbitrarily determined "base year"; then, in other years, higher price levels are represented by proportionately larger index numbers and lower levels by proportionately smaller index numbers. Inflation is indicated by an increase in the price index from one time period to the next. The percentage change in the price index over time is the *inflation rate*.

Three major types of general price indices are among those reported by U.S. official sources. The first, the most popularly known, is the *Consumer Price Index* (CPI), which measures the general price level for a basket of goods and services (such as food, clothing, housing, transportation, fuels, medical services, medications) purchased by a typical urban family. Consumer price indices are also available for specific items (e.g., fuel costs or housing). The second index is the *GDP implicit price deflator* (or simply the GDP deflator), the price index for all final goods and services produced by the national economy. The third is the *Producer Price Index* (PPI), which is calculated for production commodities and is reported for the aggregate production sector as well as for specific industries and commodities.[2]

When adjusting for inflation in a cost-benefit analysis, it is important to use the appropriate index. There is some debate, however, as to which one is suitable. To convert nominal to real values, or vice versa, we recommend a broad-based index be employed. Cost-benefit analysis focuses on the benefits and costs to all of society; thus, the appropriate inflation measure should reflect the price changes society encounters. If all policy benefits and costs are consumption items for the typical urban family, then the CPI is a relevant measure. More often, the benefits and costs will involve a wider range of goods and services, which suggests the GDP implicit price deflator is appropriate. (The PPI is based on a narrower segment of the economy and is thus less relevant for cost-benefit analysis.) Another consideration is that often the national index is used; however, if a policy affects only members of a particular region, then the analyst should consider using the corresponding region-specific index.

When projecting prices over time, a distinction must be made between changes in the general price level and relative price changes. A common practice is (1) to assume benefits and costs will usually increase over time at the rate of inflation and then (2) to identify those particular benefits and costs whose prices will change at a different rate. When predicting price increases under the assumption in (1), we again recommend use of a broad-based price index (usually the GDP deflator) to measure the inflation rate. Then, for any benefit or cost expected to undergo a *relative price change*, as in (2), the particular price should be projected, applying the most accurate information available. This might include using a specific product index or a composite index such as the PPI or, instead, projecting the price based on historical trends, in-depth analysis and/or expert judgment.

SELECTING THE APPROPRIATE CALCULATION FORMULAS

The appropriate calculations for adjusting benefits, costs and discount rates for inflation can vary for specific analyses. When considering how to account for inflation in a particular analysis, we suggest the analyst begin by answering four questions.

- *Is the analysis ex post or ex ante? Ex post* analyses are after-the-fact analyses. These examine past policies where, potentially, observed values for the benefits, costs and inflation rates can be measured. *Ex ante* analyses, in contrast, are before-the-fact analyses. These assess future policies for which future benefits, costs and inflation rates are not yet observable and must be predicted.
- *Will any dollar values need to be converted from nominal to real prices, or vice versa?* If the collected benefit and cost data are available in different forms, with some values expressed in nominal prices and others in constant dollars, then additional calculations are required. Either nominal prices need to be converted to constant dollar values, or vice versa.
- *Will any values for benefits (or costs) need to be projected over time?* In *ex post* analyses, the analyst sometimes is able to value a particular benefit (or cost) for only a portion of the policy's time horizon. If so, he must project the values for this benefit (cost) for later and/or earlier time periods. In either projection, inflation must be taken into account. In *ex ante* analyses, projections of (unknown) future benefits and costs are an inherent part of the calculations; here also, possible adjustments for inflation must be considered.
- *Will the selected discount rates need to be adjusted for inflation?* This chapter's discussion assumes the analyst generally obtains nominal discount rates. (Rates of return reported in the *Federal Bulletin*, newspapers, and so on and borrowing costs are usually nominal.) Thus, if benefits and costs are expressed in nominal prices, then the selected discount rates need not be adjusted for inflation. However, if the analysis uses benefits and costs in constant dollars, then the nominal discount rates must be converted to real discount rates.

Upon answering these questions, the analyst is ready to identify the proper calculations for adjusting specific benefits, costs and/or discount rates for inflation. The discussion that follows begins with typical adjustments for inflation encountered in *ex post* analyses and then proceeds to consider relevant adjustments for *ex ante* analyses. Appropriate calculation formulas along with illustrative examples are presented to show how to (a) convert nominal to real prices and vice versa, (b) project dollar values through time, adjusting them as needed for inflation, and (c) adjust a nominal discount rate for inflation.

To find the correct calculation formulas for a particular analysis, the analyst can skip to the relevant chapter section. The applicable section can be determined by noting which one of the following four categories describes the analysis under consideration. For convenience, a complete listing of the section subheadings is outlined.

1. *Ex post* analysis in constant dollars (i.e, real prices)
   1a. Converting a nominal price to a price in constant dollars
   1b. Projecting a real price over time
   1c. Converting a nominal discount rate to a real discount rate

2. *Ex post* analysis in nominal prices (i.e., current dollars)
   2a. Converting a real price (in constant dollars) to a nominal price
   2b. Projecting a nominal price over time
      2b-i. Adjusting for inflation to project the nominal price in later years
      2b-ii. Adjusting for inflation to project the nominal price in earlier years

3. *Ex ante* analysis in constant dollars (i.e, real prices)
   3a. Converting a nominal price to a price in constant dollars
   3b. Projecting a real price over time
   3c. Converting a nominal discount rate to a real discount rate

4. *Ex ante* analysis in nominal prices (i.e., current dollars)
   4a. Converting a real price (in constant dollars) to a nominal price
   4b. Projecting a nominal price over time.

1. *EX POST* ANALYSIS IN CONSTANT DOLLARS (i.e., REAL PRICES)

1a. Converting a Nominal Price to a Price in Constant Dollars

For an *ex post* analysis, an analyst gathers data to estimate a policy's annual benefits and costs in past years. Suppose he finds that most of the data are expressed in constant dollars, but data for at least one benefit (or cost) are available in nominal prices (i.e., current dollars). The analyst might choose to express all benefits and costs in constant dollars, simply because fewer calculations are required to convert the small number of nominal benefits (costs) to constant dollar values than vice versa. The following example illustrates such a calculation.

The analyst is assessing a beach renourishment plan implemented in past years. Suppose he locates a study that estimates the average beachgoer was willing to pay $3 per hour (a nominal price) in 1994 to visit the renourished beach. Assume also that the rest of the benefits and costs associated with the policy are expressed in constant 1993 dollars. For consistency, the analyst chooses to express the beachgoer's willingness to pay in 1994 in constant 1993 dollars.

The general calculation formula for converting the nominal price to a price in constant dollars (*PCon$*) is as follows.

Table 12.1
GDP Implicit Price Deflator, 1990–1994

Year	Price Index (1992 = 100)	Inflation Rate (%)
1990	93.6	4.3
1991	97.3	4.0
1992	100.0	2.7
1993	102.6	2.6
1994	105.0	2.3

Source: U.S. President, *Economic Report of the President Transmitted to the Congress, February 1996* (Washington, D.C.: Government Printing Office, 1996), 286.

$$\text{PCon\$} = \frac{\text{Nom P}}{PI_1} * PI_2, \tag{12.1}$$

where *Nom P* is the nominal price (or price in current dollars), PI_1 is the price index for the year of the nominal price and PI_2 is the price index for the year of the constant dollar.

Accordingly, the analyst finds the GDP implicit price deflator. The GDP deflator index and (percentage change) inflation rates for several years are reproduced in Table 12.1. As can be seen, the index for 1993 is 102.6, and for 1994, 105.0. Substituting the values into equation 12.1, the analyst converts the nominal $3 price to a constant 1993 dollar value:[3]

$$\text{PCon\$}_{1993} = \frac{\text{Nom P}_{1994}}{PI_{1994}} * PI_{1993} = \frac{\$3}{105.0} * 102.6 = \$2.9314.$$

Thus, the average beachgoer's willingness to pay per hour visit to the renourished beach in 1994 was a nominal $3, or $2.93 in constant 1993 dollars.

Once the calculation is completed, the analyst should check his results. A common mistake is to switch the price indices, causing the calculated price to increase when it should decrease compared to the original price, or vice versa. Using the beachgoer example, let's check to be sure the calculated real price makes sense. Remember the analyst is converting a 1994 nominal price to a price in constant 1993 dollars. Considering there was inflation from 1993 to 1994, which price is expected to be smaller: the 1994 price expressed in 1993 dollars or the nominal price? In removing the inflationary effect, the price in 1993 dollars should become smaller. In fact, as the 1994 price calculated in

1993 dollars ($2.93) is less than the nominal price of $3, the calculation makes sense and appears to be correct. Reasoning through the expected price change in this manner provides an easy check for the analyst and should always be practiced.

Once the benefit estimate for 1994 has been converted to a value in constant 1993 dollars, the analyst faces one of two possibilities. First, he may be able to locate other studies that value the beachgoers' willingness to pay for the renourished beach during other years. If so, and assuming these estimates are expressed as nominal prices current to these other years, then he must convert them to a constant 1993 dollar value. He should employ the same calculation formula (12.1). Alternatively, the nominal price for 1994 may be the only valuation estimate he can find. In this case he needs to project the one value, expressed in constant 1993 dollars, forward and/or backward throughout the years of the policy's time horizon. Such a projection is considered in section (1b).

1b. Projecting a Real Price over Time

Assume the analyst again has chosen to express the policy's benefits and costs in constant dollars (i.e., in real prices). However, for one particular benefit (cost), suppose he is able to estimate or find a value for only one year, say, a middle year in the policy's time horizon. In order to complete the analysis, the analyst must project the value of this benefit (cost) forward over the later years and backward through the earlier years of the policy.

Two possibilities exist. First, it may be reasonable to assume that the value of the particular benefit (cost) increased over time at the same rate as inflation, so that the real value remained the same. Continuing with the beach valuation example as illustration, this means that the average beachgoer who in 1994 was willing to pay $2.93 in constant 1993 dollars would be willing to pay the same amount during prior and later years of the analysis. As shown in column 1 of the spreadsheet in Table 12.2, the total annual value to beachgoers was therefore $2.9314 (in constant 1993 dollars) times the incremental number of beachgoer-hours generated by the beach renourishment each year. Second, suppose instead that the available evidence suggests the price changed at a rate different from inflation. In particular, perhaps expert judgment estimates the real price increased by 1% each year. The projected yearly beachgoer values assuming a 1% annual real price increase are presented in column 2.

1c. Converting a Nominal Discount Rate to a Real Discount Rate

Suppose the analyst selects three nominal discount rates for the *ex post* analysis of a given policy. If the analyst chooses to express benefits and costs in

Table 12.2
Projected Annual Beachgoer Benefits (in constant 1993 dollars)

Year	(1) Total Annual Value to Beachgoers (real price remains same each year)	(2) Total Annual Value to Beachgoers (real price increases 1% each year)[a]
1992	$2.9314(Q_{1992}{}^{b})$	$2.8737(Q_{1992}{}^{b})$
1993	$2.9314(Q_{1993})$	$2.9024(Q_{1993})$
1994	$2.9314(Q_{1994})$	$2.9314(Q_{1994})$
1995	$2.9314(Q_{1995})$	$2.9607(Q_{1995})$

[a]The 1% annual increase for each successive year $(t + 1)$ following 1994 is calculated as (real price in year t)(1.01), and for each of the prior years $(t - 1)$ as (real price in year t)/1.01.
[b]Q_{year} is the number of incremental beachgoer-hours generated by beach renourishment during the designated year. A beachgoer-hour is a one hour stay at the beach by one beachgoer.

constant dollars, then each nominal rate must be converted to a real discount rate.

$$\text{Real discount rate} = \frac{\text{Nom } d - \text{INFL}_{\text{ave}}}{1 + \text{INFL}_{\text{ave}}}, \tag{12.2}$$

where *Nom d* is the nominal discount rate and $INFL_{ave}$ is the average annual inflation rate over the policy time horizon. The real discount rate is sometimes approximated with the simple conceptual equation, *Nom d* − $INFL_{ave}$; however, equation 12.2 is more precise.

As an illustration, suppose the analyzed policy's time horizon was five years, from 1990 through 1994, and one of the selected discount rates is 8%. Table 12.1 shows the percentage change in the GDP implicit price deflator for each year during that period. Averaging the five inflation rates yields 3.2% as the average annual inflation rate over the policy's time horizon. To calculate the real discount rate, these numbers can be substituted into equation 12.2 as follows:

$$\text{real discount rate} = \frac{\text{Nom } d - \text{INFL}_{\text{ave}}}{1 + \text{INFL}_{\text{ave}}} = \frac{.08 - .032}{1 + .032} = .0465.$$

Thus, the real discount rate is 4.65%. (The approximation formula yields a rate of 4.8%, a small but distinguishable difference.)

2. *EX POST* ANALYSIS IN NOMINAL PRICES (i.e., CURRENT DOLLARS)

2a. Converting a Real Price (in Constant Dollars) to a Nominal Price

An analyst gathers relevant data for estimating a policy's annual benefits and costs for an *ex post* analysis. Suppose most of the data are expressed in nominal prices, but data for at least one benefit (or cost) are available only in constant dollars (i.e., real prices). The analyst might choose to express all benefits and costs in nominal prices, simply because fewer conversion computations are required. The following example illustrates such a calculation.

The analyst is assessing a policy that retrofits a sewage treatment plant to undertake secondary treatment. While working on the analysis, he discovers the annual operating costs are expressed in constant 1993 dollars. However, all other benefits and costs are presented in nominal prices. To be consistent, he chooses to convert the operating costs to nominal prices.

The general equation for converting prices in constant dollars to nominal prices is as follows.

$$\text{Nom P} = \frac{(\text{PCon\$})}{PI_2} * PI_1, \tag{12.3}$$

where *PCon$* is the price in constant dollars (or the real price), PI_1 is the price index for the year of the nominal price and PI_2 is the price index for the year of the constant dollar.

Suppose annual operating costs are estimated for each year to be $50,000 in constant 1993 dollars, and the analyst wants to find the 1994 nominal price. The analyst locates the relevant GDP implicit price deflators. Referring to Table 12.1, the indices are 102.6 in 1993 and 105.0 in 1994. Substituting these values into equation 12.3, the analyst converts the $50,000 operating cost (in constant 1993 dollars) into a nominal price for 1994.

$$\text{Nom P}_{1994} = \frac{\text{PCon\$}_{1993}}{PI_{1993}} * PI_{1994} = \frac{\$50,000}{102.6} * 105.0 = \$51,169.5906.$$

The sewage plant's operating costs in 1994 are $50,000 in constant 1993 dollars, or $51,169.59 in nominal prices.

The analyst should check his calculation. Here the estimated nominal price in 1994 is larger than the price in constant 1993 dollars. Does this make sense? Consider that from 1993 to 1994, inflation occurred. It is therefore expected that the 1994 nominal price would be greater than the same price expressed in 1993 dollars. The calculation appears to be correct.

The analyst needs to perform a similar conversion for every year of operating costs. As another example, the 1991 annual operating costs were also $50,000 in constant 1993 dollars, and these should be expressed in 1991 nominal prices. As can be seen in Table 12.1, the GDP implicit price deflators are 97.3 in 1991 and 102.6 in 1993. Substituting the relevant values into equation 12.3 yields the following,

$$\text{Nom } P_{1991} = \frac{\text{PCon\$}_{1993}}{PI_{1993}} * PI_{1991} = \frac{\$50,000}{102.6} * 97.3 = \$47,417.1540.$$

As the analyst checks this calculation, he notices that the nominal price in 1991 is less than the price in constant 1993 dollars. This is reasonable since from 1991 to 1993, two years of inflation occurred. Thus, the 1991 value should be less than the same price expressed in 1993 dollars.

2b. Projecting a Nominal Price over Time

The analyst again has chosen to express the policy's benefits and costs in nominal prices. However, for one particular benefit (cost), suppose he is able to estimate or find a value for only one year. The analyst must project the value of this benefit (cost) throughout the policy's time horizon, taking inflation into account. Calculation formulas for projecting the nominal price forward into later years and back in time for earlier years, respectively, are presented in the following sections.

2b-i. Adjusting for inflation to project the nominal price in later years.

Suppose for one particular benefit (cost) the analyst is able to collect a nominal value for only one year, say, the first year in the policy's time horizon. In order to complete the analysis, the analyst must project the value of this benefit (cost) forward over the later years of the policy. He confronts one of two scenarios. First, if it is reasonable to assume the nominal price increased over time at the same rate as inflation, he must adjust this one value for inflation using each year's respective inflation rate. To inflate from one year (t) to the following year ($t + 1$), the calculation formula is as follows.

$$\text{Nom } P_{t+1} = \text{Nom } P_t + (\text{Nom } P_t) * (\text{INFL}_{t+1}) \qquad (12.4)$$
$$= \text{Nom } P_t * (1 + \text{INFL}_{t+1})$$

where *Nom P_t* is the nominal price in year t, *Nom P_{t+1}* is the nominal price in the year following year t and *$INFL_{t+1}$* is the inflation rate (%) in the year following year t.

To illustrate, a study estimates that the average Florida resident was willing to pay $15 in 1990 to ensure the endangered species, the manatee, survived during that year. Assuming the average willingness to pay increased with inflation, the analyst calculates the *nominal* value in 1991. To measure inflation, he locates the GDP deflator, but this time uses the percentage change or *inflation rate*. As can be seen in Table 12.1, the inflation rate in 1991 was 4% (or 0.04). Using equation 12.4,

$$\text{Nom } P_{1991} = \text{Nom } P_{1990} * (1 + INFL_{1991}) = \$15 * 1.04 = \$15.60.$$

To inflate the price for the second year, 1992, equation 12.4 is once again employed. With the 1992 inflation rate of 2.7% (see Table 12.1), then the

$$\text{Nom } P_{1992} = \text{Nom } P_{1991} * (1 + INFL_{1992}) = \$15.60 * 1.027 = \$16.0212.$$

A second, alternative scenario arises if evidence suggests the *relative price* changed over time, with the nominal price increasing at a rate different from inflation. Accordingly, the analyst can easily adjust equation 12.4 to project the nominal price in later years. If, for example, there is reason to believe the willingness to pay for the manatee increased at a rate different from inflation, say, 5% between 1990 and 1991, then the 1991 nominal price can be calculated by substituting 5% for the inflation rate in equation 12.4. Thus, Nom P_{1991} is $15 * 1.05, or $15.75.

2b-ii. Adjusting for inflation to project the nominal price in earlier years.

Suppose once again for a particular benefit (cost), the analyst has a nominal value for only one year, but this time for the last year in the policy's time horizon. The analyst must adjust the nominal value for inflation back through preceding years in time. Again, he must consider whether or not there was a relative price change. Suppose, first, it is reasonable to assume the price of the benefit (cost) changed over time at the same rate as inflation. Then, to adjust a nominal price from one year (*t*) to the preceding year (*t* − *1*), the following equation is used:

$$\text{Nom } P_{t-1} = \frac{\text{Nom } P_t}{1 + INFL_t}, \tag{12.5}$$

where *Nom* P_{t-1} is the nominal price in the year preceding year *t*, *Nom* P_t is the nominal price in year *t* and *INFL$_t$* is the inflation rate (%) in year *t*.

As an example, a policy benefitted jet skiers, and the average skier's willingness to pay per jet ski trip was valued at $7.50 in 1992. Suppose the analyst can reasonably assume the jet skiers' average willingness to pay was less during the prior year, 1991, than in 1992 by precisely the rate of inflation and that the inflation rate in 1992, as measured by the percentage change in GDP deflator, was 2.7% (see Table 12.1). Substituting these numbers into equation 12.5 yields the following.

$$\text{Nom } P_{1991} = \frac{\text{Nom } P_{1992}}{1 + INFL_{1992}} = \frac{\$7.50}{1 + .027} = \$7.3028.$$

The second possibility is that the relative price did change. Equation 12.5 lends itself to adaptation. For illustration, suppose the jet skiers' willingness to pay is believed to have increased by less than inflation (thus, the relative price declined). If between 1991 and 1992 it increased by, say, 2% (0.7 less than the inflation rate), then the 2% increase can replace the inflation rate in equation 12.5. Thus, Nom P_{1991} is \$7.50/1.02, or \$7.3529.

3. *EX ANTE* ANALYSIS IN CONSTANT DOLLARS (i.e, REAL PRICES)

3a. Converting a Nominal Price to a Price in Constant Dollars

For an *ex ante* analysis, an analyst seeks to estimate a proposed policy's annual benefits and costs in future years. Generally, the analyst gathers data for today and/or for past years to provide the basis for future projections. Suppose he decides to express all benefits and costs in constant dollars, but the collected data for one or more benefits (or costs) are available in nominal prices (i.e., current dollars) for different year(s). For example, he may have an estimate of the average beachgoer's willingness to pay in 1993 and the average resident's willingness to pay for manatee preservation in 1990. These estimates need to be converted so that all are expressed in constant dollars in the same year (perhaps, for instance, the entire analysis is conducted in terms of constant 1993 dollars). To convert a nominal price to a price in constant dollars, the analyst should employ the same equation (12.1) developed for *ex post* analyses in section 1a.

3b. Projecting a Real Price over Time

In addition to converting all benefits and costs to real prices, in an *ex ante* analysis the analyst must project the constant dollar values into the future over the relevant years of the policy's time horizon. Since future benefits and costs are unknown, they are predicted based on what is anticipated today. The analyst must determine whether the real price is likely to remain the same or change. If the former, then the use of constant dollars offers the advantage of employing the same real price for each progressive year, similar to column 1 in Table 12.2, which projects constant dollar values for an *ex post* analysis. The analyst is saved from making numerous calculations to adjust annual benefits and costs for inflation. For this reason, real prices are commonly recommended for *ex ante* analyses. If, instead, the real price is expected to change, then the analyst must adjust the price accordingly each year, with calculations parallel to those shown for an *ex post* analysis in column 2, Table 12.2.

3c. Converting a Nominal Discount Rate to a Real Discount Rate

Suppose the analyst selects three nominal discount rates for the *ex ante* analysis of a future policy. If the analyst chooses to express benefits and costs in constant dollars, then each nominal rate must be converted to a real discount rate. The relevant calculation formula is equation 12.2, located in section 1c, for *ex post* analyses. The one difference for *ex ante* analyses is that the average annual inflation rate for the future is (obviously) unknown. The analyst must thus predict the future rate for the policy's anticipated time horizon. To do this, the analyst might consult inflation forecasts made by federal or state governments, the OECD, specialized private consultants or investment firms. Alternatively, the analyst might average yearly inflation rates for a historical time period paralleling the length of the policy's future time horizon. For instance, annual inflation rates for the past 20 years might provide the basis for predicting the average annual inflation rate for a future policy with a twenty-year time horizon. However, the analyst must be careful to take into account the specific experiences (e.g., recessions, expansions, or economic crises) influencing the inflation rates during the past period, to consider whether these events seem likely to correspond with the expected circumstances over the policy time horizon and then to adjust the rate accordingly.

4. *EX ANTE* ANALYSIS IN NOMINAL PRICES (i.e., CURRENT DOLLARS)

4a. Converting a Real Price (in Constant Dollars) to a Nominal Price

In *ex ante* analyses, the analyst also has the option of expressing all benefits and costs in nominal prices. In gathering data for current or past years to enable an estimation of future benefits and costs, the analyst may find most data are, for instance, current to the year of analysis. However, data for one benefit (or cost) may be expressed in constant dollars (say, constant 1993 dollars). He must be consistent and convert the constant dollar value to a current (nominal) price. For this calculation, the analyst should use equation 12.3, applied in section 2a for *ex post* analyses.

4b. Projecting a Nominal Price over Time

In an *ex ante* analysis, the analyst must project the nominal benefits and costs each year over the policy's future time horizon. The analyst has to assess whether a price will increase at the same rate as future inflation or undergo a relative price change. For the former case, each future year's nominal price can be calculated using the following equation.

$$\text{Nom } P_{t+1} = \text{Nom } P_t + (\text{Nom } P_t) * (INFL_{fut}) \qquad (12.6)$$
$$= \text{Nom } P_t * (1 + INFL_{fut}),$$

where *Nom P_t* is the nominal price in year t, *Nom P_{t+1}* is the nominal price in the year following year t and *$INFL_{fut}$* is the average annual inflation rate expected for the policy's future time horizon.

As an example, suppose a small water project's maintenance expenses are estimated to be $1,000 for this year and are expected to increase with inflation in the future. If, magically, the analyst knows that the average annual inflation rate in the future will be 2.5%, then, for example, the maintenance costs for next year are projected to be $1,000 * 1.025, or $1,025, and for the following year, $1,025 * 1.025, or $1,050.625.

In actuality, however, future annual inflation rates are unknown and must be predicted. Section 3c discusses how the analyst might find the expected future rate. Given the uncertain size of future inflation rates, a *selective sensitivity analysis* might be performed to see the effects of different rates on the analysis.

If, however, evidence suggests that maintenance expenses will increase in the future at a rate different from inflation, in other words, the *relative price* will *change*, then the analyst can conveniently modify equation 12.6 to project future expenses in nominal terms. Suppose, for example, there is reason to believe nominal maintenance expenses will increase by 4% (or 1.5% above the expected inflation rate); then each successive year's expenses can be calculated by substituting 4% for the future inflation rate in equation 12.6. For instance, the maintenance expenses for next year are expected to be $1,000 * 1.04, or $1,040.

CONCLUSION

This chapter presents several ways to adjust benefits, costs and discount rates for inflation. Some of these approaches can be employed to verify Principle 12.2 and show that the analyst may choose to express the values all in nominal or all in real terms without changing the results of the analysis. Suppose the analyst performs an *ex ante* analysis for a new project, predicting the real benefits and costs for next year and the following year, then calculating the NPV. In this year's constant dollars, he projects: $C_1 = \$100$, $C_2 = \$100$, $B_1 = \$50$ and $B_2 = \$300$. To find the real discount rate, the selected discount rate of 8% and anticipated average annual inflation rate of 5% for the next two years are substituted into equation 12.2, yielding $(.08 - .05)/(1.05)$, or real d is 2.8571%. To calculate NPV, equation 10.2 is reproduced; all values are in this year's constant dollars.

$$NPV = \sum_{t=0}^{T} \frac{B_t - C_t}{(1 + d)^t} = \frac{-\$50}{(1.028571)^1} + \frac{\$200}{(1.028571)^2} = \$140.43.$$

If, instead, the analyst projects the benefits and costs in nominal terms with the 5% inflation rate, then according to equation 12.6, the projected nominal values are: $C_1 = \$105$, $C_2 = \$110.25$, $B_1 = \$52.50$ and $B_2 = \$330.75$. Applying the nominal discount rate of 8%, the NPV is calculated in nominal terms as:

$$NPV = \frac{-\$52.50}{(1.08)^1} + \frac{\$220.50}{(1.08)^2} = \$140.44.$$

As seen, when the analyst consistently expresses the benefits, costs and discount rate all in nominal or all in real values, the NPVs are identical, except for rounding error.

NOTES

1. The same methods can be applied for deflation.

2. Primary sources for U.S. price indices and inflation rates are the Bureau of Labor Statistics for the CPI and PPI, and the Bureau of Economic Analysis for the GDP deflator. Among the secondary sources are the *Economic Report of the President* (U.S. President 1996) for the CPI, GDP deflator and PPI, and *Statistical Abstract of the United States* (U.S. Bureau of the Census 1995) for the CPI and PPI. Sometimes an analysis needs recent inflation rates since the date of latest publication. Business periodicals are often a good source for up-to-date inflation rates. For instance, *The Economist* regularly publishes consumer and producer price changes for the top 15 major industrialized countries, including the rate for a recent month and quarter as well as forecasts for two years (the current and one succeeding year).

3. All calculations are carried out to four decimal places to enhance the accuracy of the final calculation.

Chapter 13

Time Horizon

INTRODUCTION

The analyst must select a suitable *time horizon*, that is, the time frame of benefit and cost streams in the analysis. Ideally, the time horizon should include the entire time period over which policy benefits and costs occur. Often the time horizon is set by the expected useful life of any capital investments, as determined by engineers or manufacturers, and/or by the length of time over which policy benefits transpire, whichever is longer. Other considerations include the time frame for any future social costs, any realistic assumptions about maintenance that might prolong an asset's functional life (such assumptions should be stated explicitly in the analysis) or, future changes, such as demographic trends in a geographical area, that may be so uncertain as to suggest a reliable analysis limit the time horizon.

Biases are possible, as an arbitrarily shortened time period is likely to lower the NPV (or B/C) by reducing the future benefit stream, while an analysis that projects benefits unreasonably far into the future may raise the decision criterion's value. Or, if the policy involves sizable future social costs, then altering the time horizon will have the opposite effects on NPV (B/C). At the same time, the application of discounting may reduce any bias as well as shorten the relevant time horizon. For any selected discount rate, there is some future date beyond which additional benefits or costs are discounted to values nearing zero and thus are rendered insignificant in the present value calculation. A glance at the discount factors in Table 11.1 in the Discount Rate chapter is illustrative. Remember that a *discount factor* is the fraction that is multiplied times a future benefit or cost to calculate present value. As seen in the table, after some 60 to 75 years, the discount factors are extremely low. For example, a benefit of $1 occurring in 60 years, if discounted at 5%, has a present value of only 5.35 cents, and if discounted at 15%, the present value is only two hundredths of a cent. Therefore, the higher the discount rate, the shorter the useful time horizon in the analysis.

Principle 13.1. Be aware of possible biases in the choice of time horizon for the analysis; the horizon should include the entire time period over which policy benefits and costs occur. At the same time, the practice of discounting reduces values occurring after some 60 to 75 years to negligible amounts, potentially limiting the relevant time horizon.

TERMINAL VALUE

Another consideration when selecting the time horizon is whether to estimate a terminal value, allowing the time horizon to be shorter than the capital asset's lifetime. For example, the decision maker may only be planning the policy for, say, three years, and nearly all benefits and costs are confined to this time period, with the exception of one purchased asset with a ten-year life. To provide the most useful information for the decision maker, the analyst can define the time horizon as three years and incorporate a *terminal value* (or *residual value*) in the third year to reflect the incremental value of the asset's remaining seven-year life.

If a terminal value is employed, the net present value equation can be adjusted as follows.

$$NPV = \sum_{t=0}^{T} \frac{B_t - C_t}{(1 + d)^t} + \frac{TrmV_T}{(1 + d)^T,} \tag{13.1}$$

where $B_t - C_t$ is the incremental net benefits in time t, d is the discount rate, T is the time horizon of the analysis and $TrmV_T$ is the terminal value at the end of year T. For the example, suppose the ten-year asset can be liquidated and resold for a market value (or for salvage value if only usable as scrap) at the end of the third year (T). The market (or salvage) value is the incremental asset value or terminal value in equation 13.1. Alternatively, if no market exists to price the asset, but the asset still has useful economic value elsewhere in the public sector, then the depreciation in the asset's economic value due to use, wear and tear and obsolescence might be calculated to determine the asset's remaining (incremental) value.[1] Once estimated, the asset's terminal value at the end of year T must be discounted to present value and added to the discounted net benefits.

For another illustration, suppose a decision maker is considering upgrading a municipal golf course. The relevant time frame for the analysis might be, say, 25 years. At the end of that time, the land will have a continued life; also, the land value will most likely be greater, at least partly because of the improvements. The land might continue in its existing use or be sold at the end of the 25th year. Assuming the latter, a market value for the land can be estimated for that year. Then, the portion of the land value associated with the improvements is the incremental asset value (terminal value) in the 25th year, which should be discounted as in equation 13.1.

One obvious concern is that the estimate for the terminal value can be hard to predict, especially if the horizon terminates far in the future. A *selective sensitivity analysis* might be performed, using high and low terminal values to assess the variable's influence on NPV. At the same time, the very fact that the value occurs far in the future means that discounting will reduce its effect on the NPV, thus rendering the precise number less influential in the analysis.

DISCOUNTING A FUTURE VALUE IN PERPETUITY

Another possibility is that a particular social benefit or cost might continue into the future indefinitely. Caution is urged, for one of the easiest ways to influence the value of the decision criterion is to assume the benefits or costs continue forever. Especially tempting is to presume a capital asset with modest annual maintenance expenditures will be maintained far into the distant future. Nonetheless, if a value is reasonably determined to continue indefinitely, then it can be estimated in perpetuity. The discounted present value of a *perpetuity*, an annual value (AV) that remains constant and continues into the future indefinitely,[2] can be calculated with the formula AV/d. The NPV equation can then be adjusted to include both the policy net benefits that occur over a finite time horizon (T) and the perpetuity, as in equation 13.2.

$$\text{NPV} = \sum_{t=0}^{T} \frac{B_t - C_t}{(1 + d)^t} + \frac{AV}{d} . \tag{13.2}$$

Suppose, for instance, one benefit of a multipurpose policy is to preserve an acre of wetland habitat. If the annual value of a preserved acre of wetlands is $800, then the present value of the acre in perpetuity, at a discount rate of 8%, is $800/.08, or $10,000.[3] Note the calculation is sensitive to the discount rate; for example, the value is $16,000 if discounted at 5%, and $5,333 if discounted at 15%. Performing a *selective sensitivity analysis* for the discount rate in the NPV analysis, as recommended in Chapter 11, will assess this effect.

Principle 13.2. Other considerations when selecting a time horizon are whether to include (1) a terminal value and/or (2) a future value in perpetuity.

COMPARING ALTERNATIVE POLICIES WITH DIFFERENT TIME HORIZONS

If the decision maker is choosing one of several policies, the decision rule for promoting efficiency is to pursue the policy with the highest NPV. A simple comparison of policy NPVs is sufficient if the time horizons of the policies are equal[4] or, should they be unequal, if what matters is achieving the policy goal, not the specific time frame of accomplishment (Zerbe and Dively 1994: 182). Suppose, however, that two policies' time horizons are not the same and it makes a difference. For example, an analyst assesses two alternatives: (1) a ring levee with, say, a 25-year life and (2) floodwalls with a 50-year life, both designed to prevent river flood damage to neighboring residential properties. The levee option would require additional capital investment expenditures to generate as many years of benefits as the floodwalls; thus, the two policies are not equivalent and therefore not immediately comparable. To enable a relative assessment of policy net benefits when time horizons differ, the analyses must be adjusted. Three methods might be used.

1. *Replication.* One or both policies might be repeated over time, with exactly the same characteristics as in the first lifetime, to equalize the time horizons in the respective NPV calculations.[5] For example, the ring levee might be replaced with a new levee at the end of the 25th year, so that the net benefits calculation for each policy is for a time horizon of 50 years. As another example, if one policy is 20 years and a second 30 years in length, then the first policy might be repeated three times, while the second is repeated two times, equalizing the time horizons at 60 years. Note, however, that depending on the respective time lengths of the two policies, the replication to achieve a common time horizon can become extremely complicated, if not unrealistic, in which case this approach is less useful.

2. *Equivalent Annual Net Benefit.* When the policies are repeatable, an alternative approach converts the NPV estimates to terms expressed in a common annual unit to permit comparability. The calculation essentially evens out a policy's net benefit stream so that each year's net benefits are the same. Specifically, the *equivalent annual net benefit* (EANB) is the constant dollar amount each year over a policy's time horizon that generates the same NPV as the policy.[6] The computational formula is:

$$\text{EANB} = \frac{\text{NPV}}{\text{annuity factor,}} \qquad (13.3)$$

where the *annuity factor* is the present value of $1 at the end of each year,[7] discounted over the same time horizon, T, and at the same rate, d, as the NPV. In equation form,

$$\text{annuity factor} = \frac{1 - (1 + d)^{-T}}{d} = \frac{1 - 1/(1 + d)^{T}}{d} \qquad (13.4)$$

Suppose, for illustration, the NPV for the 25-year ring levee is $3 million and the NPV for the 50-year floodwall is $5 million, both discounted at 8%. Then, the respective annuity factors and EANBs are as follows.

ring levee:

$$\text{annuity factor} = \frac{1 - 1.08^{-25}}{.08} = 10.674776; \text{ EANB} = \frac{\$3 \text{ million}}{10.674776}$$
$$= \$281,036.34$$

flood walls:

$$\text{annuity factor} = \frac{1 - 1.08^{-50}}{.08} = 12.233485; \text{ EANB} = \frac{\$5 \text{ million}}{12.233485}$$
$$= \$408,714.28.$$

In assessing these two policy options, the appropriate decision criterion is to select the one that generates the greater equivalent net benefits on an annual basis and thus has the higher EANB. The EANB of \$408,714 for the floodwalls is larger than that (\$281,036) for the ring levee, therefore the floodwalls are the more efficient policy option.

If consistent assumptions are applied, the EANB method yields the same conclusion as replication when comparing repeatable policies. Thus, often the approach is chosen that involves the simpler calculations for a particular comparison.

Both methods assume the policies are repeated in identical form, without considering the possible development of future technologies. When sizable technological change is likely over the relevant time frames, the policy with the shorter horizon offers greater flexibility; it provides the option of adopting a less costly (or more productive) technology sooner and more frequently.[8] Thus, in comparing the two policies, if the shorter policy has the same or larger EANB (NPV under replication), then it is deemed more efficient, recognizing the flexibility benefit. When the shorter policy's EANB (or replication NPV) is the smaller of the two, knowledge of the size of the flexibility benefit is required to determine which policy is more efficient. The analyst can then pursue one of two approaches. If measurable, the flexibility benefits might be incorporated in the shorter policy's net benefits and replication be applied to estimate NPVs for the two policies under a common time horizon. (EANBs should not be calculated in this case because the method assumes continuous identical replacement.) Alternatively, given the difficulty of predicting the value of flexibility benefits, the difference between the NPVs calculated assuming replication (with no flexibility measure) might be interpreted as a *critical value*. The decision maker can then consider whether the present value of the shorter policy's flexibility benefits is likely to be larger than the critical value. If so, then the policy with the shorter time horizon promotes efficiency.

3. *Terminal Value.* If the policies are not repeatable or if there is not a high likelihood that the policies will be replicated in actuality, then neither of the first two methods is relevant. Instead, the time horizons might be equalized by assuming the longer policy ceases and liquidates assets when the shorter policy ends (Zerbe and Dively 1994: 185–86). Suppose for an example, one policy lasts six years, while an alternative lasts three years. The NPV for the longer,

6-year policy can be estimated using equation 13.1, summing three years of discounted net benefits and a discounted *terminal value* (the incremental asset value) that occurs at the end of year 3.

Principle 13.3. When choosing one of several policies where the time horizons are not all the same, three methods are available to allow comparison. If the policies are repeatable, replication might be employed to calculate NPVs, or instead, equivalent annual net benefits (EANBs) might be computed. If it is not likely the policies will be repeated, then the longer policies' horizons might be shortened and a terminal value added when calculating NPVs. In each case, the respective decision criterion (the highest NPV or EANB) is employed to determine which policy promotes efficiency.

NOTES

1. Such an estimation can be challenging, as accounting formulas for depreciation are not relevant in a cost-benefit analysis, and as the rate of economic depreciation can vary across different assets and depends on the particular use and maintenance of the asset under the specific policy. One approach sometimes used is to assume the asset's value in year T is some stipulated percentage (e.g., 10%, 60%, 75%) of the initial costs. Unfortunately, the designated percentage can be "arbitrary" and thus bear no relation to the remaining useful value of the asset (Boardman et al. 1996: 135–36). Therefore, while this "rule of thumb" conveniently eases calculation, due precaution is prescribed in using this approach. A reasonable justification for the specified percentage should be provided.

2. If instead of remaining constant, the initial value (IV) is expected to increase at a constant growth rate (g) in perpetuity, then if d is greater than g, the discounted present value can be calculated with the equation, $IV/(d - g)$. For a constant decrease in perpetuity, a negative g is substituted in the equation (Boardman et al. 1996: 137, 151).

3. The calculation can be modified if the asset value is variable (rather than constant) over the time horizon, T. First, over the finite time horizon, the varying value can be included annually in the net benefits term. Second, for the years thereafter, if it is reasonable to assume the asset value will remain constant and continue indefinitely, then the constant annual value (perpetuity) is, again, discounted as AV/d. In this case, however, AV/d gives the value of the perpetuity at the end of year T; the value must then be discounted to present value by dividing by $(1 + d)^T$ (Boardman et al. 1996: 136–37). Thus, for the second term, the $800 acre of wetlands would have a discounted value in perpetuity of $10,000 in year T, so $10,000/(1.08)^T$ yields the perpetuity's present value.

4. If the policy horizons are lengthy and differ by, say, only one or two years, then in practice the analyst need not be too concerned about the divergence. With discounting, the effect is small. Thus, the analyst may simply calculate the NPVs with the different, though closely approximate, time horizons.

5. The term "replication" is adopted from Zerbe and Dively (1994: 183) and parallels the "replacement chain" in the private capital budgeting literature. See, for example, Moyer, McGuigan and Kretlow (1992: 439–41).

6. The net benefit stream is thus converted to "equivalent annual annuities," a term commonly used in financial management. For instance, see Moyer, McGuigan and Kretlow (1992: 441–42).

7. For financial analyses, annuity factors are sometimes calculated assuming the $1 is

received at the beginning, not the end, of each year. Thus, if consulting a table or software package, be sure to check the formula used.

8. For a related discussion in the context of private business decisions, see Emery, Finnerty and Stowe (1998: 350, 352) and Brigham and Gapenski (1988: 305).

Chapter 14

Uncertainty and Risk

INTRODUCTION

"Uncertainty" and "risk" are often used interchangeably in casual conversation, however, the risk literature distinguishes between the two as separate concepts. To illustrate the prevalence of both concepts in everyday life, daily applications are presented in defining each term.

Uncertainty exists when an individual lacks information. Two kinds of uncertainty include: (1) not knowing what will happen in the future, and (2) data inaccuracy or measurement error. For example, a businessperson may be unsure whether a car tire will blow out during the daily commute. This is a possible though unpredictable future event. Likewise, the same businessperson may read a marketing study analyzing historical sales in which the reported figures are not entirely accurate and the true historical values are not known for sure. Uncertain situations such as these are handled in various ways. For instance, the businessperson may carry a cellular phone in case of a flat tire or, when using the marketing figures for decision making, act conservatively, perhaps considering an arbitrary margin of error or another rule of thumb.

An uncertain situation entails *risk* if the relevant probabilities of different outcomes are known—examples include the probabilities of uncertain events occurring or of the events realizing different dimensions or sizes. The literature generally associates risk with the probability of an adverse outcome. Nonetheless, risk assessment also includes the probabilities of desirable outcomes. In any situation where one uncertain possibility is preferred to another, the individual faces the risk of realizing the less preferable outcome. Suppose, for instance, an artist knows there is a 60% probability of selling an expensive art work to a particular collector. Risk is involved, as there is a 40% chance the collector might not purchase the piece. Risk assessment takes into account both the 60% and 40% probabilities of the possible outcomes, respectively.

The literature thus distinguishes between uncertainty (information is lacking and probabilities are unknown) and risk (probabilities are known). Consider these definitions in the realm of cost-benefit analysis. Uncertainty may exist concerning (1) a policy's consequences—what they are or whether they will occur—or (2) the size of the quantity or economic value of the consequences. The opportunities for uncertainty are innumerable. For example, natural events, mechanical failures or accidents may be unforeseen. The intricate causal relationships influencing human behavior or natural ecosystem dynamics may not be fully understood. Market prices, start-up and operating costs and the timing of benefits and costs are all subject to change. Moreover, valuation methods yield estimates with error. All of these involve some degree of uncertainty. If the probabilities of these events can be determined, then risk can be incorporated in the cost-benefit analysis. In general, probabilities might be estimated for (1) specific uncertain consequences occurring or (2) the consequences or economic values attaining different magnitudes.

Numerous approaches have been devised for analyzing uncertainty and risk. Some are highly sophisticated, requiring intricate and extensive data analysis. These have limited applicability and can be quite expensive to perform. This chapter explores several basic techniques that lend themselves more readily to practical application. The discussion begins first with the analysis of uncertainty and then considers risk.

ECONOMIC ASSESSMENT OF UNCERTAINTY

Principle 14.1. The economic assessment of uncertainty involves two components: (1) identifying the nature of any and all uncertainty relevant to a particular analysis and (2) analyzing the implications of the uncertainty for the study's conclusions and for the decision-making process.

First, uncertainty is so prevalent in the world that every cost-benefit analysis should identify and report its possible role in shaping the quantification and valuation of policy consequences. Thorough identification follows three steps.

(a) At the outset of undertaking the analysis, the potential sources of uncertainty are distinguished.

(b) For some or all uncertain variables, the range of possible consequences are delineated.

(c) Once data are collected, the quality of the information is assessed and the accuracy (or, conversely, the possible measurement error) determined.

To perform these three steps, information is often gathered from historical policy experience as well as expert analyses, expert opinions or rules of thumb (e.g., arbitrary or working margins of error).

Second, once the uncertainty has been identified, a decision has to be made concerning whether the uncertainty seems to be sufficiently important to warrant further study. The judgment may result from a discussion between the analyst and the decision maker. They might contemplate the following:

- the information that the decision maker seeks from the analysis,
- the likely effect of the uncertainty on the assessment's conclusions,
- the political significance of the variable(s) characterized by uncertainty (for example, are interest groups likely to scrutinize the estimation of these variables?),
- the costs involved in analyzing the uncertainty (i.e., do the benefits of conducting the assessment outweigh the costs?).

If the analyst and decision maker believe that the uncertainty may have significant bearing on the analysis or is otherwise important, then formal analysis can be undertaken. To analyze uncertainty for a single policy, the most common practical procedures are selective sensitivity analysis and switching values. If mutually exclusive policies are being compared, the analyst can also display payoff and regret matrices and apply alternative decision rules to identify an appropriate policy recognizing both efficiency and uncertainty concerns. In some cases, the decision maker might consider delaying the decision until additional information can be gathered. This chapter explores these options, beginning with analysis of a single policy.

Principle 14.2. To analyze uncertainty for a single policy, the most common practical procedures are selective sensitivity analysis and switching values.

SELECTIVE SENSITIVITY ANALYSIS

Selective sensitivity analysis is frequently applied when analyzing uncertainty. It demonstrates how the decision criterion (NPV) varies when select variables independently assume different values. Thus, the analysis informs the decision maker as to the NPV's sensitivity to these uncertain variables.

Selective sensitivity analysis can be performed in four steps. First, the analyst determines which variables have uncertain values and then selects the one(s) that might be expected to influence the NPV calculation notably. For example, suppose a medical clinic located in a less developed country's rainforest considers expanding its facilities into a hospital supporting surgery and in-patient care. The planned expansion would encroach on a small neighboring village. The investment expenses thus include land, construction and technology (L,C&T) costs as well as relocation costs to move the village inhabitants. The

Table 14.1
Possible Values for Select Uncertain Variables (in millions of dollars)

Uncertain Variable	Lower Bound	Likely Value	Upper Bound
Relocation costs	0.1	1.0	8.0
Medical benefits	3.0	6.0	12.0

L,C&T costs with contingency allowance are an estimated $25 million. As for the costs of relocation, depending on political and social factors, the clinic expects to provide ample funds for one of the following three scenarios: (1) construct a new village with some modern amenities ($8 million), (2) construct a new traditional village ($1 million) or (3) merge the displaced villagers with another local village ($100,000). These investment expenses would be incurred throughout the first year.

Beginning the second year, the planned hospital would start operation. Incremental operating expenses for personnel, maintenance and supplies are estimated at $1 million annually. The new hospital is designed to treat a substantial proportion of the region's ill each year. The medical benefits are valued as the savings in these patients' productive agricultural work days resulting from receiving the hospital services. Depending on the severity of the medical illnesses treated, the medical benefit estimates range from $3 million to $12 million annually, with a likely estimate of $6 million annually.

In this example, all together four costs and benefits are measured. As the first step in selective sensitivity analysis, the values for L,C&T investment and the annual operating costs are accepted as reasonably certain, while the villager relocation expenses and medical benefits are identified as uncertain variables that might influence the analysis.

Second, for each selected uncertain variable, the analyst determines the range of possible values. The general practice is to choose each variable's likely (or "best guess") value and the upper and lower bounds. These are presented in Table 14.1.

Third, the decision criterion, NPV, is calculated with all uncertain variables assuming their respective likely values. The result is the "best estimate" of the NPV. For the proposed hospital, the likely values for relocation costs and medical benefits ($1 million and $6 million, respectively) as well as the reasonably certain values for other investment and operating costs are used. Assuming one year of construction, ten years of operation and a discount rate of 8%, the best estimate of NPV is $6.99 million.

Fourth, the sensitivity analysis checks the robustness of the calculated NPV to the uncertainty in the designated variables. For each selected variable, cal-

Table 14.2
Selective Sensitivity Analysis: NPVs for Independent Changes in Each Uncertain Variable

Uncertain Variable	Bound	Value ($ mils)	NPV ($)
Relocation costs	Upper	8.0	509,636
Relocation costs	Lower	0.1	7,824,451
Medical benefits	Upper	12.0	44,269,348
Medical benefits	Lower	3.0	-11,647,997

culate the NPV two more times, assuming the variable is at its upper or lower bound, respectively, while *holding all other variables at their respective likely or known values*. This last phrase warrants elaboration. Selective sensitivity analysis is *partial economic analysis*; it measures the effects of changes in each variable independently, holding all other variables constant, that is, *ceteris paribus*. One variable is allowed to vary by itself so that its impact is assessed independent of the other variables.

In the simplest case, only one variable is chosen for sensitivity analysis, and the decision criterion is then calculated a total of three times. When there are two or more selected variables, however, the number of calculations increases and the complexity of the sensitivity analysis expands accordingly. In this example, two uncertain variables are identified as warranting assessment; thus the decision criterion is calculated a total of five times (including two upper bounds, two lower bounds and the best estimate). Remembering the best estimate is $6.99 million, the four NPVs for the respective upper and lower bounds are conveniently presented in Table 14.2.

As seen in Table 14.2, when relocation costs range from the upper to lower bound (holding medical benefits at their likely value of $6 million and the L,C&T and operating costs at their known or accepted values), the estimated NPV changes from the best estimate of $6.99 million to as low as nearly $500,000 and as high as $7.8 million. These estimates indicate the sensitivity of NPV to the possible variation in relocation costs. Likewise the NPV's substantially greater sensitivity to the uncertain value of medical benefits is displayed. When medical benefits reach the upper or lower bound (holding relocation costs at the likely value of $1 million and the other costs at their accepted values), then the calculated NPV ranges from as high as $44.3 million to as low as −$11.6 million. Looking at the entire table of NPVs, along with the best estimate, the analyst can conclude that the proposed hospital expansion promotes efficiency in all cases except when medical benefits approach the lower bound.

To complete the efficiency assessment for the decision maker, the analyst should identify the circumstances under which the medical benefits could be so small. The severity of the region's current medical illnesses might be further investigated. Also important is the analyst's appraisal of the sources of error (or accuracy) in the collected data and valuation technique, along with his overall assessment as to whether the estimated values measure the medical benefits fully. In addition, since the proposed hospital's medical benefits may be too low, the analyst or decision maker might consider modifying the proposed hospital services or even pursuing an alternative medical clinic expansion that provides less costly (or more beneficial) services.

While considering this example, the reader may be wondering what happens to NPV if more than one variable changes at the same time? Or, instead, suppose three or more variables are identified as uncertain. Remembering that the NPV's sensitivity to the discount rate should be assessed as well, the number of calculations becomes quite cumbersome. In either case, interrelated variables might be grouped together and NPVs calculated for each given group's upper and lower bounds, respectively.

Suppose for the hospital example, relocation costs and medical benefits are combined into a group. If relocation costs should reach their lower bound ($0.1 million) and medical benefits the upper bound ($12 million), NPV would approach a high of $45.1 million. At the other extreme, upper bound relocation costs ($8 million) and lower bound medical benefits ($3 million), together, would yield a low NPV of −$18.13 million. (Both computations hold L,C&T and operating costs at their known or accepted values.) Thus, the calculated NPV ranges from −$18.13 million to $45.1 million, with a likely value of $6.99 million.

Worth emphasizing is that this section's examples to demonstrate selective sensitivity analysis involve either two uncertain variables or one group. When variables or groups are large in number, however, selective sensitivity analysis can yield an overwhelming array of NPVs. The procedure is therefore useful mainly for analyzing the one or two most important uncertain variables (or groups) and the discount rate.

SWITCHING VALUES

Another approach uses switching values to investigate which variables may significantly affect the decision criterion. Specifically, for each variable in the analysis a *switching value* or *critical value* is calculated, indicating the variable value that reduces the NPV to zero. Similar to selective sensitivity analysis, the calculation holds all other variables at their respective likely or known values.

Let's continue with the example of the proposed expansion of a rainforest medical clinic to a hospital. In Table 14.3, column 1 lists the costs and benefits,

Table 14.3
Switching Values: Assuming Independent Change in Each Variable

(1) Variable	(2) PV ($)	(3) Switching PV ($)	(4) % Change in PV
L,C&T costs	23,148,148	30,139,266	30.20
Relocation costs	925,926	7,917,044	755.04
Operating costs	6,213,038	13,204,156	112.52
Total costs	30,287,112	37,278,230	23.08
Medical benefits	37,278,230	30,287,112	-18.75

and column 2 shows the present value (PV) for the likely or known value of each. Thus, the L,C&T costs, with an accepted estimate of $25 million during the first year, have a PV of $23.15 million. The villager relocation costs (at a likely value of $1 million during the first year) have a PV of $0.93 million, while the annual operating costs and annual medical benefits have likely PVs of $6.21 million and $37.28 million, respectively.

Switching values in PV terms are displayed in column 3. Since a given cost would have to increase by exactly the amount of the NPV to lower the NPV to zero, the Switching PV is calculated by adding the *cost's PV* and the NPV. The benefit, in contrast, must decline by the NPV to reduce the NPV to zero. Thus, subtracting NPV from the *benefit's PV* obtains the Switching PV.[1] Note that each calculation assumes all other variables remain constant at their likely or known values; accordingly, the Switching PV presumes an independent change in the respective variable.

Column 4 presents the percentage change in each cost or benefit required to make the NPV fall to zero; it is calculated as

$$\frac{\text{Switching PV} - \text{PV}}{\text{PV}}, \qquad (14.1)$$

then expressed as a percentage. As can be seen in the table, raising L,C&T costs by the $6.99 million NPV (a 30.2% increase) yields a Switching PV of $30.14 million. Thus, the L,C&T costs would have to rise by 30.2%, with all other variables assuming their likely or known values, to lower NPV to zero. Likewise, NPV becomes zero if relocation costs increase to a PV of $7.92 million, or 755% over their likely value. Instead, operating costs could increase by 112.5%, or medical benefits fall 18.75% below their likely value. Any one of these changes, by itself, would generate a zero NPV.

Interpreting column 4, the small percentage changes indicate highly influential variables. In this case, two variables are identified: L,C&T costs (30.2%) and medical benefits (−18.75%). Relatively small changes in either can render the policy inefficient. Thus, the analyst or decision maker would be advised to appraise ways to ensure control of the L,C&T costs and to maintain or expand the medical benefits. Moreover, these two variables warrant the decision maker's careful consideration when determining whether to go forward with the hospital.

Large percentage changes, in contrast, suggest the associated variables are not likely to affect the NPV substantially. This may be a useful rule of thumb, yet the analyst or decision maker must decide whether the estimated change is actually possible. As indicated in column 4, relocation costs must increase by 755% for the NPV to reach zero. At face value, this figure suggests that actual changes in relocation costs are not likely to impact the NPV significantly. In this particular case, however, political and social factors might possibly dictate construction of a new village with some modern amenities, which would substantially increase villager relocation costs; thus, the variable warrants further investigation. As for operating costs, these would have to more than double (increase 112.5%) to reduce NPV to zero. The analyst must assess whether this is a reasonable possibility and, in this example, has concluded that it is not.

Using switching values differs from selective sensitivity analysis in two ways. First, switching values are estimated for all variables with known or uncertain values, and the calculations are not limited to a variable's perceived upper and lower bounds. Second, switching values estimate how much (or little) a variable would have to change to impact the assessment of the policy's efficiency, while sensitivity analysis determines the range of NPV values associated with the variable reaching its upper and lower bounds.

PAYOFF AND REGRET MATRICES AND ALTERNATIVE DECISION RULES

Both selective sensitivity analysis and switching values assess uncertainty for a single policy. Suppose several mutually exclusive policy alternatives share a common uncertain variable. To analyze the uncertainty, selective sensitivity analyses can be performed calculating three NPVs for each policy. Then, to identify the most efficient policy, all NPVs are compared. Remember that without uncertainty, the appropriate decision criterion indicates that the most efficient policy option has the largest NPV. Given uncertainty, the decision criterion can be easily applied if one policy's NPVs are consistently greater than the other policies' respective NPVs. However, what if this is not the case? Suppose for respective levels of the uncertain variable, one policy's NPVs are sometimes but not always greater than other policy NPVs. Deciding which policy is more efficient depends on decision-maker attitudes towards uncertainty. Two organizing tools, payoff and regret matrices, along with alternative decision rules, can

Table 14.4
Payoff Matrix (in millions of dollars)

Policy	Low NPV	Likely NPV	High NPV
New hospital	-11.65	6.99	44.27
Clinic expansion	0.2	4.0	14.0

help in selecting the preferred policy, recognizing both efficiency and uncertainty considerations.

To illustrate, let's return to the example of the proposed hospital for the rainforest medical clinic. Suppose upon being informed of the negative NPV associated with low medical benefits, the decision maker suggests an alternative option, expanding the existing medical clinic to serve more patients. Such an expansion would involve lower costs than the hospital, yet the expanded facility would not be equipped to address some of the most severe illnesses requiring specialized technology and care.

The analyst undertakes a selective sensitivity analysis for the expanded clinic. For a proper comparison, the calculations assume the same illness severities used to determine the range of medical benefits for the hospital. Estimates of the expanded clinics' medical benefits are calculated "low" (at the lower bound), "high" (at their upper bound) and at their likely value. (For simplicity, the comparison disregards any uncertainty in villager relocation costs and presumes these are at their likely value.)

The two policies' NPVs can be presented in a payoff matrix (Table 14.4). A *payoff matrix* is simply an organizational tool, in this case, arranging the NPVs for mutually exclusive policies with a shared uncertain variable. As seen in Table 14.4, if after policy implementation the patients' illnesses prove to be less severe, yielding "low" medical benefits and NPV, the expanded clinic promotes efficiency, for the clinic NPV of $0.2 million is greater than the hospital NPV, −$11.65 million. The hospital, however, promotes efficiency if the medical benefits (and NPV) range from "likely" to "high" (for hospital NPVs ranging from $6.99 million to $44.27 million are greater than the expanded clinic's NPVs, $4 million to $14 million, respectively). If seeking the most efficient policy, the decision maker must make a judgment.

Alternative decision rules can be applied to help the decision maker weigh the uncertain trade-offs and select a policy promoting efficiency given the uncertainty. Each rule reflects a different decision-maker outlook toward uncertainty. The three most common decision rules are the maximax, maximin and minimax criteria.

1. *Maximax criterion*. Representing a highly optimistic perspective, the maximax criterion indicates the decision maker should select the policy with the

highest NPV, thus disregarding the uncertainty. (The criterion's name derives from the process of finding each policy's maximum NPV and choosing the one that is the largest—the maximum of the maximum.) Looking at Table 14.4, the recommended policy is the new hospital with maximum NPV of $44.27 million. Observe that this criterion does not consider that the hospital's NPVs have the greater spread in value and that if the medical benefits reach their lower bound, a negative NPV results.

2. *Maximin criterion.* This criterion is cautious, focusing solely on each policy's minimum NPV and selecting the maximum of these. As Table 14.4 shows, the expanded clinic is the preferred policy, for its minimum NPV ($0.2 million) is greater than the hospital's minimum (−$11.65 million). This criterion ignores the possibility that the medical benefits could be high or at the likely level. While pessimistic in its outlook, this criterion may be useful when one policy has a possible outcome that is in some way catastrophic or otherwise unacceptable. For instance, for a private organization, the prospect that a policy might result in bankruptcy could be reason enough to omit the policy from further consideration. For the rainforest medical clinic, if the possibility of a public hospital generating a negative NPV is unacceptable, then the maximin criterion may be appropriate. In other situations, if one of the compared policies might have a catastrophic effect on human life or the natural environment, the decision choice might be resolved by applying the maximin criterion.

3. *Minimax regret criterion.* Another cautious criterion, this focuses on the regrets of making a wrong decision. A *regret* is the loss in NPV from not making the best choice. Regrets are calculated by referring to the NPVs in the payoff matrix (Table 14.4). For example, if medical benefits after policy implementation prove to be "low," in hindsight, expanding the clinic (with NPV of $0.2 million) would have been the best choice. If the clinic was expanded, there would be no (or zero) regret. However, if the hospital was built, a wrong choice would have been made, and the regret is the difference between the clinic and hospital NPVs (*clinic NPV* − *hospital NPV*). The regret is thus ($0.2 − (−$11.65)), or $11.85 million. Likewise, the regrets can be calculated in case the medical benefits are actually at the "likely" or "high" levels. In both of these circumstances, the hospital would have been the best choice. Thus, if the hospital was built, the regrets are zero, and if the clinic was expanded, the regrets are positive (*hospital NPV* − *clinic NPV*). The regrets are displayed in a *regret matrix* (Table 14.5). The minimax regret criterion recommends finding each policy's maximum regret ($11.85 million for the hospital and $30.27 million for the expanded clinic) and selecting the minimum of these. Thus, the hospital is the preferred policy.

In this example, the hospital is recommended by both the optimistic maximax criterion (focusing only on the policies' highest NPVs) and the cautious minimax regret criterion (taking into consideration all NPVs). The expanded clinic is selected by the cautious maximin criterion, which looks only at the lowest NPVs and seeks to avoid the worst outcome. Of the three criteria, no single one is

Table 14.5
Regret Matrix (in millions of dollars)

Policy	Low NPV: Regret	Likely NPV: Regret	High NPV: Regret
New hospital	11.85	0	0
Clinic expansion	0	2.99	30.27

objectively superior. Which one might be appropriate in a particular situation depends on the decision maker's perception of uncertainty. Outlining the alternative rules and their respective policy recommendations illustrates several options for decision making. This information can help the decision maker choose a policy while considering both efficiency and uncertainty.

Principle 14.3. If several mutually exclusive policy alternatives share a common uncertain variable, a selective sensitivity analysis can be performed for each alternative, with the calculated NPVs displayed in a payoff matrix. Alternative decision rules, such as the maximax, maximin or minimax regret criteria, can be applied to help identify an appropriate policy in light of both efficiency and uncertainty considerations.

DELAYING A DECISION TO GATHER INFORMATION

Economic assessment of a policy's uncertain consequences or values can provide insightful information to facilitate the decision-making process, yet as demonstrated in this chapter, in some cases the analysis cannot identify any one option as consistently most efficient, and decision-maker judgment is required. One possibility the decision maker might consider is to delay the decision until additional information can be gathered. For example, in comparing the proposed hospital and clinic expansion, the decision could be postponed until further research is conducted concerning the severity of the regional population's illnesses. Note that the estimated regrets in the regret matrix (in Table 14.5) indicate the potential costs of proceeding with either policy given the uncertainty. If the new hospital is built, then the regret could be $11.85 million, while if the clinic is expanded, then the regret might be $2.99 million or as high as $30.27 million, depending on the actual level of medical benefits. A decision delay offers the prospect of gathering information to reduce the uncertainty so as to identify the efficient policy option and avoid incurring any regret. At the same time, such a delay does not guarantee that the uncertainty will be resolved; in addition, collecting information entails costs, and the delay postpones the delivery of medical benefits to the regional population, which also imposes a cost. Determining whether such a delay might promote efficiency, therefore, requires the decision maker to engage in an informal calculation weighing the delay's likely benefits and costs.

In the environmental field, the possibility of decision delays has received growing attention, especially when a proposed policy imposes *irreversible* changes on environmental or natural resources with uncertain ecological or human consequences. For instance, suppose construction of the proposed hospital would encroach on and destroy previously pristine rainforest. Many sources of economic value would be lost forever—some measurable, others currently unknown. Perhaps future scientific discoveries would otherwise find that unique native plant species on the designated land area contain important scientific knowledge or offer a life-saving medicine. If there is reason to believe additional knowledge can be generated that reveals the forest area's economic value, the decision might be delayed. Development could be prohibited and the area preserved until such information is gathered. The value of this information, *quasi-option value* (QOV), is the benefit that may be gained by delaying a policy decision with irreversible consequences and preserving the option of using the forest area in the future (Arrow and Fisher 1974).[2]

Many environmentalists recommend adoption of the *precautionary principle* in such cases. Strictly interpreted, this principle prohibits renewable resource development (or use) if the possibility exists of significant irreversible environmental damage. In effect, as Norse promotes, the burden of proof would be placed on the developer to gather the information necessary to "demonstrate reasonably" the proposed development would do no harm before being allowed. This practice would "ensure that information necessary for informed decision making is available *before* there are irreversible losses" (1993: 180–83, 306; emphasis added). A related principle, the *safe minimum standard* (SMS), would preserve from harm the biologically critical amount of a natural resource required to ensure its renewability and survival, with the caveat that the opportunity costs (or foregone benefits) of doing so not be excessive. The SMS thereby incorporates some economic considerations. However, it is not an efficiency principle. How much the costs must outweigh the benefits before foregoing preservation is not specified and is thus left to the decision maker's interpretation.

RISK: EXPECTED VALUE

The economic assessment of uncertainty in a cost-benefit analysis is concerned solely with analyzing the implications of unknown information—unknown policy consequences or the size quantity or economic value of these consequences. When the probabilities of these events can be determined, then risk can be included in the analysis.

Principle 14.4. The standard procedure for incorporating risk within a cost-benefit analysis is to (1) estimate both the uncertain event's possible values (or magnitudes) and probabilities of occurrence and then (2) calculate the expected value of the decision criterion (NPV).

The first step, known as *risk assessment*, involves determining the size values (or magnitudes) considered possible for an uncertain event, then estimating their respective probabilities of occurrence. Numerous risk assessment procedures have been devised for different fields. These include, for example, engineering applications of "fault trees" to estimate the likelihood of technological failures, financial management analyses of investment risks, life insurance actuarial procedures for projecting life expectancies, scientific computer simulations to anticipate complex ecological changes and public health assessments of disease and mortality risks. For an illustration, Box 14.1 presents the components involved in a typical EPA risk assessment of an environmental pollutant's health effects.

In the end, the selected assessment technique obtains a *probability distribution* presenting probabilities for all magnitudes of an uncertain event. This discussion addresses the second step: how to incorporate the probabilities and magnitudes, once estimated, into a cost-benefit analysis to assess policy efficiency. The most widely used procedure is to calculate the *expected value*, the weighted mean of the uncertain values.[3]

For an example, consider again the comparison of the proposed hospital and expanded clinic, both of which share uncertain medical benefits. Suppose that based on reported illness severities in other rural indigenous communities, a distribution of probabilities is estimated for the medical benefits in this region attaining different values. For instance, the probabilities might be a 0.3 chance of the medical benefits being "low," 0.6 chance of their being the "likely" value and 0.1 chance for "high" medical benefits. The expected value of NPV, *exp NPV*, can then be calculated for each policy using the formula,

$$\text{exp NPV} = p_1 * \text{NPV}_1 + p_2 * \text{NPV}_2 + p_3 * \text{NPV}_3, \tag{14.2}$$

which weights the respective NPV associated with each level of medical benefits by the probability of its occurrence (p). Using the payoff matrix NPVs in Table 14.4,[4] the *exp NPV* for the proposed hospital is

$$0.3(-\$11,647,997) + 0.6(\$6,991,118) + 0.1(\$44,269,348) = \$5,127,206,$$

and the *exp NPV* for the expanded clinic[5] is

$$0.3(\$200,000) + 0.6(\$4,000,000) + 0.1(\$14,000,000) = \$3,860,000.$$

In order to determine which policy option is more efficient, the appropriate criterion is to select the one that maximizes the expected NPV.[6] Thus, the proposed hospital, with *exp NPV* of \$5.1 million, is assessed as more efficient than the expanded clinic (*exp NPV*, \$3.86 million).

Box 14.1
EPA Risk Assessment and Cost-Benefit Analysis

In recent years the news media has increasingly mentioned the risk assessments performed by the Environmental Protection Agency (EPA). In the 1970s, the EPA began systematic analysis of human health risks (initially focusing on cancer risks) associated with exposure to such environmental factors as pesticides, hazardous wastes and toxic chemicals. There are four components to the customary EPA risk assessment.

1. *Hazard assessment.* The analyst investigates whether an environmental factor is a hazard, that is, a potential source of risk to human health. Data are gathered and analyzed for possible links between human exposure to the environmental factor (e.g., pesticides) and an adverse health effect (e.g., cancer). Two common approaches are *animal testing*, involving scientific experiments with animals, and *epidemiological studies*, examining real-world data for humans. Both compare whether living beings exposed to a possible hazard develop a greater incidence of a health effect than those not exposed.

2. *Dose-response assessment.* Using a mathematical model, the relationship is quantified between human exposure to specific levels (doses) of the environmental factor and the number of humans who develop a health effect (the response). In the case of cancer, the cancer risk for an individual is estimated, for example, indicating that an individual has a three in one hundred chance of developing cancer from exposure to a designated dose of a pesticide over his or her lifetime, and a five in one hundred chance if exposed to a specified greater amount of the pesticide.

3. *Exposure assessment.* The analyst estimates for a given population how many individuals may actually be exposed to different levels of the pesticide. Relevant data include who is exposed (e.g., children, adults, pregnant women, ethnic minorities, urban dwellers, rural farming families), the duration of each level of exposure, and when and where the different exposure levels occur (for example, when consuming food or drinking water or when in geographical proximity to a pesticide application on a farm or lawn).

4. *Risk characterization.* Using the information gathered in the three assessments, the analyst figures the health risk for the general population and/or select population segments. Thus, for every thousand members of the farm population, an estimated ten might be likely to develop cancer during their lifetime from pesticide exposure, while the pesticide-related cancer risk for urban dwellers might be an estimated three in one thousand.

Once the risk assessment is performed, the estimated probabilities can then be incorporated in further analyses to provide additional information to aid the decision maker in managing health risks. For instance, *comparative risk assessment* applies several methods to rank different risks. Thus, for example, the cancer risk from the pesticide might be assessed as greater than the cancer risk from secondhand cigarette smoke. In *risk-benefit analysis*, the hazard's benefits are weighed against its risks. In the case of the pesticide, the benefits from improved crops and lawns and the like might be compared with the health risks related to its application. *Cost-effectiveness analysis* might estimate the costs of restricting pesticide applications along with the associated decline in cancer risk. A ratio of the cost per reduced cancer risk can then be calculated and compared with the ratios of other cancer-reducing policies to identify the (relatively) cost-effective options for reducing cancer risk. In *cost-benefit*

(continued)

Box 14.1 (continued)

analysis, the assessed risks are converted into a monetary value, either a benefit or a cost. Thus, for the pesticide example, the economic benefit of reducing each cancer case might be estimated along with the costs of reducing pesticide applications. Both values can then be included in a cost-benefit calculation to assess the efficiency of restricting pesticide applications.

- For the *decision*: choose one of several mutually exclusive policies with estimated probabilities for the occurrence of uncertain values, the appropriate *decision criterion* is: the most efficient policy maximizes the expected value of NPV

Note that this approach reduces each policy's uncertain values and probabilities to one number, the *exp NPV*, and then assesses this number without considering the various NPVs that are possible given the uncertain medical benefits. Thus, the proposed hospital is deemed the more efficient policy based on its higher expected value, even though it has the larger spread in possible NPVs (from −$11.65 million to $44.27 million). In actuality, it can be perceived as the more risky of the two policies because of this greater dispersion. Application of expected value to assess policy efficiency therefore assumes the decision maker is *risk neutral,* that is, indifferent to any added riskiness.

If, instead, the decision maker is *risk averse*—preferring (to some degree) less risky alternatives, then the expected value comparison is not applicable. Highly sophisticated techniques involving certainty equivalents and expected utilities might be performed; however, the information requirements are formidable (for example, knowing the decision-maker's preferences between expected value and dispersion).[7] For most practical purposes, therefore, the risk-averse decision maker is offered only uncertainty assessment tools, specifically, considering the payoff matrix and alternative decision rules, then evaluating the alternatives based on her own outlook toward the uncertain outcomes.

CONCLUSION

In practice, numerous cost-benefit analyses have omitted any consideration of uncertainty or risk and, in doing so, have presented economic values and NPV calculations that appear to have a greater certainty than is actually the case. To avoid misleading the decision maker, care must be taken to identify any and all uncertainty relevant to a specific analysis. Moreover, as demonstrated in this chapter, there are a few basic techniques that can be carefully applied when uncertainty is deemed sufficiently important to warrant further consideration. Also, when the probabilities of uncertain outcomes can be estimated, risk assessment can be incorporated in the analysis. In the end, decision-maker judgment is often still required in deciding the desirability of selecting a policy, or even delaying the decision, in light of the uncertainty or risk. However, where relevant, application of these techniques can provide additional information that may aid the decision maker in identifying the efficient policy alternative.

NOTES

1. Observe that if a particular benefit is smaller than the NPV, that benefit's Switching PV is negative. This simply means that the benefit would have to decline by an unrealistic amount (more than its full value to a negative PV) for NPV to fall to zero. For an example, see OECD (1995: 142).

2. For practical purposes the QOV is not a separate, measurable variable to be added to the benefits in a cost-benefit analysis, for it does not reflect individual economic preferences. Rather, it is a value that may be generated as the decision maker determines the time sequence of decision making over time (Freeman 1993a: 265; 1993b: 284).

The QOV of preservation is said to be positive when future information gains can be achieved from preservation, thus providing some support for delaying development. In a highly sophisticated theoretical literature, there is some debate as to whether the preservation QOV can be negative and relatedly, whether information can be gained from proceeding with a small amount of development and then deciding later whether to commit to full development. We refer the interested reader to Freeman (1984) and Fisher and Hanemann (1987).

3. Another technique that is sometimes applied—adjusting the discount rate to account for risk—is inappropriate for cost-benefit analysis. Mathematically, in the net benefits equation the discount rate is raised to an exponential power over time; adjusting the discount rate therefore models risk arbitrarily as increasing exponentially over time.

4. The hospital figures in the equation are more precise based on the sensitivity analysis in Table 14.2.

5. The *exp NPV* can be calculated in an alternative fashion. First, compute the expected value of annual medical benefits (*exp MedBen*) as

$$\text{exp MedBen} = p_1 * \text{MedBen}_1 + p_2 * \text{MedBen}_2 + p_3 * \text{MedBen}_3, \qquad (14.3)$$

where each level of medical benefits (*MedBen*) is weighted by its corresponding probability of occurrence (p). To illustrate, using the hospital's medical benefit values from Table 14.1, the *exp MedBen* for the proposed hospital is

$$0.3(\$3 \text{ million}) + 0.6(\$6 \text{ million}) + 0.1(\$12 \text{ million}) = \$5.7 \text{ million}.$$

Second, substitute the *exp MedBen* for the annual medical benefits in computing the hospital's NPV. Holding all other variables (relocation, L,C&T and operating costs) at their likely or accepted values, the calculation yields the same *exp NPV* ($5.1 million) as obtained with equation 14.2.

The calculations in this case are the same because risk is assessed for only one variable. When probabilities are available for two or more variables, then the proper procedure is to calculate each variable's expected value (adapting equation 14.3) and use the expected values, along with values for any other benefits and costs, to compute NPV.

6. To avoid a possible source of confusion, note that the expected (mean) values of NPV ($5.1 million and $3.9 million for the hospital and expanded clinic, respectively) and "likely" NPV values ($6.99 million and $4 million, respectively) are not the same. The "likely" value is often the mode (the most frequently observed value). This is not necessarily the calculated average (mean or expected value) of all observed values.

7. For a readable illustration of certainty equivalent adjustments in the context of private management decision making, see Hirschey and Pappas (1996: 96–101).

Chapter 15

Principles of Cost-Benefit Analysis

INTRODUCTION

Part II presents a number of practical principles for how to do a cost-benefit analysis. As a help to the reader, this chapter summarizes the principles. Listed together, these serve as a reference that can be consulted when planning, performing or reviewing a particular analysis. Let's begin by restating the definition of cost-benefit analysis.

Cost-benefit analysis (CBA) is a useful approach to assess whether decisions or choices that affect the use of scarce resources promote efficiency. Considering a specific policy and relevant alternatives, the analysis involves systematic identification of policy consequences, followed by valuation of social benefits and costs and then application of the appropriate decision criterion.

SUMMARY OF PRINCIPLES

The principles are listed in the order in which they are presented in the book. The chapter titles and principle numbers are provided to facilitate easy reference to the related chapter discussion.

Economics and Cost-Benefit Analysis

4.1 Given the focus on *efficiency*, cost-benefit analysis is relevant for those decisions (government or private) which (a) involve the use of scarce resources and (b) generate "good" and/or "bad" consequences for social welfare.

4.2 As a *decision-making tool*, cost-benefit analysis provides the decision maker with information assessing a particular policy's efficiency; however, efficiency is only one of several possible goals that the decision maker might consider worthwhile. Thus, the final decision on whether to pursue the policy is resolved by the decision maker, who must weigh the policy's relative efficiency with other competing objectives.

4.3   The analyst must conscientiously inform the decision maker of the practical implications of the cost-benefit framework's focus on efficiency and, as needed, identify relevant trade-offs between efficiency and other policy objectives.

Economic Valuation of Individual Preferences

5.1   Social benefits are valued by summing individuals' *willingness to pay* (WTP).

5.2   Social costs are valued by the *opportunity cost* of the allocated resources, defined as the foregone benefits of the resources' best alternative use. The foregone benefits, in turn, are valued by individuals' willingness to pay.

Who Is Society?

6.1   The analyst should define *society* as including all persons who benefit or incur a cost from the policy under consideration.

6.2   If the decision maker stipulates a narrow society for the net benefits estimation, then in a separate discussion the analyst should identify and quantify the *spillovers* and, ideally, note how the inclusion of spillover benefits and costs would affect the calculated net benefits.

6.3   Theoretically, future persons have *standing* in cost-benefit analysis; their preferences are ideally reflected in future benefits and costs. Empirically, however, the analysis can measure directly only the preferences of the present (or past) generations. The extent to which these are likely to reflect future preferences must be considered.

6.4   Cost-benefit analysis is *anthropocentric*, recognizing only humans in the defined society; nonhuman nature does not have standing. Therefore, only those values of nonhuman nature beheld by humans are included.

"With and Without" Analysis

7.1   Cost-benefit analysis is a *"with and without" analysis*. The analyst should first develop the *baseline scenario* (i.e., what would happen without the policy) and then identify and calculate *incremental* benefits and costs by comparing consequences "with" the policy to those "without" the policy.

7.2   The use of incremental benefits and costs provides the analyst with a choice when gathering data. The analyst might collect separate data for each of the with-policy and baseline scenarios (and then calculate the incremental differences) or instead, collect data directly measuring the incremental effects. Either approach yields the same final mathematical calculation. Therefore, the decision depends on data availability, ease of data collection and whether there is a practical reason for the analyst to present particular data in the report.

Aggregated Benefits and Costs

8.1   The analyst adds (aggregates) all policy benefits received and aggregates all policy costs incurred by everyone in society within each time period.

8.2   When a policy has important implications for distinct groups, the analyst should, where reasonable and practical, include a separate statement detailing how policy benefits, costs and net benefits are distributed among members of society. The decision maker can then weigh any adverse (or desirable) distributional consequences with the efficiency assessment of the policy's overall net benefits.

8.3   When a policy's effects are valued by individuals with greatly differing incomes, or abilities to pay, the analyst should include a separate, detailed statement showing the valuation by various income groups. Also, the analyst should state explicitly that the strength of low-income individuals' preferences is underrepresented in the analysis. The decision maker can then consider this information along with the policy's calculated net benefits.

8.4   We do not recommend the use of *distributional weights* within a cost-benefit analysis, because specific unequal weights can be subjectively chosen to influence the results. However, if a decision maker requests or approves that benefits and costs be unequally weighted, then the analyst should explicitly state which weights are selected and present justification for the specific choice. Also, in order to demonstrate the implications of using distributional weights, the analyst should calculate the net benefits without unequal weights. Even better, the analyst should undertake a *selective sensitivity analysis*, first calculating the unweighted net benefits and then assigning several different sets of weights and examining the weights' effects on the net benefits calculation. In any of these cases, a detailed listing of the distribution of benefits, costs and/or net benefits should also be reported for the decision maker's perusal.

8.5   Rather than choosing in the cost-benefit analysis to weight expert and specialist preferences more heavily than the preferences of the less-informed public, we again affirm the traditional approach whereby the preferences of all individuals, whether they have expertise or not, are simply aggregated. Although individuals may not be fully informed, their preferences provide important information to the decision maker. It is imperative that the decision maker also consider expert and specialist views, expressed in other arenas or analyses, and then subjectively weigh all information received.

Present Value of Benefits and Costs

9.1   In order to add dollars over time, future dollar values are *discounted* to obtain *present values.*

9.2   In economic analysis, dollar values incurred over time are not to be added together without discounting. *Always* discount to the present value. However, if there is some compelling reason for reporting the simple sum of benefits or costs over time, the reported sum should be kept separate from the economic analysis and should be interpreted and explained within the context of the compelling reason.

9.3   Be cognizant that present value calculations entail some error and that the analyst can affect the size of the error by carefully selecting the time distribution of policy benefits and costs for analysis. Efficiency dictates that when considering ways to reduce the error, the analyst should weigh the benefits gained from more precise data with the costs of detailed data collection and manipulation.

9.4   The analyst should explicitly indicate in the report that (1) the present value calculation assumes that all benefits and costs accrue on the last day of each time period and (2) this assumption does allow some error but greatly increases the ease of computation.

9.5   Define the *present*, that is, the beginning of the policy, as that date when policy resources are first committed and begin to generate opportunity cost.

Decision Criteria

10.1   To assess the efficiency of alternative policy options, the analyst should (1) identify the type of decision the decision maker seeks to make and (2) apply the corresponding decision criterion.

10.2   For all decision choices, the NPV is preferred in identifying which policy or policy combination promotes efficiency. In one situation only, where the decision is to choose a subset of several *independent* policies with a *budget constraint*, is the B/C recommended for supplementary information. An analysis that does not use the appropriate criterion risks mistakenly identifying a relatively inefficient policy option as the one most efficient.

10.3   Cost-benefit analysis identifies those policy alternative(s) that promote efficiency. As efficiency is only one of several possible goals that might be considered by the decision maker, it is not the intent of the analysis to dictate the final decision. Rather, the goal is to provide information that enables the decision maker to make a more *rational decision*, if desired, and to be aware of trade-offs when pursuing other goals.

10.4   It is important for the analyst and decision maker to identify and appraise all relevant alternatives. Even the most accurate, detailed cost-benefit analysis is going to be of limited value if promising alternative policies are ignored. The appropriate decision criterion indicates which policy option(s) among the ones evaluated most promote efficiency. Only if all relevant alternatives are adequately assessed does the criterion identify the efficient (or *dynamically efficient*) decision.

Discount Rate

11.1   Discounting might be performed using the pretax rate of return from the best alternative investment. The cost-benefit analysis thus assesses the decision to devote resources to a particular policy rather than to an alternative investment in the private or public sector. Efficiency is evaluated in terms of whether the policy's net benefits are greater than the foregone investment return.

11.2   If relevant, discounting might be performed with a rate measuring the cost of borrowing. The cost-benefit analysis then assesses whether a particular policy generates sufficient returns to cover the borrowing costs and thus determines whether borrowing the resources to pursue the policy promotes efficiency.

11.3   The discount rate might be selected to reflect the *social rate of time preference*, that is, society's preference for present relative to future consumption. The analysis thus assesses efficiency by determining whether the policy's future stream of social values is greater than the value society foregoes by not using the resources for present consumption.

11.4   For a given policy, the higher the discount rate used in the analysis, then (a) the lower the NPV, and (b) in some cases an otherwise positive NPV may become negative.

11.5   In comparing two or more policies, the selection of the discount rate can affect the policies' relative NPV ranking, thus changing which policy is identified as more efficient.

11.6   When comparing two or more policies, high discount rates penalize policies with large future benefits and large initial construction or start-up costs.

11.7   When analyzing two or more policies for comparison purposes, the analyst should use the same discount rate.

11.8   To enhance analytical objectivity and provide greater information to the decision maker, the analyst should conduct a *selective sensitivity analysis* for the discount rate. Three carefully selected discount rates should be applied in separate present value calculations; the resulting NPVs can then be compared to assess their sensitivity to the choice of discount rate.

11.9   Suppose that, for a particular policy, the decision maker or interested parties hold ethical or environmental concerns that suggest the future should be assigned the same weight as the present. The analyst can address their concerns, while simultaneously enhancing the objectivity of the analysis, by using a zero discount rate as a fourth rate in the selective sensitivity analysis.

Inflation

12.1   The use of monetary values requires careful consideration and possible adjustment for inflation. Adjusting for inflation is sometimes confused with discounting to present value. To clarify, inflationary adjustments acknowledge the declining purchasing power of the dollar as the general price level increases over time. Discounting reflects a dollar's greater value in the present than in the future, due to one of the following: the present dollar's ability to earn a return from alternative investments, society's preference for present consumption or the future repayment of borrowing costs.

12.2   The analyst can express benefits and costs either all in nominal prices (i.e., current dollars) or all in real prices (i.e., constant dollars), as long as the discount rate is expressed the same way. Specifically, use of nominal benefits and costs requires a *nominal discount rate*. If, instead, the benefits and costs are real, then a *real discount rate* adjusted for inflation must be employed.

Time Horizon

13.1   Be aware of possible biases in the choice of *time horizon* for the analysis; the horizon should include the entire time period over which policy benefits and costs occur. At the same time, the practice of discounting reduces values occurring after some 60 to 75 years to negligible amounts, potentially limiting the relevant time horizon.

13.2   Other considerations when selecting a time horizon are whether to include (1) a *terminal value* and/or (2) a future value in *perpetuity*.

13.3   When choosing one of several policies where the time horizons are not all the same, three methods are available to allow comparison. If the policies are repeatable, *replication* might be employed to calculate NPVs, or instead, *equivalent annual net benefits* (EANBs) might be computed. If it is not likely the policies will be repeated, then the longer policies' horizons might be shortened and a terminal value added when calculating NPVs. In each case, the respective decision criterion (the highest NPV or EANB) is employed to determine which policy promotes efficiency.

Uncertainty and Risk

14.1   The economic assessment of uncertainty involves two components: (1) identifying the nature of any and all uncertainty relevant to a particular analysis and (2) analyzing the implications of the uncertainty for the study's conclusions and for the decision-making process.

14.2   To analyze uncertainty for a single policy, the most common practical procedures are *selective sensitivity analysis* and *switching values*.

14.3   If several mutually exclusive policy alternatives share a common uncertain variable, a selective sensitivity analysis can be performed for each alternative, with the calculated NPVs displayed in a *payoff matrix*. Alternative decision rules, such as the *maximax, maximin* or *minimax regret criteria*, can be applied to help identify an appropriate policy in light of both efficiency and uncertainty considerations.

14.4   The standard procedure for incorporating risk within a cost-benefit analysis is to (1) estimate both the uncertain event's possible values (or magnitudes) and probabilities of occurrence and then (2) calculate the *expected value* of the decision criterion (NPV).

Part III

Benefits and Costs: Identification and Valuation

Chapter 16

Identifying Benefits and Costs

INTRODUCTION

A cost-benefit analysis should thoroughly determine a given policy's implications for human society. Two steps are involved: identify, first, all policy consequences, and second, all related benefits and costs. Each step is discussed along with two classification schemes to help in systematically determining which consequences are (and which are not) appropriately considered to be social benefits and costs.

The chapter concludes by introducing the task of valuation. The challenge of valuing hard-to-measure effects and the possibility of interpreting the calculated NPV as a critical value for unvalued benefits (or costs) are addressed. Then, the valuation techniques presented in upcoming chapters are briefly stated.

IDENTIFY POLICY CONSEQUENCES, THEN BENEFITS AND COSTS

Principle 16.1. The analyst should identify all policy consequences, determining all of a policy's resource impacts that have good or bad consequences for social welfare and then sketching these consequences.

The analyst should be careful to consider those policy consequences recognized by the decision maker and by policy proponents and opponents, as well as any other consequences that affect human society. It is the analyst's responsibility to ensure that all relevant policy impacts are determined. This may require specialized knowledge, for example, appropriate scientific information for assessing environmental policies or familiarity with behavioral models for pre-

---

Box 16.1
To Identify All Impacts on Environmental Resources, Use a Systems Approach

Suppose an analyst assesses the construction of retention ponds to divert stormwater runoff from flowing into a local bay. The analyst carefully identifies various benefits and costs generated by the retention ponds. Included in the analysis are the costs of constructing and maintaining the retention ponds as well as the related infrastructure for diverting water to the ponds. Also, several benefits are valued that derive from the improved water quality in the bay. Has the analyst thoroughly identified all benefits and costs?

According to a *systems approach*, the answer is No. Consider again where the runoff goes: into retention ponds. And then where? Does 100% of the water remain in the ponds forever? No, some of the stormwater and the pollutants it contains will be evaporated, creating air pollution; and some will seep down into the earth's layers below the pond, possibly entering an aquifer and polluting groundwater supplies. These changes may have a negative impact on human welfare and, if so, should (ideally) be included in a cost-benefit analysis.

Underlying this approach is the First Law of Thermodynamics, which says that energy and matter cannot be created or destroyed. The retention pond project diverts polluted stormwater runoff out of the bay but does not destroy the pollutants. A systems approach recognizes the interrelatedness of different environments and considers the possibility that pollutants beneficially removed from one environment may cause harm to human welfare by entering another environment. To identify all benefits and costs of a particular policy, the analyst must take a broad perspective and consider relationships between all environments.

---

dicting human response to risk. Accordingly, the analyst should consult relevant specialists or literatures offering the necessary expertise.

The importance of carefully and thoughtfully determining relevant policy consequences should be emphasized. A properly conducted cost-benefit analysis offers a comprehensive assessment of policy effects. Identifying any unintended social consequences that might otherwise be overlooked in the decision-making process can be very helpful to the public or private decision maker. Moreover, the accuracy of the analysis depends on correctly anticipating all policy impacts. For example, in the case of a policy that affects environmental resources, a systems approach is required to ensure comprehensive identification of policy impacts (see Box 16.1).

Once the policy consequences are sketched thoroughly, the analyst should distinguish which ones are relevant for valuation as benefits and costs.

Principle 16.2. For these consequences, the analyst should identify all *benefits* and *costs*, where these represent the economic value of real changes associated with a policy. A *real change* includes a change in the physical quantity or quality of a given resource or output and/or a change in individual satisfaction (utility) derived from the resource or output.

Remember from Chapter 5 that economic value is the sum of individual preferences as expressed by consumer willingness to pay. Thus, cost-benefit analysis focuses on physical (real) resource flows, valuing resources as these are transformed into consumption opportunities.[1]

The literature offers a number of different definitional categories to aid in identifying benefits and costs. Two broad classification systems encompassing these categories are presented in this chapter. The first classification scheme distinguishes between those resources, goods and services that are priced in the market and those that are not, that is, marketed and external benefits and costs, respectively. Addressed separately are two types of market consequences, price effects and induced income changes, that generally should not be counted as benefits or costs. The second classification scheme, which originated in the context of environmental and natural resources, recognizes that resources generate two broad categories of value for individuals in society: use value and non-use value. Noting that the two schemes overlap, the analyst must take care not to double count a particular consequence's valuation. If used when appropriate, however, both schemes' categories can help the analyst systematically detect the benefits and costs to include in a thorough analysis.

MARKETED AND EXTERNAL BENEFITS AND COSTS

The first classification scheme categorizes policy impacts on physical (real) resources and output in terms of those consequences that are priced in the market and those that are not. This leads to several groupings of benefits and costs.

Marketed resource costs. These are the values of the market-priced resources or inputs used in implementing the policy. Generally included are the capital or start-up costs, operating expenses and maintenance expenses that are incurred by the government or private firms during the policy time horizon.

Marketed output benefits. These benefits represent the increased value of physical (real) goods and services that are created by the policy and sold in the market. An example can clarify. Suppose the analyst evaluates the proposed construction of a hydroelectric dam along a free-flowing river. The resulting increase in electricity sold to consumers is a change in output *quantity* and is therefore considered a marketed benefit of the dam. In addition, suppose the dam would control flooding, thereby protecting farmlands located downstream. The resulting increase in physical (real) crop output sold to consumers is also a marketed benefit. Moreover, the dam's control of the water flow might improve the *quality* of recreational rafting experiences in the river downstream. If individuals value a given rafting trip more with the dam than without it and therefore would be willing to pay the local rafting company a higher market price (and the company raises its price accordingly), then the real change in experience is a marketed benefit.

Marketed output costs. It is also possible that a policy may have negative consequences for some individuals in society. For instance, contrary to the prior example, the dam's control of the water flow might result in a reduced *quantity* of commercial rafting trips or a lower *quality* rafting experience (with a lower willingness to pay and market price). Either of these constitutes marketed costs and should be included in the analysis.

External effects. An external effect is an uncompensated gain or loss in welfare to a member of society; the effect is outside the market system and is not reflected in relative market prices. It is a *nonmarket effect.* Relevant to a cost-benefit analysis are those external effects that involve real changes related to resources or output, that is, *technological externalities.* For example, suppose the proposed hydroelectric dam would create a large reservoir lake upstream that is to be available (for free) to recreational boaters and fishers. These are real consumption opportunities that are not priced in the market and thus are external benefits. Perhaps also the dam would act as a filtration system, decreasing the amount of silt present in the river downstream. The improved water quality and appearance might provide a more aesthetically pleasing scenic view, which individuals might "consume" and value. This consumption opportunity represents an external benefit. Also possible are external costs. Suppose the periodic high water flows produced by the dam would erode the beaches along the river downstream, thereby destroying habitat and discouraging an endangered bird species from nesting. Those (human) individuals who value the preservation of this species incur an external cost.

Thus, the first classification scheme delineates four categories of benefits and costs.

Principle 16.3. Benefits and costs can be categorized in terms of impacts priced in the market and nonmarket effects. Together these include marketed resource costs, marketed output benefits, marketed output costs and technological externalities (i.e., real changes in resources or output not priced in a market).

When analyzing a policy, the analyst should seek to identify the policy consequences that result in any of these categories of real changes, for these constitute benefits and costs that should be valued in the analysis.

PECUNIARY EFFECTS AND SECONDARY BENEFITS

Two types of policy effects that are priced in markets generally should not be included as benefits or costs in a cost-benefit analysis. The first of these, *pecuniary effects* or *pecuniary externalities*, are related to price changes, rather than to real resource or output changes. To clarify the difference, let's revisit the hydroelectric dam example. Suppose the electric power produced by this new dam would be sold in sufficient quantity to lower the market price for consumers who continue to purchase the same amount of electricity from already existing power generators. It might be argued that these consumers would receive a benefit in the form of lower prices, that is, a pecuniary effect. This is true. At the same time, the electricity-generating firms would also collect lower prices, earning less per unit of electricity (also a pecuniary effect). The price change caused by the dam thus represents a redistribution of income from the firms to their consumers. One group's gain is another group's loss, with no change in social welfare. Such pecuniary effects should therefore not be included as a benefit or cost.[2]

The same can be said for changes in the prices of substitutes or complements. These too are pecuniary effects. For example, suppose in our dam example, the electricity price does indeed fall and some consumers switch to using lower-priced electricity in place of other energy substitutes, such as natural gas. The price of natural gas might then fall, and the remaining natural gas consumers would pay lower prices. It can be argued that the latter consumers obtain a benefit. True enough, yet the natural gas firms would receive lower prices. Once again, the price change caused by the dam represents a redistribution of income away from firms to their consumers, not a net change in social welfare. Thus, pecuniary effects should not be included in a cost-benefit analysis.[3]

The second set of policy consequences generally excluded from cost-benefit analysis are *secondary benefits* (sometimes referred to as *indirect benefits* in the literature). These are a type of *multiplier effect* and represent changes in income induced through linkages. For instance, returning to the example of the hydroelectric dam, suppose the dam promises to control floods, which in turn increases agricultural crop output. Income changes would be induced in both a forward direction through further processing or selling of the crop and a backward direction through changed use of inputs. An example of forward movement, also called a *forward linkage*, is the marketing of the increased crop output to the final consumer. Marketing services might be provided by merchants or intermediaries who then receive higher incomes. An example of a *backward linkage* is farmers using more inputs (seeds, fertilizers) to produce the additional crop output, yielding greater incomes to agricultural input suppliers. Another example is the construction and operation of the dam, which provide incomes to workers. The higher incomes that are induced through forward and backward linkages are often respent, generating a series of consumption expenditures. These *multiplier effects* are secondary benefits resulting from the dam. Similar to pecuniary effects, secondary benefits should generally not be incorporated in the cost-benefit calculation.

The main reason for excluding secondary benefits relates to the practice of assuming a full-employment economy and price stability. In a stabilized macroeconomy, the funds and resources used to implement the dam would otherwise be applied somewhere else in the economy, generating a parallel set of multiplier effects. Thus, the incremental secondary benefits provided by this policy over and above the alternative are believed to be negligible in size.

If, instead, an inflationary economy exists, the dam and flood control might induce higher prices, further aggravating the inflation problem, in which case the secondary benefits are negative. Only in a macroeconomy characterized by unemployment would the dam's flood control result in large positive changes in employment and incomes. Eckstein thus concludes that counting secondary benefits "must be confined to cases where it can be shown that there are unemployed and immobile resources or that there is underutilized capacity in associated economic activities" (1958: 212). At the same time, Eckstein and several other authors (for example, McKean 1958: 159–62; James and Lee 1971: 113) question including such benefits even when unemployment exists, for in an advanced economy, unemployment tends to be cyclical. It is generally unreasonable, therefore, to assume national unemployment will persist throughout the entire time horizon for long-term policies.

In addition, since secondary benefits vary in size with the state of the national economy, their quantification can be highly subjective. Simply deciding that the economy will be characterized by unemployment or inflation during the policy time horizon enables easy manipulation of the induced income changes to make a particular policy look more (or less) favorable. Some cost-benefit analyses have tracked induced income changes via multiplier studies, but the predominant view of economists is not to accept these predictions within a cost-benefit analysis. Induced income changes are instead analyzed in *input-output analyses* or *economic impact*[4] studies, which have as their primary purpose analyzing policy multiplier effects including income changes induced by linkages and/or consumer expenditures.

When a policy's objective is regional development, secondary benefits may be an especially important consideration for the decision maker. This is particularly the case if the region is depressed, with substantial unemployment. McKean concludes that under such circumstances these benefits should be described but not included in the net benefits valuation (1958: 163). The reason is that cost-benefit analysis defines society broadly. Accordingly, it recognizes that in advanced economies characterized by aggregate full employment, while the specified region may gain economic activity in the form of secondary benefits and other multiplier effects, activity is generally lost somewhere else outside the region. The region's gain is thereby offset and should not be counted in cost-benefit analysis. Eckstein concludes that even listing the region's secondary benefits can lead to possible bias and thus should be accompanied by a description of the secondary benefits lost outside the region (1958: 214). When regional considerations are an important concern, the induced income changes should be incorporated within a regional *input-output* and/or *economic impact* analysis. The decision maker can then weigh the results of the efficiency assessment provided by a cost-benefit analysis with the regional development and distributional considerations of an economic impact study.

Principle 16.4. Pecuniary (price) effects and secondary benefits (induced income changes) should generally not be included as benefits or costs in a cost-benefit analysis. Even if a policy's primary objective is regional development, secondary benefits should be listed only and not incorporated in the net benefits calculation; the diversion of secondary benefits from somewhere outside the region should also be indicated.

USE AND NON-USE VALUES

A second classification system can sometimes be helpful in illuminating all benefits and costs to be valued; it represents an alternative way of conceptualizing the same benefits and costs included in the first classification groups. The second scheme categorizes policy effects in terms of whether they generate use or non-use values.

Use value reflects the value gained from any of a broad range of consumptive uses of a particular resource, good or service. In the context of environmental and natural resources, such uses might include engaging in freshwater recreational activities, breathing clean air, observing scenic views, photographing wildlife, experiencing wilderness and the like.

The concept of *existence value* or *non-use value* (more recently termed *passive-use value*) is attributed to Krutilla (1967). Exploring the issues to be addressed when analyzing whether to preserve a natural environment or to convert the area for development, he introduced the idea of people valuing the natural area's existence. In other words, some people receive a value just knowing a particular resource exists, even though they may not now (or ever) use it.[5] This non-use value reflects the price they are willing to pay to preserve the resource's existence. Behavioral evidence that existence (or non-use) values are truly a part of individual preferences is provided by the many environmental funds and organizations that receive donations to protect endangered species; some donors may never see (use) the species, yet are willing to give money for species preservation.

While economists generally accept existence or non-use value to be a valid concept, there is little consensus as to the precise definition(s). For instance, existence and non-use values are often treated as identical, interchangeable terms; however, Freeman suggests existence value is one of several non-use values. He differentiates ''pure existence value'' as being lost when a resource no longer exists (e.g., species extinction, destruction of scenic area), while ''other non-use values'' can be lost when a resource continues to exist but is degraded in quantity or quality—such as pollution of a scenic area or early death of individual species members, where people value the area or members independent of any use value (1993a: 142, 151).

Also, the precise distinction between use and non-use values is not well defined. As Boardman and associates note, most economists likely consider behavior such as simply thinking about the resource or discussing the resource with someone else to be non-use value, while some (though not all) might deem enjoying a picture of the resource site to be a use value. These designations are not certain, however, as the exact dividing line separating use from non-use value is not clearly specified (1996: 238).

Krutilla (1967) originally presented existence and non-use values while re-ferring to unique resources subject to irreversible change. Examples of *unique* resources with no close substitutes include endangered plant and animal species, unique scenic views, incomparable wilderness experiences, and such human-made resources as precious works of art and historical sites, to name a few. As for *irreversibility*, policies might threaten, say, to eliminate a species directly or to destroy the habitat acres critical for species preservation so the species cannot recover. Another example is a policy that removes old-growth forests while promoting new growth. New forests provide a very different ecosystem than old-growth forests; thus, the forest resource, at least in its prior form, is forever changed.

At the same time, non-use values may not be limited to situations involving irreversible changes to unique resources. The growing view is that non-use val-ues can be applicable when, say, a resource is damaged and natural recuperation and regeneration occurs over a long time. Indeed, in recent assessments of the natural resource damages from oil spills, lost non-use values are measured over the period of the resource's recovery (Kopp and Smith 1993: 321–22, 326). Also, there is recognition that non-use values might be relevant for a wide range of resources, goods or services, where some individuals gain satisfaction from knowing that others benefit from a particular policy decision. Examples might include policies designed to preserve family farms or to reduce crime, poverty or transport regulation, to name only a very few. The usefulness and credibility of estimating these and other possible non-use values (as well as traditional environmental non-use values) has been the subject of debate—see Thompson (1980: 134–36, 144–45), Rosenthal and Nelson (1992) and Kopp (1992).

Despite the areas of disagreement, a number of studies' empirical estimates suggest non-use values not only exist but can be quite large in the aggregate. Thus, for those policies where non-use values are likely to be relevant, these values should not be overlooked. At the same time, the technical challenge of accurately estimating non-use values suggests caution when interpreting a par-ticular estimate. (See Freeman 1993b: 292–98 for a critical review of several studies' empirical approaches.)

Principle 16.5. A second classification scheme categorizes benefits and costs in terms of use values and non-use (or passive-use) values. Non-use values are especially relevant for unique resources subject to irreversible (or long-term) change.

VALUATION: HARD-TO-MEASURE EFFECTS

Once benefits and costs are identified, the next task is valuation. A challenge is often encountered as nonmarket effects (whether use or non-use values) by definition are not valued in the market and thus can be hard to measure.[6] Care must be taken to use appropriate valuation techniques and to avoid common valuation mistakes. (For an example of the latter, see Box 16.2.) Despite the

---

Box 16.2
Environmental Pollution Damage Is Not Properly Valued by Cleanup Costs

Suppose a proposed policy will cause water pollution that limits recreational activities at a particular site. The analyst's task is to value the pollution damage (lost recreational activities) from society's perspective. Assume that because budget and time preclude the analyst from employing a valuation technique, the pollution damage remains unmeasured. If the cost of cleaning up the water pollution is known, the analyst may be tempted to use that cost as an indicator of the pollution damage. This is not appropriate.

For example, assume the cost of cleaning up the environment is an estimated $2 million. Is this the value of the pollution damage? No. If valuation had been possible, the analyst might have found society would incur $1 million worth of damages in the form of lost recreational value. Note in this case that the estimated cleanup is not a worthwhile expenditure. Or, instead, perhaps society valued the water quality damage at $3 million, thus justifying the cleanup expense. In either case, the cost of cleaning up the pollution is not a satisfactory measure of the pollution damage.

It is thus incorrect for the analyst to include the cleanup cost as a proxy for pollution damage in the cost-benefit calculation. Instead, the analyst should report separately the $2 million cleanup estimate to the decision maker. The latter can then consider whether society's costs from the pollution damage are likely to be great enough to warrant the cleanup expense, if the policy is pursued.

---

quantification difficulties, the analyst should not neglect or omit these effects. Decision makers, when choosing between alternatives, implicitly value all relevant policy consequences, and nonmarket effects may be as important as easily measured impacts. The analyst must therefore place as accurate a value as possible on all consequences, including nonmarket effects.

Principle 16.6. When a policy has hard-to-measure effects, the analyst should (1) value as many benefits and costs as possible using monetary units; (2) if unable to assign a monetary value to a particular policy consequence, try to quantify it in physical units; and (3) in the especially difficult situation where the consequence eludes quantification of any kind, identify and describe it qualitatively.

NPV AS CRITICAL VALUE

When unable to value one or more benefits (or, instead, one or more costs), the analyst may be able to provide additional information helpful to the decision maker. The calculated decision criterion, NPV, can be interpreted as a *critical value* for non-valued benefits (costs). In effect, the NPV estimates a threshold. Intuitively, the decision maker can weigh the unmeasured benefits (costs) and consider whether or not these exceed the threshold (Pearce 1971: 56–57).

To illustrate, suppose an analyst is assessing a proposed highway that, in addition to several valued effects, will destroy a certain section of endangered mangrove habitat. The analyst calculates an NPV of $317,000 for the measured benefits and costs but is unable to value the cost associated with the habitat destruction. The analyst can report the NPV as providing a critical value for the endangered habitat. If the decision maker believes the endangered habitat to be worth more than $317,000 in present value terms then the appropriate conclusion is that the habitat damage outweighs the calculated NPV and the highway project does not promote efficiency. However, if the decision maker believes the damaged habitat to be worth less than $317,000 in present value terms, then the positive NPV appropriately indicates that the project promotes efficiency.

Likewise, suppose an analyst is assessing the benefits derived from a proposed flood control project. He is unable to value one benefit, the protection of endangered marshlands from inundation by flood waters. He completes the analysis by calculating an NPV for the measured benefits and costs, then reports to the decision maker, making clear this one benefit was not measured. Suppose the reported NPV is −$213,000. If the decision maker regards the value of the marshlands benefit as greater than $213,000, then she would conclude the benefits outweigh costs and the project promotes efficiency. However, if she believes that the preserved marshlands is not worth $213,000, she would then deduce the proposed flood control project does not promote efficiency.

Principle 16.7. At the end of the analysis, when the analyst reports the NPV, the analyst should again identify those consequences that are not valued. If these effects are *either* all benefits *or* all costs, then the analyst should explain that the NPV provides a *critical value* for the unmeasured benefits (costs).

OVERVIEW OF VALUATION TECHNIQUES

This chapter groups policy consequences into several benefit and cost categories. Once identified, a policy benefit or cost should ideally be valued. Marketed benefits and costs offer the advantage that market prices exist and often can be used for valuation purposes. However, challenges can still be encountered. First, consumer surplus should be measured and included along with the price in the valuation. Second, if government price ceilings, taxes or unemployment characterize the market for a particular resource, then the market price must be adjusted for valuation purposes. These market valuation issues are discussed in Chapter 17.

Nonmarket effects, or technological externalities, present a greater challenge, since by definition, a market price does not exist for the resource in question. Several valuation techniques are available, more than one of which may prove useful to the analyst. Chapter 18 explains the contingent valuation method where respondents are asked to *state preferences hypothetically* for a resource; for example, each respondent might be asked how much he or she would be willing to pay for the resource, assuming a market does exist. This method not only offers applications to measure use values but is also the one systematic technique for estimating non-use values. The other valuation chapters consider various *revealed preference methods*, which infer the (use) value of a nonmarket effect from observed behavior in surrogate markets. The travel cost method (see Chapter 19) analyzes the relationship between visit rates and visitor expenses incurred when traveling to and from a specific site to gain access to a resource. Alternative methods, property valuation and human life valuation, are addressed in Chapters 20 and 21, respectively. For those instances where an important benefit (or cost) cannot be valued, yet the policy consequence itself can be quantified, cost-effectiveness analysis (see Chapter 22) might be applied. Finally, Part III chapter principles are summarized in Chapter 23, providing the reader a comparative overview of the various techniques and serving as a reference to relevant chapter sections.

NOTES

1. Some sources call these *direct* benefits and costs. However, the literature attributes different meanings to the word "direct," so we do not use this term.

2. The astute economics student may at this point be wondering (correctly) about the law of demand. As the electricity price falls, basic economic theory predicts an increase in quantity demanded. Those consumers who buy additional electricity from existing firms will receive a consumer surplus over and above the price they pay. This "consumer-surplus triangle," named for its shape in a market graph, is a net gain in social welfare and, in principle, should be included as a benefit in a cost-benefit analysis. (Likewise, if the electricity price increases and consumers buy less electricity, a consumer-surplus triangle is lost and is counted as a social cost.) While theoretically important, this surplus value is generally so small that from a pragmatic perspective, the measurement costs and possible measurement error are not warranted (James and Lee 1971: 110). Thus, unless the price change is a sizable portion of the initial electricity price, the surplus triangle should be excluded from the analysis in practice.

3. Similar to the electricity market, a change in consumer surplus is also possible in the natural gas market. As consumers buy less natural gas, they lose a "triangle" of consumer surplus. This is also the case in other energy substitute markets (coal, wood, etc.) with parallel effects in important complementary markets (such as electrical consumer appliances). Given the number of related markets, estimating these surplus changes is no small challenge. How to analyze the changes has led to an extensive technical discussion in the economics literature (see, for instance, Gramlich 1990: 79–83; Boardman et al. 1996: 85–92; Nas 1996: 83–84). To summarize the discourse, the latest theory indicates that if markets are competitive, the price changes in the substitute and complementary markets will reverberate back to the electricity market as consumers continue to adjust their behavior. Thus, as adequate forecasts of future prices for the dam's electricity are likely to capture at least part of these price effects, to estimate them separately involves double counting. If, however, the related markets are distorted (for example, by taxes), separate estimates of these markets' price effects are recommended in theory. As a practical rule of thumb, however, these effects are often smaller than the likely measurement error and thus are generally omitted from cost-benefit analysis. If the effects are sizable, the analyst might consider employing a highly sophisticated general equilibrium

model that uses simultaneous equations to incorporate all relevant markets and their price effects. For discussion and applications of the model, see Gramlich (1990: 84–90).

4. Economic base multipliers are applied to analyze the series of expanded consumer expenditures and incomes deriving from a locale's "export" sector—a common topic in urban economics texts.

5. The literature ascribes several possible motives for why individuals hold non-use values, but there is no agreement. Among the hypothesized reasons are human affection, sympathy or appreciation for a natural resource (sometimes referred to as "intrinsic value" in the economics literature, but termed *inherent value* in the philosophy literature—see Chapter 6) and the desire to preserve a resource for future generations, one's heirs or others in the current generation (sometimes called *bequest value* or altruism). For differing views about possible motives, see Freeman (1993a: 143–44; 1993b: 266–67) and Pearce and Turner (1990: 131–33).

6. Some sources in the literature employ the term *incommensurables*, while others use *intangibles* to refer to hard-to-measure effects. Still other sources (Sassone and Schaffer 1978: 34–37, for example) assign these two terms to distinguish respectively between hard-to-measure economic effects and unmeasurable non-economic effects. In recent years, however, as the economics profession has progressed in developing and extending applications of valuation techniques, some of the effects previously considered to be non-economic and unmeasurable are now valued in economic terms. Thus, we find it less confusing simply to refer to a broad group of hard-to-measure effects.

Chapter 17

Market Valuation

INTRODUCTION

When policies involve a resource (good or service) that is marketed, then consumer demand, using market prices, might be analyzed to estimate the resource's market value. If the market fully reflects social preferences, then such analysis also estimates society's valuation of the resource. If, however, the market is characterized by government price ceilings, taxes or unemployment, then estimated market values do not fully equal social values and, ideally, shadow prices should be determined. This chapter explores how to estimate market demand and derive social values, assuming the market prices fully reflect social preferences. Then, the discussion considers the adjustments for valuation estimation when shadow pricing is required.

MARKET DEMAND CURVE

As introduced in Chapter 5, a resource's total value is measured by society's WTP (or Total WTP). A marketed resource offers the empirical advantage that market prices exist and often can be used for valuation purposes. In a specified geographical market area, the market price (P) and quantity (Q) purchased are directly observed. Multiplied together, as PQ, these yield the consumers' total expenditures for the resource in that market at a given time. In addition, consumers are often WTP a surplus payment, or *consumer surplus*, over and above the observed market price. (As a reminder, the reader might refer to Figure 5.1 for a graphical illustration of consumer surplus.) This value too is included as part of society's Total WTP. Thus, reproducing equation 5.4,

$$\text{Total WTP} = \text{consumers' total expenditures} + \text{consumer surplus} \qquad (17.1)$$

$$= \qquad PQ \qquad\qquad + \text{consumer surplus.} \qquad (17.2)$$

While estimating consumer expenditures can be fairly straightforward, consumer surplus is not directly observable in a market. A more sophisticated estimation approach is thus required. An informal or less sophisticated cost-benefit analysis skirts the issue by simply calculating consumers' total expenditures (PQ) and obtaining a *conservative estimate* of the resource's value. More rigorous studies employ multiple regression analysis to estimate consumer demand and find the (entire) Total WTP.

Much theoretical debate surrounds the question of the appropriate measure of consumer surplus. Alfred Marshall in the 1800s and John Hicks in the 1940s derived two different theoretically specified demand curves, each leading to alternative estimates of consumer surplus. Although many economists argue the theoretical superiority of the Hicksian function, providing supporting and elaborate mathematical derivations,[1] the Marshallian function is ordinarily estimated empirically. This chapter thus pragmatically considers estimation of the Marshallian function.

While a graphed demand curve simply shows the relationship between market price and quantity, consumer demand reflects a complex set of determinants. Demand theory identifies household income, population, prices of substitutes, prices of complements and numerous other variables relevant for specific marketed resources, such as consumer age, ethnicity and the like. To separate the effects of these variables (including market price) on demand, *multiple regression analysis* is employed. A regression equation expresses quantity demanded as a function of the demand characteristics. The analysis estimates coefficients, each of which measures the corresponding characteristic's independent effect on quantity demanded (holding all other variables constant).

Data can be gathered by consumer interviews, experiments or, more commonly, recorded data. In case of the latter, business and government records are consulted to obtain the quantity of consumer purchases at different prices as well as measurements for other consumer variables. Data might be collected for various time periods, allowing a *time-series analysis* to estimate changes in quantity demanded as price changes over time. If data are gathered for only one time period, say, for several market locations where different prices are observed, a *cross-section analysis* is performed.

Upon compiling the data, the analyst must determine the appropriate functional form that best fits the data. A number of functional forms are possible, including linear, log-linear, semilog and nonlinear, as well as others. The simplest form is a linear function that assumes that if any particular consumer variable increases, all other variables held constant, then quantity demanded changes proportionately. A general linear demand regression is specified as

$$Q = a_0 + a_1 C_1 + a_2 C_2 + a_3 C_3 + \ldots + a_n C_n, \qquad (17.3)$$

where Q is quantity demanded and C_i is demand characteristic i. The data for Q and C_i are entered into a computer, and a statistical program estimates a_0, a constant, and a_i, the respective regression coefficient for C_i. The coefficients are expressed mathematically as:

$$a_i = \frac{\Delta Q}{\Delta C_i}, \text{ for } i = 1, 2, \ldots n. \tag{17.4}$$

In the economics literature, consumer demand functions generally incorporate anywhere from a handful to a dozen characteristics. An illustrative regression equation that includes a few of the most commonly specified variables is as follows.

$$Q = a_0 + a_1 P + a_2 (Income) + a_3 (P_{substitute}), \tag{17.5}$$

where Q and P are the quantity purchased and relative price, respectively, of a particular resource, *Income* is often measured as real income per capita (or per household) and $P_{substitute}$ is the relative price of a substitute good or service. Each coefficient, a_1, thus represents the predicted change in quantity demanded associated with a unit change in the corresponding characteristic.

To graph a consumer demand curve, the coefficient of particular interest is a_1, which represents the predicted change in Q given a unit change in P. Multiple regression analysis, properly conducted, isolates the effects of the other specified variables on quantity demanded. For example, an individual's large quantity demand might reflect a high personal income rather than a relatively low resource price. Or, the price of a substitute might have increased to a high level, encouraging a large demand for the resource. Statistically removing such effects sharpens the estimation of the coefficient, a_1. In comparison, a simple (bivariate) demand regression, relating quantity demanded only to price, obtains a less precise coefficient estimate.

To facilitate a numerical example of a market demand curve, this discussion explores a simple regression estimation. Consider again the hypothetical example introduced in Chapter 5, where a government policy has supported a larger fish population and in turn an increased commercial fish catch for a number of years. These benefits are measured by society's Total WTP for the additional fish caught each year due to the policy.

Suppose the analyst gathers several years of data and determines the additional thousands of pounds of fish caught as a result of the policy. The additional annual fish catch (Q), expressed in thousands of pounds, is regressed on the measured dock-side price per pound (P) over time. Thus, a *time-series analysis* is performed. To illustrate, suppose a simple regression equation is estimated as

$$Q = 20 - 2P. \tag{17.6}$$

Figure 17.1
Market Demand Curve

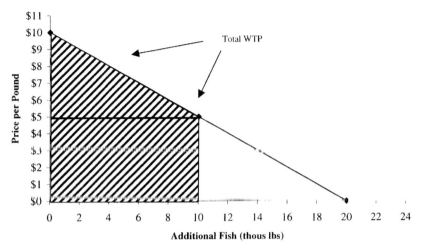

Additional Fish (thous lbs)

The regression coefficient, a_1, is thus -2. The negative sign reflects the negative relationship that economic theory expects between consumer demand and market prices. Specifically, it implies that as price increases, quantity demanded declines, all other variables held constant (i.e., *ceteris paribus*). In other words, consumers buy less of the additional fish catch at high prices and more at low prices. The numerical value of the coefficient, -2, means that for every dollar increase in the dock-side price per pound, consumers are willing to buy two thousand fewer pounds of the additional fish each year.

Regression equation 17.6 is used to predict annual quantity demanded for different prices. For example, if the price is $2 per pound, then substituting $2 for P in the equation (so $Q = 20 - 2 * 2$) predicts consumers will purchase sixteen thousand pounds of the additional fish each year. A *demand schedule* of alternative price and quantity combinations can easily be calculated. A demand schedule for his regression is listed as follows:

P ($/lb.):	$10	$8	$6	$4	$2	$0
Q (thousand lbs.):	0	4	8	12	16	20.

These P and Q combinations can be plotted graphically as points to form a market demand curve. Figure 17.1 shows a linear demand curve that connects and passes through these point combinations. (The reader might note this is an extended version of the demand curve shown in Figure 5.1.) Consider the last P, Q combination in the list. If the fish are available at a zero dockside price, then consumers would want 20 thousand pounds of the additional fish each year. Note that 20 is also the value of the constant, a_0 in equation 17.6. Given the convention in economics of graphing a demand curve with price (the independent variable) on the vertical axis and quantity (the dependent variable) on the horizontal axis, this is the curve's horizontal intercept.[2]

Total WTP, the sum of consumers' total expenditures and consumer surplus, is represented graphically as an area under the demand curve. Suppose the market price is $5. As shown in the graph, the predicted quantity demanded is 10,000 pounds of additional fish. Total WTP is the area under the curve from the origin out to 10,000 pounds (see the lined area in Figure 17.1). Consumers' total expenditures are the rectangle, PQ (or $5 per pound by 10,000 pounds), and consumer surplus is the triangular area above the market price of $5. The total area is the sum of $50,000 and $25,000 ($\frac{1}{2}$ * 10,000 * $5). Thus, society's valuation of the additional fish catch is an estimated $75,000 each year.

Principle 17.1. For a marketed resource, good or service, society's Total WTP is the sum of consumers' total expenditures and consumer surplus. Total WTP is calculated by applying multiple regression analysis to estimate market demand and computing the relevant area under the demand curve.

MULTIPLE REGRESSION ANALYSIS: AN OVERVIEW

Multiple regression analysis provides a very useful technique for estimating the total benefits for a marketed resource. Care and caution are warranted, however, in its application and interpretation, as regression analysis is a highly sophisticated statistical technique. The expertise of a professional skilled in performing the analysis is required. In addition, the decision maker and other interested parties must have a general understanding of what statistical measures to look for in order to make even the most basic assessment of a reported regression estimation. For this reason, this section provides a brief overview of several technical considerations. For greater detail, the interested reader is referred to any of the numerous econometrics and statistics texts (available from beginning to advanced levels) that address the subject.

Regression analysis is a statistical method that allows predictions of one (dependent) variable from one or more specified (independent) variables. To enable these predictions, the most basic technique, *ordinary least squares* (OLS),[3] analyzes the chosen variables' data and finds the regression line that "best fits," by minimizing the sum of squared deviations of the observed data around the line (i.e., the *least squares method*).

Once the regression coefficients are estimated, several statistics are examined to assess the validity, goodness of fit and likely accuracy of the regression equation.

1. Each *regression coefficient's sign* should be compared with economic theory, or logic, to appraise its validity. For instance, for equation 17.6, the sign for P's coefficient is negative, which is consistent with economic theory's expectation that as P increases, Q decreases. This provides evidence in support of

the validity of the estimated regression equation. In a multiple regression, the sign for every "partial" regression coefficient is similarly checked.

2. Hypothesis tests are performed on each *regression coefficient* to determine whether it is *statistically significant* (or *significantly different from zero*). In other words, for equation 17.6, the coefficient for P is -2. Given sampling variability, it is theoretically possible to obtain this result; yet in actuality, no relationship exists between the fish prices and quantities demanded and thus the true (population) coefficient is zero. What is the probability of a regression analysis of sample data obtaining a coefficient as deviant as 2, when the true population coefficient is zero? A statistical t-test can be performed to find the probability for the coefficient. If the probability is below some designated *level of significance* (often .05, although .01 or .10 is sometimes used), then the likelihood is considered so low that the analyst concludes that the coefficient is statistically significant and thus different from zero. In a multiple regression, a similar t-test should be performed for every regression coefficient.

3. The data for the independent variables in a multiple regression might be highly correlated. This *multicollinearity* is a sample phenomenon. Economic theory may postulate that for the population, all of the independent variables have a separate, independent influence on Q; yet, for a particular sample, some or all of the measured variables may be too highly correlated with each other to permit estimation of each variable's separate effect. The correlation coefficients between every two independent variables can be inspected to determine whether multicollinearity is a sizable problem. Rough rules of thumb are used. While in some fields the cut-off indicating too much multicollinearity is a correlation coefficient with absolute value exceeding .50, in economics the acceptable cut-off is often higher (at .70 or .80). When two independent variables are found to be highly correlated, then the regression coefficients cannot correctly separate and measure each variable's effect on Q. The main solution is to drop one of the two variables from the equation and reestimate the coefficients.

4. The *coefficient of multiple determination* (R^2) is often used as a summary measure of how closely the regression equation fits the data. Specifically, R^2 ranges in value from 0 to 1 and measures the proportion of total variability in Q that is predicted by the regression equation. R^2 can be used to compare the "closeness of fit" of different regression equations and select the one with the closest fit. Also, R^2 can be adjusted for the number of independent variables in the equation. Despite the popular use of R^2, this *adjusted* R^2 is the preferred statistic for assessing and comparing the "fit" of the regression equation to the data.

5. An F statistic can be calculated for the regression equation to test the statistical significance of R^2 and determine whether R^2 is significantly different from zero. The F test (or *goodness of fit test*) tests the hypothesis that in actuality, the population Q is unrelated to all of the specified independent variables. If indeed this is the case, what is the probability, given sampling variability, of

getting this specific F statistic? If the probability is below some designated level of significance (usually .05), then the analyst concludes that the equation as a whole is statistically significant.

6. When applying the regression equation to make predictions of the dependent variable (Q in the market demand equation), the likely size error is indicated by the *standard error of estimate*, which measures the variability (standard deviation) of the observed data around the regression line. In simpler terms, it measures the approximate average error. Thus, for example, for equation 17.6, if the standard error is 1, then when P is $2, the prediction that Q is 16 thousand pounds involves on average an error of approximately $\pm$ 1 thousand pounds.

In addition, a *residual plot*, a graphical scatterplot of the residuals (or errors) for each of the predicted Q's for the sample data should be examined to see if there are any patterns. This practice can help detect several different problems in the regression estimation.

7. *Specification bias* is said to exist when the regression is incorrectly specified, either with an inappropriate functional form or the omission of important variables. The variables included in the equation should be directly examined to see if any theoretically important variables are omitted. In addition, a visual look at the residual plot can check for systematic patterns suggesting misspecification of the equation. If found, then the regression coefficients are inaccurately estimated, and the equation needs to be respecified.

8. The residual plot can also be checked to see if each frequency distribution of residuals has the same spread or standard error (indicating, as assumed in the analysis, these are *homoscedastic*). If not, *heteroscedasticity* exists and the regression estimates are not accurate. In such a case, the problem can be corrected with sophisticated statistical procedures.

9. In time-series analysis, a *Durbin-Watson* statistic can identify whether successive residuals vary in value in a random (independent) manner, or instead, whether there is a systematic pattern (and thus *autocorrelation* or *serial correlation*) between successive residuals, indicating they are not independent. The Durbin-Watson statistic ranges in value from 0 to 4. If the calculated Durbin-Watson statistic is 2, there is zero autocorrelation, and the residuals are randomly distributed. A value less than 2 suggests positive autocorrelation (a value less than 1 identifies a substantial degree of positive autocorrelation). A value between 2 and 4 indicates negative autocorrelation (more than 3, a substantial degree). Autocorrelation denotes values for one time period are correlated (positively or negatively) to values in another time period, resulting in inaccurate estimation of the regression coefficients. Sophisticated regression techniques are required to correct for serious autocorrelation.

As the reader can see, a number of technical details must be considered when reviewing any reported regression's results. Thus, caution is advised not to accept a regression estimation at face value, but rather to seek relevant statistics summarizing the regression equation's technical dimensions.

SHADOW PRICES

Regression analysis offers a sophisticated empirical technique for estimating market demand and, in turn, society's value of a marketed resource. However, if the resource's market is characterized by government price ceilings, taxes or unemployment, then adjustments in the valuation estimation are needed to determine the resource's true value to society. Ideally, the resource's *shadow price*, the price that would be observed in the market without these distortions, is estimated. Let's consider each case.

1. Suppose an effective maximum price (or *price ceiling*) constrains the market. Then, according to basic economic theory, the market price is artificially held below the demand curve. The analyst should estimate the shadow price, and in turn, the true consumer demand to find society's Total WTP.

2. If *taxes*, such as a sales tax, increase the amount consumers pay for the resource, these should be incorporated along with the observed (pretax) market price, to estimate Total WTP.

3. Suppose a market is characterized by *unemployment* or *underemployment*. Consider, for example, the labor market. The social cost of hiring workers is each worker's opportunity cost, or foregone wages from alternative employment. Despite the existence of unemployment, if the particular laborers hired would otherwise be employed, then the full wages paid count as social costs of the policy. Alternatively, if the hired laborers would otherwise be underemployed, then their opportunity cost in the form of foregone wages (the true social value) is less than the paid wage. The market wage should thus be adjusted to estimate the true *shadow wage rate*. Or, instead, if the laborers would otherwise be unemployed, then their opportunity cost is zero. Caution is prescribed, however, as it must be reasonably evident that the hired labor would not otherwise be employed during the entire policy time horizon. Only then can a zero shadow wage rate be used in the analysis.[4] If a positive probability exists that the unemployed worker might eventually find other work during the time horizon, then the wage rate should be adjusted accordingly. (The same reasoning applies to the land, capital and other resource markets that might be characterized by unemployment.)

In actuality for each of these cases, the difficulties of determining the true shadow price can be quite challenging. Thus, for all practical purposes, the analyst should consider economic theory's indication as to whether the shadow price is expected to be above or below the market price and use detailed information about the market to identify a possible (reasonable) range of values for the true shadow price. Some level of analytical judgment is required. Therefore, given the uncertain value of the shadow price, the analyst should employ a *selective sensitivity analysis*, with the actual market price providing the upper or lower bound as indicated by theory, and two possible shadow prices selected as the likely value and the other bound at the opposite end of the range (Sassone and Schaffer 1978: 50–51, 64, 66).

Principle 17.2. When price ceilings, taxes or unemployment characterize a market, then selective sensitivity analysis is recommended, with adjustments in market values to reflect possible shadow prices.

CONCLUSION

Valuation of marketed resources is facilitated by the availability of market prices. Regression analysis estimating consumer demand enables a calculation of society's Total WTP, including consumer surplus along with consumer expenditures. However, when price ceilings, taxes or unemployment characterize a market, then performance of selective sensitivity analysis is recommended, allowing adjustments for shadow pricing.

Another circumstance that warrants shadow pricing is when a marketed resource generates a technological externality. In addition to the market valuation, conducted as described in this chapter, shadow prices for the externality might be estimated using one of the alternative valuation techniques, contingent valuation, travel cost method, property valuation or human life valuation. These are the respective topics of the next four chapters.

NOTES

1. Both demand curves represent the relationship between price and quantity. The difference is that the Hicksian demand curve "compensates" for the changes in buyer income that result from price changes and thus traces the association between changing price and quantity while holding consumer utility constant. The theoretical derivation of this demand curve yields four measures of consumer surplus. These include *compensating variation*, the minimum amount the consumer must be compensated for a price change to maintain the same level of utility and *equivalent variation*, the maximum amount the consumer would be willing to pay to avoid a price change and keep utility constant, along with respective parallel concepts, *compensating surplus* and *equivalent surplus*, when quantity is also held constant (as is the case in reality for many public goods). In contrast, the Marshallian demand curve simply relates quantity demanded to changing market prices with no adjustment for the "income effect." The interested reader can consult any of a number of advanced microeconomics or cost-benefit analysis texts (for example, see Hanley and Spash 1993) that explain consumer welfare theory in detail.

2. If a multiple (rather than bivariate) regression is performed, the P and Q combinations are generated by plugging into the multivariate equation alternative values of P along with the mean data values for the other demand characteristics. For each P, the equation is solved for the predicted Q. The various P and Q combinations are then plotted as points to form a demand curve.

3. A number of other techniques, including maximum likelihood, Box-Cox transformation, other nonlinear techniques, logit, probit and tobit, are also available for application.

4. It might be argued, reasonably, that if a worker is otherwise unemployed, the opportunity cost is foregone leisure time. Theoretically, leisure can be valued by observing

or asking how much individuals would spend to save leisure time. However, a common practice is to use unemployment payments to value leisure; and since these are transfers, and thus also represent government costs, in net, they yield a zero shadow wage (Schofield 1987: 58).

Chapter 18

Contingent Valuation Method

INTRODUCTION

Suppose a policy preserves a natural resource or species, improves water quality, enhances a scenic view, increases recreational opportunities or generates some other nonmarket effect or technological externality that, by definition, is not priced in a market. One technique that might be applied to value such technological externalities is the *contingent valuation method*. A survey asks individuals to imagine a market exists for a particular resource, good or service and, contingent upon this hypothetical market, to state their valuation of the associated benefits and costs.

Principle 18.1. To value nonmarket effects or technological externalities, the contingent valuation method asks survey respondents to state their preferences hypothetically, indicating their valuation as if a market for the particular resource, good or service actually exists.

Since its development, application of the method has received much scrutiny (both favorable and critical) from academic economists and, in recent years, government, legal, corporate and environmental interests. An understanding of the issues is crucial to appreciating the care that must be devoted to the successful design, implementation and interpretation of a contingent valuation survey.

Similar to other sample surveys, a suitable sample must be selected and an appropriate survey instrument chosen. In addition, a contingent valuation survey involves three other components. First, a hypothetical market scenario provides information simulating market conditions for the resource, good or service in question. Second, valuation question(s) are asked to elicit individual preferences. The most frequently asked valuation question concerns the individual's *maximum willingness to pay* (WTP) to receive a benefit (or reduced cost) from the resource, good or service. Third, additional information is gathered about respondents' characteristics and preferences; statistical analysis of these traits can test the validity and reliability of WTP responses as well as sharpen estimation of the aggregate WTP.

The chapter begins with a historical overview of the academic and real-world discussions concerning the method's validity and reliability. Then it addresses each of the method components, presenting the various choices that must be made in designing and interpreting the survey and considering the potential biases or other difficulties that might be encountered. Several principles for crafting a well-designed survey are recommended.

CONTINGENT VALUATION'S VALIDITY AND RELIABILITY: HISTORICAL OVERVIEW

From the method's initial formulation and continuing to the present day, lively discourse has surrounded contingent valuation's application in valuing economic preferences. For many years, academic discussions in economics debated contingent valuation's validity and reliability in estimating use values. Then in the 1970s, the method's application expanded to include non-use (or passive-use) values. By the late 1980s, some federal government agencies as well as the courts accepted the method's assessments of polluter liabilities for natural resource damages (including lost non-use values). Given the financial and other stakes involved, the method has come under intense scrutiny, not only within the academic community but also in the "real world" by legislators, regulators, lawyers, corporations and environmentalists. In order to understand the issues, this section overviews the discussions, beginning first with the earlier academic debate concerning contingent use values.

Use Values: Academic Discussion

At the heart of the academic debate is the method's elicitation of hypothetical statements—an approach differing from the usual economic techniques. Traditionally, economic analysis has focused on measuring consumer preferences by observing actual behavior in private markets. When seeking to value nonmarket effects, a logical step would be to develop techniques to measure *revealed preferences*, that is, inferring nonmarket values either directly or indirectly from observed market behavior. Contingent valuation departs from these approaches by focusing on *stated preferences*. Can hypothetical statements (rather than actual, observed human behavior) provide valid and reliable estimates of economic preferences? This is the key question underlying the academic discussion. As for the answer, some economists are convinced the method is invalid and unreliable, while others believe that appropriate, well-designed survey instruments can provide valid, reliable information about individual preferences. Given the degree to which contingent valuation diverges from the conventional approach, it is not surprising that much debate has surrounded the technique's application since its inception.

The method originated with an idea expressed by Ciriacy-Wantrup (1947: 1189) followed nearly two decades later by the first known application (Davis 1963). Since then, hundreds of contingent valuation studies have been performed. The large number published suggests many in the economics profession are confident in this survey technique. However, the studies have applied different levels of sophistication, yielding a variability that has only added fuel to the academic debate. In response, several publications (most notably, Cummings, Brookshire and Schulze 1986; and a comprehensive reference text, Mitchell and Carson 1989) provide extensive information to facilitate the careful design, implementation and interpretation of contingent valuation surveys. Together, these establish a foundation enabling the method to evolve into maturity.

The debate focuses attention on an important consideration in designing a survey, specifically whether the survey method is valid and reliable. The survey technique can be considered *valid* if it measures what it claims, in this case, the respondents' actual valuation of the specified resource, good or service. In other words, a survey's validity reflects the degree to which survey measurements are free of systematic error or bias. *Reliability* refers to the method's consistency, that is, whether repeat applications of the method can measure the same value. Reliability is the lack of random error in measurements (Drummond, Stoddart and Torrance 1987: 117–18; Weiers 1988: 163).

There are four ways the validity of contingent valuation surveys might be checked (Mitchell and Carson 1989: 189–209). First, the content of the survey's scenario and questions can be assessed qualitatively to judge its appropriateness (*content validity*). Second, *criterion validity* is determined by comparing survey results with actual behavior. This, however, is difficult for nonmarketed resources, goods and services. Instead, a small number of studies have performed experiments, undertaking contingent valuation surveys for private market goods, and then comparing consumers' hypothetical responses with actual buying behavior. So far, the conclusions are mixed (Diamond and Hausman 1994: 54; Hanemann 1994: 30–31), and additional experiments are needed. Third, survey results might be compared with other methods' estimates to assess *convergent validity*. In a meta-analysis, Carson and associates examine 83 studies that compare hundreds of contingent use values with estimates obtained from revealed preference methods. They find a strong correlation between the two sets of estimates, with the contingent values ''smaller, but not grossly smaller'' than the revealed preference estimates overall (1996: 93). These comparisons indicate a convergence of the various methods' estimates, suggesting the general validity of both contingent and revealed preference use values. Fourth, WTP responses can be statistically related to various respondent characteristics to check for consistency with theoretical expectations (*theoretical validity*). This is an increasingly common practice in contingent valuation studies.

Reliability might be assessed with several approaches. To see the degree to which the results are repeatable, the same respondents might be questioned more than once with the identical survey (*test-retest* technique) and/or the survey might be administered to different large samples (*interpenetrating sampling*). As Mitchell and Carson note, however, these two approaches are expensive, and thus individual contingent valuation surveys are more likely to employ alternative techniques. First, regression analysis is increasingly performed to determine the coefficient of multiple determination (R^2) and measure the unexplained variability (randomness and thus possible "noise") in a survey sample's responses. Second, a clear, realistic survey enhances reliability; thus, the designer often pretests the scenario and survey questions. Third, a number of contingent valuation surveys undertake split-sample tests to check specific survey components; a modified survey is issued to different subsamples, and the responses are compared to determine their sensitivity to the survey changes. Fourth, sample size can be increased to improve the estimation's precision. Fifth, outliers can be statistically identified and removed to generate a more reliable estimate (1989: 212–29).

All together, great strides have been taken in establishing the validity and reliability of carefully designed contingent valuation surveys in estimating use values. With these steps in progress, a new application during the 1970s foreshadowed an added dimension for debate.

Non-use Values: Real World and Academic Discussion

In the 1970s, the contingent valuation method was applied to estimate non-use (i.e., passive-use or existence) values. *Non-use value*, by definition, is the value received by an individual who wishes to preserve a natural resource simply to sustain its existence, quantity or quality unrelated to use of the resource. Non-use values are thus not associated with behavioral activities. These values can possibly be estimated by contingent valuation, which elicits individual valuations under hypothetical conditions, but not by revealed preference methods that analyze individual behavior expressed in markets.

Principle 18.2. Contingent valuation is the only systematic method offering the potential for estimating non-use values.

In some cases donations to appropriate environmental organizations may provide information concerning non-use values. However, as Freeman notes, three difficulties may be encountered. First, if a charitable organization provides a magazine, calendar, notecards or other private goods to its contributors, then it is not apparent how much of the donation reflects a WTP for the environmental resource as opposed to the private goods. Second, contributions may reveal the donor's desire to preserve or enhance a resource for future use rather than for non-use value. Third, some individuals are expected by economic theory to be *free riders*, choosing to donate less than the non-use (and use) values they receive (1993a: 158–59).

The application of contingent valuation to estimate non-use values was initially confined to the academic literature. Sizable estimates, however, suggested non-use values should not be ignored in any comprehensive assessment of unique environmental resources. Then, during the mid-to-late 1980s and early 1990s, both the arena of discussion and the political and financial stakes involved in the application of contingent valuation expanded considerably. Two federal regulatory agencies, a court decision and the extensive Exxon Valdez accident focused the attention of "real world" legislators, regulators, lawyers, corporations and environmental groups on the possible inclusion of lost non-use (or passive-use) values in the assessment of natural resource damages in liability cases.

In 1986, the Department of the Interior (DOI) issued regulations specifying the compensable damages and permissible valuation techniques for assessing damages from hazardous material emissions, in compliance with the 1980 Comprehensive Environmental Response, Compensation, and Liability Act (CERCLA), commonly known as the Superfund law. The new regulations provided qualified acceptance of both the contingent valuation method and recovery of lost non-use values (specifically, non-use values counted only if use values could not be measured). A legal challenge resulted in a 1989 decision by the District of Columbia Court of Appeals[1] that directed the DOI to alter the regulations to count non-use values in addition to use values and to accept "more seriously" the contingent valuation method as a damage estimation technique (Portney 1994: 7).

Then in March 1989 the *Exxon Valdez* spilled oil off the coast of Alaska. For this discussion, the accident had two implications. First, the size of Exxon's liability received notable scrutiny. Aware of the new regulations for hazardous materials, corporations and environmentalists considered the prospect that if Exxon had been required to compensate for lost non-use (or passive-use) values, its already extensive liability would have increased considerably. Representing competing viewpoints, these groups took an interest in the contingent valuation method's validity and reliability. Second, the oil spill focused the nation's attention on the risks of natural resource damages resulting from ocean-going supertankers. Accordingly, Congress passed the Oil Pollution Act of 1990, which included provisions for the government to recover compensation from the relevant oil company for future oil spill damages. The National Oceanic and Atmospheric Administration (NOAA) was assigned a task paralleling that of the DOI: to develop regulations concerning damage assessment for oil spills. Recognizing the economists' debate, as well as the political stakes, NOAA appointed an advisory expert panel to assess contingent valuation's reliability in estimating lost non-use values as part of natural resource damage assessment (Portney 1994: 8).

The academic debate, meanwhile, had expanded to address whether the contingent valuation method could estimate non-use values with validity and reliability. Although contingent non-use values cannot be compared with estimates obtained by revealed preference methods or actual economic behavior, experiments are possible. A small number have been performed, creating artificial situations to compare actual and hypothetical donations[2] to support a specified environmental cause. So far, the results are mixed (Hanemann 1994: 31), and additional experiments are needed to draw conclusions. More applicable for specific non-use estimates is to assess content validity (qualitative judgment of the survey content) and theoretical validity (statistical analysis of the valuation responses). As for reliability, contingent valuation surveys can apply regression analysis and inspect the R^2, ensure sufficient sample size, remove outliers and undertake survey pretests and split-sample tests.

In assessing the contingent valuation method, the NOAA panel considered the published literature and listened to experts from both sides of the controversy. The panel's report, submitted to NOAA in January 1993, determined that a survey conducted according to a carefully specified series of guidelines can "convey useful information" for damage assessment. "Thus, the Panel concludes that CV studies can produce estimates reliable enough to be the starting point of a judicial process of damage assessment, including lost passive-use values. . . . [A] well-conducted CV study . . . contains information that judges and juries will wish to use, in combination with other evidence, including the testimony of expert witnesses" (Arrow et al. 1993: 4610–11).

The following year, NOAA proposed and DOI reproposed regulations encouraging or requiring compliance with a number of the advisory panel's recommended guidelines.[3] Not surprisingly, contingent valuation's opponents and proponents expressed differing views. Opponents are dismayed by the panel's support of the method's potential reliability,[4] while some proponents find the guidelines too stringent. The guidelines are ambitious; as one panel member later wrote: "the panel hoped to elevate considerably the quality of future studies." (Portney 1994: 10).

This chapter is in agreement with the NOAA panel's assessment that a carefully designed survey can be reliable. Surveying consumers' hypothetical statements may not be the traditional method of economics. However, the approach is regularly employed in market research to estimate the demand for new yet-to-be-marketed commercial products. Once a new product is introduced to the market, the research estimates can be compared with actual consumer behavior and generally are "moderate overestimates of actual willingness to pay" (Arrow et al. 1993: 4609). Such overstatements encourage greater attentiveness in research design, not an abandonment of market research. Moreover, extensive experience and knowledge have been gained by behavioral scientists in the field of survey research methods. Conscientious application of these survey techniques in the area of contingent valuation can provide relevant and useful information. Thus, our conviction is that the contingent valuation procedure, if suitably applied, is a worthwhile method for valuing numerous nonmarket effects (both use and non-use values). For this reason, as well as recognizing the disagreements about the method's validity and reliability, this chapter details several procedures for properly constructing a contingent valuation survey.

OVERVIEW OF THE SURVEY METHOD

Principle 18.3. The contingent valuation method consists of the following components:

* hypothetical market scenario
* sample selection
* survey instrument
* valuation question(s)
* valuation estimation
* response validity and reliability tests

The design or implementation of these components can involve three new characters. These include (1) the *survey designer*, who may or may not be the analyst; (2) *interviewers*, who conduct the interviews if in-person or phone survey instruments are employed; and (3) *respondents*, who are the individuals or participants, usually representing households, asked to answer the survey questions. Contingent valuation can be subjectively influenced by any of these individuals; thus, caution and awareness of the potential biases and influences in the contingent valuation method are clearly required.

In designing a contingent valuation survey, overriding concerns are to be clear, realistic and conservative.

Principle 18.4. The designer should construct a clear, realistic survey that appears plausible to respondents, while taking appropriate precautions whenever possible to be conservative and avoid overestimating economic values.

The chapter examines each component of a contingent valuation survey and in each case identifies various considerations, biases or problems that might be encountered. Several options the designer might apply to address these challenges and to devise a realistic and conservative survey are explored. The chapter's recommendations are generally consistent with the NOAA guidelines. However, at times, we present a wider range of options as specific circumstances may warrant a variation in the survey procedure. In the end, the survey designer must justify the choices made in planning a specific survey.

In addition, the designer should assess the survey's content and theoretical validity with qualitative judgment and statistical analysis, respectively. He can also appraise or enhance survey reliability by checking a regression equation's R^2, ensuring sufficient sample size, removing outlier responses and applying survey pretests and split-sample tests. Moreover, the survey designer should verify the lack of bias or other problems; and wherever a particular influence remains, the report should explain the likely effect on the final valuation.

Principle 18.5. The survey designer must justify the design of a specific survey and assess the survey's validity and reliability.

HYPOTHETICAL MARKET SCENARIO

Introduction

At the beginning of a contingent valuation survey, a *hypothetical market scenario* is presented to the respondent. This scenario is comprised of information specifying the conditions under which the hypothetical market operates for the nonmarketed resource, good or service. Such a scenario is necessary to enable the respondent to state preferences (contingent values). Key is to make the scenario, though hypothetical, sufficiently realistic and informative to enhance respondent accuracy. As a number of influences might affect a respondent's answer, the scenario must be devised carefully. The discussion examines several considerations for designing a hypothetical scenario, including the information to provide and the relevant biases and problems to address, along with the need for pretests and follow-up questions to assess the scenario.

Six Considerations

Principle 18.6. The hypothetical market scenario should be designed with consideration of the following possible influences on respondents' answers: hypothetical valuation, information presented, incremental valuation, embedding problem, strategic bias and payment vehicle bias.

1. *Hypothetical valuation.* Since respondents do not actually pay (or receive) the values they indicate, the respondents' stated valuations based on hypothetical conditions may differ from their actual market behavior. One of the main challenges for the scenario is to engage respondents in a careful, thoughtful process so that their hypothetical responses are as close as possible to reflecting what they would actually do if a market really existed. A statement such as the following might be presented to the respondent.

- We would like to ask you to indicate your valuation of the proposed policy under hypothetical conditions, assuming a market exists. We understand that the valuation process may seem unnatural, but we would nonetheless ask that you think seriously and carefully about your response. This hypothetical market valuation is one way we can gather relevant data. Thus, it is very important for your response to reflect what you would actually do if a market really existed.

In addition, the survey should include follow-up questions to determine whether respondents take the valuation process seriously.

2. *Information presented.* Respondent answers are influenced by the amount and quality of information provided in the hypothetical market scenario, coupled with the respondents' interpretation of that information. If respondents have no personal experience using a particular resource or site, for example, misperceptions may influence their answers. The survey designer must take care to provide sufficient information to make the scenario plausible and realistic as well as to ensure appropriate interpretation by each respondent.

3. *Incremental valuation.* The objective of the hypothetical market scenario is to simulate actual market conditions. In reality, markets value goods and services at the *margin*, pricing individual units of a particular resource. To approximate this incremental valuation, respondents must either have prior experience varying the quantity (or quality) of the resource, or they must learn how to do so during the survey, perhaps from the scenario presentation. For instance, Schulze and associates valued incremental changes in visibility at the Grand Canyon associated with varying degrees of air pollution. Respondents were shown five photographs depicting different visibility levels (in increasing order) and asked to value the improved visibility between select paired photographs (1983).

Another interesting example is suggested by Mitchell and Carson's study measuring the value of water quality. Interviewers showed respondents a diagram picturing a "water-quality ladder," with ascending rungs representing improved quality. Select ladder rungs were associated with water designated as safe for boating, fishing, swimming or drinking, respectively. Each respondent was asked to indicate the maximum willingness to pay for each quality level, allowing the analyst to infer the respondent's incremental valuation for improvements from one water quality level to the next (1986: App. A).

4. *Embedding problem.* The estimates obtained by some contingent valuation studies suggest that total willingness to pay does not increase with the quantity (scale or scope) of the resource, good or service—a relationship inconsistent with rational choice. For a hypothetical example, suppose two studies estimate a region's willingness to pay for saving the lives of sea otters from a severe oil spill. One survey mentions saving 500 while the other asks about saving 100,000 sea otters, and they both estimate a total willingness to pay of around $1 million. Critics of the contingent valuation method assert that such results indicate the surveys are not really measuring willingness to pay for the specific resource, good or service, since surely saving a hundred times more otters is worth substantially greater value. Instead, it is claimed, the obtained survey responses reflect the respondents' approval of the policy "embedded" with a "warm glow" from giving. In other words, similar to charitable donations, the valuation

(in part or in total) is measuring the pleasure of giving to a worthy cause—perhaps *any* worthy cause—rather than a valuation of a particular policy to save a specific number of sea otter lives.

Critics claim that such an *embedding phenomenon* or *problem* exists and complicates the task of estimating willingness to pay (economic valuation) for the specific policy in question. Some supporters of the contingent valuation method respond, in contrast, that such survey results are not indicative of any so-called embedding problem, but rather reflect shortcomings in the specific studies, which did not present the alternative sizes or scales clearly. In either case, the task for a contingent valuation survey is to summon responses valuing the specific policy given its quantified consequences rather than any "warm glow" from the pleasure of giving. In accord with a NOAA panel recommendation (Arrow et al. 1993: 4614), the survey needs to present to respondents the relevant substitutes, which may well include not only alternative policies for reducing oil spill damages but also other charitable activities (e.g., reducing global warming, preserving rainforest habitat) that might create a "warm glow" effect.[5]

5. *Strategic bias.* Strategic bias occurs when respondents overstate or understate their true valuations in an effort to alter the conclusion of the analysis. For instance, suppose recreational fishers have clamored for the last five years over the increased pollution that has invaded freshwater Loon Lake, killing a once-thriving large-mouth bass population. Assume the county government will sponsor a proposed cleanup and bass-stocking program only if respondents place a sufficiently high value on the improvements. If asked, a local bass fisher might strategically overstate the policy's value in order to regain the lake's large-mouth bass population. At the same time, neighboring property owners who live on the lake may not want a dirty, polluted lake, but they might prefer to avoid the increase in traffic and mayhem arising from recreational fishers visiting the lake. Accordingly, they may understate the policy's value. Such strategic responses could notably alter survey estimates. A task for the survey designer is to structure the survey analysis to reduce the role of such strategies.

To reduce strategic bias, the analyst might be able to include appropriate statements in the hypothetical scenario. For example, Hammack and Brown, in a much cited waterfowl hunting questionnaire, provided assurances to the respondents that their replies would not strategically influence policy decisions (1974: 202). In the Loon Lake example, if the goal is to value the improved water quality and proposed stocking as part of a valuation study, without any specific real-world policy being considered for possible implementation, a similar disclaimer might also be effective. However, once the scenario states that a particular government proposal is under consideration, the potential influence of strategic answers is apparent to all. In this case, the analyst needs to alter other aspects of the survey design to control for strategic bias.

6. *Payment vehicle bias.* The *payment vehicle* is the method of payment used hypothetically to pay the stated value. Possibilities include taxes, market prices,

utility bills, user fees and the like. In order for valuation questions to seem realistic to respondents, it is important for the analyst to select a payment vehicle that respondents associate with the change being valued. For example, taxes are sometimes paid to cover water-pollution control expenses; thus, respondents might be asked to value additional water quality in terms of higher taxes.

The choice of payment vehicle, however, may influence respondent answers (known as *payment vehicle bias*), for respondents may be sensitive to the selected method. As an example, suppose the survey does ask for the respondent's willingness to pay in higher taxes. A respondent who is very upset about paying high taxes might respond negatively to the thought of paying even one extra tax dollar for the particular benefit being valued; yet if asked about the willingness to pay a $1 entrance fee or $1 surcharge on an electricity bill for the same benefit, the respondent might reply positively. The analyst thus needs to be careful to select a payment vehicle that does not give rise to such bias. To test for payment vehicle bias, studies can vary the payment method and see if the average (mean) bid changes.

Information to Include

In developing a hypothetical scenario, several specific areas of information should be included to portray a market-like situation effectively. These are listed here.

1. *Describe the resource, good or service* affected by the policy. The scenario should be as specific as is practical. For instance, it is not adequate to talk of "fish" if the questions refer to a game species such as large-mouth bass; at the same time, the scenario need not detail the many biological characteristics of the species.

2. *Describe the incremental change* in the resource, good or service resulting from the policy. The survey designer must consider by what size increment to vary the quantity or quality of the resource and then ensure the respondent is thinking in terms of the same incremental unit when determining values. If the policy is to stock a body of water with fish, for example, the description might specify the precise (incremental) quantity of fish to be stocked if this information is likely to be meaningful to respondents; or it might be sufficient to indicate that a currently barren lake will be well-stocked with the fish.

3. *Describe the specific site or geographic location.* The scenario should provide the respondent with a clear impression of the geographic area or location of the resource, good or service.

4. *Displays might be presented* to augment the respondent's image of the resource, good or service or the specific site. The survey designer should consider the possibility of employing displays with some caution, however. While displays can effectively present information, their "dramatic nature," especially in the case of photographs, "may have much more emotional impact than the rest of the questionnaire" (Arrow et al. 1993: 4612).

5. *Discuss the characteristics and quality of experience* associated with the resource, good or service. Specifically, identify opportunities that might change for the respondent (or others) and describe relevant characteristics of the geographical area or site, such as congestion, environmental quality and facilities, as well as any other aspect that would impact a user's experience or non-user's perception.

6. *State the duration* of the policy impact or user's experience. Whether it be years, months, days, hours or minutes, the survey should be very clear about how long the relevant impact or experience will last.

7. *Describe the substitutes or alternatives already in existence and available to the respondent.* To approximate a realistic market situation, the scenario should explicitly identify existing, already available substitutes. For instance, if alternative sites offer a very similar resource, good or service, these should be specified. As an example, when valuing beach preservation, the miles of nearby and more distant beach shorelines might be indicated. If the respondent does not consider available alternatives, the stated valuation may be larger than otherwise. Indeed, according to NOAA panel guidelines, a list of substitutes should be presented "directly prior" to asking the valuation question to encourage respondents to consider the available options when determining their valuation for the designated policy (Arrow et al. 1993: 4608–9).

8. *Identify the specific payment vehicle* (or method of payment, e.g., taxes, utility bills, seasonal license fees) and whether this is a one-time-only payment or a repeated payment (monthly, seasonally, annually, per trip). The vehicle should be familiar to the respondent.

9. *Indicate that payments collected will be used solely to finance the designated policy.* As respondents may not believe that the monies will really be allocated and spent where indicated, reassurance is necessary (Hufschmidt et al. 1983: 235).

10. Respondents may also want to know *how much others in the community are going to pay*, as they do not want to pay more than their fair share for benefits (or reduced costs) that are advantageous for the general society (OECD 1994: 112). Accordingly, the scenario might stipulate, for example, that everyone else (e.g., taxpayers, resource users) will pay the same price as the respondent.

11. *Remind* the respondent that *a willingness to pay* for the resource, good or service is determined within the context of his or her budget constraint and *involves foregoing other expenditures*. Other expenditure options should be considered by the respondent as part of recognizing a finite budget constraint. Indeed, the respondent might be asked to think in terms of which current or possible future expenses he or she would choose to reduce when deciding how much to pay for the policy under discussion (Arrow et al. 1993: 4605).

12. *Specify that other expenditure options include paying for alternative hypothetical scenarios for different nonmarket effects.* While a survey elicits values for one policy, say, to support a bass fishery in Loon Lake, in reality there are other opportunities and problems in the world to which the resources might be allocated. These can include stocking bass in some other water body, preserving endangered marine mammals, alleviating human hunger and so on, to name only a few. Respondents should be reminded of such alternatives, for when a specific policy is presented by itself, respondents are often willing to pay a few dollars—perhaps simply because asked

about a policy (any policy). It is not always evident they are consciously considering the value of the stated policy relative to other options (Arrow et al. 1993: 4605, 4613). By presenting a specific scenario within a broader context of alternative hypothetical scenarios, the survey encourages the respondents to be more realistic and conservative when expressing their values.

13. *Some scenarios might provide a real-world benchmark or anchor* indicating how much respondents currently pay per capita for corresponding kinds of goods or services or for alternative expenditure options. For some scenarios such information may be very important, as the respondent may not otherwise have any foundation for conceiving a realistic, meaningful valuation for the resource, good or service. Keeping in mind that a nonmarket effect is not priced in a market, the survey designer must consider on what basis the respondent can reasonably answer the valuation question posed. A caveat exists, however. By providing a benchmark, the survey might influence the respondents to answer with the anchor in mind, rather than their own individual valuation, thereby engendering *starting point bias*. Pretests using different benchmark values can check for such bias.

This section identifies information that should be detailed clearly and explicitly in a hypothetical market scenario. Providing sufficient information is key to helping the respondents understand exactly what they are being asked to value and thus enhances the survey's validity and reliability.

Pretests and Follow-Up Questions for the Hypothetical Market Scenario

The survey designer must ensure that the hypothetical scenario effectively presents information and that the respondents both understand and accept the scenario. The definition of "accept" warrants elaboration, for it means to acknowledge and believe fully the scenario's details (Arrow et al. 1993: 4605, 4613). In the Loon Lake example, for instance, the respondent might understand the proposed policy, yet think that without the policy fewer pollutants will enter the lake over time and the lake waters' assimilative capacity will improve water quality. Or, the respondent may believe that the proposed policy will be insufficient to improve water quality enough to allow a return of the bass fishery. In either case, the respondent undervalues the policy in contradiction to the information available to the government and analyst, for supposedly scientific studies indicate that without the policy the lake pollution will continue at high levels, but with the policy the pollution can be reduced to a level that supports a bass population.

Principle 18.7. To determine whether respondents have understood and accepted the scenario's details as well as to identify other influences on respondent answers, the survey designer should (1) pretest the hypothetical scenario (including any displays) and (2) include follow-up questions at the end of the survey.

The principle recommends two practices. First, pretests can allow the survey designer to alter the scenario and increase its effectiveness. Second, detailed follow-up questions during the survey should offer respondents the opportunity to criticize or disagree with any aspect of the scenario. Their comments can then provide the analyst with a basis for assessing the respondents' grasp of the scenario. If respondents do not understand and accept the information, then their answers are really valuing some other situation and thus are not reliable values for the scenario at hand. Such responses can then be eliminated from further analysis.

SAMPLE SELECTION

In designing any survey method, a decision must be made as to whom to survey. Surveying the entire population (or society) of interest is usually too expensive and is also prone to inaccuracy. Fortunately, probability sampling of a subset of individuals or households using well-accepted procedures can enable reasonably accurate generalizations about the population's WTP. In designing the sample, a professional statistician should be consulted. For smaller analyses, however, such services may be too expensive. Also, the decision maker and other interested parties must have a basic understanding to be able to assess an analysis once performed, for contingent valuation surveys and related subsample tests have sometimes been conducted with samples of insufficient size. For these reasons, this section explores two technical fundamentals: the appropriate sample size to achieve a specified degree of precision in estimating WTP and the implications of the nonresponse rate.

Precision and Sample Size

Precision can be defined as how close a sample's average (mean) WTP is to the population mean. With sampling variability, the mean WTP from any one sample is unlikely to be identical to the true population mean WTP. A measure of the sample's precision is the *error*, defined as the difference between the sample and population means. For a carefully executed probability sample, an increase in the number of individuals or households surveyed (i.e., the *sample size*) raises the likelihood of obtaining a sample mean closer to the population mean and thereby reducing the error. This relationship can be used to calculate the size sample needed to generate a designated allowable error.

Principle 18.8. In selecting a probability sample (whether simple random, stratified or clustered), the sample size can be determined to attain a desired degree of precision.

To estimate the sample size, n, of a *simple random sample*, three pieces of information are needed.

1. *Allowable error:* The decision maker should be asked how much error is allowable, in other words, the *desired maximum likely error, E*. Thus, the decision maker might designate that the sample mean should be within, say, $5, $10, $20, $50 or some other amount, of the true population mean WTP. The smaller the desired error, the larger is the required sample.

2. *Level of confidence: E* is the maximum *likely* error because there is always a positive probability of selecting a sample that errs more than the specified amount. Thus, the decision maker must also indicate the desired likelihood of obtaining a sample with an acceptable error, in other words, the level of confidence in the sampling procedure. Most commonly, a confidence level of 95% or 99%, or occasionally 90%, is set. (In statistical methods, the level can be represented with a z-score or student's t. For a confidence level of 95%, which is used in this discussion, $z = 1.96$.) The greater the desired confidence, the larger must be the sample.

3. *Population standard deviation*, σ: Within the population it would be most surprising to discover every individual is WTP the same dollar amount; thus the individual WTPs will undoubtedly vary. The greater the variability, the larger is the sample size needed for a desired level of precision. Variability can be measured by σ, the standard deviation of the individual WTPs around the population mean WTP. If unknown, σ might be approximated based on the estimated sample standard deviations (unbiased estimates of σ) reported by earlier studies. Without prior reliable estimates, professional judgment or small exploratory surveys (of maybe 50) might provide some information about σ (Weiers 1988: 136; Lind and Mason 1997: 244). Mitchell and Carson report that the variation in WTP tends to be greater for "large heterogeneous populations" with a "diversity of opinion," such as the national or general population, and smaller for "homogeneous subgroups, such as fishermen or hunters" (1989: 224 n.11).

Suppose the decision maker indicates an allowable error of $5 with a desired confidence level of 95% ($z = 1.96$). Also, based on prior contingent valuation studies, assume σ is believed to be $70. Then, the following statistical equation can be applied to determine the sample size, n.

$$n = \frac{Z^2 * \sigma^2}{E^2} = \frac{(1.96)^2 * (\$70)^2}{(\$5)^2} = 753. \tag{18.1}$$

Worth noting is that n is the number of usable sample responses; for the example, the survey designer should plan to select a random sample with enough individuals to obtain 753 usable responses. Equation 18.1 illustrates the relationship between the desired precision and n. If the allowable error is reduced to $2.50 (thus multiplied by $\frac{1}{2}$), then the requisite sample size, n, increases four times (by 2^2) to 3,012.

Equation 18.1, based on the *absolute allowable error*, is one equation that might be used. For WTP estimates, a similar equation using the *relative allowable error* may be of greater interest (Mitchell and Carson 1989: 224). The main reason is that as individual WTPs get larger, the variability of responses increases, making σ volatile. Thus, reasonable values for σ and E are hard to anticipate in advance of estimating the mean. A simple solution is to express both relative to the population mean.

First, the maximum likely error, E, is represented as a percentage (%E) or proportion (propE) of the population mean WTP. The decision maker is asked to indicate whether the sample mean should be within, say, 5%, 10%, 15% (or other) of the actual population mean. Mitchell and Carson suggest ''[r]easonable values'' for proportional E ''lie between .05 and .3'' (1989: 225 n.14).

Second, correspondingly, σ is converted to a percentage (or proportion) of the population mean, and the new term is called the *coefficient of variation* (V). Based on past contingent valuation studies, Mitchell and Carson report that V ''tends to be much more stable'' than σ (1989: 224); estimates of σ are ''almost always'' between .75 and 6 (225 n.13), while most V's (using proportions) range from 1.0 to 3.0[6] (362). When estimating the required sample size, Mitchell and Carson suggest that a value ''of at least 2'' be used for V (225 n.13).

Suppose, for example, the decision maker considers a 25% error at the 95% confidence level to be acceptable. Also, assume an initial V is 2 (or 200%). Then, the sample size of usable responses, n, can be calculated as follows (using proportions).

$$n = \frac{z^2 * V^2}{propE^2} = \frac{(1.96)^2 * (2)^2}{(.25)^2} = 246. \qquad (18.2)$$

To see the effects of greater desired precision, suppose the decision maker believes that at most a 5% error is allowable. Then, the required sample size of usable responses, n, increases to 6,147. By reducing the maximum likely error to one-fifth of its value, the sample size must expand nearly 25 (or 5^2) times!

Once n is calculated, the sample size might be reconsidered for four reasons.

First, in both equations 18.1 and 18.2, the sample size, n, is not determined by population size; n is the same whether the population is 150,000 or several million people. However, if the calculated sample size is 5% to 10% or more of the population (Cochran 1963: 24), then a ''finite population correction factor'' can be applied to reestimate n. To illustrate, again assume the decision maker allows a 25% error with a 95% confidence interval, V is assumed to be 2 and the calculated n is 246. Suppose the population size, N, is only 1,500, then the sample would be more than 16% of the population. Using the finite population correction factor, the sample size can be recalculated as follows.[7]

$$n = \frac{V^2}{\dfrac{propE^2}{z^2} + \dfrac{V^2}{N}} = \frac{2^2}{\dfrac{.25^2}{1.96^2} + \dfrac{2^2}{1,500}} = 211. \qquad (18.3)$$

In this case, the adjustment is modest. In comparison, for a maximum allowable error of only 5%, the calculated sample size of 6,147 (using equation 18.2) more than exhausts the small population of 1,500! Application of the finite population correction reduces the requisite sample size to 1,206—a considerable reduction, although the sample remains a substantial percentage of the small population.

Second, keeping in mind that n estimates the number of usable WTP responses needed for a particular degree of precision, the survey designer must expand the planned sample to allow for the anticipated unusable responses (e.g., nonresponses, unrealistically high values, protest zeros and the like).

Third, if the required sample size outstrips the decision maker's budget or planned time frame, the survey designer and decision maker face a potentially difficult choice: (1) increasing the budget and/or time commitment, (2) reducing the size and thus the sample's precision in order to lower the monetary or time expense, or (3) discontinuing the survey, perhaps until additional financial resources can be acquired[8] (Cochran 1963: 73; Carlson and Thorne 1997: 455).

Fourth, assuming sampling does proceed, then after responses are gathered from the selected sample, the size should be reassessed. If the sample V is less than initially estimated (here 2), then the task is completed, although note that the sample was larger and thus more expensive than needed to achieve the specified maximum likely error. On the other hand, if the sample V is greater than 2, then sampling of additional individuals must resume to obtain the desired precision (Lind and Mason 1997: 245).

This discussion concerning sample size assumes a simple random sample. Alternative sample selection methods might be considered, including a *stratified random sample* if the population can be divided into strata (such as different income or age groups) with widely differing WTPs or a *cluster sample* if, for example, the population is dispersed over a broad geographical area, entailing high sampling costs. To determine the size and design of such samples, an advanced sampling methods text or expert must be consulted.

Nonresponse Rate

Beyond anticipating the number of nonresponses when planning sample size, an even greater consideration is the meaning of the nonresponses themselves. When interpreting survey results, a key issue becomes who chose to respond, who did not and why. Would the nonrespondents' valuations follow the same or a different distribution than the responses received? If different, then the obtained results do not fully reflect the entire population's true valuation. A high nonresponse rate is therefore a cause for concern, suggesting possible bias, *nonresponse bias*, in the survey results. For credibility, the analyst should always report the response rate to the survey. More important, in the survey design careful attention should be devoted to reducing the nonresponse bias by matching the respondents' characteristics with population characteristics to ensure a representative sample.

Principle 18.9. When devising the survey, the designer should make every reasonable effort to minimize the nonresponse rate and bias.

SURVEY INSTRUMENTS

In any survey method, an instrument (in-person interview, telephone interview or written questionnaire) must be selected. In addition, a decision is made as to where the survey will take place or be distributed. For example, an in-person interview might be conducted at home or at relevant sites, and telephone interviews most likely would be at home. A questionnaire might be distributed any of a number of ways, including being mailed to respondents, handed to respondents at particular site(s) or perhaps left on vehicle windshields on site for respondents to fill out and drop off at a collection center or return by mail.

This discussion focuses on the choice of survey instrument. In the literature there is some disagreement as to which survey instrument is preferred. For example, the OECD indicates that each can be suitable depending on the circumstances (1994: 94). In contrast, the 1993 NOAA panel endorses in-person interviews "of significant duration" as the preferable choice. The panel notes some advantages of telephone interviews (e.g., lower costs, centralized supervision), but it considers the lengthier conversations that tend to characterize in-person interviews to be superior. As for mail surveys, the panel questions their reliability, indicating that if used, a subsample's responses should be validated by personal or telephone interviews. At the same time, the panel acknowledges that the high cost of personal interviews limits their usability (Arrow et al. 1993: 4607–8, 4611). Professionally conducted personal interviews are unaffordable for small budgets and irrational for decisions involving small economic values.

Recognizing that circumstances can vary for each specific case, we remain unconvinced that any single survey format is always superior. For example, when the decision maker's budget is limited, is no information on individual preferences better than the information gathered from lower-cost mail surveys? This is a question to be answered by the designer in the context of considering a number of factors, including the other controllable survey design characteristics, the defined society and the particular decision under assessment. Thus, we summarize the key advantages and disadvantages of each survey instrument, noting that the choice and the burden of justification belong to the analyst. It is the analyst's task to enumerate the strengths and weaknesses of his chosen survey instrument, to explain how the selected instrument (in the context of the overall survey design) effectively addresses possible biases and to assess the instrument's influence on the survey results obtained.

Principle 18.10. Survey instruments (i.e., in-person interview, telephone interview or written questionnaire) are distinguished in terms of the following characteristics: interactive or not interactive, ability to show displays, sample selection, nonresponses and costs.

Interactive or Not Interactive

A survey is said to be *interactive* when it permits a dialogue between the respondent and the interviewer.

- In-person and telephone interviews are interactive.
- Written questionnaires are not interactive.

The selection of an instrument that is (or is not) interactive can have important implications for survey responses. Either choice involves a trade-off. An interactive instrument facilitates information presentation, hypothetical valuation and some control of strategic bias, while potentially creating another bias, interviewer effects. A noninteractive survey does the opposite.

How does an interactive instrument enhance survey validity and reliability?

- A dialogue can facilitate the presentation of information by providing the respondent the opportunity to clarify any questions that arise, while allowing the interviewer to observe and perhaps identify any confusion on the respondent's part.
- The interviewer can see the seriousness with which the respondent approaches the survey and might thereby detect the extent to which the hypothetical aspect of the valuation question influences the responses.
- Interaction enables the interviewer to control the order in which the respondent receives information and responds to questions. This can help reduce the opportunity for *strategic bias*, as the interviewer can ask the respondent to agree to answer survey questions before the specific policy is revealed.

In contrast, when the respondent has the opportunity to review the survey content before deciding to respond, as is the case with a noninteractive written questionnaire, those most interested in the specific policy may decide to participate, while those less interested may not respond. As a result, the sample response may be unrepresentative, with a high percentage of the respondents having a strategic interest in the survey outcome.

- The interviewer can also ensure that a single respondent (without "help" from friends or other household members) provides all of the answers. The role of interaction in addressing these considerations helps explain the NOAA panel's strong endorsement of (interactive) in-person or phone surveys over mail questionnaires.

At the same time, interaction may generate another type of bias.

- Interaction allows for the possibility of *interviewer effects*, where the interviewer's presence or delivery of the information and questions affects the response. In particular, "overly compliant" respondents may want to please or be helpful, giving the answers they think the interviewer wants to hear. The NOAA panel recommends pretests for interviewer effects, asking subsamples of individuals to respond to interviewer questions in sealed or mailed ballots (Arrow et al. 1993: 4611–12).

Option of Showing Displays

- In-person interviews and written questionnaires allow displays.
- Telephone interviews do not permit displays.

The use of displays can enhance the information provided in the hypothetical scenario. Moreover, if any displays are included in the survey, then selecting an instrument that is also *interactive* (i.e., in-person interviews) permits the interviewer to encourage the respondent to take time to utilize them.

Sample Selection

The choice of survey instrument can affect the ability to select a random sample that represents the defined society (or population).

In-person interviews:
- involve physical identification of housing structures or individuals (when the latter, say, are visiting a particular site). This process can facilitate selection of a random sample. However, if interviewers exert any personal preference in selecting (or avoiding) specific housing units or individuals, then *interviewer bias* is introduced.
- might employ cluster sampling to lower selection costs, although a larger sample is then required, partially offsetting the cost decrease.

Telephone interviews:
- can use random digit dialing, which greatly aids the selection of a representative sample (although excluding households without phones). Instead, a sample might be selected with a telephone directory, but this approach omits unlisted numbers, newly assigned but not-yet-published numbers as well as phoneless households.
- require a phone system (which may preclude its use in some rural or less developed areas of the world).

Written questionnaires:
- can select a sample from a telephone directory; however, this excludes all households with unlisted numbers, newly assigned numbers or no phones; if available, a more inclusive mailing list might be used to select a sample.
- exclude functionally illiterate individuals.

Overall, the in-person interview is generally considered to be the instrument that most facilitates representative sample selection. However, the relatively recent development of random digit dialing has increased the competitiveness of telephone interviews in this regard. Greater concerns remain about written questionnaires, depending on the availability of an inclusive mailing list.

Nonresponses

The survey instruments often generate different nonresponse rates. For comparison purposes, national surveys of all kinds during the 1970s "usually" reported nonresponse rates of 25% to 35% (Schuman and Presser 1996: 331). In addition to the number of nonresponses, a related concern is who does not respond. In other words, do the nonrespondents' preferences deviate from and thus not represent those of the population? If so, then nonresponse bias is the result.

In-person interviews:

• usually generate the lowest nonresponse rates, because (1) respondents generally find it harder to refuse an in-person request and (2) persuasive interviewers can motivate many individuals to take the time to respond to the survey.

• introduce less nonresponse bias as respondents who decline an interview do so without knowing the topic.

Telephone interviews:

• often generate low nonresponse rates as the interviewer can encourage participation; however, the rates are generally a little higher than in-person interviews—mainly because the phone call's timing can be inconvenient and individuals find it easier to decline an interview or hang up the phone.

• introduce less nonresponse bias, as respondents who decline an interview do so without knowing the topic.

Written questionnaires:

• traditionally have resulted in high nonresponse rates—for instance, Mitchell and Carson list a number of 1970s and 1980s contingent valuation studies yielding nonresponse rates of from 40% to more than 70% (1989: 281). At the same time, application of the latest (more expensive) techniques can yield "more respectable" nonresponse rates of 30–50% (Carson 1991).[9]

• can be subject to serious nonresponse bias, as respondents can see the survey's focus, and those who are least interested are less likely to respond. The returned responses therefore tend to underrepresent select groups of society and, accordingly, are not generalizable to the population.[10]

Costs

Worth emphasizing is the relationship between the level of interaction and expenses, as greater interaction is generally associated with higher costs. In addition, a number of other factors contribute to the costs of employing different survey instruments.

All three instruments:

- require expertise in developing survey questions and compiling and analyzing the resulting data.

In-person interviews:

- incur training expenses and (the more expensive) decentralized supervision for the interviewers.
- require interviewer wages for longer interviews.
- involve travel time and expenses, which can be especially high for a geographically dispersed sample.

Telephone interviews:

- incur training expenses and (the less expensive) centralized supervision for the interviewers.
- need interviewer wages for the usually shorter interviews.
- may include long distance calls.

Written questionnaires:

- entail costs for printing, distribution, staffing, and perhaps postage and envelopes, depending on the selected distribution method.

Summary

Table 18.1 presents the three survey instruments and five characteristics for easy comparison. To summarize for each instrument:

In-person interviews facilitate more extensive interaction with the respondents, thereby enhancing information presentation, realistic hypothetical valuation and some control of strategic bias yet also providing the opportunity for interviewer effects to influence the survey results. The in-person interview offers the added advantage of allowing the survey to include displays, along with appropriate interaction to support accurate interpretation. It also facilitates random sample selection, and interviewer motivation can often reduce nonresponse rates. Unfortunately, professionally conducted in-person interviews involve high costs, potentially limiting this instrument to policies that are sufficiently large to warrant expensive analysis.

Telephone interviews facilitate less extensive interaction with the respondents, thus providing less (yet still some) of interaction's advantages while simultaneously providing a moderate opportunity for interviewer effects to influence the survey results. Displays cannot be used. Application of random digit dialing can enable representative sample selection (although excluding households with-

Table 18.1
Summary: Comparison of Survey Instruments

Characteristics	In-Person Interview	Telephone Interview	Written Questionnaire
Interactive	Longer interaction	Short interaction	Not interactive
Aids information presented and hypothetical valuation, reduces strategic bias, yet allows interviewer effects	✓ (more)	✓ (less)	Has opposite effects
Displays			
Are possible	✓		✓
Can be explained (interactive)	✓		
Sample Selection			
Facilitates selecting representative sample	Facilitates most, subject to interviewer bias	Facilitates more, with random digit dialing	Facilitates less, depending on mailing list
Survey requirements		Phone system	Literacy
Nonresponses			
Nonresponse rate	Lowest rate	Lower rate	Higher rate
Nonresponse bias			Can be serious
Costs	Higher costs	Lower costs	Lowest costs
Expertise to develop questions, compile and analyze data	✓	✓	✓
Train interviewers	✓	✓	
Supervise interviewers	Decentralized (higher cost)	Centralized (lower cost)	
Interviewer time and wages	✓ (more)	✓ (less)	
Other	Travel time and expenses	Any long distance calls	Printing, any envelopes and postage, staff

out phones), while phone calls attain moderately low nonresponse rates. Expenses are lower than for in-person interviews.

The *written questionnaire*, while not offering the advantages of interaction, does avoid any bias introduced by interviewers asking questions. In addition, the questionnaire allows some displays to be used. Concerns are raised about the ability to select a representative sample, depending on the inclusiveness of available mailing lists. Moreover, nonresponse rates can be high and nonresponse bias quite serious, underscoring the importance of employing the latest techniques to encourage responses. The strongest appeal of this instrument is the cost savings compared to the other instruments.

VALUATION QUESTION DESIGN

The primary reason for undertaking a contingent valuation survey is to ask respondents about their valuation of a resource, good or service given the conditions specified in the hypothetical market scenario. To elicit accurate valuations, suitably designed questions must be employed.

Principle 18.11. When devising the valuation question(s), the survey designer should consider the following choices: (1) type of valuation question (WTP, WTS, WTA), (2) question format (open-ended question, question with checklist, iterative bids or referendum question) and (3) actual payment question(s).

Then, after a respondent answers a valuation question, the survey should follow up and check the reliability of the response.

Principle 18.12. The survey should ask respondents to indicate the reasons for their answer(s) to the valuation question. The stated reasons should be coded and reported. In addition, an individual's reasons provide a basis for determining whether specific valuation answers are not credible and should be omitted by the analyst when estimating the social valuation.

This section explores the choices involved in designing valuation questions to elicit valid and reliable responses.

Choice of Valuation Questions: WTP, WTS or WTA?

Several valuation concepts exist. If a resource, good or service provides a benefit, respondents can be asked for their maximum willingness to pay (WTP) and/or minimum willingness to sell (WTS). If, instead, the resource imposes a cost, respondents can be questioned about their maximum WTP to have the cost removed and/or the minimum amount of compensation they are willing to accept (WTA) to tolerate the cost.

Principle 18.13. A respondent might be asked one or more of the following types of valuation questions.

- What is the *maximum* amount you are *willing to pay (WTP)* for a resource benefit (or to reduce a resource cost)?
- What is the *minimum* amount you must be paid to be *willing to sell* (WTS) or voluntarily forego a benefit, assuming you hold the property right to the resource?
- What is the *minimum* amount of compensation you are *willing to accept* (WTA) to tolerate a resource cost?

Which type of question should the analyst use? How do WTP, WTS and WTA estimates compare?

Simple logic suggests that values for WTA and WTS can be greater than for WTP. Unlike WTA and WTS, WTP is restricted by the respondent's income and wealth. For example, a bass fisher with $10,000 in annual disposable income cannot realistically claim to be willing to pay more than that per season for an improved fishing opportunity. In contrast, assuming ownership of the new fishing opportunity, the same fisher might sincerely state he or she must receive a value greater than $10,000 to be willing to sell the fishing right (or to be compensated for environmental pollution destroying the fish population). Thus, compared to WTS or WTA, WTP values are likely to be the more *conservative estimates.*

While a difference is expected, many contingent valuation studies have estimated considerable differentials. For example, the estimated WTS is eighteen times the WTP in Thibodeau and Ostro's study valuing wetlands preservation in the Charles River Basin (1981: 26) and four times WTP with Hammack and Brown's waterfowl hunting questionnaire (Dwyer, Kelly and Bowes 1977: 73). Likewise, a survey of several studies found the WTA to range from 1.6 to 16.6 times the WTP estimates (Cummings, Brookshire and Schulze 1986: 35).

The sizable differences have generated debate. Two views are expressed in the literature. According to traditional economic theory, the difference should be very small. Economic theory assumes a symmetric response in individual valuation with an individual's WTP to *gain* an incremental unit nearly equal[11] to the WTS to *lose* that same unit. According to this view, the contingent valuation estimates of WTS and WTA are unrealistically high. These overestimates reflect flawed contingent valuation studies—a failure to design a survey instrument encouraging respondents to state their valuation accurately.

In contrast, a theory in the field of psychology suggests that wide differentials between WTP and WTS (or WTA) can and do accurately reflect human behavior. According to *prospect theory*, people behave differently than economic theory has assumed. Individuals attach greater weight to incurring a loss (measured by WTS or WTA) than to receiving a gain (WTP) relative to current circumstances. Thus, prospect theory expects asymmetrical responses, with WTS and

WTA each greater than WTP (Kahneman and Tversky 1979; Levy 1992).[12] From this perspective, the estimates reported in contingent valuation studies are consistent with expected human behavior.

Of concern are the practical implications of these two views for the design, interpretation and application of a contingent valuation survey.

- If traditional economic theory is correct, then the empirical estimates of WTA and WTS are unrealistically high and should not be used when valuing social benefits or costs. WTP is the only suitable valuation option.
- If, instead, prospect theory is correct, then the appropriate valuation measure varies depending on whether the analyst is assessing a gain or a loss. When valuing a gain, the applicable measure is WTP for the benefit; WTS or WTA to forego the benefit overestimates the gain. When measuring a loss, on the other hand, WTP to receive the lost resource's value underestimates the individual's valuation of the damage done; WTS (or WTA compensation for the loss) are the realistic measures.

Clearly, further research needs to be undertaken to determine the reason for the differences between WTP and WTS (or WTA) estimates. In the meantime while the issue is unresolved, what should the conscientious survey designer do? Since WTP provides the conservative valuation estimate, the safest strategy is to ask a WTP question. (Notably, this choice is strongly advocated by the NOAA panel (Arrow et al. 1993: 4608).) If the survey, instead, asks only about minimum WTS or WTA, the resulting valuation estimate invites scrutiny with the likely challenge that it overstates the value of the resource, good or service.

In practice, WTP is the valuation concept most commonly employed. Indeed, even in damage assessments that include lost non-use values, contingent valuation studies typically do not measure respondents' minimum WTA compensation for these losses. Instead, surveys ask for the respondents' WTP to prevent a hypothetical scenario involving similar damage in the future.[13] If prospect theory proves to be accurate, then the current practice may underestimate society's value of the damage done; however, until the disagreement is resolved, a study exhibiting caution should pose a WTP question and provide a conservative valuation.

Principle 18.14. If the survey asks only one type of valuation question, then conservative estimation dictates that the choice is to elicit maximum willingness to pay (WTP).

An additional possibility the survey designer might consider is whether to ask more than one type of valuation question in a survey. For instance, when valuing a loss, since no consensus exists as to the accuracy of traditional economic theory as opposed to prospect theory, the survey designer might consider following a WTP question with a WTS or WTA question. The latter estimate could give the decision maker an idea as to how high society's valuation might rise.

Also, in some cases, there may be a reasonable concern that the finite incomes of an important segment of the defined society may be too restrictive. For example, in applying cost-benefit analysis to analyze a decision whether to preserve the Navajo Nation's traditional areas, the analyst immediately confronts the challenge of trying to compare the value of mineral development on these lands with the preservation value held by many Navajo, whose per capita income and thus WTP are relatively low. Certainly, one option is not to place a dollar value on the traditional areas. Suppose, however, a measure of economic preferences is desired for comparison purposes. The decision maker may want an indication of the strength of Navajo preferences without the income constraint. Asking the Navajo for their minimum WTS or WTA compensation to allow the development and alteration of the traditional areas, along with their WTP for preservation, then generates additional valuable information for the decision maker.

We suggest these possibilities, while noting that care and extreme caution must be exercised when incorporating WTA or WTS estimates into a cost-benefit analysis. The predominant, accepted practice is to use WTP to measure economic value. Moreover, asking too many questions can tire the respondent, resulting in less meaningful responses. Thus, only with due cause, suitably explained, might an analyst be justified in using WTS[14] or WTA values in the analysis; and these should be incorporated in addition to a measure of WTP. In effect, a *selective sensitivity analysis* is performed for the valuation estimate by using WTP as a lower bound and WTS or WTA as an upper bound.

Principle 18.15. In some cases, with justification, asking more than one type of valuation question may provide additional useful information for the decision maker.

When asking the chosen valuation question(s), respondents should explicitly be presented with the possibility of responding with NO ANSWER. This can lower the chances that a respondent offers a meaningless value simply to comply with the request to answer the question. The panel also recommends asking respondents to explain why they select the NO ANSWER response and tabulating the reasons (Mitchell and Carson 1989: 219; Arrow et al. 1993: 4609, 4612).

A final consideration in devising a valuation question concerns uncertainty. The valuation questions discussed in this section all assume certainty exists. Instead, the survey designer might consider the possibility that the individual respondent is *uncertain* as to whether at some future date he or she will want to use the particular resource or whether the resource will actually be available. If so, then the relevant question (using WTP as an example) becomes: What is the maximum amount the individual is WTP now, before a proposed resource change occurs, given his or her uncertainty? Such a question measures *option price*, a concept derived from the financial literature on option value. The basis for applying this concept in economic valuation was initially formulated by Weisbrod (1964) and then developed in an extensive, highly sophisticated theoretical literature. Much debate still continues over the concept of option price and its theoretical relationship to *option value* (a risk premium the risk-averse respondent is WTP to reserve the option of future use or availability).

A practical illustration of a valuation question asking for the respondent's option price is provided by Brookshire, Eubanks and Randall. They sought to estimate society's WTP to preserve grizzly bears and bighorn sheep in Wyoming, specifically valuing proposed new hunting areas stocked with maintained herds of grizzly bears (or bighorn sheep). Respondents were asked for the maximum price they would be WTP annually for a 90% probability they could begin hunting (or observing) grizzly bears (or bighorn sheep) at a specified date in the future. Some respondents were given five years, others fifteen years. Respondents who did not expect either to hunt or observe were asked for the maximum price they would be WTP to ensure, with a 90% probability in five or fifteen years, the existence of a sizable herd of one or the other species. Brookshire, Eubanks and Randall thus requested each respondent's option price by specifying a level of uncertainty as to the proposed policy's future success in herd maintenance (1983).

While many economists argue that option price is the appropriate valuation concept for an *ex ante* cost-benefit analysis of a proposed policy, it is not clear that a valuation question specifying uncertainty can be posed in a meaningful way to respondents in most instances. Thus, applications remain limited.

Valuation Question Format

A given valuation question might be presented to the respondent in any of a number of different formats. Thus, upon determining which type of valuation question to ask, the survey designer must then select an appropriate question format. Possible formats include an open-ended question, a question accompanied by a checklist, a series of iterative bids and a referendum question. All have been used in professional valuations. In recent years, several literature sources, including the NOAA panel, recommend the referendum question as the preferred alternative. Recognizing that other formats also have advantages, we note it is the survey designer's task to weigh the trade-offs and decide which format is most suitable for a given analysis. To help in this matter, the discussion identifies the advantages and disadvantages of each format. Among the elements of comparison are the following:

- ease or difficulty of responding
- starting point bias
- strategic bias
- simulation of market experience
- approximate or precise values
- statistical analysis requirements.

(When discussing each format, we refer to WTP questions assuming the reader understands that the formats can be applied to WTS or WTA questions.)

(a) Open-ended question. In an open-ended question, the respondent is asked: What is the maximum amount you are willing to pay for . . . ? With no suggestion concerning what would be a reasonable reply, the answer is left open.

Advantages:

- Straightforward. Respondents are asked precisely what the analyst wants to know—their maximum WTP.

- Does not lead (or bias) the respondent to a particular answer.

Disadvantages:

- Difficulty in responding. Typically, respondents do not have experience placing a dollar value on the policy or resource in question and thus have a limited basis for providing a realistic answer. Respondents may also find it unfamiliar to think in terms of their "maximum" WTP.

- Strategic bias. Respondents may strategically understate or overstate their valuation, sometimes answering at an extreme, indicating a willingness to pay zero or an unrealistically high amount. Open-ended questions tend to result in more widely dispersed answers (with a higher standard deviation) than the other question formats (Hufschmidt et al. 1983: 235; Arrow et al. 1993: 4606).

(b) Question with checklist. The interviewer provides the respondent a written checklist specifying alternative price intervals (e.g., $0 to $25.00, $25.01 to $50.00, and so on, up to a designated high price, along with the option of indicating an amount not listed), then asks the respondent to check the interval that contains his or her maximum willingness to pay. A checklist can be included either as part of a written questionnaire or on a card handed to the respondent during an in-person interview. A relatively short checklist might be read to the respondent over the phone.

Advantages:

- Ease of response. Providing a list of possible prices to consider makes it easier for the respondent to identify a maximum price.

- Does not lead (or bias) the respondent to a particular answer.

Disadvantages:

- Starting point bias. Showing respondents the list of price intervals may affect the responses, making them higher (or lower) than otherwise.

- May engender a quick, unconsidered answer. The respondent may rapidly check one interval with little thought.

- Approximate data values. Respondents are asked to identify a price interval rather than a single precise value.
- Strategic bias. Respondents may strategically understate or overstate their valuation.

The survey designer must choose the particular price range (highest and lowest values) and size intervals to specify on the checklist. To some extent the choices are arbitrary. Pretests of the questionnaire or interview provide an excellent opportunity to try alternative checklists. The survey designer can inspect for *starting point bias* as well as see which value range and intervals fit most responses. In addition, the higher the participant's income, the greater may be the willingness to pay. Thus, a single checklist may be extended to include a wide range of prices relevant for all income groups. Another possibility is for an interviewer to carry a number of checklists prepared for different income groups and hand the relevant list to each respondent.

(c) Iterative bid approaches. Several formats engage the respondent in making a series of bids. This discussion examines three such iterative bid formats.

Multiple yes/no responses (also called the converging-bid approach). This format can be lengthy and requires interaction between interviewer and respondent, thus limiting its use to interviews. To determine the WTP, the interviewer suggests the first price, the *starting point bid*, and asks whether the respondent is willing to pay that price (usually a low price). An iterative procedure follows. If the respondent is willing to pay the low bid, then the price is increased and the respondent is asked again, and so on, until the respondent declares the price is too high. Next, the interviewer lowers the price (down toward the previous highest agreeable bid) and continues until it is low enough the respondent is willing to pay. This last accepted bid is the maximum WTP.[15]

A difficulty is encountered, however, that limits effective use of the multiple bid approach. There is no predetermined end to the iterative process, and respondents are inclined to get impatient if asked to respond to too many bids. A more useful version of the iterative bid process is therefore explored.

Full-bidding game (three yes/no responses). A full-bidding game engages the respondent in interactive bidding while limiting the respondent to three YES/NO responses. Thus, unlike the multiple-bid approach, the game recognizes behavioral and time constraints and provides a more practical iterative format.

To illustrate how a full-bidding game works, let's look at a hypothetical example. Suppose the interviewer seeks to determine a recreational fisher's willingness to pay a user fee for each fishing day at Loon Lake. In a pretest, the survey designer concludes most respondents' values fall within a range of $0 to $12. The survey designer then divides the maximum value, $12, into three equal intervals, yielding three values, $4, $8 and $12. The survey designer decides to begin with a low *starting point bid* and thus starts with $4. In an effort to converge toward the respondent's maximum willingness to pay, whenever a respondent answers YES to a particular bid, the interviewer then raises the bid by $4. Whenever a respondent answers NO, the interviewer lowers the bid halfway back toward the prior accepted bid (or halfway toward $0, if no prior bid has been accepted). The iterative process continues, increasing or decreasing halfway. With a limit of only three YES/NO responses, the question-response interaction can follow one of four possibilities. These are presented for illustration. (Note that the questions are asked by the interviewer, while the respondent's answers are capitalized.)

(1) Would you be willing to pay $4? YES
    Would you be willing to pay $8? YES
    Would you be willing to pay $12?
    —if YES, then $12 is the valuation attributed to the respondent.
    —if NO, then $8 is used as the respondent's maximum willingness to pay.

(2) Would you be willing to pay $4? YES
    Would you be willing to pay $8? NO
    Would you be willing to pay $6?
    —if YES, then $6 is the respondent's valuation employed by the analyst.
    —if NO, then $4 is used as the respondent's maximum willingness to pay.

(3) Would you be willing to pay $4? NO
    Would you be willing to pay $2? YES
    Would you be willing to pay $3?
    —if YES, then $3 is accepted as the respondent's valuation.
    —if NO, then $2 is used as the respondent's maximum willingness to pay.

(4) Would you be willing to pay $4? NO
    Would you be willing to pay $2? NO
    Would you be willing to pay $1?
    —if YES, then $1 is the respondent's valuation.
    —if NO, then $0 is used as the respondent's maximum willingness to pay.

The full-bidding game is not limited to interviews; it can also be presented using a questionnaire, although the respondent may find the iterations somewhat tedious. For a possible layout of questions in a written iterative process, see OECD (1994: 115–16).

The advantages and disadvantages of the full-bidding game, as compared to other valuation question formats, are outlined.

Advantages:

• Ease of response. Asking the respondent to consider a series of possible prices is a familiar process.

• Simulates market experience. The iterative process asks the respondent to think longer and thus more carefully about the valuation, thereby enhancing realistic and incremental valuation and reducing the embedding problem.

• Limits strategic bias. Restricting the range of prices to three iterations gives the respondent only a constrained opportunity to answer strategically.

- Engages respondent in iterations. The iterative process may facilitate valuation in cultures that practice bargaining (OECD 1994: 116).

Disadvantages:

- Starting point bias. The first bid suggested by the interviewer may affect the responses. An overly compliant respondent may think the starting bid is the answer the interviewer wants to hear and respond accordingly. Likewise, an initial YES reply may serve to "anchor" the second or third response toward a low value. Bidding games tend to result in a narrower range of responses (with a lower standard deviation) than an open-ended question (Hufschmidt et al. 1983: 235). Studies can check for starting point bias by offering subsamples different starting bids as well as letting some respondents make the first bid.
- Approximate data values. The three YES/NO responses allow the bidding to approach the respondent's maximum WTP, but do not guarantee convergence precisely at the maximum.

Full-bidding game (three yes/no responses) and follow-up open-ended question. Recognizing that three YES/NO responses have the disadvantage of yielding approximate values, some studies have employed a variant. In this approach, the interviewer asks for a YES/NO response to each of three bids and then concludes with an open-ended question: What is the maximum amount you are willing to pay?

Advantage:

- Precise data value. Respondents answer with their maximum WTPs.

It may be wondered, of course, if the open-ended question allows for greater precision, why not simply ask an open-ended question by itself? Adding a full-bidding game offers two advantages:

- Ease of response. Asking the respondent to consider a series of possible prices is a familiar process and can facilitate determining the actual maximum WTP.
- Simulates a market experience. The iterative process can engender a more realistic valuation by the respondent, enhancing incremental valuation and reducing the embedding problem.

Disadvantage:

- Starting point bias. The iterative process may affect the responses.

(d) Referendum question. The referendum question consists of asking each respondent for a single YES/NO response (or "vote"). The respondent is asked once: Are you willing to pay $8 (or some other specified price)? The respondent can then answer: YES, NO or NO ANSWER. The survey designer randomly selects a different price for specific subsamples. By counting the number of YES

responses for each price asked, the survey designer can generate a function showing how many individuals are WTP different prices.

A referendum (or dichotomous) question simulates the political referendum process where voters are asked to vote for or against a specified public expenditure. Many economists are expressing a growing preference for the referendum question, arguing that political markets are the appropriate basis for contingent valuation of public goods. However, some also note that consumer markets are relevant for "quasi-private goods" that can be offered to individuals at a price (such as access to a wilderness area or the opportunity to engage in a recreational activity). For both views, see Mitchell and Carson (1986: 3/1–3/3; 1989: 91–97). The NOAA panel endorses the referendum question as the preferable format, noting the strong advantages of the dichotomous approach.

Advantages:

- Ease of response. The respondent is given one price to consider in a process paralleling the political referendum, which is already familiar to voters.

- Eliminates strategic bias. Since the survey designer determines the one price, the respondent is not given the opportunity to overstate or understate the value of the resource in question.

- Eliminates starting point bias. The random selection of prices for different respondents avoids such bias.

At the same time, there are several disadvantages to using the referendum question.

Disadvantages:

- May engender a quick, unconsidered response. The "take-it-or-leave-it" question might not engage respondents in a thoughtful valuation process but rather encourage a snap judgment.

- Statistical analysis. To perform a rigorous, sophisticated analysis interpreting and testing the responses, a larger sample size is needed for cross-tabulations; and a highly technical regression analysis, different from the regression techniques suitable for the other valuation questions, is applied. (See the chapter sections on valuation estimation and on response validity and reliability tests.)

- Abrupt response. In cultures where bargaining is prevalent, a single YES/NO answer might be considered abrupt or rude (OECD 1994: 112).

(e) Comparison of question formats. The chapter considers five different question formats as possible alternatives for the survey designer (omitting a sixth, the multiple iterative bid process, which is outperformed by the full-bidding game). This section, along with accompanying Table 18.2, provides a comparative summary of the formats organized in terms of select characteristics.

The amount of iteration and respondent thought vs. time. Repetitive bidding asks the respondent to value the resource several times, each time comparing

Table 18.2
Summary: Comparison of Valuation Question Formats

Characteristics	Open-ended Question	Question with Checklist	Full Bidding Game (3 Yes/No Responses)	Full Bidding Game with Open-ended Question	Referendum Question
Amount of iteration, respondent thought and time	1 Response	1 Response	3 Responses	4 Responses	1 Response
Strategic bias	Allows strategic bias	Allows strategic bias	Limits strategic bias	Limits strategic bias	Eliminates strategic bias
Difficult to respond vs. starting point bias	Difficult to respond	A little of both	Starting point bias	Starting point bias	Neither
Precision of response	Precise value	Interval of values	Approximate value	Precise value	Approximate value
Statistical analysis	Recommended	Recommended	Recommended	Recommended	Recommended
					Cross-tabulations require larger sample; regression analysis is more advanced.

trade-offs between the resource in question and other goods and services. This process simulates the market whereby preferences that might be originally exaggerated are modified (Brookshire and Coursey 1987: 565). As seen in Table 18.2, the full-bidding games (with and without the open-ended question) involve the larger number of iterations (four and three, respectively) and thus engage the respondent in a greater amount of thought when valuing the resource in question. Simultaneously, respondents generally do not favor long surveys which entail a lot of time. Some may answer questions quickly, with little thought, to end the experience. A trade-off therefore exists with the number of iterations, for the greater number of responses generally require more respondent time.

Eliminating or allowing strategic bias. The open-ended question and question with checklist allow respondent strategies to affect valuations, while the full bidding games partially limit the bias. The referendum question is the one format that eliminates strategic bias.

Starting point bias vs. difficulty of responding. At issue is who determines the starting value. If the survey designer, then the possibility of starting point bias is introduced. If the respondent, then he or she may encounter difficulties in answering. At one end of the spectrum, the open-ended question successfully avoids starting point bias, yet offers no help to the respondent in determining a maximum price in the valuation process. At the other end, the full-bidding games aid the respondent by identifying three prices for consideration; however, the games allow starting point bias. The referendum question is the one format that successfully avoids the trade-off; the respondent is offered a single price in a form familiar to voters, while the random selection of prices eliminates starting point bias. This adds to the referendum question's appeal.

Precision of response. The two formats involving an open-ended question (by itself and combined with a full-bidding game) both conclude with a respondent stating a precise value. (In other words, the stated value comes as close to the respondent's true preferences as the individual is willing to reveal.) Other formats, by the strictures of the questioning process, do not allow the respondent to reveal fully his or her actual valuation. The simple full-bidding game and referendum question end with an approximate value that may or may not be close to what the respondent would actually be willing to pay. The question with checklist format generally reports an interval of values, containing the respondent's actual WTP.

Statistical analysis. When interpreting survey results, statistical analysis is generally recommended. In the case of the referendum question, a larger sample and a different, highly technical regression analysis along with the related expertise, time and expense are required for a sophisticated analysis.

In the final report the designer should justify his choice of valuation question format, explaining the format's advantages and disadvantages. Table 18.2 provides a reference to facilitate easy comparison of the five formats' strengths and weaknesses.

Actual Payment Question(s)

Principle 18.16. If actual market payments can be identified that are in some way related to the hypothetical scenario under consideration, then respondents should be asked whether they have made such payments and, if so, how much they paid.

Including questions about any relevant market payment(s) can enhance the hypothetical valuation in two ways. First, more thoughtful answers may be generated. As the respondent considers different market trade-offs and decisions, additional reflection is encouraged, which may make the hypothetical valuation more realistic. Second, the analyst may be able to detect inaccuracies in a given respondent's valuations. For example, the Hammack and Brown questionnaire asked four different questions to value waterfowl hunting, rotating between hypothetical and actual payments: (1) WTS the right to hunt waterfowl, (2) actual hunting costs (as defined by the respondent), (3) WTP for the right to hunt waterfowl, and (4) actual payments to hunt on private land (1974: 201–4). Comparing a respondent's four answers sometimes revealed unrealistic valuations, which could then be excluded from further analysis.

VALUATION ESTIMATION

Once the survey has been designed and administered to the selected sample, the collected sample data are given to the analyst, who then estimates the population's valuation of the nonmarketed resource, good or service. To make inferences from the sample to the population, contingent valuation studies employ different aggregation methods with varying levels of statistical sophistication.

Principle 18.17. The population's aggregate value (or Total WTP) for a nonmarketed resource, good or service can be estimated from sample data using any of a number of different statistical techniques, including:

- mean or median WTP
- frequency distribution of WTP
- aggregate bid (or demand) schedule
- valuation function (multiple regression analysis)

This section presents each approach using the hypothetical Loon Lake example. To help a county government assess the benefits of a proposed cleanup and bass-stocking program for Loon Lake, a contingent valuation survey is administered. County residents are expected to be the predominant visitors who will engage in recreational fishing and other activities at the lake; in addition, environmentally concerned individuals in the county may value the proposed program for its environmental improvements. Accordingly, a random sample is selected from the county population.

Out of a total of 2,200 county households selected for personal interview (at their residences), suppose 550 do not respond. In a few cases, housing units are discovered to be vacant. In others, individuals are not at home despite repeated interviewer attempts to establish contact, and some individuals when contacted refuse the interview. Without these households, all together 1,650 respondents are interviewed, yielding a response rate of 75%.

Furthermore, the responses of those interviewed are not always usable. Some respondents answer "do not know" to the valuation question. Others indicate dollar amounts that are not credible and thus do not reflect the respondent's true WTP for the resource in question. For instance, when protesting some aspect of the scenario or valuation question, respondents sometimes offer zero bids. The analyst must therefore determine whether any given zero response is such a *protest zero*. In addition, some WTP responses may be judged as unrealistically high (*outliers*). Also, interviewer assessment might indicate the respondent was uncooperative, had difficulty grasping the valuation question, or did not seem to take the question seriously. It is not uncommon for such responses to be dropped from the survey results for further analysis.

In the hypothetical Loon Lake example, respondents who indicated a zero WTP were then asked why. Some said that this is what the proposed cleanup and stocking program was worth to them or that they did not have enough money to offer a payment—suggesting their responses are valid economic values. Other responses signaled protest bids. These were offered by the following:

1. a few lakeside households who valued the proposed cleanup and bass stocking program but were weary (unduly, according to government expectations) of the disturbances they anticipated from the recreational fishers who would visit the lakeside neighborhood,

2. some recreational fishers who contended that they should not have to pay and instead the polluters should be charged,

3. respondents who expressed disbelief in either the county government or the proposed program's ability to clean the lake,

4. individuals who opposed any policy involving additional government intervention, and

5. a number of individuals who indicated that assigning a monetary value to an environmental attribute is unethical or immoral.

In addition to designating these five sets of Loon Lake responses as protest zeros, the analyst identifies some other bids as unrealistically high. Most notably, several recreational fishers offered a WTP of infinity, a million dollars or a disproportionately large percentage of their household's annual pretax income.[16] Also, the interviewers reported a small number of respondents as uncooperative or offering poorly considered bids. All together, dropping the protest zeros, unrealistic values and other questionable responses from the Loon Lake analysis leaves 1,500 usable responses.

Proper reporting of such adjustments to the sample responses is important to enable accountability of the analysis. The exclusion of the various bids should be justified in the analyst's report. Also, ideally, the analysis is undertaken both with these responses included as well as dropped in order to see their impact on the estimated Total WTP. (For simplicity, the illustration in this chapter considers only the usable responses.)

With the sample responses narrowed, the analyst must address whether the remaining (usable) responses are representative of the population as a whole. Did specific groups of individuals respond more than others? In other words, are certain groups underrepresented among the respondents who provided credible and plausible WTP bids? This is a question addressed, to varying degrees, by each of the statistical techniques applied to estimate the county population's valuation of the proposed Loon Lake improvements.

Mean or Median WTP

The county government's proposal includes an initial year of clean up and stocking of the lake, followed by annually recurring efforts to sustain both the improved water quality and bass population. Thus, the survey asks the respondents to indicate an annual maximum WTP for the proposed improvements. Use of an open-ended valuation question yields a specific WTP from each respondent. In data analysis, the mean for the usable WTP responses is calculated as $21.45 per year. An alternative summary statistic is the median WTP, which in this example is $15. Thus, 50% of the responses are $15 or less, while the average household is WTP $21.45 per year. Since the upper bound on the responses can extend quite high, it is not uncommon for the mean to be greater than the median. Despite the apparent skewness of the responses, the statistic most frequently used in contingent valuation studies to summarize valuation responses is the sample mean.

The objective in surveying the sample is to estimate the county population's WTP for the lake improvements. To generalize from the sample results to the county population, the sample's representativeness of the population must be determined. A common approach is to match the respective demographics for the sample and the population. For example, the survey might collect data measuring respondent age, gender, education, household size, pretax household incomes and other variables. These data are then compared with parallel data for the county population. (A more sophisticated analysis can perform t-tests to determine if there is any statistical difference.) If the demographics do not correspond closely, then a multiple regression estimation of the valuation function is required to predict the population's WTP using the sample data. If the demographics do correspond, the sample mean might be interpreted as the population mean. The estimated Total WTP is calculated as (estimated population mean) * (population). Assuming a county population of 100,000 households, the estimated Total WTP is $21.45 * 100,000, or $2,145,000.

The stability of the estimate given sampling variability can be assessed. Use of a probability sampling technique provides 95% confidence that a sample is selected with the population's true mean falling within a 95% confidence interval around the sample mean. A 95% *confidence interval* (CI) for the sample mean is calculated with the following formula,

$$CI = \text{mean} \pm z * s/\sqrt{n}, \tag{18.4}$$

where z is a z-score (1.96 for a 95% CI), s is the estimated sample standard deviation (19.08975 for the sample) and n is the sample size (1,500). Thus, the

$$
\begin{aligned}
95\% \text{ CI} &= \$21.45 \pm 1.96 * 19.08975/\sqrt{1,500} \\
&= \$20.4839 \text{ and } \$22.4161.
\end{aligned}
$$

The probability sampling technique therefore yields 95% confidence that the county population's true mean WTP falls between $20.48 and $22.42 per household and hence 95% confidence that the population's true Total WTP is somewhere between $2.048 million and $2.242 million.[17] The three Total WTPs calculated with the sample mean and the CI's upper and lower limits, respectively, might all be employed as estimates for the county population's valuation of the proposed Loon Lake improvements. A *selective sensitivity analysis* is thus performed to assess the estimates' effects on the calculated NPV.

Alternatively, the Total WTP might be estimated using the median. Given a median of $15, the estimated Total WTP for the population of 100,000 households is $1.5 million. The two Total WTPs calculated with the mean and the median can provide the upper and lower bounds, respectively, in a *selective sensitivity analysis*. Or instead, recognizing the skewness of the sample responses, some studies prefer to employ the Total WTP estimated with the median value, along with the confidence interval around the median. Substituting the median value for the mean in equation 18.4 yields a 95% CI ranging from $14.03 to $15.97 per household or from $1.403 million to $1.597 million for the population. Again, a *selective sensitivity analysis* can demonstrate the estimates' effects on the NPV for Loon Lake's improvements.

Frequency Distribution of WTP

A *frequency distribution* summarizes the overall distribution of WTP responses gathered from the sample and thus provides a quick overview of all (usable) survey responses. In Table 18.3, columns 1 through 4 present the frequency distribution of WTPs for the Loon Lake sample. For easy summary, the 1,500 responses are grouped into intervals (see column 1). Columns 3 and 4 list the number and percentage, respectively, of respondents who are WTP an annual

Table 18.3
Frequency Distribution: Willingness to Pay for Loon Lake Improvements

Willingness to Pay per Year		Respondents			
(1)	(2)	(3)	(4)	(5)	(6)
	Interval			Estimated	Total
Interval	Midpoint			Population	WTP[a]
($)	($)	Number	%	(hhs)	($)
0.00	0	225	15	15,000	0
0.01 to 10	5	450	30	30,000	150,000
10.01 to 20	15	300	20	20,000	300,000
20.01 to 30	25	225	15	15,000	375,000
30.01 to 40	35	90	6	6,000	210,000
40.01 to 50	45	150	10	10,000	450,000
more than 50	110[b]	60	4	4,000	440,000
Total		1,500	100	100,000	1,925,000

[a]Calculated as (interval midpoint WTP)(estimated population households) or column (2) times column (5).
[b]The approximate mean for bids greater than $50.

dollar amount within the corresponding interval. As can be seen, 15% of the sample are WTP $0 for the proposed lake improvements, 65% are WTP $0.01 to $30 per year, another 16% are WTP up to and including $50 and the remaining 4% are WTP more than $50 each year. Not indicated in the table, the over-$50 bids are concentrated from $60 to $150 with a handful ranging in the $200s and $300s, and one bid at $500 per year. The frequency distribution of WTPs using respondent percentages is illustrated graphically in Figure 18.1. As clearly seen, the majority of respondents are WTP an annual amount within ± $15 of the $15 median, while a smaller number of respondents are WTP notably more.

If the sample and population demographics are comparable, then the frequency distribution might be used to estimate the population's Total WTP. Assuming the respondent percentages are identical for the population, the number of population households who are WTP different amounts can be estimated. As shown in column 5, if, for instance, 15% of the sample is WTP $0, then 15,000 population households (15% * 100,000) are estimated as WTP the same amount. Likewise, an estimated 30% * 100,000, or 30,000 households, are WTP from $0.01 to $10, and so on for each interval.

Figure 18.1
Frequency Distribution of Willingness to Pay

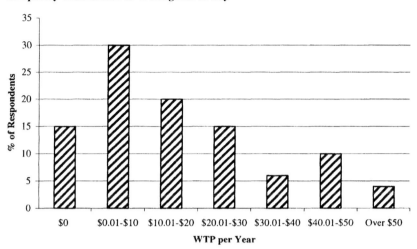

Total WTP (in column 6) is then calculated by multiplying the estimated population households by the midpoint WTP (shown in column 2) for the respective interval. Thus, for the interval $.01 to $10, the estimated 30,000 population households are assumed to be WTP $5, for a total of $150,000. Making similar computations for all of the intervals, and then adding, the Total WTP is an estimated $1.925 million. (Note that given the grouping of responses into intervals, the estimation of Total WTP based on the frequency distribution uses a rough approximation, interval midpoints, of the sample data. In contrast, estimating Total WTP from the mean makes precise use of all sample data.)

Aggregate Bid (or Demand) Schedule

An aggregate demand curve for the Loon Lake improvements can be derived from the frequency distribution. The demand relationship shows the cumulative number of county households who are WTP different dollar amounts for the improvements. In other words, a point on the demand curve represents the number of households WTP a given amount (say, $20.01) or more. Table 18.4 presents the *aggregate bid (or demand) schedule* for the Loon Lake improvements. The schedule is derived from Table 18.3, specifically, the lower limits of the WTP intervals (column 1) and corresponding estimated population number (column 5). The derivation begins with the greatest WTP interval and cumulates to smaller value intervals. Thus, referring to Table 18.3, 4,000 households are WTP more than $50. This becomes the first point in the aggregate bid schedule. For the second point, find the number of households WTP at least $40.01. In this case, 14,000 (4,000 + 10,000) are WTP $40.01 or more.

Table 18.4
Aggregate Bid Schedule for Loon Lake Improvements

Willingness to Pay per Year	Cumulative Population (hhs)
$50.01 or more	4,000
$40.01 or more	14,000
$30.01 or more	20,000
$20.01 or more	35,000
$10.01 or more	55,000
$ 0.01 or more	85,000
$ 0.00 or more	100,000

The derivation continues, cumulating with the entire population, 100,000 households, being WTP $0 or more.

These points are plotted graphically to form the *aggregate bid curve* (see Figure 18.2). As illustrated, the points are connected with linear segments. (A more sophisticated analysis might fit a rounded curve to the points.) The curve begins off the graph at a vertical intercept just above $500, the highest bid offered by any respondent. It then extends down to lower dollar amounts until reaching $0, an amount that technically the entire population of 100,000 households is WTP. As displayed in Figure 18.2, the curve overall has a negative slope, showing that as the dollar amount falls, a larger number of the population households are WTP for lake improvements. In this particular example, a segment of the demand curve flattens along the horizontal axis as the last 15,000 population households (from 85,000 to 100,000) are WTP only $0.

The aggregate population's Total WTP is calculated as the area under the demand curve. In Figure 18.2, the relevant area is below the curve from the origin (0) to the entire population (100,000 households). By dividing the area into rectangles and triangles and computing the size of each, the total area is calculated to be approximately $1.915 million. Thus, the 100,000 county households are WTP an estimated $1.915 million in the aggregate for the lake improvements. This Total WTP corresponds closely to that calculated from the frequency distribution, from which the aggregate bid curve is derived.

In some cases the aggregate bid curve provides additional useful information. For example, suppose the Loon Lake survey had limited its focus to estimating WTP only for access to use the improved lake (thus omitting any non-use value generated by the improvements). Then, the demand curve would indicate how

Figure 18.2
Aggregate Bid Curve

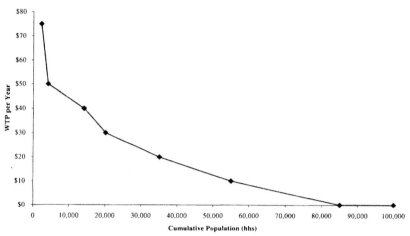

many households are WTP different dollar amounts for each entry to the lake after the improvements. Accordingly, the demand curve shows the implications of charging a user fee for entry to the lake (if exclusion is possible). The aggregate bid curve predicts how the number of users and, in turn, revenues would change for different entry fees.

Valuation Function

The techniques discussed so far for estimating Total WTP all assume that the sample is representative of the county population and thus the sample results can be directly generalized to the population. If the sample is not representative—for example, characteristics for the respondents and the population do not correspond closely—then such simple generalization can be misleading. An alternative approach is to undertake multivariate estimation of a valuation function using the gathered sample data. This function can then be applied, along with data measuring population characteristics, to predict the population's Total WTP.

The *valuation function* relates the sample respondents' WTP to several variables representing socioeconomic, demographic and attitudinal characteristics of the respondents. Relevant variables might be selected from the following: age, household size, household income, gender, race, education, occupation, political party affiliation, environmental attitude, scenario acceptance, recreational participation, prior site visits and likely future site visits. Data for the chosen variables are collected as part of the contingent valuation survey. Each variable's independent relationship with WTP can be measured using *multiple regression analysis*.[18]

In analyzing the sample data, the analyst must determine the appropriate functional form that best fits the data. For simplicity, this discussion assumes a linear function. A general formula for a linear valuation function is

$$\text{WTP} = a_0 + a_1 C_1 + a_2 C_2 + a_3 C_3 + \ldots + a_n C_n, \tag{18.5}$$

where C_i is respondent characteristic i. The data for WTP and C_i are entered into a computer statistical package, which then estimates a_0, a constant, and a_i, the respective regression coefficient for C_i. Each coefficient represents the change in WTP associated with a unit change in the corresponding characteristic C_i. The coefficients are expressed mathematically as:

$$a_i = \frac{\Delta \text{WTP}}{\Delta C_i}, \text{ for } i = 1, 2, \ldots, n. \tag{18.6}$$

Valuation functions in the literature include anywhere from a handful to a dozen or so characteristics. For illustrative purposes, a linear valuation function for the Loon Lake example might be specified as follows.

$$\text{WTP} = a_0 + a_1(\text{Age}) + a_2(\text{Income}) + a_3(\text{Education}) + a_4(\text{Env}) + \tag{18.7}$$
$$a_5(\text{RecFish}) + a_6(\text{FutVisit}),$$

where *Env* indicates whether the respondent considers himself or herself to be a strong environmentalist, *RecFish* identifies recreational (freshwater) fishers and *FutVisit* measures the respondent's likely future visits to Loon Lake after the proposed improvements.

Once the coefficients are determined, the analyst can use the valuation function to predict the population's Mean WTP, taking into account the characteristics of the county population. Specifically, the mean population value, *Mn*, for age, pretax household income and education might be determined from county census data. The mean number of future annual visits and the proportion, *Prp*, of the population who are declared environmentalists and recreational freshwater fishers might be obtained from a recent countywide poll. If available, these values are plugged into the valuation function to predict the county population's Mean WTP as follows.

$$\text{Mean WTP} = a_0 + a_1(\text{MnAge}) + a_2(\text{MnIncome}) + \tag{18.8}$$
$$a_3(\text{MnEducation}) + a_4(\text{PrpEnv}) +$$
$$a_5(\text{PrpRecFish}) + a_6(\text{MnFutVisit}).$$

If population data are not available for particular variable(s), the relevant sample mean or proportion might be used (adjusted as appropriate to reflect any discernible differences between the sample and population). Once the Mean WTP is estimated, it is then multiplied by the county households to obtain Total WTP. For a professional application, see, for instance, Schulze and associates (1983).

The multiple regression analysis must be performed with due care, checking for multicollinearity, specification bias, data accuracy and other statistical considerations discussed in Chapter 17. If the analysis is conducted properly, then the resulting Total WTP figure is considered the most credible of any of the Total WTP estimates obtained with the techniques examined in this chapter.

In addition, the valuation function (equation 18.7) can be adapted to incorporate the respondent answers that were dropped from the analysis and to determine the effect on the estimated Mean WTP of their inclusion or omission. For instance, a dummy variable (*Prot*) might be created, assigning a value of one to responses categorized as *protest responses*. Similar dummy variables might be devised for such variables as the perceived success of the proposed cleanup and bass-stocking program (*Suc*) and unrealistically high values (*High*). These are added to the independent variables in equation 18.7, yielding the equation,

$$WTP = a_0 + a_1(Age) + \ldots + a_6(FutVisit) + a_7(Prot) + a_8(Suc) + \qquad (18.9)$$
$$a_9(High).$$

Incorporating the data measuring the dropped respondents' answers, equation 18.9 is estimated several times. First, all variables are included as specified to estimate the regression coefficients. Then, one at a time, a dummy variable is set to zero and the regression coefficients are reestimated. Next, equation 18.8 is adjusted to include the three dummy variables, and each set of regression coefficients is plugged in to obtain a series of Mean WTP estimates. The predicted Mean WTPs can be compared to see the effect of including or excluding each of the dummy variables. See Carson and associates (1992: 106–17) for an application.

Conclusion

All together, this chapter section presents four different techniques for estimating the county population's Total WTP for Loon Lake improvements. The mean and frequency distribution are particularly useful in summarizing the sample responses for the layperson. When demographic data suggest the responding sample is representative of the population, then these or the aggregate bid curve can also be applied to obtain initial rough estimates of the Total WTP. A more credible aggregate estimate is yielded by applying the fourth statistical technique, multiple regression analysis of the valuation function. Estimation of the valuation function, therefore, is recommended to increase the rigor of a contingent valuation study. However, when time or resources are limited and a "ballpark" figure is sufficient for decision-making purposes, one of the first three approaches may be acceptable.

Whichever of the four techniques is used, the possible error must be assessed and explained in the analyst's report, and the resulting estimate should be interpreted and used accordingly by the decision maker. The estimated Total WTP can then be considered by the county government when determining whether annual budget allocations are warranted to improve Loon Lake's water quality and maintain a bass-stocking program.

RESPONSE VALIDITY AND RELIABILITY TESTS

A rigorous contingent valuation study takes the final step of testing the survey WTP responses to assess their validity and reliability. As a reminder, *theoretical validity* reflects the responses' consistency with theoretical expectations, while *reliability* refers to the repeatability of the survey measurements or, in other words, the lack of random error in the sample responses. Contingent valuation studies employ a number of different statistical approaches to test the validity and reliability of WTP responses.

Principle 18.18. The theoretical validity of WTP estimates can be explored by testing the relationship between WTP and various socioeconomic and demographic variables, using alternative statistical techniques including:

- cross-tabulations and
- valuation function (multiple regression analysis).

Evidence concerning the estimates' reliability is provided by:

- the valuation function's R^2.

Cross-Tabulations: Theoretical Validity

Evidence that the WTP responses are theoretically valid can be provided by examining *cross-tabulations* of the WTP responses with the respondents' different socioeconomic, demographic and attitudinal characteristics. With this technique, respondents are divided into groups according to specified characteristics; mean WTPs are calculated for the respective groups and then compared to see if they are consistent with theoretical (or logical) expectations.[19] Table 18.5 presents a cross-tabulation of the usable WTP responses for the Loon Lake improvements. Data for the variables are gathered by the survey. For illustration purposes, the same variables specified in the valuation function (equation 18.7) are included in the cross-tabulation. As can be seen from the mean WTPs for different age groups, older respondents on average are WTP less than younger respondents. Also shown in the table, as income or education increases, WTP increases for the Loon Lake improvements. Respondents who consider them-

Table 18.5
Cross-Tabulation of Willingness-to-Pay Responses with Respondent
Characteristics, Loon Lake Survey

Respondent Characteristics	% of Respondents	Mean WTP ($ per year)
Age (years)		
18-29	15	26
30-54	50	24
55+	35	15
Household income (pretax)		
$0-$19,999	30	10
$20,000-$39,999	35	18
$40,000-$59,999	20	25
$60,000-$79,999	10	40
$80,000+	5	60
Education (last grade completed)		
Grade school	7	10
Some high school	10	15
High school graduate	60	18
College graduate	15	35
Post graduate degree	8	40
Strong environmentalist		
Yes	55	26
No	45	15
Recreational fisher		
Yes	45	30
No	55	14
Likely future visits (number per year)		
Zero	30	10
1-5	40	15
6-11	20	35
12-24	8	50
25+	2	75

selves strong environmentalists are WTP more than non-environmentalists. Likewise, recreational freshwater fishers and respondents anticipating frequent future visits are WTP more than respondents not in these respective categories. These results are generally consistent with demand theory and logical expectations, providing evidence of the survey responses' validity.

Cross-tabulations present additional summary information that may be useful to the decision maker. The procedure identifies which variables appear to affect respondent WTP and thus which respondents are WTP more (or less) for the Loon Lake improvements. At the same time, the technique involves only modest statistical analysis and the multiple grouping of respondents does not separate each variable's effect independent of the others. As a result, the analysis ignores the possible interrelationships between variables; also, each variable's relative importance in influencing WTP is not apparent. Thus, estimation of a valuation function using multiple regression analysis to separate each variable's effects provides more information.

Valuation Function: Theoretical Validity

A more sophisticated statistical technique for relating WTP responses to respondent characteristics involves estimating the general valuation function (equation 18.5) and testing both the sign and statistical significance of each of the regression coefficients.[20] Suppose the valuation function specified for Loon Lake (equation 18.7) is estimated and yields the following regression:

$$\text{WTP} = 10 - 0.235 * \text{Age} + 0.6 * \text{Income} + 0.7 * \text{Education} + \qquad (18.10)$$
$$(-2.21) \qquad\quad (3.85) \qquad\qquad (3.18)$$
$$3.0 * \text{Env} + 12.0 * \text{RecFish} + 4.0 * \text{FutVisit},$$
$$(2.93) \qquad\ (5.24) \qquad\qquad (4.38)$$

where each number in parentheses is a t-ratio for the corresponding regression coefficient. As can be seen, the absolute values of all of the t-ratios are greater than 2—a rough rule-of-thumb value for the critical t at a 95% confidence level. Thus, all of the coefficients are statistically significant (or significantly different from zero).

The values of the coefficients can be interpreted. As defined in equation 18.6, each regression coefficient predicts the change in WTP associated with a unit change in the corresponding variable. Thus, for example, the coefficient for age indicates that a respondent is WTP on average $0.235 less per year for each additional year of age. Also consider the coefficient for income (where income is measured in thousands of dollars). The coefficient of 0.6 predicts that for every thousand dollars of annual pretax household income, the respondent is WTP an additional $0.60 per year. The positive relationship between income and WTP satisfies a general expectation of economic theory. Likewise, the positive coefficient for education is as anticipated. Also logical, the respondents are WTP an additional $4 for each likely visit to the Lake after improvements. For the remaining variables, the regression coefficients indicate that on average the strong environmentalist is WTP $3 more per year than the non-environmentalist and the recreational fisher is WTP $12 more per year than the non-fisher. All of these coefficient signs are consistent with expectations, thus providing strong evidence in support of the theoretical validity of the survey's WTP responses.

The Valuation Function's R^2: Reliability

An indication of the survey's reliability is provided by the valuation function's coefficient of multiple determination, R^2. R^2 measures the variability in WTP responses predicted by the regression equation. $1 - R^2$, the unpredicted variability (or randomness) in the sample WTPs, is a cause for concern; it suggests that with sampling variability, the true population Total WTP may be very different from the Total WTP estimated using the sample. Accordingly, the reliability of the valuation estimates is compromised.

In general, R^2 ranges in size from 0 to 1, with values greater than 0.7 generally suggesting a strong relationship between the equation's independent variables and the dependent variable. In contingent valuation studies, R^2s are generally low, commonly less than 0.6, suggesting a relatively large amount of "noise" and thus randomness in WTP responses. As a rule of thumb, Mitchell and Carson suggest an R^2 of 0.15 as the cut-off, with a contingent valuation study's reliability "open to question" if the R^2 is less than 0.15 (1989: 213).

Conclusion

The "state of the art" for the contingent valuation method has advanced in recent years. It is now reasonable to expect studies to provide some evidence of the theoretical validity and reliability of the WTP responses gathered by a survey. Cross-tabulation assesses the responses' theoretical validity, without requiring extensive statistical analysis. Thus, the application is readily understandable by the noneconomist. Multiple regression analysis, undertaken to estimate a valuation function as well as to test the coefficients and inspect the R^2, is a more rigorous yet expensive alternative. For sizable surveys that are supported with considerable financial resources and time, this last technique should be applied to assess both the study's validity and its reliability.

CONCLUSION

Contingent valuation is a survey method that elicits stated, hypothetical valuations from respondents in order to estimate the economic value of a nonmarket effect. Since the method's inception, its validity and reliability have received scrutiny. This chapter identifies a number of influences on respondent answers, along with several survey adjustments, that the survey designer must take into account in order to devise a valid and reliable survey. Table 18.6 provides an overview summarizing the various options that might be considered to address each influence. The table thus serves as a reference. The reader can then consult specific chapter sections in order to remember the details and consider any trade-offs associated with a given option.

Moreover, the growing practice in contingent valuation studies is to test statistically the validity and reliability of survey responses. In addition, several levels of statistical analysis, from simple mean calculations to sophisticated regression analysis, are available for estimating society's valuation of a particular resource. Thus, contingent valuation is in the process of evolving into a highly sophisticated and well-tested valuation method.

Table 18.6
Summary: Survey Designer's Options to Address Each Influence on Respondent Answers

Source of Influence	Hypothetical Market Scenario	Pretests	Sample Selection	Survey Instrument	Valuation Question[a]	Follow-up Questions and Eliminate Problem Answers
Hypothetical valuation	✓	✓		Interactive	Iterative bids, actual payment question	✓
Information presented	✓	✓		Interactive, displays		✓
Incremental valuation	✓	✓			Iterative bids, actual payment question	✓
Embedding problem	✓	✓			Iterative bids	✓
Strategic bias	✓	✓		Interactive	Referendum question	✓
Payment vehicle bias	✓	✓				✓
Protest bias, unrealistically high values, uncooperative respondents			Sample size	Interactive		✓
Nonrepresentative sample			Probability sample, sample size, nonresponse rate	Interactive		
Interviewer effects		✓		Noninteractive (written questionnaire)		✓
Starting point bias		✓			Open-ended question, referendum question	✓

[a]Only format(s) that most effectively address a particular influence are listed.

NOTES

1. *State of Ohio v. Department of the Interior*, 880 F.2nd 432 (D.C. Cir. 1989).

2. Depending on donor objectives, these may reflect use and non-use values.

3. Specifically, NOAA in January 1994 encouraged analysts to use in-person interviews and the referendum format, while both NOAA and DOI (in May 1994) required "scope tests" designed to determine the responses' sensitivity to different amounts of damage (Portney 1994: 10).

4. For example, Diamond and Hausman believe that individual responses to survey valuation questions do not reflect "true" economic preferences (1994: 47, 63) and thus that contingent valuation is "deeply flawed" in measuring non-use values (62). For elaboration, along with a straightforward and (we find) convincing counterargument by Hanemann (1994), we refer the interested reader to the two articles, noting these at times use technical jargon.

5. As one approach, Bendle and Bell apply *top-down disaggregation*, asking respondents first for their WTP for an array of alternatives (specifically, their willingness to give money or time to various environmental causes), then gradually narrowing the scope until eventually asking respondents for their WTP to protect the endangered manatee—the study's specific focus (1995).

6. "The few that are much larger than 3.0 were calculated from samples which included a number of gross outliers or aberrant cases, or both, which the researcher usually dropped before conducting the data analysis. The few studies having coefficients of variation much smaller than 1.0 tended to be from small samples of homogeneous populations" (Mitchell and Carson 1989: 362).

7. If the sample size is calculated using the absolute allowable error (equation 18.1), then to recalculate n with the finite population correction, equation 18.3 can be easily adjusted by simply substituting E for *propE* and σ for V.

8. For an economic model that determines sample size by weighing the trade-off between precision benefits and sample size costs, see Carlson and Thorne (1997: 457–59).

9. A number of options, including prior communication, an updated current mailing list, a skillfully devised questionnaire, extensive pretests, a noncommercial sponsor (such as a university or government), monetary incentives, numerous design techniques for the cover letter, envelope and enclosures and follow-up postcards to nonrespondents, as well as respondents perceiving a connection to the valued resource, can help lower the nonresponse rate (Mitchell and Carson 1989: 279–80; Weiers 1988: 233–39).

10. When interpreting a questionnaire's results, Mitchell and Carson indicate "the most defensible way" to address the nonresponse bias is to assume that nonrespondents attach zero value to the resource in question (1989: 282).

11. Using a sophisticated theoretical derivation, Willig suggests the difference should be no greater than approximately 5% (1976).

12. Hanemann, in a highly technical mathematical derivation, suggests that under certain assumptions (specifically, the existence of few substitutes for the valued resource), economic theory does derive a sizably larger WTA than WTP (1991).

13. This approach was taken, for example, by the contingent valuation study assessing the lost non-use values of the *Exxon Valdez* damage (Carson et al. 1992: 1/7–1/8).

14. Also, keep in mind that WTS questions can be more challenging to frame; the

respondent must be able to relate to holding the property right to the resource in question and thus be in a position to consider selling the resource.

15. In determining the WTA or WTS, the process works in reverse. The interviewer usually starts with a relatively high starting point bid, systematically lowers the price until the respondent is no longer WTA or WTS and then ascends until reaching (converging on) the respondent's minimum WTA or WTS.

16. Sometimes an arbitrary cut-off, say, 5%, 10% or 20%, of pretax income is established to identify outliers. Caution is suggested in setting any particular cut-off, as it allows subjectivity to influence the valuation estimation.

17. The relatively small size of the interval reflects two factors: (1) the sample designer's decision to select a sizable sample yielding a fairly large number of usable responses in order to obtain a small maximum likely error and increase the estimate's precision, and (2) the sample responses yielding a relatively low coefficient of variation, V, of 0.89 ($s/mean$ = 19.08975/21.45). See the section on precision and sample size for further discussion.

18. If a referendum question is asked eliciting a YES/NO response, then an alternative regression model is required. WTP is a dummy variable, usually with the value of one assigned to a YES response and zero to NO. The discontinuity of the numerical values (0,1) requires a different equation. A *logit* or *probit model* can be applied to estimate the valuation function and then the population's Total WTP derived. See Hanemann (1984) and Mitchell and Carson (1986: 3/17–3/22) for a demonstration of the highly technical logit approach. Also, Cameron (1988) presents a maximum likelihood estimation procedure as an alternative to the logit model. See McConnell (1990) for a comparison.

19. If a referendum question is asked, a very large sample is required for cross-tabulations. To understand, remember with this question format the WTP responses are divided into subsamples according to the specific price presented to respondents. Cross-tabulations involve breaking these subsamples into smaller groups, which, if too small, hinder discerning any pattern related to a given characteristic.

20. If the survey asks a referendum question, then a model relevant for a discontinuous WTP variable (such as logit or probit) can be estimated. For example, see Hanemann (1984). For an alternative approach, see Carson and associates (1992) where double YES/NO responses are analyzed with Weibull and logarithmic functions.

Chapter 19

Travel Cost Method

INTRODUCTION

When resource(s) are located at a particular site and access is not adequately priced in the marketplace, then the travel cost method may be an appropriate valuation technique. In contrast with contingent valuation, where individuals are asked hypothetically to state their preferences, the travel cost method is a *revealed preference method*. It values preferences indicated by actual behavior in a *surrogate market*. Specifically, an individual expends time and resources when traveling to and from a particular resource site. The travel cost method might be applied when individuals voluntarily visit a site for one of the following:

- to use recreational resources (e.g., lake, fish, forest, canyon view),
- to collect resources (e.g., fuelwood, water), or
- to deposit wastes (e.g., hazardous or toxic household wastes, recyclable materials).

The travel cost method recognizes that visitors incur different travel costs to visit a site, and the size of the costs in turn affect the number of visits. Generally speaking, travel costs and visitation rates are inversely related; the larger the travel costs, the smaller the visitation rate. This relationship is estimated and applied to derive WTP, assuming visitation rates respond the same to changes in monetary admission prices as they do to changes in travel costs.

Principle 19.1. The travel cost method may be applicable when a nonmarketed resource, good or service is located at a specific site. The method employs regression analysis to estimate the relationship between visitation rates and travel costs incurred to and from the site. It then applies this relationship to derive how the population would respond to alternative site admission prices, thereby inferring society's willingness to pay for the site's nonmarketed resource, good or service.

This chapter defines the components of travel costs and develops an example illustrating how to use a travel cost technique, specifically the Clawson-Knetsch method, to estimate willingness to pay. The discussion then considers the information that a detailed travel cost survey should gather and concludes by identifying the advantages and disadvantages of the travel cost method in comparison with the contingent valuation method.

TRAVEL COSTS DEFINED

A visitor's travel costs consist of several costs. First, the visitor is sometimes, but not always, charged an admission price (or user fee). Generally this is a nominal fee set well below the market-clearing price. Thus, this price does not reflect fully the market's estimation of individual willingness to pay for access to the site.

Second, the visitor incurs transportation expenses that are directly attributed to traveling to and from the site. If travel is by car or truck, these can include the costs of operating the vehicle plus any tolls over the round-trip distance along with any parking fees at the site. Or if travel is by commercial vehicle, such as bus, train or plane, then the round-trip fare paid by the site visitor constitutes the transportation expenses. Some travel cost studies include expenditures on such items as overnight motel rooms and meals over and above what the visitor would otherwise pay without taking the trip; however, we urge caution, as these expenditures often generate utility independent of the resource site's value and, if so, should not be incorporated in the analysis. (For a related discussion, see Box 19.1.)

Third, the visitor incurs a time cost when traveling to and from the site. Using the economic concept of *opportunity cost*, travel time can be valued in terms of the return foregone from its next best alternative use. In other words, the visitor might otherwise have worked and earned wages or, instead, engaged in another leisure activity and received utility. In traveling to and from the site, the visitor is foregoing one (or some combination) of these returns.

Fourth, the visitor spends time at the site and likewise incurs an opportunity cost. In travel cost studies the opportunity cost of on-site time is sometimes but not always included. It seems reasonable that the time on site could have been spent pursuing some other leisure or income-generating activity; thus, the visitor's decision to forego that alternative provides an indication of how much the visitor is willing to spend to gain access to the site. We therefore include a valuation of on-site time as part of the travel cost.

There is some question whether on-site time and travel time have the same opportunity cost. According to the traditional theoretical view, the value of time spent at the site directly reflects the site's value, but the value of time spent

Box 19.1
Expenditure Method

An alternative valuation technique that is sometimes mistakenly used is the *expenditure method*. The expenditure method equates the value of a resource site with the sum of all consumer expenditures (e.g., food, lodging, equipment and transportation) incurred as a part of enjoying the site's resource opportunities. As plausible as this approach may appear, its application to value a given site is misleading. The main criticism is the expenditures do not measure how much an individual is willing to pay for admission to a particular resource area—which is the relevant indication of use value for a cost-benefit analysis.

Consider the inclusion of such a broad group of expenditures to infer a resource site's value. Suppose, for example, visitors go winter skiing on mountain slopes for a weekend, and during the visit they buy food and pay for overnight lodging. At least some portion of the food expenditures would be incurred regardless of whether the visitors visit the site. In addition, food and lodging provide utility in and of themselves. Therefore, it must be asked whether the amount that visitors are willing to pay for food reflects their preference for the site or for the particular food. The same can be said regarding the expenditures on lodging. Does the willingness to pay for five-star accommodations reflect utility for being able to ski on the mountain slopes or a preference for superior lodging? It is difficult to claim that food and lodging expenditures measure the value of the particular ski slopes.

Likewise, expenditures on such items as recreational equipment are generally not applicable. Suppose, for instance, the visitors either bring their own skis or buy them at the lodge's ski shop. The purchased equipment was most likely purchased for use at more than one site. Theoretically, the marginal cost of the skis for the one visit is relevant; however, in practice it is difficult to measure. In addition, the visitors might enjoy being ski owners or receive utility when perceived by others as committed skiers; or perhaps they purchase expensive, high-quality skis because they take pleasure in owning very good equipment. In either case, their willingness to pay for skis does not reflect their valuation of the ski slope for the weekend excursion (Dwyer, Kelly and Bowes 1977: 189).

Note that some of these expenditures may be useful in measuring the impact of the mountain ski slopes on regional expenditures and incomes. Thus, these could be very important in assessing the role of the ski slopes in regional development. The relevant expenditures should be included as part of an *economic impact analysis*, however, not a cost-benefit analysis.

traveling can reflect both the site's value and the utility gained (or lost) from traveling (Freeman 1979: 206–7). For people who enjoy traveling, the estimated opportunity cost of travel time should be reduced to represent only the valuation for visiting the site.[1] When visitors find traveling to be unpleasant, their willingness to incur this disutility in order to visit the site should be added to the estimated opportunity cost of their travel time. However, Smith, Desvousges and McGivney review the theoretical literature and conclude it does not justify, without ambiguity, valuing travel time differently than on-site time (1983b:

262). Thus, given the practical difficulties of estimating each visitor's travel (dis)utility, it seems reasonable to value travel time at the estimated opportunity cost of time. Nevertheless, care and caution are warranted, especially when there is evidence that many visitors to a particular site receive (dis)utility from the travel itself.

To calculate travel costs, therefore, the various costs are added together. In equation form,

$$\text{total travel costs of one visit } = \qquad\qquad\qquad\qquad (19.1)$$
$$\text{admission price (or user fee) + transportation expenses +}$$
$$\text{opportunity cost of travel time + opportunity cost of site time.}$$

INTRODUCTION TO THE ILLUSTRATIVE EXAMPLE

The travel cost method involves gathering and analyzing survey data for visitors from various zones or geographic areas located at varying distances from the resource site. A number of analytical procedures have been used in the literature; the most commonly applied, the *Clawson-Knetsch method*,[2] is presented in this chapter.

Principle 19.2. The Clawson-Knetsch method estimates the following elements:

- visitation rates for different zones
- travel costs
- visitation rate function
- demand curve for the resource site.

The chapter presents each of these components using a hypothetical example. Suppose a state park and historical battleground located in Kentucky is a well-known landmark that has long been a part of Kentucky's heritage. Assume in 1995 the state reconsidered budgetary expenditures, with state legislators asking whether the citizens of Kentucky placed sufficient value on this landmark to warrant its preservation. Suppose at the time the State of Kentucky commissions an analyst to estimate the site's value to citizens. The travel cost method lends itself quite nicely for this valuation, for many families visit the park and battleground each year, incurring different travel expenses. Thus, based on the relationship between travel costs and visitation rates, the analyst can predict society's willingness to pay.

A short time frame for completing the valuation prohibits the analyst from undertaking his own specially designed survey. Suppose, however, he obtains 1993 data collected as part of an attendance survey by the Park Service for the hypothetical park and historical battleground. Also, the analyst has access to the

Table 19.1
Distance, Travel Time and Visitation Rates by Zone

Zone	(1) Distance (miles)	(2) Travel Time (hours)	(3) Number of Visitors	(4) Population (thousands)	(5) Visitors Per 1,000[a]
I	50	1	140,000	700	200
II	100	2	90,000	600	150
III	150	3	45,000	450	100
IV	200	4	25,000	500	50
Total			300,000	2,250	

[a]Calculated as (number of visitors)/(population thousands) or column (3)/column (4).

Statistical Abstract of the United States, population census data, a road map and his own knowledge of road and driving conditions en route to the site. These sources provide the data for this particular illustration. The example thus serves to demonstrate the fundamentals of the technique as well as to illustrate what the technique can offer in a context where a "rapid appraisal"[3] is all that time or budgetary resources allow. After presenting this application, the discussion then considers the information that a more extensive survey should collect and how such information would contribute to sharpening the analysis.

VISITATION RATES FOR DIFFERENT ZONES

The 1993 Park Service survey recorded the county from which each visitor had traveled to and from the park. The analyst groups the counties into four zones. Using a road map, he estimates the average (mean) round-trip distance for individuals originating in each zone (50, 100, 150 and 200 miles, respectively). He then considers typical speeds and road conditions for a variety of routes and figures that with an extensive interstate road system, the average visitor could be expected to travel 50 miles per hour or one, two, three and four hours round trip from each respective zone. These estimates for the mean distance and traveling time (round trip) are presented in Table 19.1, columns 1 and 2, respectively.

Visitation rates are calculated as the number of visitors per thousand of each zonal population.[4] ("Visit" and "visitor" are used interchangeably; thus, an individual who visits multiple times is counted as multiple visitors.) The analyst tabulates the number of visitors recorded by the park survey along with zone populations gathered from county census data. As reported in columns 3 and 4 of Table 19.1, park attendance in 1993 was a total of 300,000 visitors out of a surrounding population of 2.25 million people. Column 5, obtained by dividing column 3 by column 4 for each zone, shows the visitation rate for Zones I through IV to be 200, 150, 100 and 50 visitors per 1,000 people, respectively.

TRAVEL COSTS

Remember from equation 19.1 that total travel costs include any admission price, transportation expenses, travel time costs and on-site time costs spent visiting a site. For the park and battleground, these are first calculated per vehicle and then converted to per visitor estimates.

Cost of Admission to the Site per Vehicle

Suppose the park charged a $3.00 entrance fee for each adult and $1.00 for each child under the age of twelve in 1993. Moreover, the Park Service's attendance survey for that year reported that each vehicle averaged four visitors (two adults and two children). Thus, the admission fees per vehicle were $8 (two adults @ $3 and two children @ $1).

Transportation Expenses per Vehicle

The 1993 survey revealed that the visitors arrived almost exclusively by car or truck rather than by commercial vehicle. The survey also indicated that few tolls or related expenses were incurred, and the park itself provided free parking. Thus, the relevant transportation expense for the visitors was the cost of operating their vehicles.

To estimate vehicle operating costs, two pieces of information are needed: vehicle operating costs per mile and distance traveled. Vehicle operating costs refer to those vehicle costs directly attributable to the trip, that is, *variable costs*. Variable operating costs include such incremental expenses as gas and oil, maintenance, and tire "wear and tear" incurred in traveling a specific trip. Other vehicle costs, such as insurance, depreciation, and licensing, are associated with vehicle ownership and are *fixed costs*. These must be paid whether or not the trip is taken and thus are not considered in the calculation. Table 19.2 reproduces part of a *Statistical Abstract* table showing the fixed and variable costs of owning and operating an automobile in 1993. As can be seen, the (bolded) variable operating costs in 1993 were 9.3 cents per mile.

The vehicle costs per round trip are calculated for each zone.

$$\text{Vehicle operating costs} = \qquad\qquad (19.2)$$
$$\text{(variable operating costs per mile) * (round-trip distance).}$$

As shown in Table 19.1, the four zones are located an estimated 50, 100, 150 and 200 miles, round trip, respectively, from the park. Multiplying these dis-

Table 19.2
Costs of Owning and Operating an Automobile, 1993

Item	Unit	1993
Variable cost	**Cents/mile**	**9.30**
Gas and oil	Cents/mile	6.00
Maintenance	Cents/mile	2.40
Tires	Cents/mile	0.90
Fixed Cost	**Dollars**	**4,486**
Insurance	Dollars	724
License and registration	Dollars	183
Depreciation	Dollars	2,883
Finance charge	Dollars	696

Source: U.S. Bureau of the Census, *Statistical Abstract of the United States: 1995*, prepared by the Chief of the Bureau of Statistics (Washington, D.C.: Government Printing Office, 1995), 640, Table no. 1038 (bold added).

tances by 9.3 cents, the corresponding operating costs per vehicle in 1993, round trip, were $4.65, $9.30, $13.95 and $18.60, respectively, for each zone.

Opportunity Cost of Travel Time per Vehicle

Besides transportation expenses, visitors to the park and battleground also incurred time costs traveling to and from the site. In valuing the opportunity cost of time, some studies use the full wage rate, reflecting the wages foregone by taking the trip rather than engaging in labor. However, Cesario maintains that the eight-hour workday distorts the labor-leisure choice. He questions whether the individual could realistically be working and earning income in place of taking the trip, or if, instead, the trip is at the expense of participating in another leisure opportunity (1976: 34). In situations where the trade-off is a leisure alternative, Cesario recommends the following benchmarks to value time: one-third of the wage rate for an adult,[5] and 25% of an adult's time value for a child under twelve (38).

This example follows Cesario's recommendation.[6] For a precise calculation, the analyst should find each adult visitor's income. Such data were not collected in the Park Service survey, although the survey did determine that the visitors were predominantly from Kentucky; also, park employee observations during the survey period suggested the majority of visitors were middle-income earners with smaller numbers of lower and upper income visitors. The analyst decides to approximate the average adult visitor salary with Kentucky's disposable personal income per capita.[7] (*Disposable income*, or income after taxes are deducted, is appropriate because the income value lost to the visitor by taking the trip is the foregone, after-tax, spending money.)

To calculate the hourly opportunity cost of travel time, the analyst finds the annual disposable income statistic, converts it to an hourly wage and then applies Cesario's recommended benchmarks. In equation form, the

$$\text{value of adult travel time per hour} = .3333 * \frac{\text{annual disposable income}}{2,000 \text{ hours}} \qquad (19.3)$$

The disposable personal income per capita for Kentucky in 1993 was $14,715 (U.S. Bureau of the Census 1995: 462). Substituting this amount in equation 19.3 yields an estimated value of adult travel time of $2.4523 per hour.[8] In turn, the value of child travel time per hour is 25% of $2.4523, or $0.6131 per hour. Thus, on average, each vehicle of two adults and two children incurred an estimated hourly opportunity cost in travel time of $6.1308 (2 @ $2.4523 and 2 @ $0.6131) in 1993.

This hourly cost is converted to the round-trip travel time value. For the average vehicle, the opportunity cost is $6.1308 times the average round trip length of one, two, three and four hours (from Table 19.1), respectively, for each zone. Therefore, the opportunity cost of (round-trip) travel time per vehicle in 1993 was $6.13, $12.26, $18.39 and $24.52 for Zones I through IV, respectively.

Opportunity Cost of Time Spent on the Site per Vehicle

Suppose the Park Service survey reported the average visitor spent six hours visiting and touring the park and battleground in 1993. Using the value of one hour's time, $6.1308, computed for a vehicle of two adults and two children, the on-site time value for the six hours was $36.7848 per vehicle.

Total Travel Costs per Vehicle and per Visitor to the Site

Table 19.3 summarizes the estimated components of travel costs for the average vehicle of two adults and two children in 1993. As can be seen in the table, the largest of the travel costs was on-site time value ($36.78 for all zones), followed by round-trip travel time value ($6.13 to $24.52, varying with zone

Table 19.3
Travel Costs per Vehicle and per Visitor in 1993

		Per Vehicle					
	(1) Vehicle Operating Costs	(2) Travel Time Value	(3) On-Site Time Value	(4) Entry Fee	(5) Total Cost	(6) Per Visitor Total Cost	(7) Visitors Per
Zone	($)	($)	($)	($)	($)	($)	1,000
I	4.65	6.1308	36.7848	8	55.5656	13.8914	200
II	9.30	12.2616	36.7848	8	66.3464	16.5866	150
III	13.95	18.3924	36.7848	8	77.1272	19.2818	100
IV	18.60	24.5232	36.7848	8	87.9080	21.9770	50
Beyond IV	--	--	--	--	--	24.6722	0

proximity to the park). Vehicle operating costs ranged from $4.65 to $18.60, depending on zone, while the average vehicle of passengers paid a combined admission or entry fee of $8.

The travel costs per vehicle are totaled in column 5. On average, two adults and two children incurred a combined cost ranging from $55.57 to $87.91, depending on zone of origin, to visit the park and battleground in 1993. Also shown in Table 19.3 are the travel costs per visitor for each zone. These are calculated by dividing the per vehicle travel costs (column 5) by the four visitors per vehicle. Listed in column 6, the per visitor total costs in 1993 were $13.89, $16.59, $19.28 and $21.98 for Zones I through IV, respectively.

VISITATION RATE FUNCTION

The visitation rate function in its simplest form relates visitation rates with travel costs. For the Kentucky park, each zone's visitation rate is reproduced in column 7 of Table 19.3 to facilitate comparison with the per visitor travel costs (column 6). Comparing the two columns reveals that as total costs per visitor rise, the visitation rate declines. For the given numbers, the reader can verify that total costs per visitor increase by a constant amount of $2.6952 from one zone to the next, while the visitation rate declines by 50 visitors per 1,000. Using this relationship, the travel costs can be projected for the geographical area beyond Zone IV, where the reported number of visitors was zero in 1993. With the visitors per 1,000 falling from 50 in Zone IV to 0 beyond Zone IV, the per visitor total cost rises by an estimated $2.6952 to $24.6722 (also shown in Table 19.3). This suggests that visitors in 1993 were not willing to incur travel costs as high as $24.67 per person to attend the park and battleground.

To analyze the relationship between travel costs and visitation rates, a curve is fitted to these numbers. To facilitate the illustration, the values in columns 6 and 7 have a perfectly linear relationship, with every observation falling precisely on a straight line. In reality, it is unlikely an analyst would generate estimates that line up so perfectly; thus, a regression must be estimated to find the equation that best fits the relationship. When analyzing only the two variables, a simple regression is employed.

A more sophisticated approach is to collect data for additional variables and perform a multiple regression analysis relating the visitation rate to these variables as well as travel costs. The analyst must determine the appropriate functional form that best fits the gathered data. Several forms (log, semilog, linear)[9] are used in the literature. To simplify the explanation, the linear version is presented here. A linear *visitation rate function* is expressed as

$$V = a_0 + a_1C + a_2C_s + a_3S_3 + a_4S_4 + \ldots + a_nS_n, \tag{19.4}$$

where data are organized by zone, V is the zone visitation rate, C is total travel costs per zone visitor, C_s is an index of travel costs or distance to substitute sites per zone visitor and S_i (where $i = 3, 4, \ldots, n$) are variables such as average zone visitor income, education and age, zone urbanization and other socioeconomic characteristics that influence the visitation rate. The data for V, C, C_s and S_i are entered into a statistical program that then estimates a_0, a constant, and a_1, a_2 and a_i, the respective regression coefficients for variables C, C_s and S_i. The coefficients are expressed mathematically as:

$$a_1 = \frac{\Delta V}{\Delta C}, a_2 = \frac{\Delta V}{\Delta C_s}, \text{ and } a_i = \frac{\Delta V}{\Delta S_i}, \text{ for } i = 3, 4, \ldots, n. \tag{19.5}$$

The coefficient of particular interest for the travel cost method is a_1, which represents the change in visitation rates (ΔV) associated with a change in per visitor travel costs (ΔC) across the zones. Multiple regression analysis, if carried out carefully, isolates the effects of the other variables on the visitation rate. For instance, a high visitation rate for a particular zone may reflect a populace with high mean education level or few available proximate substitute sites, rather than low travel costs. Statistically removing such effects sharpens the estimation of the coefficient a_1. In comparison, a simple regression relating only travel costs to visitation rates obtains a less exact coefficient estimate.[10]

For the travel cost and visitor data in columns 6 and 7 of Table 19.3, the numbers fall along a straight line forming the simple visitation rate function,

$$V = 457.7063 - 18.5515C. \tag{19.6}$$

Note that the coefficient -18.5515 is equal to $-50/2.6952$, representing a decrease in 50 visitors per 1,000 population for an increase of $2.6952 in per visitor travel costs across zones. The coefficient -18.5515 thus means that the visitation rate declines by 18.5515 per 1,000 population for each $1 increase in travel costs. This coefficient and function can be used to derive a demand curve for the historic park and battleground.[11]

DEMAND CURVE FOR THE RESOURCE SITE

The *resource site demand curve*, or what Clawson and Knetsch called the "recreation resource demand curve" (1966: 77–85), shows the relationship between price and quantity of visits to the site. Specifically, the curve relates the different monetary prices (P) that visitors are willing to pay per admission with the total number of visitors ($TotV$) to the park. Using the Clawson-Knetsch technique, the demand curve is derived one point at a time. Each point is obtained by, first, reinterpreting the visitation function coefficient and applying the simple function equation (19.6), and second, adjusting the measurement units from the visitation rate (V) to the total number of visitors ($TotV$). Let's look at these two steps more closely.

First, the coefficient (-18.5515) in the visitation function indicates that for each $1 increase in travel costs, the visitation rate declines by an estimated 18.5515 per 1,000 people in each zone. The travel cost method assumes that the visitation rate responds the same to additional monetary or admission fees as it does to additional vehicle operating costs and time opportunity costs. Accordingly, the coefficient is reinterpreted to mean that for each $1 increase in monetary (admission) price to the park, the visitation rate would decline by 18.5515 per 1,000 people in each zone. Given this new interpretation, suppose the admission price (and thus visitor travel cost, C) increases by a specified dollar amount. The new visitation rate, V, for each zone can be predicted by applying the simple visitation rate function (equation 19.6). This calculation is performed zone by zone.

Second, each zone's estimated new visitation rate is multiplied by that zone's population and converted to the total number of zone visitors. Summing across all zones yields the aggregate total visitors ($TotV$). Thus, for a given new admission price, P, the total number of visitors, $TotV$, is predicted—providing one point for the resource site demand curve.

To illustrate the numerical calculations, several points on the demand curve for the park and battleground are derived. The starting point is based on observation; it is the existing price and quantity during the survey period. The other points are each obtained by following the two steps.

Observed starting point. In 1993, 300,000 visitors attended the park and battleground, paying an admission price of $3 for adults and $1 for children. Remembering that half of the visitors were adults and half were children, the weighted average is an admission price of $2. Thus, a starting point for the

Figure 19.1
Resource Site Demand Curve

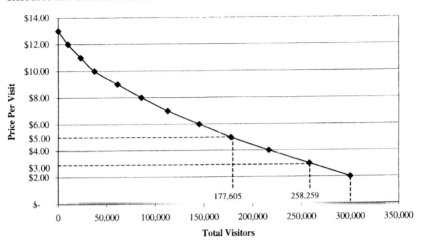

demand curve is $P = \$2$ and $TotV = 300,000$ visitors (see Figure 19.1). (Note that if no admission price were charged, the point would be 300,000 visitors at a zero price, providing an x-intercept for the demand curve.)

Suppose the admission price, P, increases by \$1 (to \$3). A series of calculations are required to estimate $TotV$. Consider, for example, Zone I. Before the price increase, the average Zone I visitor incurred a travel cost of \$13.8914 (reported in Table 19.3). With the \$1 increase in admission price, the travel costs per visitor, C, also increase \$1 to \$14.8914. Assuming the new C, the visitation rate can be recalculated using equation 19.6. Thus for Zone I,

$$V = 457.7063 - 18.5515 * 14.8914 = 181.4485 \text{ visitors per } 1,000.$$

Given a zonal population of 700 thousand (from Table 19.1), the new number of visitors from Zone I is (181.4485 * 700) or 127,014. Having found Zone I's total visitors, similar calculations are repeated for Zones II through IV. The series of calculations for $P = \$3$ are presented in the top block of Table 19.4. For each zone, the per visitor travel costs are assumed to increase by \$1 to generate the new costs, C. Given C, each zone's visitation rate is calculated using equation 19.6 and then multiplied by the zonal population to get the zone's total visitors. Once the number of visitors is figured for each zone, these are summed, yielding a predicted total of 258,259 visitors to the park and battleground. Thus, a second point on the resource site demand curve is $P = \$3$, $TotV = 258,259$ visitors (see Figure 19.1).

Suppose P increases to \$5 (\$3 over the 1993 average price). As reported in the second block of Table 19.4, application of the simple V function (equation

Table 19.4
Calculations for Four Points on the Resource Site Demand Curve

P=$3 (+$1):

Zone	New Costs, C (+$1)	Visitors per 1,000[a]	Population (thousands)	Visitors[b]
I	$ 14.8914	181.4485	700	127,014.00
II	$ 17.5866	131.4485	600	78,869.10
III	$ 20.2818	81.4485	450	36,651.83
IV	$ 22.9770	31.4485	500	15,724.25
				258,259.10 = TotV

P=$5 (+$3):

Zone	New Costs, C (+$3)	Visitors per 1,000[a]	Population (thousands)	Visitors[b]
I	$16,8914	144.3455	700	101,041.90
II	$19.5866	94.3455	600	56,607.30
III	$22.2818	44.3455	450	19,955.48
IV	$24.9770	0.00	500	0.00
				177,604.60 = TotV

P=$8 (+$6):

Zone	New Costs, C (+$6)	Visitors per 1,000[a]	Population (thousands)	Visitors[b]
I	$19.8914	88.691	700	62,083.70
II	$22.5866	38.691	600	23,214.60
III	$25.2818	0.00	450	0.00
IV	$27.9770	0.00	500	0.00
				85,298.30 = TotV

P=$11 (+$9):

Zone	New Costs, C (+$9)	Visitors per 1,000[a]	Population (thousands)	Visitors[b]
I	$22.8914	33.0365	700	23,125.55
II	$25.5866	0.00	600	0.00
III	$28.2818	0.00	450	0.00
IV	$30.9770	0.00	500	0.00
				23,125.55 = TotV

[a]Calculated using equation 19.6.
[b](Visitors/1,000)(population thousands).

19.6), followed by adjustment for the zonal population, indicates the number of visitors from Zone I would be 101,042. Similar calculations are made for Zones II and III. Consider Zone IV. With a $3 increase in P, C rises from the 1993 per visitor cost of $21.977 to $24.977. This is greater than the travel costs of $24.6722 determined in Table 19.3 as too high for visitors to be willing to make the trip to the park and battleground. Thus, the predicted Zone IV visitors are zero. For all zones, the total visitors, $TotV$, is 177,605 at the P of $5—a third point for the demand curve (see Figure 19.1).

Similar computations are made, increasing P one dollar at a time to $6, $7, and so on up to $13. The calculations for $P = $8 and $11 are presented in Table 19.4 for further illustration.

At $P = $13 ($11 over the 1993 average price), the per visitor travel costs, C, for every zone rise above $24.6722. Thus, the total number of park visitors is zero. $P = $13, $TotV = 0$ is the y-intercept of the demand curve (see Figure 19.1).

In Table 19.5, the demand schedule lists alternative prices and total visitors for the park and battleground. Each P and $TotV$ is a point that is plotted in the graph (in Figure 19.1) with a connecting line to form the resource site demand curve.

Remember the 1995 State of Kentucky legislators were interested in the citizens' valuation of the park and historic battleground. To infer society's aggregate WTP in 1993, the analyst estimates the area under the resource site demand curve. In Figure 19.1, the relevant area is below the curve, from the origin to 300,000 visitors (the actual number of visitors). By dividing the area into rectangles and triangles and figuring the size of each, the total area is calculated to be $1,877,005. Thus, the 300,000 visitors in 1993 were willing to pay an estimated $1.877 million in the aggregate for the park and battleground. This converts to approximately $25 per vehicle of two adults and two children, or, with rounding, $6.26 per visitor in 1993. These estimates can be considered by the State of Kentucky legislators as they determine whether further budget allocations to preserve and operate the park are warranted (and if so, how much). In addition, note that the demand curve can be used to assess the attendance and revenue implications of increasing the park's admission price, should the decision makers wish to consider that option.

To assess the travel cost estimation of WTP, the assumptions underlying the analysis must be considered.

Principle 19.3. The prediction of WTP based on visitor travel costs is premised on the following:

- the assumption that visitors respond the same to changes in monetary admission prices as they do to changes in travel costs, and
- the corollary that the most distant visitor's travel costs is the maximum that any visitor might be WTP.

Table 19.5
Resource Site Demand Schedule

Price ($)	Total Visitors[a] (TotV)
2	300,000
3	258,259
4	216,518
5	177,605
6	145,140
7	112,674
8	85,298
9	61,181
10	37,064
11	23,126
12	10,140
13	0

[a]Rounded to whole number.

Both of these premises are demonstrated in the park and battleground example. The derivation of the resource site demand curve from the visitation rate function assumes equivalent responses to dollar increases in monetary prices and travel costs. As a corollary, the estimated visitation rate function predicts that a zero visitation rate is associated with a per visitor travel cost of $24.6722; the analysis then infers the average visitor is not WTP as much as $24.6722 for access to the park. To the extent that these assumptions are not realistic, then the travel cost estimation inaccurately values WTP.

Additional considerations in assessing the estimates are the data quality and sophistication of the analysis—both of which can be enhanced by designing a thorough visitor survey. The discussion therefore considers the data to be gathered in a detailed survey.

TRAVEL COST SURVEY INFORMATION

The travel cost method is a valuation technique that requires survey data. The survey designer must make several choices, including the following:

1. Select a representative visitor sample to achieve the desired precision. The determination of sample size involves the same steps as discussed for a contingent valuation survey (Chapter 18).
2. Identify location(s) at which to survey visitors. Visitors might be surveyed on site, en route from the site or at their residences.
3. Design the survey instrument. Similar to contingent valuation surveys, visitors can be

surveyed in person, by questionnaire (perhaps distributed on site) or by phone (if at home).

In addition, the designer must determine the survey's content. In the illustrative example, the analyst does the best he can with limited data. However, in several instances, data precise to the park are not available and the analyst uses approximations. In the end the travel cost valuations are only as accurate as the numbers employed. A thorough attendance survey would have facilitated the accuracy of the calculated values. The basic information for a proper survey to collect is listed.

Information from site records (or surveyor observation):
- admission fee (and any breakdown, e.g., children under twelve, adults, seniors)
- total number of visitors (by breakdown) for a given time period
- total number of vehicles.

Information from visitor sample:
- number of adults and children traveling together (per vehicle, if relevant)
- frequency of visits
- how long they stayed at the site for the visit
- the place where the trip to the site originated[12]
- other sites visited during the trip
- other reasons for traveling to the site area (e.g., to visit friends or family, business)
- travel time to reach the site (one-way or round trip)
- transport mode used (e.g., personal car or truck, commercial bus, plane)
- types of costs and dollar expenditures incurred traveling to the site
- substitute sites visited in the past
- types of costs and dollar expenditures incurred visiting substitute sites
- attitudes (e.g., pleasure, displeasure) toward travel
- alternatives the visitors might have pursued instead of visiting the site (e.g., work for income, visit another site, engage in other leisure activity)
- socioeconomic indicators, demographics (e.g., age, income, gender, education).

Gathering this information facilitates applying regression analysis to estimate the multivariable visitation rate function (equation 19.4). Remember that compared to a simple two-variable regression, a carefully executed multiple regression can obtain a more precise estimate of the coefficient a_1, relating travel costs to visitation rates. In addition, the calculation of the travel costs themselves is enhanced with more exact measures of foregone income and travel and on-site times for each visitor. For instance, incomes may vary by zone, in which case the opportunity cost of time, both for travel and on site, differs across zones.

Likewise, an extensive survey might find that visitors from different zones stay on site varying lengths of time. Inclusion of such detailed estimates determines more accurately the points plotted to derive the demand curve and, in turn, the predicted willingness to pay.[13] Finally, an in-depth survey can also identify responses that violate the method's assumptions. The analyst can then consider whether adjusting or excluding specific responses is appropriate as well as whether the travel cost method is applicable in valuing a particular resource site.

ADVANTAGES AND DISADVANTAGES OF THE TRAVEL COST METHOD IN COMPARISON WITH THE CONTINGENT VALUATION METHOD

When valuing a particular benefit or cost, the analyst must select an appropriate valuation method. The literature has devoted much attention to comparing the relative strengths and disadvantages of the travel cost method and contingent valuation method. To facilitate the analyst's assessment as to which of the two methods (if either) to apply for a particular valuation, this section explores the advantages and disadvantages of the travel cost method, considering these in comparison with the contingent valuation method.

1. *Survey responses based on actual behavior.* The travel cost method is perceived by many as advantageous in that survey responses are based on actual behavior rather than being contingent on hypothetical circumstances. In addition, there is less concern that field personnel, simply by the way they ask respondents questions, might influence valuations. Therefore, proponents believe the travel cost method can more easily gather reliable data.

2. *Site specific.* The travel cost method is applicable when estimating values for resource opportunities at specific sites. In contrast, contingent valuation has greater versatility; it can estimate values for particular sites as well as for designated resources or activities within broader geographical areas. For example, contingent valuation can be used to estimate the value of national water quality levels, a particular wildlife species within a region or specific regional or even national recreational activities.

3. *Single purpose trips.* The travel cost method assumes the round trip distance and travel time are all incurred for the single purpose of visiting the one site. If in actuality the trips are multipurpose, then the calculated values overstate willingness to pay for the resource site. Should a small number of visitors travel to a given site as one of multiple destinations or purposes, their responses might be dropped or excluded from further analysis. If, however, a substantial number of visitors do so, then the travel cost method is subject to *multiple destination bias* and estimates become "unstable" (Smith and Kopp 1980). This is especially likely for sites, such as the Grand Canyon, that attract cross-country travelers who generally visit several sites during the long-distance trip. In order to use each multiple destination response, the analyst might attribute only a portion of the visitor's travel costs to each of the multiple sites. Determining the exact

proportion is arbitrary, although there is some support for simply averaging the distance traveled for all sites visited (Haspel and Johnson 1982). Alternatively, the analyst might employ the contingent valuation method, which does not encounter this bias.

4. *Omits use values for non-visitors.* As illustrated for the hypothetical park and battleground, the travel cost method includes only the site visitors' valuation; non-users are omitted from the survey. Individuals who did not travel to the park in 1993, even though they might value the site's preservation for possible current or future visits, are excluded. In that respect, the travel cost method underestimates the value of preserving the park and battleground.

In terms of statistical regression, the sample is said to be truncated, as it is not fully representative of the broader population, which includes visitors and non-visitors. Information as to why individuals do not visit a particular site can enhance understanding of what determines visitation. Omission of such information can lead to *truncation bias*, yielding a biased coefficient in the visitation rate function and thereby affecting the derived demand curve and willingness to pay.

The exclusion of non-visitors can be especially significant when a site is characterized by congestion or pollution. The travel cost method assumes there is zero site congestion and pollution. If either exists, discouraging interested individuals from visiting the site, the travel cost method underestimates the willingness to pay for site benefits. If the congestion or pollution is substantial, then the contingent valuation method, with non-visitors included in the survey sample, can offer useful information.

5. *Excludes non-use values.* The travel cost method omits non-use values—for both non-users and visitors. The value any individual holds for preserving the park and battleground simply to know it exists is not measured. When there is reason to believe these values are sizable, estimation of the total willingness to pay should include a contingent valuation of non-use values.

6. *Assessment of site quality changes.* The travel cost method, as illustrated, analyzes site visitation given the site's existing characteristics. Unknown is how visitation would change if the site's quality changes. The literature offers several variations of the method to value changes in site quality. One modification is for the travel cost survey to include some *contingent activity questions*,[14] eliciting (hypothetically) how many times visitors would visit the site if specified quality changes were achieved. This information is then used to generate a resource site demand curve and to estimate total WTP for each designated quality level. The difference in WTPs associated with changes in site quality can then be calculated (McConnell 1986).

Most other method variations require extensive data measuring the travel costs incurred to visit a number of different sites. Highly sophisticated techniques are applied to infer the WTP for different site qualities. Noting the methods' complexity, we highlight several methods and refer the interested reader to relevant sources providing application or critique.

- As one of the earliest efforts, Cesario and Knetsch (1976) developed a *gravity model* incorporating into a single equation the interactions between the travel costs to different sites, including an "attractiveness" variable for each site.

- Another approach, a *varying parameter model* or *generalized travel cost model*, estimates several visitation rate functions (equation 19.4), one for each alternative site, and then regresses the functions' respective travel cost coefficients, a_1, on the sites' quality attributes (Smith, Desvousges and McGivney 1983a; Smith and Desvousges 1985).

- *Random utility models* and *participation models*, often applying a *logit* model, relate each individual's decision choice, whether or not to visit specific sites, to the sites' characteristics. Freeman overviews these two approaches (1993a: 469–72, 474–79).

- A *hedonic travel cost method* values specific site characteristics in a two-stage process. First, distance (or travel time) is regressed as a function of various site characteristics to estimate the implicit (or hedonic) price for each trait. Second, additional statistical analysis is applied to derive the demand for each site characteristic (Brown and Mendelsohn 1984; Smith and Kaoru 1987; Bockstael, McConnell and Strand 1991: 233–34).

A caveat to all of these approaches is the exclusion of non-visitors from the estimation. In order to predict society's response to quality improvements, a sample should include both visitors and non-visitors, for improvements may well attract current non-visitors to the site (Freeman 1979: 204). In this regard, the contingent valuation method is advantageous.

Principle 19.4. Similar to contingent valuation, the travel cost method surveys respondents, in this case, visitors to a specific site. Unlike contingent valuation, visitor responses to travel cost questions are based on actual rather than hypothetical behavior. Travel cost proponents perceive the method's elicitation of revealed preferences as enhancing reliable estimation. At the same time, the analyst should consider applying contingent valuation as an alternative or supplement to the travel cost method when a resource, good or service is any of the following: available independent of a specific site, one of multiple destinations for individual visitor trips, valued for use by numerous non-visitors, located at a congested or polluted site or associated with sizable non-use values. Likewise, to value site quality changes, the analyst may employ sophisticated variations of the travel cost method or, instead, apply the contingent valuation method.

NOTES

1. For example, a visitor might take a scenic route involving a longer distance and travel time than the faster, more direct routes. The travel costs for the direct routes are the relevant measure.

2. The method originally explained in Clawson and Knetsch (1966) has evolved in the literature, incorporating time costs as well as the role of substitute sites in determining visitation to a particular site. Such modifications are incorporated in the chapter.

3. This term is borrowed from Chambers (1985) and refers to shortcuts in information gathering that preclude the most thorough and sophisticated academic research but are cost effective for timely decision making.

4. This measurement unit is commonly used when population members typically visit the site once or not at all during the designated time frame. In cases where individuals generally visit several times in a given period, then visitation rates might be expressed as the number of visits per individual. For an illustrative example, see Boardman and associates (1996: 326–28).

5. Cesario selected the factor of one-third based on many empirical studies that reported values of leisure time between one-fourth and one-half of the average wage rate (1976).

6. Discussion continues regarding whether to use the full wage rate or Cesario's recommendation in valuing travel time. Smith, Desvousges and McGivney present a theoretical analysis that "provides formal support" for Cesario's recommendation; however, their empirical analysis found both Cesario's recommendation and the full wage rate to be "plausible" values for travel time (1983b: 275–76).

7. Per capita income is admittedly a rough indicator. When visitor incomes are not known, yet sufficient data are available concerning visitor traits, such as age and education as well as job and residential area characteristics, the analyst might consider applying a statistically estimated *hedonic wage model* to predict visitor wages. See Smith, Desvousges and McGivney (1983b).

8. All calculations are carried out to four decimal places to enhance the accuracy of the final calculation.

9. In a number of studies, the semi-log form (with the log of V regressed on C and other explanatory variables) fits the data best.

10. Whether performing a simple or multiple regression analysis, the analyst must check carefully for the regression's goodness of fit, specification bias, multicollinearity, statistical significance, data accuracy and so on, as discussed in Chapter 17.

11. Note that the inverse of this equation is the function $C = f(V)$, and in this case, $C = 24.6722 - .0539V$. The coefficient $(-.0539)$ measures $\Delta C/\Delta V$ and indicates that if the visitation rate increases by one visitor per 1,000, travel costs decrease by $0.0539. The constant, $24.6722, is the per visitor travel cost associated with zero visitors. This function is sometimes graphed (with C on the vertical axis and V on the horizontal axis) to present the per visitor travel costs incurred at different visitation rates, or what Clawson and Knetsch called the "whole outdoor recreation experience demand curve" (1966: 64–77).

12. Visitors might be asked the number of miles traveled to reach the site, either one-way or round trip. However, people often do not keep track of precise mileage; thus, their answers are likely to be inaccurate. If, instead, visitors are asked to identify the place of origin for the trip to the site, then the surveyor can estimate the mileage. Also, organizing visitors by county, city or town enables the analyst to use available government data for population size and socioeconomic characteristics. Or, the surveyor may designate zones on an area map and ask the respondent to indicate the zone of origin. For example, concentric zones might be drawn around the site so that a visitor leaving from any point within a given zone would travel approximately the same distance. Another suggestion is that visitors traveling from home might be asked to indicate their residential zip code.

13. The reader might note in the illustrated example that inclusion of the constant on-site time value does not affect the estimated regression coefficient, for there is no relationship between changing visitation rates and a constant on-site value. Thus, the practice in some studies of excluding on-site time value has no effect on the analysis if in actuality

the on-site time value is constant across zones. However, if it is variable, then the omission of on-site time value does change the coefficient as well as the derived demand and predicted willingness to pay. We recommend inclusion of the on-site time value in any case, for it is part of the full value of a visitor's travel costs.

14. "Contingent activity questions" is a term used by Freeman (1993a: 461).

Chapter 20

Hedonic Pricing Method: Property Value Approach

INTRODUCTION

Principle 20.1. The property value approach infers WTP for a nonmarket effect from observed behavior (revealed preferences) in property markets. It is thus relevant only when the studied nonmarket effect influences property values.

The method views property as a fixed asset that provides a "bundle" of uses simultaneously. The property thus holds a value equal to the discounted present value of future net benefits from the many uses of the property. When a property enables a new owner to receive the benefits (or incur the costs) of some nonmarket effect, such value is therefore included in the purchase price. Property buyers are assumed to have the mobility to choose between sites as well as the knowledge to perceive different levels of the nonmarket effect at alternative property sites and to value the respective properties accordingly.[1]

The following examples suggest some of the many possible applications of the property value approach.

- To value air pollution: compare property values in residential areas impacted by different levels of sulfur dioxide, particulates or other pollution indicators.[2]

- To value increased water quality: compare the values of waterfront properties bordering high-quality water bodies with waterfront properties adjacent to low-quality water bodies.

- To value a beach: compare the values of beachfront properties with properties located at various distances from the shoreline.

- To value natural habitat in a condominium development: compare the values of condominium properties that have nature preserves with those that do not.

• To value a mass transit system: compare how property values change with proximity to the transit line.

This chapter describes the estimation techniques commonly employed by the property valuation method and considers how to interpret the empirical results. It should be noted that professional skills in statistical regression analysis are required to undertake proper estimation. The objective of this discussion is to provide the decision maker, beginning analyst or interested party a basic understanding of the technique and thereby to enable each to decide for themselves whether such an analysis is appropriate or useful in assessing a particular policy.

THE HEDONIC PRICE RELATIONSHIP

Analyzing property values to derive individual willingness to pay for a nonmarket effect involves two steps. Estimate, first, hedonic prices and second, willingness to pay. Within these steps are three conceptual components. These are:

• the hedonic price function,
• the hedonic prices of the nonmarket effect, and
• the willingness-to-pay function.

Once estimated, the willingness-to-pay regression can then be used to predict welfare changes for individual households (property buyers) due to changes in the nonmarket effect.

Hedonic Price Function

The idea that property values can reflect individual valuation of particular nonmarket effects is fairly straightforward and simple. At the same time, empirical estimation recognizes that a complex set of determinants influences any given property value. Suppose the analyst is comparing the value of large homes located in areas with high-quality (relatively clean) air with smaller homes in high-smog areas. The difference in property values cannot be attributed entirely to the variation in air quality. Indeed, even if the analyst was comparing large homes at all sites, there are numerous other characteristics (e.g., number of bedrooms, number of bathrooms, house age, lot size, neighborhood safety, local school quality, proximity to stores or employment and many other factors) that can affect property values. The analyst must isolate the air quality's impact from other characteristics' effects.

The variables' effects can be separated statistically by estimating a *hedonic price function* using *multiple regression analysis*. The hedonic price regression relates various property values to a number of property characteristics (including the nonmarket effect). The analysis determines several regression coefficients that measure, at the margin, each respective characteristic's independent effect on property value.

Concerning data collection, the common practice is to use available records of residential property transactions that indicate the actual sale price and pertinent house and lot characteristics.[3] Data trends might be analyzed over time, as in a *time series* analysis; however, difficulties are encountered trying to account for the many variables that affect property values over time. Thus, most hedonic price regressions are *cross-section analyses*, evaluating data for selected pieces of property for a designated time period.

Once data are gathered, the analyst must determine the appropriate functional form that best fits the data. The simplest is a linear function that assumes that if any specific property characteristic increases, all other variables held constant, then the property value changes in steady (linear) proportion. It is not uncommon, however, for property value studies to find the relationship to be nonlinear. Indeed, a common functional form used in property valuation studies is the log-linear model.[4] A general formula for a log-linear hedonic price function is

$$\ln P = a_0 + a_1 \ln C_1 + a_2 \ln C_2 + a_3 \ln C_3 + \ldots + a_n \ln C_n, \tag{20.1}$$

where *ln* is the natural log, *P* is the property value (or price) and C_i is property characteristic *i*. The data for *P* and C_i are entered into a computer, and a statistical program estimates a_0, a constant, and a_i, the respective regression coefficient for C_i. In the log-linear model, each coefficient represents the percentage change in property value associated with a percentage change in the corresponding characteristic C_i. The coefficients are expressed mathematically as:

$$a_i = \frac{\% \, \Delta P,}{\% \Delta C_i}, \text{ for i } = 1, 2, \ldots, \text{ n.} \tag{20.2}$$

A residential property can be differentiated by hundreds of characteristics. Hedonic regressions in the literature therefore sometimes include more than ten variables. In general, the variables can be categorized in five broad groups representing characteristics of the house, lot, neighborhood, accessibility and nonmarket effect. For illustrative purposes, a simple hedonic price function is presented with an environmental attribute, *EA*, as the nonmarket effect. The example is:

$$\ln P = a_0 + a_1 \ln(\text{Floor Area}) + a_2 \ln(\text{\#Bathrooms}) + a_3 \ln(\text{Lot Size}) + \tag{20.3}$$
$$a_4 \ln(\text{Job Proximity}) + a_5 \ln(\text{Crime Rate}) + a_6 \ln(\text{EA}).$$

Of particular interest for valuing the nonmarket effect is coefficient a_6; it measures the percentage change in property value for each percentage change of the environmental attribute, other variables held constant. To illustrate, suppose in a coastal metropolitan area the environmental asset of concern is air quality. Numerous properties have coastal views with varying visibility levels due to air pollution. Accordingly, visibility is monitored at several sites, and visibility levels are used as EA. Assume a_6 is estimated as .05. Then, a 1% increase in visibility is associated, on average, with a .05% (one-twentieth of a percent) increase in property value. (Likewise, a 1% decrease in visibility is related to a .05% decrease in property value.)

Hedonic Prices of the Nonmarket Effect

The coefficient a_6 can be used to derive the *hedonic price*[5] of the environmental attribute, r_6, for each property. Each hedonic price is appropriately interpreted as the change in a particular property value associated with a marginal increase in EA, other variables held constant. Mathematically, r_6 is the slope (or derivative) of the hedonic price function with respect to EA. Given equation 20.3, the relevant slope is:

$$r_6 = a_6(P/EA). \tag{20.4}$$

Equation 20.4 is calculated by multiplying the estimated regression coefficient, a_6, by a ratio of the original data for each property value, P, and the EA specific to that property. Accordingly, the equation generates a series of hedonic prices, r_6, for the environmental attribute.

For the visibility example, remember a_6 is .05. Suppose one property has a property value, P, of \$150,000; also, it is located near a monitoring site measuring a mean visibility level (EA) of ten miles per year. Substituting these values into equation 20.4, the hedonic price for visibility, r_6, for this property is .05(\$150,000/10) or \$750. Thus, for an average annual increase of one mile of visibility, this particular property's value, P, is predicted to increase by \$750.

Consider a second property located at a site with greater visibility—specifically, a mean visibility level of fifteen miles per year. If the property value is \$180,000, then the property's hedonic price for visibility, r_6, is \$600 or .05(\$180,000/15). For this property, an average annual increase of one mile of visibility is associated with a \$600 increase in the property value, P.

Note the relationship between r_6 and EA. Comparing these two properties, as EA increases (from ten to fifteen miles), r_6 decreases (from \$750 to \$600). This illustrates the general relationship expected in equation 20.4. As shown in the equation, each hedonic price of the environmental attribute r_6 varies with the level of EA (as well as P).[6] In words, the change in property value associated with a marginal increase in visibility varies for each visibility level. Specifically, in smog-prone neighborhoods with lower visibility levels, a marginal increase in visibility is predicted to raise property values a relatively large amount, while in "clean air" neighborhoods with high levels of visibility, property values increase less as visibility improves further.

As defined, r_6 is the change in property value associated with a marginal increase in *EA*. Therefore, for marginal (very small, infinitesimal) changes in *EA*, a hedonic price, r_6, can be interpreted as the change in an individual household's willingness to pay. In reality, however, most environmental changes (or other nonmarket effects) of sufficient interest to warrant such an analysis are too sizable to be considered marginal. In order to value these environmental changes, a second regression analysis is required.

Willingness-to-Pay Function

A willingness-to-pay function must be estimated in order to predict the change in WTP that results from a nonmarginal change in the environmental attribute. To understand why, let's again consider the hedonic price function. As expressed in equations 20.1 or 20.3, the hedonic price function analyzes the property value (price) as a function of property characteristics, while neglecting the traditional determinants of consumer demand, such as household income, tastes, age and the like. Thus, each property's hedonic price, r_6, may reflect not only the quantity of the environmental attribute but also the corresponding household's socioeconomic characteristics and consumption preferences.

In the unlikely event that all households share the same incomes and preferences, then each household's demand for the environmental attribute is identical. In such a case, each hedonic price for a property can be interpreted as the respective household's willingness to pay for a change in the environmental attribute (Freeman 1979: 80). However, in reality, incomes and preferences do vary across households. According to demand theory, households with higher incomes, for example, are likely to be WTP more than lower-income households for a positive improvement in environmental quality. In order to analyze household demand for the environmental attribute, *EA*, the calculated hedonic prices, r_6, are statistically regressed on the environmental and household attributes. This regression is called an *inverse demand function*.[7]

In specifying the equation, the appropriate functional form must be determined. Assuming a log-linear function for illustration, then a simple version of the household *willingness-to-pay function* can be written as

$$\ln r_6 = b_0 + b_1 \ln EA + b_2 \ln Income + b_3 \ln(\# \text{ Household Dwellers}). \quad (20.5)$$

(The equation can be easily expanded with additional household characteristics that affect consumer demand for residential housing property.)

Once the coefficients b_i are estimated, the regression equation is then used to predict each individual household's WTP for a nonmarginal change in the environmental attribute. First, plug into the estimated equation the specific values for a given household's characteristics to find that individual household's demand. Second, calculate the area under the household's demand curve for a specified nonmarginal change in the environmental attribute, *EA*. This area is the individual household's total WTP for the change. Third, make a similar estimate for each household, and sum across all households to determine the aggregate total WTP for the change in environmental attribute.[8]

The calculation procedure is sketched because of the theoretical desirability of employing a willingness-to-pay function. Sometimes, however, property value studies do not estimate this household inverse demand function. Rather the hedonic prices, r_6, are interpreted as each individual household's respective WTP. The reader should be aware that such estimates are approximations and are likely to be overestimates (Freeman 1979: 145; 1993a: 401).

Principle 20.2. The property value approach applies multiple regression techniques to analyze property values. The approach first estimates a hedonic price function to determine the amount of property value associated with the nonmarket effect, separated from other property characteristics. Second, the hedonic prices of the nonmarket effect are regressed on the household demand characteristics and nonmarket effect to determine the willingness-to-pay function. This function is used to calculate the change in total WTP for a change in the nonmarket effect.

INTERPRETING PROPERTY VALUATION ESTIMATES

When using the hedonic pricing method to infer the property owners' WTP for an environmental attribute (or other nonmarket effect), care is needed in interpreting the results. First, the regression analyses must be performed with adequate consideration as to goodness of fit, functional form, specification bias, multicollinearity, statistical significance, data accuracy and the like, as discussed in Chapter 17. Second, property values are in present value terms; they are the discounted values of future net benefits each owner expects from using the property. In the NPV calculation, therefore, the inferred WTPs should be treated as values that have already been discounted; these are not annual values, and in this way they differ from most other benefits and costs.

Third, the inferred WTPs should not be incorporated in a cost-benefit analysis if they represent *pecuniary effects*. For example, suppose a new sports stadium is constructed in a metropolitan area and benefits are measured in the form of local citizens' and spectators' willingness to pay. Arguments that the stadium also increases surrounding property values may be accurate; however, these are price effects that, as explained in Chapter 16, "Identifying Benefits and Costs," should generally not be included in a cost-benefit analysis. Caution is therefore required to verify whether property value estimates are inferring willingness to pay for a nonmarket effect or whether they represent a price change in the related property market and thus are a pecuniary effect. Moreover, to the extent that the owners of nearby properties have indicated their preferences as citizens or attenders at the sports events, their valuation of the availability and close proximity of the events may have already been measured. If so, inclusion of property values involves *double counting*.

Fourth, the question as to whose values are counted needs further consideration. In the case of valuing a lake's water quality, for example, property values near the lake can reflect such use benefits as the pleasure of the view and easy access to engage in specific recreational activities (e.g., boating, swimming). However, these property values include only the valuation held by residents adjacent to or near the water body. The valuation of any "nonresidents" who might use the lake is excluded from the property value approach. When the objective is to estimate the total social benefits associated with the lake's water quality, the values of nonresidents must also be included. One solution is to undertake a separate estimate of recreational benefits, say, through contingent valuation interviews of swimmers, boaters and other visitors to the lake. However, be wary of double counting. Only the responses from those who do not own property near the lake should be counted in combination with the property valuation of water quality. Alternatively, given the limited scope of the property value approach for this case, along with the time, effort and costs of undertaking two different valuation methods, the analysis might be better served by foregoing property valuation. Instead, choosing the one approach that includes the most members of society who benefit from the lake may be rational. Furthermore, property valuations measure use values only, thereby excluding existence or other non-use values.

Fifth, the factor causing the nonmarket effect may have additional effect(s) on property values. If so, these should be identified and accounted for in the analysis. For instance, suppose an analyst seeks to estimate the impact of noise pollution from a nearby airport on residential property values. The differential in property values between noise impacted and non-impacted areas could reflect two other distinct influences by the airport: employment accessibility and air pollution. If sufficient data are available, three variables should be included in the hedonic price regression to measure these independent effects. When data are unobtainable, the analyst must take care in designing the analysis. As one possibility, a student analyzed a regional airport's noise pollution but found employment data for respective properties were not available. The student designed a sample to control for employment accessibility by using noise contours to identify noise impacted and non-impacted residential areas, respectively, and chose areas located approximately the same distance from the airport. In this manner, the analyst ensured the differential in property values between the two areas reflected airport noise and not employment accessibility (Smith, M. 1988). Similarly, in any property value analysis, care is required to control for all related effects.

CONCLUSION

The property value approach is one method for valuing individual WTP for a nonmarket effect. It is most applicable when the relevant policy consequence is site specific and property owners constitute a substantial percentage of society's members who experience the benefit or cost.

The method entails extensive data collection and sophisticated regression analysis, along with careful interpretation of the empirical results. Thus, it can be expensive in both time and budgetary resources. At the same time, the approach offers the advantage of inferring WTP from observed behavior in well-established markets for an asset long accepted as pricable. While some discussion in the literature questions the validity of the approach (often focusing on the theoretical assumptions), the technique has generally been accepted as one that, with due care in data collection, regression analysis and interpretation, can yield useful information for inclusion in cost-benefit analysis.

Principle 20.3. The hedonic pricing method analyzes the actual behavior of property buyers, usually measured with market values. The method's use should be checked to ensure it is (appropriately) valuing WTP for a nonmarket effect, rather than valuing a pecuniary effect. Moreover, its application is limited to valuing a policy consequence that affects a well-defined site area and to estimating the use values of property owners. Thus, additional valuation methods are required to estimate any nonresidents' use values (with due caution to avoid double counting property owner values) as well as any non-use values.

NOTES

1. For a discussion of these and other theoretical assumptions involved in the approach, see Freeman (1979, 1993a). Readers with advanced economic knowledge might refer to Rosen (1974) for the original theoretical exposition of hedonic prices.

2. In the literature, the property value method has been applied most often to value air pollution. Studies have been published in several journals, especially in the *Journal of Urban Economics* and *Journal of Environmental Economics and Management*. Smith and Huang (1995) provide a ''meta-analysis'' of 37 studies' estimates of the marginal WTP to reduce total suspended particulates in the air.

3. Freeman notes such market data are ''preferable'' to professional property appraisals or census data that tabulate responding homeowners' valuations of their own properties. Limitations of the latter include the accuracy of self-estimates, the small number of reported property characteristics and the aggregation of census tract data (1979: 130–32; 1993a: 375–76).

4. For a discussion of alternative functional forms, see Freeman (1979: 139–142) and Cropper, Deck and McConnell (1988). Freeman (1993a: 379–81) overviews several applications of Box Cox transformations.

5. Hedonic price is also called *implicit price* or *implicit marginal price* in the literature.

6. This variation reflects the nonlinearity of the original hedonic price function. If equation 20.3 was linear, the respective regression coefficient, a_6, would be the change in P for a unit change in EA or, in other words, the hedonic price; and it would remain constant for all levels of EA. Moreover, if linear, there would be no further derivation beyond the hedonic price function. An easily readable linear regression example is provided by the initial property valuation study, Ridker and Henning (1967).

7. By definition, in an inverse demand function, Price is the dependent variable—a function of quantity, income and other household characteristics. Two alternative ways to estimate willingness to pay are to employ a demand function with quantity demanded as the dependent variable or to use simultaneous demand and supply equations. Freeman suggests these techniques' respective assumptions generally do not pertain to housing. However, in urban areas with rapid growth and quick housing supply adjustments, the latter approach might be appropriate (1979: 125–27).

8. An approximation is sometimes calculated by plugging the mean values for all households' characteristics into the estimated willingness-to-pay regression, calculating the relevant area under the average household's demand curve and multiplying by the total number of households.

Chapter 21

Valuation of Human Life

INTRODUCTION

Perhaps one of the most challenging tasks for the analyst is presented when a policy results in a saved or lost human life or a change in the probability (risk) of human death. Cost-benefit analysis seeks to compare the efficiency of allocating scarce resources to save (or inadvertently lose) lives with achieving alternative objectives. In order to weigh the change in lives with the other policy benefits and costs, human life is expressed using the same yardstick, or unit of measurement, that is, monetary value. Several techniques exist to infer the value of human life.

For most people, however, the concept of placing a dollar value on a human life is unacceptable. If asked, many would say the value is infinite, or the sacredness of human life cannot be captured in monetary valuation. It is important to realize that economists make no claim to estimate the intrinsic value of a human life. Rather, at issue is how decision makers must choose between alternative policies within the context of finite resources. If one policy saves one human life, and another policy provides social benefits but none is life-saving, does this mean that the decision maker should automatically pursue the former policy? Should this be the case even if the former costs 100 times as much as the latter policy, while the latter benefits thousands of individuals? If the answer is yes, then society would be placing substantially more resources toward new medical procedures and multimillion-dollar equipment that promise to prolong one human life, and none toward football stadiums and sports arenas, which, no matter how beneficial, are not known to save lives. Every time individuals drive a car, ride a bicycle or travel by plane, they are indicating a willingness to accept a positive risk of an accident resulting in death. By not installing a security alarm system with triple locks on all doors and windows in every home and office, individuals are suggesting that they are not willing to incur infinite costs to ensure a long life. By these and countless other decisions, individuals demonstrate that although they value life, they are not willing to take every precaution and devote every possible resource toward preserving their lives.

Principle 21.1. In the context of scarce resources, numerous individual choices reveal a willingness to forego some expenditures that might ensure preservation of one's own or someone else's life in order to achieve other desired objectives. Such trade-offs provide the basis for economists to infer a monetary valuation of human life.

The question economists thus ask is: In the context of scarce resources, how many resources are to be devoted toward saving human lives or reducing life-threatening risks? In this sense, how much is a human life worth? It may be tempting to infer a value from past public expenditures to save lives or from court awards or state law compensations for the premature loss of a life. However, there is little reason to expect that these decisions reflect economic preferences. Likewise, life insurance premiums, although a readily obtainable market value, are not suitable. These measure an individual's willingness to pay for compensation to family and dependents upon an untimely death, rather than the individual's valuation of remaining alive. Seeking an appropriate measure, the economics literature has developed two different valuation concepts. The first, estimating expected future income earnings, is not recommended for cost-benefit analysis, while the second, valuing mortality risk, is consistent with the cost-benefit technique.

EXPECTED FUTURE INCOME EARNINGS

In the first approach, economists attach a dollar value to human life by estimating the present value of expected future earnings over an individual's lifetime. Known as the *human capital method*, this approach infers an economic value in terms of an individual's contribution to national income, specifically by measuring the human's labor productivity as priced in the market and estimating the present value of the individual's expected future earnings. A related variant subtracts the individual's expected future consumption to determine the net monetary value to others of the individual's life. The latter version is commonly used in wrongful death court cases. Suppose, for example, a spouse is killed in a truck collision, the surviving spouse sues the truck driver for wrongful death and the court awards damages to the complainant. Estimated damages generally consist of two components. The first is set by the court to acknowledge the living spouse's pain and suffering. The second reflects compensation for the foregone net income that otherwise would have accrued to the still-living spouse if the deceased had been able to work over an expected lifetime, that is, the human capital method.

The application of either variant of the human capital method within cost-benefit analysis encounters difficulties, however. Perhaps most apparent, the method values the lives of individuals who earn low incomes or who are unemployed (such as children, retired persons, housewives/husbands, chronically ill persons) at a value much below that for the wealthy, and sometimes at zero value. This may be appropriate for wrongful death suits that address the loss to a complainant of a specific, identifiable individual whose particular income-earning capability directly affects the size of the economic loss. However, cost-benefit analysis takes the perspective of human society as a whole. When assessing a policy's social benefits, attributing zero value to the saved lives of the retired or permanently unemployed is of dubious merit. Even more problematic, the human capital method violates the fundamental tenet that valuation in cost-benefit analysis is based on individual economic preferences. An individual's expected income earnings (or net earnings) do not reflect individual preferences—either the individual's own valuation of remaining alive or others' valuation of saving the individual's life (and preventing premature death). For these reasons, the human capital method is not appropriate for valuation of human life in a cost-benefit analysis.[1]

Principle 21.2. The human capital method, which estimates the present value of expected future earnings or net earnings over an individual's lifetime, should not be used to value a human life in a cost-benefit analysis.

VALUE OF MORTALITY RISK

A newer approach is to estimate the value individuals place on a small change in the probability of death, or *mortality risk*. As Schelling (1968) asserts, rather than assessing the certain death of a specific individual (arguably of infinite value), the relevant measure for most policies is a *statistical death*, where some subset of unnamed individuals is expected to die with (or without) a policy. Each member of the population (or society) thus faces a probability (risk) of being among those in the subset.

A simple example can illustrate how valuation of this risk allows calculation of the value of a human life. Suppose in a population of 1 million, each individual is willing to pay $40 for a policy that is expected to reduce the death rate from 90 to 70 per million, thus saving 20 members of the one-million population. All together, the aggregate population is willing to pay $40 million, or ($40)(1 million people), to save the 20 lives. The *implied value* of the 20 statistical lives is thus $40 million or $2 million per life saved. The implied value is the amount the aggregate society is WTP to reduce each member's probability of death by a small amount.

In everyday life, individuals do express preferences about exposure to different risks of death. All together, three different analytical techniques have been applied to measure these preferences. First, the *wage compensation method* is often used by studies to estimate individual *willingness to accept* (WTA) a small increase in risk on the job. This method recognizes a differential in wages is often paid to compensate individuals for voluntarily choosing jobs with higher mortality risks. Since wage differentials are influenced by a number of factors, these must be separated statistically to isolate the mortality risk's effect. The primary approach is to apply multiple regression analysis to estimate a *hedonic wage equation*, relating wage rates to fatality risks and a number of other wage determinants including nonfatal health risks.[2] Given the increasing availability of data concerning individual workers' risk levels and wages, this method is the most frequently applied of the three techniques.

Second, a smaller number of studies estimate the individual consumer's *willingness to pay* (WTP) for a reduction in mortality risk. These studies employ a variety of approaches. Some analyze the higher market prices consumers are willing to pay for consumption goods with lower mortality risks. These studies apply multiple regression analysis to estimate the *hedonic price equation* for a particular consumption good, where price is a function of other consumer variables in addition to mortality risk. Alternative approaches value non–price-related changes in consumer behavior to reduce risk. As examples, Ippolito and Ippolito analyze how over past years the quantity demand for cigarettes changed with growing reports of the health hazards associated with smoking (1984); and Blomquist values voluntary individual decisions to buckle seat belts by estimating the value (opportunity cost) of time devoted to perform the task (1979).

These two revealed preference methods (wage compensation and consumer WTP analyses) assume individuals in the labor and consumption markets have *perfect information* concerning the mortality risk associated with their choices. The wage compensation method also assumes *mobility* within the labor market; thus, an individual can move easily to a job with greater (or lesser) mortality risk. Mobility implies, among other things, that poor individuals do not have to accept a high-risk job because of their low income; as they too have mobility, their job and income choices are voluntary. (Note that this assumption implicitly indicates that the income distribution resulting from such choices is acceptable.) In addition, market behavior reflects *voluntary* choices. In contrast, many government policies address involuntary exposures (such as breathing lead particulates in the air). Individuals may be WTP more to avoid involuntary than voluntary risks; if so, the revealed preference estimates understate WTP when involuntary risks are involved.

Recognizing some of the limits of the revealed preference methods, a few studies employ a third technique, *contingent valuation surveys*, to estimate individual WTA compensation or WTP for a change in life-threatening risk. Contingent valuation surveys offer the possibility of shaping the hypothetical valuation questions to address particular policy concerns, including risks that are not priced in markets. Caution is warranted, however. Critics question whether respondents can meaningfully value small changes in mortality risk specified in a hypothetical scenario. Careful survey design must ensure respondents accurately understand and can realistically value the specified change in mortality risk.

Compared to the human capital method, these three techniques are founded on the appropriate valuation principle for cost-benefit analysis: valuing individual economic preferences for human life, and specifically, WTA compensation or WTP for small changes in mortality risk. Ideally, application of these techniques would measure an individual's valuation of reducing his or her own risk as well as that of others. In actuality, labor wages generally compensate for an individual's own risk, while consumer WTP can, but does not always, include some valuation of the risk to others. Contingent valuation surveys offer the prospect of asking the respondent to value both risks; however, this is not yet the common practice. Another difference is whose preferences are reflected in the various measurements. Individuals who accept jobs involving greater risk exposures are generally less risk averse than the general population. Wage compensation studies thus tend to reflect this group's preferences. Consumer analyses and contingent valuation studies can include other, often broader, segments of the population.

As indicated, each of the three techniques has its strengths and weaknesses. Despite the differences, literature review articles have found a perhaps surprising amount of consistency across the different techniques' value-of-life estimates, especially between wage compensation and contingent valuation analyses. The reviews conclude with suggested value ranges that they consider ''defensible'' or ''reasonable.'' Such value-of-life ranges include, as examples, $1.6 million to $8.5 million in 1986 dollars (Fisher, Chestnut and Violette 1989: 96) and $3 million to $7 million in 1990 dollars (Viscusi 1993: 1942), where all dollar values are discounted to present value.

That the literature obtains a range of values (rather than one precise value) for a human life is not surprising. Risk preferences vary for any given individual as well as across individuals, depending on the risk level, risk type, individual's risk averseness and other individual characteristics, such as income. Therefore, independent of differences in analytical technique, value estimates vary with the particular individuals and risk circumstances included in the study. For this reason, when applying such estimates to assess a particular policy, the specifics of the policy situation (level of risk, whether voluntary or involuntary risk, characteristics of exposed population, etc.) must be compared with those for the value-of-life study, and the study's value estimates must be interpreted accordingly.

Principle 21.3. The appropriate principle for human life valuation is the willingness to pay (WTP) or willingness to accept (WTA) compensation for a small change in mortality risk. Accordingly, estimation techniques infer a value of life from revealed preferences (by analyzing a hedonic regression for wage rates or consumer prices or investigating non-price-related changes in consumer behavior) or, instead, from surveys eliciting contingent values.

CONCLUSION

Public policies allocate substantial resources to address a wide range of health and safety risks as well as environmental threats to human life; moreover, any of a number of additional opportunities to save lives might be pursued. Faced with budget constraints and competing objectives, decision makers may understandably seek information assessing which policy alternatives are economically rational.

To identify the efficient allocation of resources, all benefits and costs must be expressed in a common unit. Only then is it possible to compare the relative value of saving human lives with achieving competing policy objectives, such as increased education, enhanced transport, preserved environmental habitat and the like. This is the primary rationale for assigning dollar values to human lives.

The appropriate valuation concept is to measure individual preferences for saving a statistical life (or reducing mortality risk). A relatively new and growing empirical literature is beginning to establish a range of such estimates. While there is no agreement as to a precise value, Viscusi emphasizes the estimates' usefulness as a "broad index" that might help identify policies that entail excessively high costs to save a life. As he concludes, "the estimates do provide guidance as to whether risk reduction efforts that cost $50,000 per life saved or $50 million per life saved are warranted" (1993: 1943).

The importance of economic assessment is suggested by rising complaints of the high costs imposed by government health, safety and environmental regulations that are designed to save lives. At the same time, public interest groups are perhaps appreciably weary of the political implications and possible biases in an analysis that recommends limits to improvements in health, safety and environmental quality. Likewise, many individuals are reluctant to accept the assigning of a dollar value to human life.

One analytical technique that appears to avoid monetary measurement, while still providing some rational economic assessment, is *cost-effectiveness analysis*. This technique does not explicitly assign a dollar value to the benefits of saving human life. Rather, it estimates the costs of saving each life or, more likely, each life year or quality-adjusted life year (QALY). The analysis then enables a comparison of alternative policies to determine their relative costs per life (or life year) saved. However, as explained in Chapter 22, the decision maker must still employ some implicit value of human life to determine which policy options are relatively cost effective. Thus, empirical value-of-life estimates are still a valuable contribution to policy assessment.

NOTES

1. The approach is still applied, however, in many studies when assessing nonfatal illnesses (*morbidity*). The practice derives from cost-of-illness analyses (COIAs) that measure the effect of an illness, or its eradication, on a country's national income. Stud-

ies, for example, estimate the social benefits of avoiding an illness by valuing the related reduced medical costs, reduced absenteeism and increased labor productivity—all of which are viewed as generating economic value for society.

2. For a detailed exposition of the relevant considerations when specifying the equation, see Viscusi (1993: 1916–22).

Chapter 22

Cost-Effectiveness Analysis

INTRODUCTION

While several valuation techniques have been developed, there are times when an analyst might not value a particular hard-to-measure, nonmarket effect. These include cases where:

- a specific policy consequence cannot be valued with any of the still evolving techniques,
- the costs of collecting the relevant data may be deemed too high,
- the data may be collected, but large estimation error generates extreme uncertainty,
- the valuation of a particular consequence may generate such controversy that a quantitative analysis that sidesteps the dispute may be beneficial to the decision-making process, or
- the decision maker may perceive a moral obligation or other commitment to achieve a particular objective without compromise (e.g., preserving an animal or plant species, protecting a fundamental human right such as not being exposed to a health risk without consent or achieving a given level of income redistribution), where the cost-benefit trade-off is not relevant for decision-making purposes.

In any of these cases, the analyst might consider performing a cost-effectiveness analysis.

Similar to cost-benefit analysis (CBA), cost-effectiveness analysis values policy consequences in monetary terms; the difference is that at least one policy consequence is not valued but instead is quantified in physical units. For example, in evaluating a life-saving medical procedure, instead of assigning a dollar value to the benefits of preserving a human life, the analysis might simply quantify the number of life years saved and then calculate that the procedure costs, say, $30,000 per saved human life. The analysis thus undertakes economic assessment, while avoiding the challenge of valuing a hard-to-measure effect. This may be appealing. At the same time, the analysis provides less information to the decision maker. The quantified effect (the saved life year, in the example) is presented to the decision maker, who must then determine its value. Is saving a human life year worth $30,000? Without explicit measurement of society's valuation, the answer is left to the decision-maker's own personal valuation, perception of society's valuation or other yardstick.

The analysis might also address how the costs change with expanded use of the medical procedure; at the margin, does saving each additional life year cost $30,000? Or do the marginal costs increase (decrease) with each additional life year saved? Furthermore, the analyst or decision maker might compare this medical procedure with other alternatives to determine whether there are any less expensive (or more effective) ways to save human life years. Such is the information that cost-effectiveness analysis can provide.

Principle 22.1. Cost-effectiveness analysis can (1) value the costs and quantify the effect[1] of a single policy so the decision maker can then decide whether pursuing the policy is worth it, and/or (2) assess a number of policies and/or policy levels to identify which one(s) (a) minimize the costs of achieving a given effect or (b) maximize effectiveness for a given budget or set of resources.

The analysis can therefore aid the decision maker in answering the following questions:

- *whether* to pursue a policy (or achieve an effect),
- *how much* (i.e., which scale or level) of a policy to pursue,
- *which* among a number of policies to pursue.

COST-EFFECTIVENESS ANALYSIS DEFINED

Principle 22.2. Cost-effectiveness analysis (CEA) is one approach to assess decisions or choices that affect the use of scarce resources. Similar to CBA, this method considers a specific policy and relevant alternatives and involves systematic identification of policy consequences. However, unlike CBA, each consequence is then expressed either in monetary units (as a cost) or in one common physical unit measuring the effect. The analysis then compares the costs and effect of each policy alternative, applying the appropriate decision criterion to aid the decision maker in determining which alternative(s) are (relatively) cost effective.

Consider this definition[2] more closely.

1. Similar to CBA, cost-effectiveness analysis is a decision-making tool, assessing "decisions or choices" to provide information to aid decision makers.

2. Once all policy consequences are identified, each is either valued as a "cost" or quantified as an "effect." Costs in traditional cost-effectiveness analysis are defined as social costs; however, the analysis is increasingly performed recognizing the costs to only specifically designated segments of society. For instance, sometimes only budgetary expenses are included, ignoring other social costs, as some decision makers are particularly interested in weighing policy effects with budget costs. As another example, in the health field, analyses often assess a policy from the perspective of either insurance companies, hospitals, physicians or patients. As Udvarhelyi and associates emphasize, to enable correct interpretation of the results, an analysis should state explicitly the segments of society included in determining a policy's costs (1992: 239).

As for quantifying the effect, the analyst must carefully choose the measurement unit; considerations include the feasibility and expense of measurement as well as whether the measurement unit facilitates comparison of the assessed policy with other policy choices. For example, a health intervention's "effect" might be the number of cases treated for a particular disease; this allows assessment relative to other treatments of the same disease. Measuring the number of life years saved broadens the possible comparison to other life-saving interventions, while estimating the number of quality-adjusted life years (QALYs)[3] enables comparison with interventions that save lives or enhance the quality of life.

Traditionally, negative consequences are valued as costs, while positive consequences are expressed in terms of the common physical unit measuring the effect. However, policy consequences do not always lend themselves to such simple classification. For example, some positive consequences may not be measurable in terms of the common physical unit but can be conveniently valued in monetary terms; these are sometimes treated as negative costs, which are then aggregated in the analysis with any positive costs. Also, some negative consequences (for example, environmental destruction) may not lend themselves to valuation yet can be quantified in physical units as a negative effect.

3. Cost-effectiveness analysis "compares the costs and effect" of a policy alternative. This is emphasized because mistakes are occasionally made. Applications in the literature sometimes misinterpret cost-effectiveness analysis as identifying the policy alternative that minimizes costs (with no regard to the policy's effectiveness) or that maximizes effectiveness (with no regard to costs). As indicated in Principles 22.1 and 22.2, both costs and effect are considered in a cost-effectiveness analysis.

4. The reader may have noticed that the word "efficiency" is not included in the definition. Similar to CBA, cost-effectiveness analysis assesses the allocation of "scarce resources" and identifies and values costs from an efficiency perspective. However, unlike CBA, society's valuation of at least one consequence is not estimated. For this reason, cost-effectiveness analysis does not necessarily identify the policy alternative that promotes efficiency (or increases

social welfare). The designated alternative promotes efficiency only if the un-valued effect is deemed sufficiently worthwhile by society; however, such information is not provided by the analysis.

5. Instead of efficiency, the analysis seeks to identify which policy alternative(s) are "cost effective." The "appropriate decision criterion" involves two components: first, calculation of the appropriate *cost-effectiveness (C/E) ratio* for each policy alternative, where the ratio[4] can generally be expressed as

$$C/E = \frac{Costs}{Effect,} \tag{22.1}$$

and, second, comparison of the ratio(s) with the decision maker's willingness to pay. This second component, sometimes disregarded in the literature, should not be overlooked. Which particular policy is cost effective depends on the decision-maker's subjective valuation. Does the decision maker believe a policy's effect is worth it? Is she willing to pay (or recommend others pay) the costs? "Cost effective" is therefore a relative term that is not determined solely by the C/E ratios but varies with each particular decision maker's valuation. For example, a large organization with extensive resources may well consider one specific policy alternative to be cost effective while a small organization with a limited budget might identify a different option (Doubilet, Weinstein and McNeil 1986: 254). For this reason, the goal of the analysis is to "aid the decision maker in determining" which policy alternative(s) are "relatively cost effective."

6. Cost-effectiveness analysis compares a policy with "relevant alternatives." The analysis explicitly compares one or more of the following policy alternatives.

- *Policy vs. no policy.* Is it more cost effective to pursue a policy or not to pursue that policy?
- *Different scales or levels of a policy.* Which scale or level is more cost effective?
- *A number of different policies.* Which policy or policies are more cost effective?

DECISION CRITERIA

Principle 22.3. In performing a cost-effectiveness analysis, the analyst should:

- identify the type of decision the decision maker is considering,
- calculate the appropriate *cost-effectiveness ratio* for each policy or policy level, and
- apply the correct decision criterion to determine which policy alternative(s) are cost effective.

Table 22.1
Decision Types and Cost-Effectiveness Ratios

Decision Type	C/E Ratio
(1) One policy: implement?	Average C/E
(2) Subset of independent policies	Average C/E
(3) One of several levels of a policy	Marginal C/E
(4) One of mutually exclusive policies	Incremental C/E
(5) Subset of dependent policies	Incremental C/E

In general, five decision types can be distinguished. The decision maker might be considering

1. whether (or not) to pursue a policy,
2. which subset of several independent policies to pursue,
3. which scale or level (i.e., how much) of a policy to pursue,
4. which one of several mutually exclusive policies to pursue,
5. which subset of several dependent policies to pursue.

All together, there are three different cost-effectiveness ratios: the average C/E, marginal C/E and incremental C/E. Table 22.1 matches each decision type with the appropriate ratio.

In practice, errors have sometimes been made in the selection of the cost-effectiveness ratio and decision criterion; as a result, the analysis provides inaccurate information to the decision maker. This section explains the appropriate ratio and criterion for each decision type using illustrative examples.[5]

In the examples, the reader might notice the costs are discounted, while the effects are not. There is some disagreement in the literature as to whether effects distributed over time should be discounted. We use undiscounted effects to simplify the illustrative examples, not to endorse a particular practice. A key decision the analyst must make is whether to discount the policy effect (and if so, which discount rate to apply). The issue of discounting is addressed in another section of the chapter.

1. One Policy: Implement or Not?

Suppose an alcohol rehabilitation center considers offering outpatient counseling services to former alcoholics. One year's present value cost is $50,000, with the likely result that an estimated ten recovering alcoholics will choose not to take even one drink during the year's time due to the counseling. The appropriate cost-effectiveness ratio is the *average C/E* (often simply called C/E). Note that the (average) C/E ratio is essentially a "with and without" calculation. It compares the costs and effect of pursuing a specific policy with not pursuing the policy (in this case, providing counseling services with not offering the services). For this example,

$$\text{average C/E} = \frac{\text{PV Total Costs}}{\text{Total Effect}} = \frac{\$50,000}{10} = \$5,000. \qquad (22.2)$$

Thus, the cost is an average of $5,000, discounted, per recovering alcoholic who, as a result of the counseling services, chooses not to drink during one year.

With a C/E of $5,000, are the counseling services cost effective? Answering this question involves a subjective judgment by the decision maker. Is the rehabilitation center willing to pay (or recommend others pay) $5,000 in present value for counseling to result in one recovering alcoholic not drinking over a year? Does the center think the outcome is worth the expenditure? If so, then this is a cost-effective policy for the center to pursue.

• For the *decision*: whether or not to implement one policy, the appropriate *decision criterion* is: policy implementation is cost effective if the decision maker is WTP the (average) C/E.

2. Several Independent Policies: Choose a Subset

Suppose an international health organization considers implementing a number of health interventions (e.g., malaria treatment, AIDS prevention campaign, measles inoculation, etc.) in various rural African communities. The interventions are believed to be *independent*, with the cost and effectiveness of any one policy not varying with the implementation of any other policy. Also, any combination or subset of policies can be pursued together, that is, the policies are *mutually compatible*. The organization thus seeks to identify which subset of policies is cost effective.

Table 22.2 presents the costs and effect for each of five health interventions, A through E, where the effect is measured in terms of the number of life years saved. The list assumes each intervention is *not repeatable*. In other words, full implementation of intervention A, for example, costs $5 million in present value and saves 5,000 life years; expanding A to save additional life years is not an option.

To assess cost effectiveness, each policy's (average) C/E is calculated; the ratios are also presented in Table 22.2. Each (average) C/E is calculated "with and without," comparing the costs and effect of pursuing a particular policy

Table 22.2
Average C/E Ratios for Independent Health Interventions

Health Intervention	PV Costs ($)	Effect (life years saved)	Average C/E ($)
A	5,000,000	5,000	1,000
B	10,000,000	2,500	4,000
C	25,000,000	1,000	25,000
D	30,000,000	5,000	6,000
E	40,000,000	8,000	5,000

relative to not pursuing that policy. Thus, implementing intervention A rather than maintaining the status quo costs $1,000 in present value per life year saved. In comparison, pursuing intervention B rather than the status quo costs a discounted $4,000 per life year saved, and so on. Ranking the interventions according to the cost-effectiveness ratio yields the following (from lowest to highest average C/E): A, B, E, D, C. Once the policies are rank ordered, the decision criterion varies depending on whether there is a budget constraint.[6]

(2a) Independent policies, without budget constraint. When financial resources are sufficient to afford all policies under consideration, the decision approach is similar to evaluating one policy. A subjective judgment by the decision maker is required. What is the cost the decision maker is WTP for a saved life year?[7] Once answered, a cost-effective subset of policies can be chosen. To do so, proceed in order of the ranking (from lowest to successively higher average C/E ratios); select each policy, one by one, until the (average) C/E reaches as high as the decision maker's WTP (or *cut-off*). Thus, for example, if the decision maker is WTP $10,000 in present value for each saved life year, then interventions A, B, E and D are cost effective.

• For the *decision*: choose a subset of several independent policies with no budget constraint, the appropriate *decision criterion* is: all policies with an (average) C/E less than or equal to what the decision maker is WTP are cost effective.

(2b) Independent policies, with budget constraint. Suppose a well-defined budget is insufficient to finance all policies under consideration. To determine which policies are cost effective, first select the policy with the lowest average C/E and then, one by one, choose policies with successively higher average C/Es, until the budget is exhausted. If for this example the budget is $55 million

(in present value), then interventions A, B and E, ranked in order of average C/E, exhaust the budget. Together these generate a total of 15,500 life years saved, thereby achieving the maximum effect for the given budget. (The reader can verify by looking at Table 22.2 that no other affordable combination of policies yields a greater number of life years saved.) Thus, A, B and E are cost effective in this example.[8]

The analysis provides an additional piece of information. Suppose that a new affordable policy (intervention F) is proposed and competes for some of the already allocated $55 million budget funds. Would it be more cost effective to pursue intervention F than any of the already selected interventions (A,B,E)? This question can be answered by recognizing that the average C/E for the last policy selected in the analysis provides a *cut-off*[9] that can be used to assess any new affordable policies. In this example, the cut-off is $5,000 in present value, the average C/E for intervention E. Suppose the average C/E for intervention F is $5,500 (or any number greater than $5,000), discounted, per life year saved. Then F is not a cost-effective substitute for E, as intervention E saves a life year at a lower per unit cost. In contrast, if intervention F's average C/E is some number less than $5,000 (say, $4,500) in present value, then implementing F as a priority to E is the more cost effective use of the budget funds.[10] The cut-off is therefore the maximum allowable average C/E for any new affordable policy options that might be proposed for this particular budget.

- For the *decision*: choose a subset of several independent policies with a budget constraint, the appropriate *decision criterion* is: the cost-effective policies are those selected in succession from lowest to highest (average) C/E until the budget is exhausted.

3. Several Levels (or Scales) of a Policy: Choose One

Suppose doctors prescribe differing doses of a particular medication to individuals diagnosed with pancreatic cancer. A medical researcher gathers data measuring four doses' costs and effects, with the effects expressed in terms of the number of life years saved. To identify which dosage (or policy level) is cost effective, the data are organized, as in Table 22.3, in order of increasing dosage (or policy level). The table also presents two C/E ratios, the average and marginal C/E, for each dosage. Both ratios play a role in analyzing cost effectiveness for this decision.

The *marginal*[11] C/E is a "with and without" calculation comparing the cost-effectiveness of each successive policy level (in this case, dosage) with the one before it. The general equation is

$$\text{marginal C/E} = \frac{\text{change in costs between successive levels}}{\text{change in effect between successive levels.}} \qquad (22.3)$$

Table 22.3
Average and Marginal C/E Ratios for Alternative Dosages of a Medication

Daily Dosage (mg)	PV of Total Costs ($ mils)	Total Effect (life years saved)	Average C/E ($)	Marginal C/E ($)
25	100	7,000	14,286[a]	14,286[a]
50	150	12,500	12,000	9,091[a]
75	210	15,000	14,000	24,000
100	280	16,000	17,500	70,000

[a]Rounded to nearest dollar.

Thus, for example, the marginal C/E for 50mg is calculated using the change in (discounted) costs and effect between 25mg and 50mg, which yields the following:

$$\frac{(\$150 \text{ million} - \$100 \text{ million})}{12,500 - 7,000} = \frac{\$50 \text{ million}}{5,500} = \$9,090.9090.$$

This means that, compared to 25mg of the drug, the 50mg dosage costs an added $9,091 in present value for each additional life year saved. A similar calculation is performed for every two successive policy levels. (The lowest dosage, 25mg, is compared with 0mg dosage.)

To determine which dosage is cost effective, the marginal C/Es are compared with the maximum cost the decision maker is WTP to save a life year. Suppose the decision maker considers $40,000 in present value to be the *cut-off* for a life year. Select the last dosage with the marginal C/E that is closest and less than or equal to the cut-off. A glance at Table 22.3 identifies 75mg, with a marginal C/E of $24,000 in present value.

To see why marginal, and not average, C/E is the guiding ratio, look again at Table 22.3. Focusing only on the Average C/E column, the average C/E that is closest to (and less than) the decision maker's WTP of $40,000 (in present value) is $17,500 per life year saved. Thus, the dosage of 100mg appears to be the cost-effective dosage. However, compare 100mg with 75mg. The 75mg dosage costs $210 million, discounted, and saves 15,000 life years (at an average C/E of $14,000). In comparison, 100mg saves an additional 1,000 life years with an added $70 million, discounted, in total expense. The marginal C/E for 100mg is therefore ($70 million/1,000) or $70,000 in present value for each additional life year saved. This amount is far too costly given the decision maker is WTP a maximum of $40,000 in present value. The 100mg dosage is therefore not cost effective. Thus, the marginal C/E is the appropriate indicator and identifies the 75mg dosage with a marginal C/E of $24,000 as potentially cost effective.

A caveat must be added, however. The condition to select the closest marginal C/E less than or equal to the cut-off is necessary but not sufficient for identifying the cost-effective dosage. A final step is required. Verify that for the designated dosage (or policy level), the average C/E is also less than or equal to the cut-off (DHHS 1992: 25–29). In this case, as the 75mg dosage has an average C/E of $14,000, which is less than the $40,000 cut-off in present value, the 75mg is indeed the cost-effective dosage.

To understand why this last condition is added to the decision criterion, let's assess a different cut-off. Assume the decision maker is WTP no more than $10,000 in present value for a life year. Find the last dosage with the marginal C/E closest (less than or equal) to $10,000. Looking at Table 22.3, the 50mg dosage has the closest smaller marginal C/E ($9,091) and is thus identified as cost effective. However, consider the average C/E for 50mg. At $12,000 in present value, it is greater than the cut-off. What does this mean? Remember the average C/E compares the 50mg dosage with no dosage (no policy). Since the average ratio is greater than the cut-off, the cost-effective option is to prescribe no dosage (0mg) of the drug.

How can the average C/E be greater than the cut-off while the marginal C/E is less? Note the high costs ($100 million in present value) for the lowest dosage (25mg). This policy entails large start-up or fixed costs which are incurred whether small or large dosages of the medication are produced. Also, the expensive 25mg dosage has an effectiveness (7,000 life years saved) that is insufficient to warrant applying the drug and paying these costs. Increasing the dosage from 25mg to 50mg raises the effectiveness notably and lowers the marginal C/E to below the cut-off. Nevertheless, as indicated by the average C/E, the increased life years are still too small in number to warrant the high start-up costs (DHHS 1992: 27). Thus, if the decision maker is WTP a maximum of $10,000 in present value for a life year, the cost-effective decision is not to prescribe or use this drug for pancreatic cancer.

• For the *decision*: choose one of several policy levels (or scales), the appropriate *decision criterion* is: the cost-effective policy level is the last one with marginal C/E closest (less than or equal) to the decision maker's WTP, subject to verification that the level's average C/E is also less than or equal to the cut-off.

4. Mutually Exclusive Policies: Choose One

Suppose a coastal community seeks to protect the endangered seagrass habitat in nearby waters. Recent damage has been caused by several factors, including propeller scars inflicted as motorboats run aground on the seagrass beds.[12] The

Table 22.4
Incremental C/E Ratios for Mutually Exclusive Policies to Prevent Seagrass Damage

Policy	PV of Total Costs ($)	Total Effect (% of boaters to change behavior)	Incremental C/E ($)
Signs	10,000	33	303[a]
Pamphlets	35,000	33	Eliminated
Signs & pamphlets	45,000	73	875
Area closure	1,332,000	99	49,500

[a]Rounded to nearest dollar.

community considers four policy alternatives (boater warning signs, boater education pamphlets, signs and pamphlets combined and area closure to internal combustion engines), each of which is designed to change boater behavior to reduce further damage. The decision-making objective is to determine which one of these *mutually exclusive* policies to pursue.

Table 22.4 presents the costs and effect for each policy. The first two policies involve the costs of making and posting signs and of printing and distributing pamphlets to registered boaters, respectively. The third policy, signs and pamphlets, combines both sets of costs. While these three policies cost less than $50,000 each in present value, the fourth policy, area closure, is substantially more expensive. If the seagrass areas are closed to motorboat traffic, over $1 million in resource costs, discounted, would be incurred. These include reduced commercial fish catches and fisher relocation expenses as well as closure enforcement and signs. The estimate thus includes social costs. As for effectiveness, given the difficulty of quantifying the seagrass damage caused by boats, the effect is measured using expert estimates as to each policy's expected change in boater behavior. Thus, signs or pamphlets are expected to alter the behavior of 33% of the boaters, the combined signs and pamphlets, say, 73%,[13] and the area closure promises 99% effectiveness in changing boater behavior.

The analysis assumes the policies are *not repeatable* and are *divisible* with *constant returns to scale*. An assessment of cost effectiveness first orders the policies from lowest to highest cost, as in Table 22.4. The list is then checked to see if any policy has the same costs and a smaller effect (or more costs and the same effect) as the prior policy. Looking at the table, the pamphlets cost more while achieving the same 33% effectiveness as the signs. Therefore, pamphlets can be ruled out as not cost effective and are eliminated from the list.

To identify which of the remaining options is cost effective, the appropriate ratio is the *incremental C/E*. The incremental C/E is a "with and without" calculation comparing the cost-effectiveness of each successive policy with the one listed before it. A policy's incremental C/E is therefore determined by the particular policy chosen for comparison and must always be interpreted with reference to that policy. The formula is

$$\text{incremental C/E} = \frac{\text{change in total costs between successive policies}}{\text{change in total effect between successive policies.}} \quad (22.4)$$

In Table 22.4, begin with the lowest cost policy. Signs cost $10,000, discounted, and alter the behavior of 33% of the boaters. Compared to pursuing no policy (with zero costs and zero effect), signs yield an incremental C/E of $10,000/33% or $303 in present value for each 1% of affected boaters. Signs and pamphlets combined, not surprisingly, cost more and yield a greater effectiveness than signs alone. The question asked by the analysis is whether the additional effectiveness warrants the extra cost. The relevant ratio is the incremental C/E. Compared to signs, the combination policy costs an additional $35,000 ($45,000 − $10,000), discounted, and alters the behavior of an added 40% (73% − 33%) of the boaters. The result is an incremental C/E of $875 ($35,000/40%) in present value for each additional one percent of boaters who change their behavior. Finally, the fourth policy, area closure, offers even greater effectiveness. It influences another 26% of the boaters, in comparison to the combined signs and pamphlets, at an additional cost of $1.287 million ($1,332,000 − $45,000) in present value. Area closure's incremental C/E is thus $1,287,000/26% or $49,500 in present value for each additional percentage point.[14]

To determine which policy is cost effective, a subjective judgment by the decision maker is required. What is the maximum the decision maker is WTP (or willing for society to pay) to influence a percentage of the boaters (1%) to stop motoring over seagrass beds? The cost-effective policy is the one with incremental C/E closest (less than or equal) to this maximum WTP. Thus, if the WTP is $49,500 or more in present value, then area closure is the cost-effective policy. If, instead, the WTP is less than $49,500 yet greater than or equal to $875 in present value, then the combined signs and pamphlets are cost effective. Finally, if the WTP is less than $875 but greater than or equal to the signs' incremental C/E of $303 in present value, then the signs are cost effective.

• For the *decision*: choose one of several mutually exclusive policies, the appropriate *decision criterion* is: the policy with incremental C/E closest (less than or equal) to the decision maker's WTP is cost effective.

5. Several Dependent Policies: Choose a Subset

Suppose a decision maker is considering several policies where the effectiveness of one varies if any of the others are implemented. These policies are said to be *dependent*. In order to determine which policy or policies are cost effective, the dependence between the policies' effects must be taken into account.

(5a) Dependent policies, without budget constraint. If the decision is not constrained by the budget, then the simplest approach is to find all possible combinations of the policies and calculate the total costs and effect for each. Then, determine the one combination that is cost effective. The decision is thereby converted to choosing one of several (mutually exclusive) policy combinations and can be analyzed in the same manner as mutually exclusive policies.

Let's revisit the seagrass example, where a community seeks to change boater behavior in order to preserve the remaining seagrass beds. Suppose the decision maker is considering two policies: boater warning signs and boater education pamphlets. These policies are dependent, assuming warning signs have extra effectiveness for boaters who read the pamphlets, as the latter explain the importance of not boating over seagrass beds. Likewise, the pamphlets can be more effective for boaters who encounter warning signs near the seagrass beds.

The analyst's task is to identify all possible policy combinations and then list these combinations in order from lowest to highest cost. Refer again to Table 22.4. The first three policies listed represent all possible combinations of these two policies: each policy separately and the two together, appropriately arranged by increasing cost. (For this example, ignore area closure, the fourth policy in the table.) Eliminate any policy with the same costs and a smaller effect (or more costs and the same effect) as the prior policy. Thus, pamphlets are removed from the list. To assess cost effectiveness, the incremental C/E between each successive combination is calculated, then the combination with incremental C/E closest (less than or equal) to the decision-maker's WTP is identified. This is the cost-effective combination. Thus, using the numerical estimates in Table 22.4, if the decision maker is WTP $1,000 in present value for each one percent of boaters who change behavior, the cost-effective policy is the combined signs and pamphlets with incremental C/E of $875.

• For the *decision*: choose a subset of several dependent policies with no budget constraint, the appropriate *decision criterion* is: find all possible combinations and the one with incremental C/E closest (less than or equal) to the decision-maker's WTP is the cost-effective combination.

(5b) Dependent policies, with budget constraint. If the budget is insufficient to finance all possible policy combinations, then the decision criterion is modified slightly. The one change is to identify all affordable combinations, thus eliminating any combinations that overspend the budget. Then, the analysis proceeds exactly the same: order the affordable combinations from lowest to highest cost and eliminate any combination with the same costs and smaller effect (or greater costs and same effect) as a prior combination. Next, calculate the incremental C/Es between each two successive combinations and identify which incremental C/E is closest (less than or equal) to the decision maker's WTP.

Table 22.5
Summary: Decision Types and Criteria for Cost-Effectiveness Analysis

Type of Decision	Decision Criterion [a]
1. One policy: implement?	Average C/E ≤ decision maker's WTP
2. Independent policies: choose subset	
a. No budget constraint	All with average C/E ≤ decision maker's WTP
b. Budget constraint	Rank lowest to highest average C/E, find affordable subset
3. Levels of a policy: choose one	Last marginal C/E closest (≤) to decision maker's WTP, verify average C/E ≤ WTP
4. Mutually exclusive policies: choose one	Incremental C/E closest (≤) to decision maker's WTP
5. Dependent policies: choose subset	
a. No budget constraint	Find possible combinations; incremental C/E closest (≤) to decision maker's WTP
b. Budget constraint	Find affordable combinations; incremental C/E closest (≤) to decision maker's WTP

[a] Assumes the policy effect is positive. For a negative effect, policies are ranked in order from highest to lowest ratio. Also, the inequality in the criterion is reversed; the relevant C/E ratio ≥ decision maker's WTP indicates relative cost effectiveness.

- For the *decision*: choose a subset of several dependent policies with a budget constraint, the appropriate *decision criterion* is: find all affordable combinations and the combination with incremental C/E closest (less than or equal) to the decision maker's WTP is cost effective.

Summary: Cost Effectiveness Defined

A summary of the appropriate criterion to assess cost effectiveness for each type of decision is presented in Table 22.5. As can be seen in the last column, all together three alternative C/E ratios are available for application. When interpreting the C/E ratios, it is important to remember that similar to CBA, cost-effectiveness analysis is a "with and without" analysis. Each of the three C/E ratios compares a policy with a different baseline scenario. Thus, the average C/E (sometimes called C/E in the literature) compares a policy with the option of not pursuing that policy; the marginal C/E compares one policy level (scale) with another level of the same policy; and the incremental C/E compares a policy with some other policy. For a given policy, therefore, a ratio measuring cost effectiveness can vary in value depending on the specific policy alternative used for comparison. As Doubilet, Weinstein and McNeil emphasize, if the baseline is not stated explicitly, a reported ratio can lead to misleading conclusions as to whether or not the assessed policy is cost effective (1986: 255) When considering any C/E ratio, the reader must immediately ask about the frame of reference. In other words, this ratio is assessing cost effectiveness compared to what alternative?

Principle 22.4. For clarity and accurate interpretation, the analyst should identify the particular C/E ratio (i.e., average, marginal or incremental) being reported and specify the "without-policy" or baseline scenario, in other words, the exact alternative with which the policy is being compared.

Given the different C/E ratios and criteria that might be applied in assessing cost effectiveness, what does it mean to say a policy is "cost effective"? The term has been used and misused with a variety of meanings in the literature. A synthesis of the decision criteria discussed in this chapter leads to the following definition.

Principle 22.5. Pursuing a policy (combination) is *cost effective*

(1) compared to no policy, if the cost per unit of effect (average C/E) is less than or equal to the decision maker's WTP, or

(2) compared to other levels (scales) of the same policy, if its marginal C/E is closest (less than or equal) to the decision maker's WTP (and the corresponding average C/E is also less than or equal to WTP), or

(3) compared to other policies, if its incremental C/E is closest (less than or equal) to the decision maker's WTP.

Each of these conditions, (1), (2) and (3), selects the policy or policies that maximize the effect attainable for given total costs (or budget) or minimize the costs of achieving a given effect.

DISCOUNTING AND COST-EFFECTIVENESS ANALYSIS

As discussed in Chapter 11, the customary practice in economic analysis is to discount future monetary values to present value. In a CBA, the future streams of benefits and costs are generally discounted at a rate chosen in accordance with one of two conceptual rationales: (1) the return foregone by diverting policy funds from the best alternative investment or (2) society's preference for present over future consumption.

Likewise, in a cost-effectiveness analysis, a logical extension of the practice is to discount future costs to present value. A question is raised, however, concerning the other, quantified component of a C/E ratio. Should future effects too be discounted? This question has generated substantial discussion in the literature.

Many onlookers find the idea of discounting future effects to be unacceptable. In particular, discounting human lives that are lost or saved at some future date is challenged. Does it make sense to discount a life at the best alternative investment return? Are future lives to be valued less than present lives? For many, the answers to both questions are negative. However, the growing view in the academic literature is that, yes, future effects should be discounted, even if the effect is the future loss or saving of a human life. In the latter case, it is argued that individuals can, and do, invest in health, thus it is reasonable to compare the return from this investment with foregone returns from alternative investments. Also, surveys indicate that individuals do place a higher value on saving a life today compared to in the future. For example, suppose two policies cost the same, where one will save 100 lives this year while the other will save 100 lives in three years time. Which policy should the decision maker choose? An answer of the first policy suggests a positive time preference for human life in the present. Accordingly, although disagreement continues, many cost-effectiveness analyses discount future human lives as well as other future effects.

If future effects are to be discounted, the next question becomes: at what rate? Should the discount rate be the same as for future costs? or a different rate? Much discussion and research continues regarding the answer. A detailed exposition of the related technical issues goes beyond the scope of this chapter. The interested reader is referred to a number of sources, including Weinstein and Stason (1977), Keeler and Cretin (1983), Lipscomb (1989) and Viscusi (1996).

Given the controversy about whether to discount effects, as well as the particular discount rate to apply, a pragmatic recommendation is adapted from DHHS (1992: 126). Specifically, the analyst should extend the usual *selective sensitivity analysis*, where three different rates (low, moderate and high) are applied to discount future costs; for each of the three rates, the future effects are then discounted at the same rate as well as zero. Thus, all together, six different NPV calculations are undertaken. Using d_c and d_e as the rates for discounting future costs and effects, respectively, the NPV is calculated with each of the following discount rate combinations:

1. d_c = low, d_e = 0
2. d_c = low = d_e
3. d_c = moderate, d_e = 0
4. d_c = moderate = d_e
5. d_c = high, d_e = 0
6. d_c = high = d_e.

Principle 22.6. Given the disagreement as to whether future effects should be discounted and the uncertainty as to the appropriate discount rate for this purpose, a carefully performed, objective cost-effectiveness analysis should apply a range of discount rates. Specifically, the recommended selective sensitivity analysis for discounting monetary values should be extended, allowing the rate for discounting effects to vary from zero to the same rate selected for discounting costs.

COST-EFFECTIVENESS ANALYSIS OR COST-BENEFIT ANALYSIS: WHICH TO PERFORM?

Cost-effectiveness and cost-benefit analyses offer two alternative forms of economic assessment. A key decision, therefore, is which one should be performed to analyze a particular policy. The decision maker and analyst in their consultations together should discuss both alternatives. At the time of their initial conversations, however, it may not be apparent which analysis is the more suitable for the task at hand. If so, then as the research progresses, the gathered information should shed light to identify the appropriate analysis.

Principle 22.7. In comparing cost-benefit with cost-effectiveness analysis, CBA provides the greater information to the decision maker by valuing society's preferences concerning all policy consequences that generate benefits or costs. Also, CBA assesses a policy's relative efficiency, while the relatively cost-effective policy identified by CEA is not necessarily the more efficient policy. The difference is that CEA does not measure society's preferences regarding the quantified "effect"; thus, these cannot be weighed along with the other preferences to determine efficiency.

At the same time, when valuation of a particular consequence is controversial, CEA can be advantageous in avoiding explicit valuation (although the decision maker must then employ an implicit value). Moreover, CEA may be the only practicable tool when limited data preclude valuation of particular policy consequence(s) with an acceptable level of precision or when moral obligations (or other commitments) render the cost-benefit trade-off irrelevant.

The choice between the two analyses is fairly straightforward when, at one end of a spectrum, all of a policy's benefits and costs can be valued with sufficient precision, affordable expense and little controversy. Unless a moral commitment to achieve a given policy goal dictates otherwise, CBA is the more informative technique. At the spectrum's other end, suppose the analyst cannot value any of a policy's benefits (or, instead, any of the costs)—perhaps because of limitations in the data, valuation technique or available budget. If these can be quantified in a common unit as an "effect," then CEA is favored.

Less clear cut is when, say, some benefits can be valued but others not. For instance, construction of a highway may save traveler time and vehicle operating expenses while destroying native forest and plant areas inhabited by wildlife. Suppose the benefits to travelers can be valued, but monetary values for the natural areas are not obtainable. The analyst and decision maker must give careful consideration as to which analysis to employ. Two possibilities are sketched.

1. If the main policy objective is to provide traveler benefits, then a CBA might be performed without valuing the environmental destruction. The calculated NPV can then be interpreted as a *critical value*. If the NPV is positive, the analyst can report to the decision maker that if society's value of the destroyed habitat is greater than the NPV, then the proposed highway does not promote efficiency. The decision maker can weigh this information with her own perceptions as to society's preferences regarding the habitat. (If the NPV is negative, then the highway project is deemed inefficient, even without considering the habitat destruction.)

2. Suppose, instead, a primary policy objective is to construct an environmentally sensitive highway. If it is possible to quantify the habitat damage in a common physical unit, a CEA can be conducted to calculate the net benefits gained in travel time per unit of habitat destroyed. Such an analysis might calculate the incremental C/Es of alternative routes for the proposed highway to find the cost-effective option—the route that generates the greatest net benefits per unit of habitat destroyed (or, the same thing, the route that minimizes the habitat destroyed per dollar of net benefit).

In all, the analyst and decision maker should consider several factors when choosing between the two analyses. Among these are the following:

- the policy objective(s),
- the desired information to be gained from the economic analysis,
- the feasibility of monetary or quantitative measurement, and
- the relevance of the cost-benefit trade-off to the policy decision.

NOTES

1. Some sources in the literature use the words (positive) "effect" and "benefit" interchangeably. We accept this for informal discussion; however, in a formal definition

or analysis we reserve the use of the word "benefit" for the monetary valuation of a positive consequence and use the word "effect" for the same consequence quantified in a physical, nonmonetary unit.

2. A number of conflicting definitions are presented in the literature. Some of the differences reflect expanded application of the analysis over time. Other variations represent differing perceptions as to which policy alternatives (e.g., several policies, single policy vs. no policy) are relevant for comparison. To reflect this versatility, we use a broad, inclusive definition. For concise overviews and critiques of several different definitions, see Thompson (1980: 225–26) and DHHS (1992: 5–7).

3. A QALY reflects individual preferences for a particular health state, expressed in utilities. Accordingly, when QALYs are employed, the effectiveness analysis is called *cost-utility analysis*. Generally, a QALY ranges from 0 to 1, with a healthy life year assigned a QALY of 1, death assigned a QALY of 0, and intermediate health states a fraction between 0 and 1. For an explanation of the concept, see Drummond, Stoddart and Torrance (1987: 112–48) and Kaplan (1996: 31–60).

4. Sometimes the specific numbers in a particular analysis lend themselves to more convenient expression as E/C, which is interpreted as: effects per unit of cost. If employed, the analyst should be careful to reverse the appropriate decision criterion to determine cost effectiveness.

5. For additional examples illustrating the appropriate ratios and criteria for the various decisions, see Weinstein (1996: 78–91), DHHS (1992: 9–31) and Thompson (1980: 227–40). Note that each criterion assumes a positive effect. If an effect is negative, the decision criterion should be reversed.

6. With or without a budget constraint, the decision criterion is derived assuming all interventions or policies are *divisible* with *constant returns to scale*. This means if budgetary considerations or the decision maker's willingness to pay the total cost limits full implementation of a given policy, the possibility exists to pursue only a portion of the policy (or intervention) and achieve the same (constant) effectiveness per dollar spent. For instance, every $1,000 in present value spent on intervention A in Table 22.2 will save one life year, regardless of whether the full $5 million policy or only a portion is implemented. This assumption allows every single dollar of the budget or decision-maker total WTP to be spent.

For those instances when policies are *indivisible* or "lumpy," complex algorithms may be required to identify the cost-effective subset. These instances are few, however. As DHHS notes, when the policies with C/E ratios close to the criterion "cut-off" can be expanded or reduced in scale, modest recalculations of costs and effects can usually accommodate any lumpiness. Moreover, for decisions where individual policies spend a tiny portion of the budget, any lumpiness has only a slight effect on the decision choice (1992: 14).

7. For an analysis performed without a particular decision maker in mind, or if the decision maker has not yet determined the maximum WTP, the analyst might use a value that has emerged in the literature as a reasonable "cut-off" or standard.

8. Likewise, the reader can confirm from Table 22.2 that if the goal is to save 15,500 life-years at least cost, the answer is the same: pursue interventions A, B, E.

9. The cut-off is sometimes called the threshold, critical value or standard.

10. Policy *divisibility* ensures that if F requires a greater total cost than E, then part of F can be pursued; or if F is less expensive than E, then F can be implemented in its entirety and the remaining budget monies can be allocated to some portion of E.

11. While some sources use the term "incremental," a common practice in economics is to refer to the additional unit changes for a given policy as "marginal," reserving "incremental" for comparisons between alternative policies.

12. This example is based on an insightful student analysis (Welch 1992); for mathematical simplicity, most numbers are only approximate to Welch's detailed estimates; and for illustrative purposes, some additional information is hypothesized.

13. The hypothesized combined effect of 73% is greater than the simple sum of the two policies' separate effects because signs and pamphlets are presumed to be *dependent policies*.

14. Not included in this example is a possibility explicitly recognized by DHHS (1992: 16). If there is any intervention in the list with a greater incremental C/E than the next successive intervention, the former should be eliminated, assuming policy divisibility with constant returns to scale. Thus, for example, if there is some Policy E that can achieve 99.5% effectiveness in changing boater behavior, at a discounted total cost of, say, $1.335 million, area closure is then removed from the list.

To see this, the reader can verify that the incremental C/E for Policy E, relative to area closure, is $3,000/0.5% or $6,000, which is lower than area closure's incremental C/E of $49,500 in present value. With a lower incremental C/E, Policy E is the more cost effective of the two policies. Therefore, area closure, deemed less cost effective, is eliminated from further consideration. The incremental C/E for Policy E is then recalculated, comparing Policy E with the remaining prior policy on the list: signs and pamphlets combined. Policy E's new incremental C/E is $1,290,000/26.5% or $48,679, rounded, in present value. Note how a given policy's incremental C/E varies in value with the specific policy comparison. The new ratio is notably larger than before. However, it remains lower than area closure's incremental C/E calculated relative to the signs and pamphlets option; this is as expected from the determination that Policy E is more cost effective than area closure.

Chapter 23

Principles for Identifying and Valuing Benefits and Costs

INTRODUCTION

Part III offers several principles for identifying benefits and costs as well as specifying a number of techniques for estimating the economic values. The decision maker, the analyst and interested persons must be familiar with each technique in order to determine which might be appropriate when assessing a particular policy's benefits and costs. To enable a quick overview and comparison of the valuation methods, this chapter presents both the identification and the valuation principles. These are listed in order of appearance in the text, along with chapter titles to facilitate easy reference.

SUMMARY OF PRINCIPLES

Identifying Benefits and Costs

16.1 The analyst should identify all policy consequences, determining all of a policy's resource impacts that have good or bad consequences for social welfare and then sketching these consequences.

16.2 For these consequences, the analyst should identify all *benefits* and *costs*, where these represent the economic value of real changes associated with a policy. A *real change* includes a change in the physical quantity or quality of a given resource or output and/or a change in individual satisfaction (utility) derived from the resource or output.

16.3 Benefits and costs can be categorized in terms of impacts priced in the *market* and *nonmarket effects*. Together these include *marketed resource costs, marketed output benefits, marketed output costs* and *technological externalities* (i.e., real changes in resources or output not priced in a market).

16.4   *Pecuniary* (price) *effects* and *secondary benefits* (induced income changes) should generally not be included as benefits or costs in a cost-benefit analysis. Even if a policy's primary objective is regional development, secondary benefits should be listed only and not incorporated in the net benefits calculation; the diversion of secondary benefits from somewhere outside the region should also be indicated.

16.5   A second classification scheme categorizes benefits and costs in terms of *use values* and *non-use* (or *passive-use*) *values*. Non-use values are especially relevant for unique resources subject to irreversible (or long-term) change.

16.6   When a policy has hard-to-measure effects, the analyst should (1) value as many benefits and costs as possible using monetary units; (2) if unable to assign a monetary value to a particular policy consequence, try to quantify it in physical units; and (3) in the especially difficult situation where the consequence eludes quantification of any kind, identify and describe it qualitatively.

16.7   At the end of the analysis, when the analyst reports the NPV, the analyst should again identify those consequences that are not valued. If these effects are *either* all benefits *or* all costs, then the analyst should explain that the NPV provides a *critical value* for the unmeasured benefits (costs).

Market Valuation

17.1   For a marketed resource, good or service, society's Total WTP is the sum of consumers' total expenditures and consumer surplus. Total WTP is calculated by applying *multiple regression analysis* to estimate market demand and computing the relevant area under the demand curve.

17.2   When price ceilings, taxes or unemployment characterize a market, then selective sensitivity analysis is recommended, with adjustments in market values to reflect possible *shadow prices*.

Contingent Valuation Method

18.1   To value nonmarket effects or technological externalities, the contingent valuation method asks survey respondents to state their preferences hypothetically, indicating their valuation as if a market for the particular resource, good or service actually exists.

18.2   Contingent valuation is the only systematic method offering the potential for estimating non-use values.

18.3   The contingent valuation method consists of the following components:

- hypothetical market scenario
- sample selection
- survey instrument
- valuation question(s)

- valuation estimation
- response validity and reliability tests

18.4   The designer should construct a clear, realistic survey that appears plausible to respondents, while taking appropriate precautions whenever possible to be conservative and avoid overestimating economic values.

18.5   The survey designer must justify the design of a specific survey and assess the survey's *validity* and *reliability*.

18.6   The *hypothetical market scenario* should be designed with consideration of the following possible influences on respondents' answers: hypothetical valuation, information presented, incremental valuation, *embedding problem, strategic bias* and *payment vehicle bias*.

18.7   To determine whether respondents have understood and accepted the scenario's details as well as to identify other influences on respondent answers, the survey designer should (1) pretest the hypothetical scenario (including any displays) and (2) include follow-up questions at the end of the survey.

18.8   In selecting a probability sample (whether simple random, stratified or clustered), the sample size can be determined to attain a desired degree of *precision*.

18.9   When devising the survey, the designer should make every reasonable effort to minimize the *nonresponse rate* and *bias*.

18.10   *Survey instruments* (i.e., in-person interview, telephone interview or written questionnaire) are distinguished in terms of the following characteristics: interactive or not interactive, ability to show displays, sample selection, nonresponses and costs.

18.11   When devising the valuation question(s), the survey designer should consider the following choices: (1) type of valuation question (WTP, WTS, WTA), (2) question format (open-ended question, question with checklist, iterative bids or referendum question) and (3) actual payment question(s).

18.12   The survey should ask respondents to indicate the reasons for their answer(s) to the *valuation question*. The stated reasons should be coded and reported. In addition, an individual's reasons provide a basis for determining whether specific valuation answers are not credible and should be omitted by the analyst when estimating the social valuation.

18.13   A respondent might be asked one or more of the following types of valuation questions.

- What is the *maximum* amount you are *willing to pay* (WTP) for a resource benefit (or to reduce a resource cost)?
- What is the *minimum* amount you must be paid to be *willing to sell* (WTS) or voluntarily forego a benefit, assuming you hold the property right to the resource?
- What is the *minimum* amount of compensation you are *willing to accept* (WTA) to tolerate a resource cost?

18.14   If the survey asks only one type of valuation question, then conservative estimation dictates that the choice is to elicit maximum willingness to pay (WTP).

18.15   In some cases, with justification, asking more than one type of valuation question
may provide additional useful information for the decision maker.

18.16   If actual market payments can be identified that are in some way related to the
hypothetical scenario under consideration, then respondents should be asked
whether they have made such payments and, if so, how much they paid.

18.17   The population's aggregate value (or Total WTP) for a nonmarketed resource,
good or service can be estimated from sample data using any of a number of
different statistical techniques, including:

- mean or median WTP

- frequency distribution of WTP

- aggregate bid (or demand) schedule

- valuation function (multiple regression analysis)

18.18   The theoretical validity of WTP estimates can be explored by testing the relationship between WTP and various socioeconomic and demographic variables,
using alternative statistical techniques including:

- cross-tabulations and

- valuation function (multiple regression analysis)

Evidence concerning the estimates' reliability is provided by:

- the valuation function's R^2

Travel Cost Method

19.1   The *travel cost method* may be applicable when a nonmarketed resource, good
or service is located at a specific site. The method employs regression analysis
to estimate the relationship between visitation rates and travel costs incurred to
and from the site. It then applies this relationship to derive how the population
would respond to alternative site admission prices, thereby inferring society's
willingness to pay for the site's nonmarketed resource, good or service.

19.2   The Clawson-Knetsch method estimates the following elements:

- visitation rates for different zones

- travel costs

- visitation rate function

- demand curve for the resource site

19.3   The prediction of WTP based on visitor travel costs is premised on the following:

- the assumption that visitors respond the same to changes in monetary admission prices as they do to changes in travel costs, and
- the corollary that the most distant visitor's travel costs is the maximum that any visitor might be WTP

19.4   Similar to contingent valuation, the travel cost method surveys respondents, in this case, visitors to a specific site. Unlike contingent valuation, visitor responses to travel cost questions are based on actual rather than hypothetical behavior. Travel cost proponents perceive the method's elicitation of revealed preferences as enhancing reliable estimation. At the same time, the analyst should consider applying contingent valuation as an alternative or supplement to the travel cost method when a resource, good or service is any of the following: available independent of a specific site, one of multiple destinations for individual visitor trips, valued for use by numerous non-visitors, located at a congested or polluted site or associated with sizable non-use values. Likewise, to value site quality changes, the analyst may employ sophisticated variations of the travel cost method or, instead, apply the contingent valuation method.

Hedonic Pricing Method: Property Value Approach

20.1   The *property value approach* infers WTP for a nonmarket effect from observed behavior (*revealed preferences*) in property markets. It is thus relevant only when the studied nonmarket effect influences property values.

20.2   The property value approach applies multiple regression techniques to analyze property values. The approach first estimates a *hedonic price function* to determine the amount of property value associated with the nonmarket effect, separated from other property characteristics. Second, the *hedonic prices of the nonmarket effect* are regressed on the household demand characteristics and nonmarket effect to determine the willingness-to-pay function. This function is used to calculate the change in total WTP for a change in the nonmarket effect.

20.3   The hedonic pricing method analyzes the actual behavior of property buyers, usually measured with market values. The method's use should be checked to ensure it is (appropriately) valuing WTP for a nonmarket effect, rather than valuing a pecuniary effect. Moreover, its application is limited to valuing a policy consequence that affects a well-defined site area and to estimating the use values of property owners. Thus, additional valuation methods are required to estimate any nonresidents' use values (with due caution to avoid double counting property owner values) as well as any non-use values.

Valuation of Human Life

21.1   In the context of scarce resources, numerous individual choices reveal a willingness to forego some expenditures that might ensure preservation of one's own or someone else's life in order to achieve other desired objectives. Such trade-offs provide the basis for economists to infer a monetary valuation of human life.

21.2   The *human capital method*, which estimates the present value of expected future earnings or net earnings over an individual's lifetime, should not be used to value a human life in a cost-benefit analysis.

21.3   The appropriate principle for human life valuation is the willingness to pay (WTP) or willingness to accept (WTA) compensation for a small change in *mortality risk.* Accordingly, estimation techniques infer a value of life from revealed preferences (by analyzing a hedonic regression for wage rates or consumer prices or investigating non–price-related changes in consumer behavior) or, instead, from surveys eliciting contingent values.

Cost-Effectiveness Analysis

22.1   Cost-effectiveness analysis can (1) value the costs and quantify the effect of a single policy so the decision maker can then decide whether pursuing the policy is worth it, and/or (2) assess a number of policies and/or policy levels to identify which one(s) (a) minimize the costs of achieving a given effect or (b) maximize effectiveness for a given budget or set of resources.

22.2   *Cost-effectiveness analysis* (CEA) is one approach to assess decisions or choices that affect the use of scarce resources. Similar to CBA, this method considers a specific policy and relevant alternatives and involves systematic identification of policy consequences. However, unlike CBA, each consequence is then expressed either in monetary units (as a cost) or in one common physical unit measuring the effect. The analysis then compares the costs and effect of each policy alternative, applying the appropriate decision criterion to aid the decision maker in determining which alternative(s) are (relatively) cost effective.

22.3   In performing a cost-effectiveness analysis, the analyst should:

- identify the type of decision the decision maker is considering,
- calculate the appropriate *cost-effectiveness ratio* for each policy or policy level, and
- apply the correct decision criterion to determine which policy alternative(s) are cost effective

22.4   For clarity and accurate interpretation, the analyst should identify the particular C/E ratio (i.e., average, marginal or incremental) being reported and specify the "without-policy" or baseline scenario, in other words, the exact alternative with which the policy is being compared.

22.5   Pursuing a policy (combination) is *cost effective* (1) compared to no policy, if the cost per unit of effect (*average C/E*) is less than or equal to the decision maker's WTP, or (2) compared to other levels (scales) of the same policy, if its *marginal C/E* is closest (less than or equal) to the decision maker's WTP (and the corresponding average C/E is also less than or equal to WTP), or (3) compared to other policies, if its *incremental C/E* is closest (less than or equal) to the decision maker's WTP.

22.6   Given the disagreement as to whether future effects should be discounted and the uncertainty as to the appropriate discount rate for this purpose, a carefully performed, objective cost-effectiveness analysis should apply a range of discount rates. Specifically, the recommended selective sensitivity analysis for discounting monetary values should be extended, allowing the rate for discounting effects to vary from zero to the same rate selected for discounting costs.

22.7   In comparing cost-benefit with cost-effectiveness analysis, CBA provides the greater information to the decision maker by valuing society's preferences concerning all policy consequences that generate benefits or costs. Also, CBA assesses a policy's relative efficiency, while the relatively cost-effective policy identified by CEA is not necessarily the more efficient policy. The difference is that CEA does not measure society's preferences regarding the quantified "effect", thus, these cannot be weighed along with the other preferences to determine efficiency.

At the same time, when valuation of a particular consequence is controversial, CEA can be advantageous in avoiding explicit valuation (although the decision maker must then employ an implicit value). Moreover, CEA may be the only practicable tool when limited data preclude valuation of particular policy consequence(s) with an acceptable level of precision or when moral obligations (or other commitments) render the cost-benefit trade-off irrelevant.

Bibliography

Alviani, Joseph D. 1980. ''Federal Regulation: The New Regimen.'' *Environmental Affairs Law Review* 9 (2): 285–309.

Armstrong, Susan J., and Richard G. Botzler, comps. 1993. *Environmental Ethics: Divergence and Convergence.* New York: McGraw-Hill.

Arrow, Kenneth, and Anthony C. Fisher. 1974. ''Environmental Preservation, Uncertainty, and Irreversibility.'' *Quarterly Journal of Economics* 88 (May): 312–19.

Arrow, Kenneth, Robert Solow, Edward Leamer, Paul Portney, Roy Randner and Howard Schuman. 1993. ''Appendix I—Report of the NOAA Panel on Contingent Valuation.'' *Federal Register* 58 (January 15): 4602–14.

Baldwin, G.R., and C.G. Veljanovski. 1984. ''Regulation by Cost-Benefit Analysis.'' *Public Administration* 62 (Spring): 51–69.

Baumol, William J. 1968. ''On the Social Rate of Discount.'' *American Economic Review* 58 (4): 788–802.

Beatley, Timothy. 1994. *Ethical Land Use: Principles of Policy and Planning.* Baltimore, Md.: Johns Hopkins University Press.

Bendle, Bradley J., and Frederick W. Bell. 1995. *An Estimation of the Total Willingness to Pay by Floridians to Protect the Endangered West Indian Manatee through Donations.* Prepared for the Save the Manatee Club (Maitland, Fla.) and the Florida Department of Environmental Protection (Tallahassee, Fla.).

Bierman, Harold, Jr., and Seymour Smidt. 1988. *The Capital Budgeting Decision: Economic Analysis of Investment Projects.* 7th ed. New York: Macmillan.

Blomquist, Glenn. 1979. ''Value of Life Saving: Implications of Consumption Activity.'' *Journal of Political Economy* 87 (3): 540–58.

Boardman, Anthony E., David H. Greenberg, Aidan R. Vining and David L. Weimer. 1996. *Cost-Benefit Analysis: Concepts and Practice.* Upper Saddle River, N.J.: Prentice Hall.

Bockstael, Nancy G., Kenneth E. McConnell and Ivar Strand. 1991. ''Recreation.'' In

Measuring the Demand for Environmental Quality, ed. J.B. Braden and C.D. Kolstad, 227–70. Amsterdam: Elsevier.

Bradford, David F. 1975. "Constraints on Government Investment Opportunities and the Choice of Discount Rate." *American Economic Review* 65 (5): 887–99.

Brent, Robert J. 1996. *Applied Cost-Benefit Analysis*. Brookfield, Vt.: Edward Elgar.

Brigham, Eugene F., and Louis C. Gapenski. 1988. *Financial Management: Theory and Practice*. 5th ed. New York: Dryden Press.

Brookshire, David, and Don L. Coursey. 1987. "Measuring the Value of a Public Good: An Empirical Comparison of Elicitation Procedures." *American Economic Review* 177 (4): 554–66.

Brookshire, David S., Larry S. Eubanks and Alan Randall. 1983. "Estimating Option Price and Existence Values for Wildlife Resources." *Land Economics* 59 (1): 1–15.

Brown, Gardner M., Jr. 1982. "Recreation." In *Economics of Ocean Resources: A Research Agenda*, ed. Gardner M. Brown, Jr., and James A. Crutchfield, 144–63. Seattle: University of Washington Press.

Brown, Gardner M., Jr., and Robert Mendelsohn. 1984. "The Hedonic Travel Cost Model." *Review of Economics and Statistics* 66 (3): 427–33.

Browner, Carol. 1995. Interview by Monroe Karmin. National Press Club Luncheon. *Federal News Service*. Transcript of program on C-SPAN and National Public Radio, April 20.

Bullard, Robert D., ed. 1994. *Unequal Protection: Environmental Justice and Communities of Color*. San Francisco: Sierra Club Books.

Callicott, J. Baird. 1993. "On the Intrinsic Value of Nonhuman Species." In *Environmental Ethics: Divergence and Convergence*, comp. Susan J. Armstrong and Richard G. Botzler, 66–70. New York: McGraw-Hill. First published in *The Preservation of Species: The Value of Biological Diversity*, ed. B.G. Norton, 138–72. Princeton, N.J.: Princeton University Press, 1986.

Cameron, Trudy Ann. 1988. "A New Paradigm for Valuing Non-market Goods Using Referendum Data: Maximum Likelihood Estimation by Censored Logistic Regression." *Journal of Environmental Economics and Management* 15: 355–79.

Carlile, William H. 1994. "States Are Closing Firms' 'Candy Store': Laws Tighten Incentives, Seek Accountability for Subsidies." *The Arizona Republic*, 24 July, final chaser edition, business section.

Carlson, William L., and Betty Thorne. 1997. *Applied Statistical Methods for Business, Economics, and the Social Sciences*. Upper Saddle River, N.J.: Prentice Hall.

Carson, Richard T. 1991. "Constructed Markets." In *Measuring the Demand for Environmental Quality*, ed. J.B. Braden and C.D. Kolstad, 121–62. Amsterdam: Elsevier.

Carson, Richard T., Nicholas E. Flores, Kerry M. Martin and Jennifer L. Wright. 1996. "Contingent Valuation and Revealed Preference Methodologies: Comparing the Estimates for Quasi-Public Goods." *Land Economics* 72 (1): 80–99.

Carson, Richard T., Robert C. Mitchell, W. Michael Hanemann, Raymond J. Kopp, Stanley Presser and Paul A. Ruud. 1992. *A Contingent Valuation Study of Lost Passive Use Values Resulting from the Exxon Valdez Oil Spill*. A Report to the Attorney General of the State of Alaska. La Jolla, Calif.: Natural Resource Damage Assessment, Inc.

Cesario, Frank J. 1976. "Valuation of Time in Recreation Benefit Studies." *Land Economics* 52 (1): 32–41.

Cesario, Frank J., and Jack L. Knetsch. 1976. "A Recreation Site Demand and Benefit Estimation Model." *Regional Studies* 10: 97–104.

Chambers, Robert. 1985. "Shortcut Methods of Gathering Social Information for Rural Development Projects." In *Putting People First: Sociological Variables in Rural Development*, ed. Michael M. Cernea, 399–415. Published for the World Bank. New York: Oxford University Press.

Ciriacy-Wantrup, S.V. 1947. "Capital Returns from Soil-Conservation Practices." *Journal of Farm Economics* 29 (November): 1181–96.

Clawson, Marion, and Jack L. Knetsch. 1966. *Economics of Outdoor Recreation*. Published for Resources for the Future. Baltimore, Md.: Johns Hopkins Press.

Cochran, William G. 1963. *Sampling Techniques*. 2nd ed. New York: John Wiley and Sons.

Cropper, Maureen L., Leland B. Deck and Kenneth E. McConnell. 1988. "On the Choice of Functional Form for Hedonic Price Functions." *Review of Economics and Statistics* 70 (4): 668–75.

Cummings, R.G., D.S. Brookshire and W.D. Schulze. 1986. *Valuing Environmental Goods: An Assessment of the Contingent Valuation Method*. Totowa, N.J.: Rowman and Allanheld.

Davis, Robert Kenneth. 1963. "The Value of Outdoor Recreation: An Economic Study of the Maine Woods." Doctoral thesis in economics, Harvard University, Cambridge, Mass.

DHHS (U.S. Department of Health and Human Services). Office of Disease Prevention and Promotion. 1992. *A Framework for Cost-Utility Analysis of Government Health Care Program*, by Mark S. Kamlet. Washington, D.C.: Government Printing Office.

Diamond, Peter A., and Jerry A. Hausman. 1994. "Contingent Valuation: Is Some Number Better than No Number?" *Journal of Economic Perspectives* 8 (Fall): 45–64.

Dinwiddy, Caroline, and Francis Teal. 1996. *Principles of Cost-Benefit Analysis for Developing Countries*. New York: Cambridge University Press.

Doubilet, Peter, Milton C. Weinstein and Barbara J. McNeil. 1986. "Use and Misuse of the Term 'Cost Effective' in Medicine." *New England Journal of Medicine* 314 (4): 253–56.

Drummond, Michael F., Greg L. Stoddart and George W. Torrance. 1987. *Methods for the Economic Evaluation of Health Care Programmes*. New York: Oxford University Press.

Dupuit, Jules. 1952. "On the Measurement of the Utility of Public Works." Translated from French by R.H. Barback. *International Economic Papers* 2: 83–110. Originally published as "De la Mesure de l'Utilité des Travaux Publics," *Annales des Ponts et Chaussées*, 2nd series 8 (1844).

Durham, T.R. 1979. *An Introduction to Cost-Benefit Analysis for Evaluating Public Programs*. Croton-on-Hudson, N.Y.: Policy Studies Associates.

Dwyer, John F., John R. Kelly and Michael D. Bowes. 1977. *Improved Procedures for Valuation of the Contribution of Recreation to National Economic Development*. Research Report no. 128. University of Illinois at Urbana–Champaign Water Resources Center, September.

Eckstein, Otto. 1958. *Water-Resource Development: The Economics of Project Evalua-tion*. Cambridge, Mass.: Harvard University Press.

———. 1961. "A Survey of the Theory of Public Expenditure Criteria." In *Public Finances: Needs, Sources and Utilization*, ed. James M. Buchanan, 439–94. Princeton, N.J.: Princeton University Press.

Emery, Douglas R., John D. Finnerty and John D. Stowe. 1998. *Principles of Financial Management*. Upper Saddle River, N.J.: Prentice Hall.

EPA (U.S. Environmental Protection Agency). 1992. *Environmental Equity: Reducing Risk for All Communities*. Vol. 1, *Workgroup Report to the Administrator*. EPA 230-R-92–008. Washington, D.C.: EPA, June.

Epstein, Marc J. 1994. "Viewpoints: A Formal Plan for Environmental Costs." *New York Times* 3 April, late edition, sec. 3.

Feldstein, Martin S. 1974. "Distributional Preferences in Public Expenditure Analysis." In *Redistribution through Public Choice*, ed. Harold M. Hochman and George E. Peterson, 136–61. Published in cooperation with The Urban Institute, Washington, D.C. New York: Columbia University Press.

Fisher, Ann, Lauraine G. Chestnut and Daniel M. Violette. 1989. "The Value of Re-ducing Risks of Death: A Note on New Evidence." *Journal of Policy Analysis and Management* 8 (1): 88–100.

Fisher, Anthony C., and W. Michael Hanemann. 1987. "Quasi-Option Value: Some Misconceptions Dispelled." *Journal of Environmental Economics and Manage-ment* 14: 183–90.

Freeman, A. Myrick, III. 1979. *The Benefits of Environmental Improvement: Theory and Practice*. Published for Resources for the Future. Baltimore, Md.: Johns Hopkins University Press.

———. 1984. "The Quasi-Option Value of Irreversible Development." *Journal of En-vironmental Economics and Management* 11: 292–95.

———. 1993a. *The Measurement of Environmental and Resource Values: Theory and Methods*. Washington, D.C.: Resources for the Future.

———. 1993b. "Nonuse Values in Natural Resource Damage Assessment." In *Valuing Natural Assets: The Economics of Natural Resource Damage Assessment*, ed. Raymond J. Kopp and V. Kerry Smith, 264–303. Washington, D.C.: Resources for the Future.

Gramlich, Edward M. 1981. *Benefit-Cost Analysis of Government Programs*. Englewood Cliffs, N.J.: Prentice Hall.

———. 1990. *A Guide to Benefit-Cost Analysis*. 2nd ed. Englewood Cliffs, N.J.: Prentice Hall.

Greer, Linda E. 1995. "The Role of Risk Assessment and Cost Benefit Analysis in Regulatory Reform." Prepared testimony before the Senate Commitee on Gov-ernment Operations. *Federal News Service*, 15 February.

Hammack, Judd, and Gardner Mallard Brown. 1974. *Waterfowl and Wetlands: Toward Bioeconomic Analysis*. Washington, D.C.: Resources for the Future.

Hanemann, W. Michael. 1984. "Welfare Evaluations in Contingent Valuation Experi-ments with Discrete Responses." *American Journal of Agricultural Economics* 66: 322–41.

———. 1991. "Willingness to Pay and Willingness to Accept: How Much Can They Differ?" *American Economic Review* 81 (3): 635–47.

———. 1994. "Valuing the Environment through Contingent Valuation." *Journal of Economic Perspectives* 8 (Fall): 19–43.

Hanley, Nick, and Clive Spash. 1993. *Cost-Benefit Analysis and the Environment*. Brookfield, Vt.: Edward Elgar.

Harberger, Arnold C. 1976. "On Measuring the Social Opportunity Cost of Public Funds." *Project Evaluation: Collected Papers*, 94–122. Chicago: University of Chicago Press. First published in *The Discount Rate in Public Investment Evaluation*. Conference Proceedings of the Committee on the Economics of Water Resources Development, Western Agricultural Economics Research Council, Report No. 17, Denver, Colorado, 17–18 December 1969, 1–24.

Hare, R.M. 1987. "Moral Reasoning about the Environment." *Journal of Applied Philosophy* 4 (1): 3–14.

Haspel, Abraham E., and F. Reed Johnson. 1982. "Multiple Destination Trip Bias in Recreation Benefit Estimation." *Land Economics* 58 (3): 364–72.

Haveman, Robert H. 1968. "Comment (on Weisbrod)." In *Problems in Public Expenditure Analysis*, ed. Samuel B. Chase, Jr., 209–13. Washington, D.C.: Brookings Institution.

Hirschey, Mark, and James L. Pappas. 1996. *Managerial Economics*. 8th ed. New York: Dryden Press.

Hitch, Charles J., and Roland N. McKean. 1961. *The Economics of Defense in the Nuclear Age*. Cambridge, Mass.: Harvard University Press.

———. 1967. *Elements of Defense Economics*. Washington, D.C.: Industrial College of the Armed Forces.

Howe, Charles W. 1971. *Benefit-Cost Analysis for Water System Planning*. Water Resources Monograph 2. Washington, D.C.: American Geophysical Union.

Hufschmidt, Maynard M., David E. James, Anton D. Meister, Blair T. Bower and John A. Dixon. 1983. *Environmental, Natural Systems, and Development: An Economic Valuation Guide*. Baltimore, Md.: Johns Hopkins University Press.

Ippolito, Pauline M., and Richard A. Ippolito. 1984. "Measuring the Value of Life Saving from Consumer Reactions to New Information." *Journal of Public Economics* 25: 53–81.

James, L. Douglas, and Robert R. Lee. 1971. *Economics of Water Resources Planning*. New York: McGraw-Hill.

Kahneman, Daniel, and Amos Tversky. 1979. "Prospect Theory: An Analysis of Decision under Risk." *Econometrica* 47 (2): 263–91.

Kaplan, Robert M. 1996. "Utility Assessment for Estimating Quality-Adjusted Life Years." In *Valuing Health Care: Costs, Benefits and Effectiveness of Pharmaceuticals and Other Medical Technologies*, ed. Frank A. Sloan, 31–60. New York: Cambridge University Press.

Keeler, Emmett B., and Shan Cretin. 1983. "Discounting of Life-Saving and Other Nonmonetary Effects." *Management Science* 29 (3): 300–306.

Kopp, Raymond J. 1992. "Why Existence Value *Should* Be Used in Cost-Benefit Analysis." *Journal of Policy Analysis and Management* 11 (1): 123–30.

Kopp, Raymond J., and V. Kerry Smith. 1993. "Natural Resource Damage Assessment: The Road Ahead." In *Valuing Natural Assets: The Economics of Natural Resource Damage Assessment*, ed. Raymond J. Kopp and V. Kerry Smith, 307–36. Washington, D.C.: Resources for the Future.

Krutilla, John V. 1967. "Conservation Reconsidered." *American Economic Review* 57 (4): 777–86.

Krutilla, John V., and Otto Eckstein. 1958. *Multiple Purpose River Development: Studies in Applied Economic Analysis.* Published for Resources for the Future. Baltimore, Md.: Johns Hopkins Press.

Leopold, Aldo. 1949. "The Land Ethic." In *A Sand County Almanac, And Sketches Here and There*, 201–26. New York: Oxford University Press.

Lesser, Jonathan A., Daniel E. Dodds and Richard O. Zerbe, Jr. 1997. *Environmental Economics and Policy.* New York: Addison-Wesley.

Levy, Jack S. 1992. "An Introduction to Prospect Theory." *Political Psychology* 13 (2): 171–86.

Lind, Douglas A., and Robert D. Mason. 1997. *Basic Statistics for Business and Economics.* 2d ed. Chicago: Irwin.

Lind, Robert C. 1982a. "A Primer on the Major Issues Relating to the Discount Rate for Evaluating National Energy Options." In *Discounting for Time and Risk in Energy Policy*, by Robert C. Lind, Kenneth J. Arrow, Gordon R. Corey, Partha Dasgupta, Amartya K. Sen, Thomas Stauffer, Joseph E. Stiglitz, J. A. Stockfish and Robert Wilson, 21–94. Washington, D.C.: Resources for the Future.

———. 1982b. "Introduction." In *Discounting for Time and Risk in Energy Policy*, by Robert C. Lind, Kenneth J. Arrow, Gordon R. Corey, Partha Dasgupta, Amartya K. Sen, Thomas Stauffer, Joseph E. Stiglitz, J. A. Stockfish and Robert Wilson, 1–19. Washington, D.C.: Resources for the Future.

———. 1990. "Reassessing the Government's Discount Rate Policy in Light of New Theory and Data in a World Economy with a High Degree of Capital Mobility." *Journal of Environmental Economics and Management* 18: S8–S28.

Lipscomb, Joseph. 1989. "Time Preference for Health in Cost-Effectiveness Analysis." *Medical Care* 27 (3): 5233–53.

Little, I.M.D., and J.A. Mirrlees. 1969. *Manual of Industrial Project Analysis for Developing Countries.* Vol 2. Paris: Organization for Economic Co-operation and Development.

———. 1974. *Project Appraisal and Planning for Developing Countries.* London: Heinemann Educational Books.

Lynch, Claudia. 1991. "An Analysis of the Social Costs of a Prenatally Drug Exposed Child in Pinellas County." Senior economics comprehensive, Eckerd College, St. Petersburg, Fla.

Lyon, Randolph M. 1990. "Federal Discount Rate Policy, the Shadow Price of Capital, and Challenges for Reforms." *Journal of Environmental Economics and Management* 18: S29–S50.

Maass, Arthur, Maynard M. Hufschmidt, Robert Dorfman, Harold A. Thomas, Jr., Stephen A. Marglin and Gordon Maskew Fair. 1962. *Design of Water-Resource Systems: New Techniques for Relating Economic Objectives, Engineering Analysis, and Governmental Planning.* Cambridge, Mass.: Harvard University Press.

Mack, Ruth P. 1968. "Comment (on Weisbrod)." In *Problems in Public Expenditure Analysis*, ed. Samuel B. Chase, Jr., 213–22. Washington, D.C.: Brookings Institution.

Marglin, Stephen A. 1962. "Objectives of Water-Resource Development: A General Statement." In *Design of Water-Resource Systems: New Techniques for Relating*

Economic Objectives, Engineering Analysis, and Governmental Planning, by Arthur Maass, Maynard M. Hufschmidt, Robert Dorfman, Harold A. Thomas, Jr., Stephen A. Marglin and Gordon Maskew Fair, 17–87. Cambridge, Mass.: Harvard University Press.

———. 1963a. "The Social Rate of Discount and the Optimal Rate of Investment." *Quarterly Journal of Economics* 77 (February): 95–111.

———. 1963b. "The Opportunity Costs of Public Investment." *Quarterly Journal of Economics* 77 (May): 274–89.

Markandya, Anil, and David Pearce. 1988. *Environmental Considerations and the Choice of the Discount Rate in Developing Countries.* Environment Department Working Paper no. 3. Washington, D.C.: World Bank, May.

McConnell, Kenneth E. 1986. *The Damages to Recreational Activities from PCBs in New Bedford Harbor.* Prepared for the Oceanic Assessment Division, National Oceanic and Atmospheric Administration. Cambridge, Mass.: Industrial Economics, Inc.

———. 1990. "Models for Referendum Data: The Structure of Discrete Choice Models for Contingent Valuation." *Journal of Environmental Economics and Management* 18: 19–34.

McKean, Ronald N. 1958. *Efficiency in Government through Systems Analysis with Emphasis on Water Resources Development.* New York: John Wiley and Sons.

Mitchell, Robert Cameron, and Richard T. Carson. 1986. *The Use of Contingent Valuation Data for Benefit/Cost Analysis in Water Pollution Control.* Prepared for the U.S. Environmental Protection Agency. Washington, D.C.: Resources for the Future.

———. 1989. *Using Surveys to Value Public Goods: The Contingent Valuation Method.* Washington, D.C.: Resources for the Future.

Moyer, R. Charles, James R. McGuigan and William J. Kretlow. 1992. *Contemporary Financial Management.* 5th ed. New York: West Publishing Co.

Nas, Tevfik F. 1996. *Cost-Benefit Analysis: Theory and Application.* Thousand Oaks, Calif.: Sage Publications.

Norse, Elliott A., ed. 1993. *Global Marine Biological Diversity: A Strategy for Building Conservation into Decision Making.* Washington, D.C.: Island Press.

OECD (Organization for Economic Co-operation and Development). 1994. *Project and Policy Appraisal: Integrating Economics and Environment.* Paris: OECD.

———. 1995. *The Economic Appraisal of Environmental Projects and Policies: A Practical Guide.* Paris: OECD.

OMB (U.S. Office of Management and Budget). 1992. "Guidelines and Discount Rates for Benefit-Cost Analysis of Federal Programs." Circular No. A-94. Revised. Washington, D.C.

Orr, David W. 1994. *Earth in Mind: On Education, Environment, and the Human Prospect.* Washington, D.C.: Island Press.

Pearce, D.W. 1971. *Cost-Benefit Analysis.* London: Macmillan.

———. 1983. *Cost-Benefit Analysis.* 2d ed. New York: St. Martin's Press.

Pearce, D.W., and Dominic Moran. 1994. *The Economic Value of Biodiversity.* London: Earthscan Publications Ltd.

Pearce, D.W., and C.A. Nash. 1981. *The Social Appraisal of Projects: A Text in Cost-Benefit Analysis.* New York: John Wiley and Sons.

Pearce, D.W., and R. Kerry Turner. 1990. *Economics of Natural Resources and the Environment.* Baltimore, Md.: Johns Hopkins University Press.

Pearce, David, Anil Markandya and Edward B. Barbier. 1989. *Blueprint for a Green Economy.* A Report for the U.K. Department of the Environment. London: Earthscan Publications.

Portney, Paul R. 1994. "The Contingent Valuation Debate: Why Economists Should Care." *Journal of Economic Perspectives* 8 (Fall): 3–17.

Ragland, Linda S. 1993. "A Socially Responsible Choice: An Analysis of the Florida Aquarium's Proposed Parking Lot Design as a Stormwater Management Technique." Senior thesis in environmental studies, Eckerd College, St. Petersburg, Fla.

Ray, Anandarup. 1984. *Cost-Benefit Analysis: Issues and Methodologies.* Published for the World Bank. Baltimore, Md.: Johns Hopkins University Press.

Ridker, Ronald G., and John A. Henning. 1967. "The Determinants of Residential Property Values with Special Reference to Air Pollution." *Review of Economics and Statistics* 49 (2): 246–57.

Rolston, Holmes, III. 1993. "Values Gone Wild." In *Environmental Ethics: Divergence and Convergence*, comp. Susan J. Armstrong and Richard G. Botzler, 56–65. New York: McGraw-Hill. First published in *Inquiry* 26 (1983): 181–207.

Rosen, Sherwen. 1974. "Hedonic Prices and Implicit Markets." *Journal of Political Economy* 82 (1): 34–55.

Rosenthal, Donald H., and Robert H. Nelson. 1992. "Why Existence Value Should *Not* Be Used in Cost-Benefit Analysis." *Journal of Policy Analysis and Management* 11 (1): 116–22.

Rowe, Robert D., Ralph C. d'Arge and David S. Brookshire. 1980. "An Experiment in the Economic Value of Visibility." *Journal of Environmental Economics and Management* 7 (1): 1–19.

Sagoff, Mark. 1988. *The Economy of the Earth.* New York: Cambridge University Press.

Sassone, Peter G., and William A. Schaffer. 1978. *Cost-Benefit Analysis: A Handbook.* New York: Academic Press.

Schelling, Thomas C. 1968. "The Life You Save May Be Your Own." In *Problems in Public Expenditure Analysis*, ed. Samuel B. Chase, Jr., 127–62. Washington, D.C.: Brookings Institution.

Schofield, J. 1987. *Cost-Benefit Analysis in Urban and Regional Planning.* Boston: Allen and Unwin.

Schulze, William D., David S. Brookshire, Eric G. Walther, Karen Kelley MacFarland, Mark A. Thayer, Regan L. Whitworth, Shaul Ben-David, William Malm and John Molenar. 1983. "The Economic Benefits of Preserving Visibility in the National Parklands of the Southwest." *Natural Resources Journal* 23 (January): 149–73.

Schumacher, E.F. 1975. *Small Is Beautiful: Economics as if People Mattered.* New York: Harper and Row.

Schuman, Howard, and Stanley Presser. 1996. *Questions and Answers in Attitude Surveys: Experiments on Question Form, Wording, and Context.* Thousand Oaks, Calif.: Sage Publications.

Self, Peter. 1975. *Econocrats and the Policy Process: The Politics and Philosophy of Cost-Benefit Analysis.* London: Macmillan Press.

Seneca, Joseph J., and Michael K. Taussig. 1984. *Environmental Economics*. 3d ed. Englewood Cliffs, N.J.: Prentice-Hall.

Shenk, Joshua Wolf. 1995. "The Case for Some Regulation; Republican Anti-Business Regulation Stance." *Washington Monthly* 27 (3): 26.

Smith, Michelle. 1988. "The Economic Impact of Airport Noise Pollution on the Sarasota-Bradenton Area: A Property Value Approach." Senior thesis in economics, Eckerd College, St. Petersburg, Fla.

Smith, V. Kerry, and William H. Desvousges. 1985. "The Generalized Travel Cost Model and Water Quality Benefits: A Reconsideration." *Southern Economic Journal* 52 (2): 371–81.

Smith, V. Kerry, William H. Desvousges and Matthew P. McGivney. 1983a. "Estimating Water Quality Benefits: An Econometric Analysis." *Southern Economic Journal* 50 (2): 422–37.

———. 1983b. "The Opportunity Cost of Travel Time in Recreation Demand Models." *Land Economics* 59 (3): 259–78.

Smith, V. Kerry, and Ju-Chin Huang. 1995. "Can Markets Value Air Quality? A Meta-Analysis of Hedonic Property Value Models." *Journal of Political Economy* 103 (1): 209–27.

Smith, V. Kerry, and Yoshiaki Kaoru. 1987. "The Hedonic Travel Cost Model: A View from the Trenches." *Land Economics* 63 (2): 179–92.

Smith, V. Kerry, and Raymond J. Kopp. 1980. "The Spatial Limits of the Travel Cost Recreation Demand Model." *Land Economics* 56 (1): 64–72.

Squire, Lyn, and Herman G. van der Tak. 1975. *Economic Analysis of Projects*. Published for the World Bank. Baltimore, Md.: Johns Hopkins University Press.

Staman, Mathew. 1992. "PRIDE at Zephyrhills Correctional Institution, Cost-Benefit Analysis." Senior economics comprehensive, Eckerd College, St. Petersburg, Fla.

Stevens, William K. 1995. "Congress Asks, Is Nature Worth More Than a Shopping Mall?" *New York Times*, 25 April, late edition, sec. C.

Stokey, Edith, and Richard Zeckhauser. 1978. *A Primer for Policy Analysis*. New York: W.W. Norton and Co.

Sugden, Robert, and Alan Williams. 1978. *The Principles of Practical Cost-Benefit Analysis*. New York: Oxford University Press.

Thibodeau, Francis R., and Bart D. Ostro. 1981. "An Economic Analysis of Wetland Protection." *Journal of Environmental Management* 12: 19–30.

Thompson, Mark S. 1980. *Benefit-Cost Analysis for Program Evaluation*. Beverly Hills, Calif.: Sage Publications.

Tierney, John. 1995. "Different Drummers; One Man's Parade, Another's Parking Lot." *New York Times*, 7 May, late edition, sec. 1.

Tietenberg, Tom. 1996. *Environmental and Natural Resource Economics*. 4th ed. New York: HarperCollins College Publishers.

Tresch, Richard W. 1981. *Public Finance: A Normative Theory*. Plano, Tex.: Business Publications.

Udvarhelyi, I. Steven, Graham A. Colditz, Arti Rai and Arnold M. Epstein. 1992. "Cost-Effectiveness and Cost-Benefit Analyses in the Medical Literature: Are the Methods Being Used Correctly?" *Annals of Internal Medicine* 116: 238–44.

UNIDO (United Nations Industrial Development Organization). 1972. *Guidelines for Project Evaluation*. New York: United Nations.

U.S. Bureau of the Census. 1995. *Statistical Abstract of the United States: 1995.* Prepared by the Chief of the Bureau of Statistics. Washington, D.C.: Government Printing Office.

U.S. House. 1995. House Republican Conference. "Legislative Digest—Week of February 27, 1995." *Congressional Press Releases* 24 (8), 26 February.

U.S. President. 1996. *Economic Report of the President Transmitted to the Congress, February 1996.* Washington, D.C.: Government Printing Office.

Viscusi, W. Kip. 1993. "The Value of Risks to Life and Health." *Journal of Economic Literature* 31 (December): 1912–46.

———. 1996. "Discounting Health Effects for Medical Decisions." In *Valuing Health Care: Costs, Benefits, and Effectiveness of Pharmaceuticals and Other Medical Technologies,* ed. Frank A. Sloan, 125–47. New York: Cambridge University Press.

Weiers, Ronald M. 1988. *Marketing Research.* 2d ed. Englewood Cliffs, N.J.: Prentice Hall.

Weinstein, Milton C. 1996. "From Cost-Effectiveness Ratios to Resource Allocation: Where to Draw the Line?" In *Valuing Health Care: Costs, Benefits and Effectiveness of Pharmaceuticals and Other Medical Technologies,* ed. Frank A. Sloan, 77–97. New York: Cambridge University Press.

Weinstein, Milton C., and William B. Stason. 1977. "Foundations of Cost-Effectiveness Analysis for Health and Medical Practices." *New England Journal of Medicine* 296 (13): 716–22.

Weisbrod, Burton A. 1968. "Income Redistribution Effects and Benefit-Cost Analysis." In *Problems in Public Expenditure Analysis,* ed. Samuel B. Chase, Jr., 177–209. Washington, D.C.: Brookings Institution.

———. 1964. "Collective-Consumption Services of Individual-Consumption Goods." *Quarterly Journal of Economics* 78 (3): 471–77.

Welch, Julia. 1992. "Cost-Effectiveness Analysis of Three Proposals to Save the Fort DeSoto Seagrass." Research paper for natural resource and environmental economics course, Eckerd College, St. Petersburg, Fla.

Willig, Robert D. 1976. "Consumer's Surplus without Apology." *American Economic Review* 66 (4): 589–97.

Zerbe, Richard O., Jr., and Dwight D. Dively. 1994. *Benefit-Cost Analysis in Theory and Practice.* New York: HarperCollins College Publishers.

Index

About the Authors

DIANA FUGUITT is Professor of Economics and a Coordinator of an interdisciplinary Environmental Studies major at Eckerd College, St. Petersburg, Florida. She has directed numerous economic and environmental studies students in the techniques of cost-benefit analysis, and received the Robert A. Staub Distinguished Teaching Award in 1992. She has also presented and published papers in African agricultural development and habitat valuation.

SHANTON J. WILCOX is a Senior Consultant for a top management consulting firm. He recently completed a warehousing cost-benefit analysis as a logistical consultant for an engineering and architectural firm.